The Modern Writer's Handbook

The Modern Writer's Handbook

Second Edition

Frank O'Hare

The Ohio State University

Macmillan Publishing Company

New York

*Credit acknowledgments follow the Dedication page
and precede the Contents.*

Macmillan Publishing Company
866 Third Avenue, New York, New York 10022

Library of Congress Cataloging-in-Publication Data

O'Hare, Frank.
    The modern writer's handbook / Frank O'Hare.—2nd ed.
      p. cm.
    Includes index.
    ISBN 0-02-389101-7
    1. English language—Rhetoric. 2. English language-
  -Grammar—1950- I. Title.
PE1408.037 1989   88-9303
808'.042—dc19   CIP

Printing: 5 6 7   Year: 1 2 3 4 5

To my parents
Frank O'Hare
and
Theresa Sutherland O'Hare
for their encouragement and support
and for their love

Grateful acknowledgment is given to authors and publishers for permission to reprint excerpts from the following:

Preface

To the Instructor

To make the second edition of *The Modern Writer's Handbook* a straightforward, convenient, accessible, and comprehensive handbook, I have reorganized the text and introduced a new design that will enable students to work independently and to find information quickly. I have also updated and improved this new edition by adding the following: methods of avoiding the use of sexist language, instruction on the use of a computerized index in library research and a sample entry, the advantages of word processing, additional grammatical principles, new examples and exercises, and detailed explanations and examples of both the MLA and APA documentation formats. These additions and improvements are designed to reinforce the first edition's fundamental premise that revision is central to the writing process.

New Organization

In this second edition, I have revised the order of presentation in order to focus on the writing process itself. This edition begins with a discussion of the stages in the composing process, from the initial conception of an idea through multiple drafts to the final, important step—proofreading. The text then focuses on the grammar of the sentence, punctuation, and mechanics. It next moves to the process of completing the research paper, with two student sample research papers (using the MLA and APA style manuals, respectively) that illustrate each stage of the writing and documentation process. That section is followed by a discussion of the fundamentals of business writing. The text closes with a glossary of usage and a glossary of grammatical terms.

Each part of the handbook's eight parts is subdivided into units and then further subdivided into sections that contain a rule followed by examples, cross-referenced to appropriate sections in the text, and where appropriate, exercises that allow for practical application of the subject matter. Model paragraphs and essays contribute to this emphasis on realistic applications. There are more than forty paragraphs by professional writers in addition to two sample research papers by students. One of the papers is a literary analysis of William Faulkner's novel *As I Lay Dying* that follows MLA rules of documentation; the other is an essay on the ethics of animal experimentation, written in APA style. In tandem, these papers provide a broad illustration of problems in documentation, demonstrate effective use of in-text citations, and offer practical applications of earlier textual coverage of both MLA and APA documentation styles.

New Design

To make *The Modern Writer's Handbook* more practical and accessible, we have provided a new design. Colored tab indexes appear at the top of every text page, highlighting the unit symbol and section number of the material appearing on that page and thus providing students with an easy reference. Information can be accessed by simply flipping through the pages. The front endpapers include a detailed revision checklist students can refer to as they work on their papers and an indexed chart of correction symbols they can consult as they review their corrected papers. Back endpapers contain an abbreviated table of contexts that incorporates tab symbols found within the text for easy location of material. The revised glossaries of usage and grammatical terms and the detailed index and cross-referenced material further enable students to locate information with ease.

Exercises and Examples

In response to reader and reviewer comments, many of the exercises have been written and updated. All of the exercises consist of related sentences that give students practice proofreading in paragraph form.

Supplements

This new edition of *The Modern Writer's Handbook* is accompanied by an expanded and comprehensive supplementary package. *The Modern Writer's Workbook* (with accompanying answer key) by Marie-Louise N. Matthew of Bronx Community College offers additional exercises, tabs that correspond to those found in the handbook, and a cross-referencing index on the front endpapers that allows for easy integration of the handbook and workbook. The *Test Item File* by Marie-Louise N. Matthew and Katie B. Davis includes diagnostic and achievement tests and a comprehensive test. It is available in printed form as an 8½ × 11 booklet with perforated pages and as a MICROTEST software program for the IBM computer. *The Macmillan Electronic Handbook*℗, developed by Technology Training Associates, Inc., Cambridge, Massachusetts, is an on-line reference program which incorporates the key elements of the handbook. The program can be used with any word processing system on the IBM-PC and is available to adopters of the second edition of *The Modern Writer's Handbook.*

Acknowledgments

I would like to express my gratitude to those who helped make this second edition possible, particularly Barbara Carson of the University of Georgia, contributing editor of this edition. Barbara's hard work and dedication to the quality of the text have both strengthened and, indeed, improved the presentation of the concepts presented within these pages. Her expertise in grammar and her skills as a teacher are evident throughout the text. Her advice and contributions to the development of the supplements accompanying the book are also appreciated.

I must also thank William J. Kelly of Bristol Community College and Deborah C. Andrews of the University of Delaware for their expert advice. We are grateful to Peter Conlin and Sheila Roxanne Woody for granting us permission to use their research papers and to their respective instructors, Professor David Payne and Dr. Stuart Katz.

Thanks must also be extended to John Campbell, Reference Librarian at the University of Georgia, for his assistance in preparing the computer search and documentation section of the text. And, of course, we recognize the reviewers, whose advice helped guide us through this revision: Victoria Aarons, Trinity University; Lucien L. Agosta, California State University–Sacramento; Vivian Brown, Laredo Junior College; Barbara Fine Clouse, Youngstown State University; William Coyle, Florida Atlantic University; Robert DiYanni, Pace University; Harriette Y. Dodson, Florida Community College of Jacksonville; Sylvia Gengenbach, University of Wisconsin–Stout; Casey Gilson, Broward Community College; Polly S. Glover,

University of Tennessee at Martin; Donna Gorrell, St. Cloud State University; Edward A. Kline, University of Notre Dame; Donna J. Quinn, University of Minnesota–Duluth; Helen Quinn, University of Wisconsin–Stout; and Raymond A. St. John, Bob Jones University.

I also wish to express my gratitude to the dedicated staff at Macmillian: Sharon Balbos, associate development editor; Amy K. Davis, editorial assistant; Aliza Greenblatt, production supervisor; Eileen Burke, assistant art and design director; and Barbara A. Heinssen, English editor.

Frank O'Hare
Ohio State University

To the Student

How to Use This Book

This book has been designed to help you learn to write effectively. It does not pretend to give you a sure-fire formula for an essay or a quick answer on how to avoid all errors. There are no such shortcuts. Instead, *The Modern Writer's Handbook* provides a plan for learning that begins by illustrating general writing strategies and proceeds to aid you in working through the stages of planning, drafting, revising, and proofreading. The suggestions offered are not laws, but options. It is not wrong, for example, to write a draft of an essay without outlining first, but since some people find outlining helpful, we describe strategies for outlining in Unit 2.

Organization

This book begins with a general overview of the writing process that includes how to plan, draft, and revise your essay. It then deals with the surface features of the language, with the important conventions that educated readers expect to encounter when they read your work. The text concludes by introducing you to specialized writing tasks you'll encounter in college or in the world of commerce and industry: research and business writing.

Part I offers advice about the writing process, including preparation for writing, producing a first draft, and revising. Then the parts of the essay are considered in detail with coverage of paragraph development and transitions within and between paragraphs. Sentences are also covered with suggestions for variety in structure, clarity, and effective emphasis. Part I ends with a discussion of critical thinking and faulty reasoning. Parts II through VI of the book examine the principles of grammar, sentence form, punctuation, spelling, and diction. If you are already familiar with grammatical principles and terms and the conventions of usage, you will use this section as reference only. If your familiarity with this material is limited, you may use these sections to help you master the conventions of grammar and usage. Part II, "Grammar," presents the principles and terms; Part III, "Sentence Form," examines problems that often appear if the principles established in the grammar section are violated; and Part IV explains the conventions of punctuation and mechanics. Part V on spelling and Part VI on diction conclude this section.

Part VII explains and illustrates how to write a research paper. The emphasis here is on the research writing process: how to conduct research, how to plan and write the paper, and how to document according to styles recommended by the Modern Language Association (MLA) and the American Psychological Association (APA). Two sample research papers are included: one utilizes the MLA style; the other, APA. Part VIII, "Business Writing," explains and illustrates memo and letter writing, the resume, and the job application, with samples of memos, business letters, and résumés for guidance.

The text is arranged first into parts, then into units. Each unit contains sections that explore in detail the subject matter at hand. For instance, Part V, "Spelling," contains the following subdivisions: unit 37, spelling rules; unit 38, troublesome words; unit 39, capitalization, unit 40, the apostrophe; and unit 41, the hyphen. Each of these units is further subdivided. Thus, unit 37 covers the following: 37a on doubling the final consonant; 37b on dropping the silent *e*; 37c on changing the *y* to *i*; 37d on choosing between *ei* and *ie*; 37e on forming noun plurals. Each of these subsections will provide you with rules to follow, examples for clarification, and practice exercises.

How to Find the Information You Need Quickly and Efficiently

- Colored "tabs" at the top of every text page contain the particular unit symbol and section number on the page and enable you to locate the information you seek by simply thumbing through the book.

- Top-of-page titles containing the particular unit title or section identification simplify locating material. Headings on the left-hand pages spell out the unit title; right-hand page headings give you more specific guidance.

- These unit symbols correspond to items listed in the abbreviated table of contents on the back endpapers and in the correction symbol index on the inside of the front cover. Instructors often use these symbols when responding to your papers. You can then consult several sources for a description or explanation of the error: the top-of-page tabs, the abbreviated table of contents at the rear of the book, the detailed table of contexts at the front of the book, or the correction symbol list. For instance, if your instructor marked "agr" in the margin of your paper, you could look to the correction symbol list on the inside of the front cover and note that this abbreviation indicates faulty agreement and turn to the section number indicated, 15. The detailed index at the back of the text could also direct you to the page on which you would find a discussion of subject-verb agreement. You could also flip through the pages of the text until you found the abbreviation "agr" in the colored tabs in Unit 15 on subject-verb agreement. Sections 15a through 15i elaborate further on subject-verb agreement with examples and exercises on compound subjects (section 15a), intervening phrases and clauses (section 15b), and so forth.

You cannot learn to write well without writing often. *The Modern Writer's Handbook* aims to be a guide to all the steps in the writing process and with continued use will help you grow in competence and confidence. Paradoxically, the more diligently you use this small book, the less you need it.

Frank O'Hare
Ohio State University

Contents

Part II
Grammar

Part III
Sentence Form

Part IV
Punctuation and Mechanics

Part V
Spelling

Part VI

Diction

Part VII
Writing the Research Paper

Part VIII
Business Writing

Part I

The Process
of Writing

1 Preparation for Writing

Few people can pick up a tennis racket for the first time and nail a perfect serve across the net without thinking. Such competence in athletics is rare, however, and the same is true among writers. Like the tennis serve, writing requires a combination of skills perfected over time. It requires coordination of thought, language, and hand, and most of us are no more naturally adept at making the three work together than we are at making our arm muscles, our eyesight, and a racket put a tennis ball where we want it. So, like the tennis player, we must discover the strategies for learning to write and then practice. Writing strategies are prewriting, drafting, and revising, and each of them is itself a series of steps. In the beginning of the process of writing—prewriting—three activities are especially useful: keeping a journal, reading, and writing letters.

1a Keeping a Journal

A journal differs from a diary because it goes beyond recounting the events of the writer's day to recording what the writer *thought* about the events or about some information. For example, a diary entry might read:

May 17

> Met Juanita at the ice cream parlor yesterday p.m. She had a bandaged knee from falling off her bicycle and couldn't keep our date for the dance. Ralph's girlfriend offered to call a friend of hers for me, but I stayed with Juanita and went with her to a movie and Burger King instead.

A journal entry, on the other hand, might read like this:

> Juanita had to break our dance date the other night because she had damaged her knee in falling off her bike. She piled up,

of course, because she was riding no-hands the way she always does on her heavy class days. Nothing I say seems to convince her that a backpack would be much better for hauling her books around than four texts under each arm and a prayer that God will steer and brake for her. She says the backpack would look sloppy, and I have to admit she dresses well. But why wear a boutique on your shoulders and live dangerously? I suppose there is something to be said for going in style, but she ought to realize as well that pride goeth before a fall.

You need not keep a journal on a daily basis, but you should keep it with some regularity if you are to gain any benefit from it. The journal gives regular practice in coordinating thought, language, and hand; it also provides a reservoir of ideas for future writing. In the sample entry above, there is an abundance of raw material to develop into an essay: the sacrifice of safety and practicality to appearance, the futility of arguing for a change in a person's basic values, the theme of pride's leading to a fall. That great authors like Henry David Thoreau, F. Scott Fitzgerald, Henry James, George Sand, and many, many others kept journals is no accident. The practice of thinking things out in a journal is invaluable writing preparation.

1b Reading

Travel with a book. When you are stuck in traffic, waiting for a bus, or standing in line at the bank or the supermarket, read everything—books, newspapers, magazines, poems, billboards. Learn through reading what others have experienced and learned. What you read becomes part of your own experience for later use.

As you read, do more than absorb information; think about the way the author writes, about the turns of phrase, about the rhythm of sentences and how the author avoids—or fails to avoid—a monotonous delivery. Try to store up particularly effective passages as models for your own prose. Read critically. Learn to argue with the printed word. A disagreement with another's point of view is a potential starting point for an essay. Read looking for grammatical mistakes and errors of punctuation. If you can spot the faults of others, you will proofread your own work more accurately. Read to discover the author's tone and purpose, and how they complement each other. Use your journal to record what you think about what you read.

1c Writing Letters

Writing letters to friends and relatives is excellent writing practice. The recipient of a letter is a clearly defined audience for the writer, and we usually adjust our letters consciously or unconsciously to the likes and dislikes of the person we are writing to. Think of the adjustments you find yourself making in such letters. Ask yourself why you wrote to Great-Uncle Herman about the "minor automobile accident" that prevented you from attending Gretchen's wedding, and why you described the same occurrence as "a stupid fender-bender" to your friend Dee. Work at making your letters entertaining. Invent new ways of saying "nothing much has happened here"—and remember, something always has.

Exercise 1

Set yourself the goal of writing at least 150 words a day for a month. The writing can be of any sort as long as it is not required academically or professionally. Count personal letters and journal entries as part of the exercise. Write more than 150 words if you like, but don't write 1,000 words on Tuesday evening and call it a week's work. Instead, spread your writing out so that you'll gain more from the practice.

Exercise 2

Keep a record for one week of everything you read. (Don't count advertisements and notices.) At the end of the week, review your record and select the piece of reading that sticks most clearly in your mind. Write a brief discussion of your choice, explaining why you remember it so well. Look at it again and evaluate the way it is written. Is there anything in the author's writing that makes the piece stand out?

2 The Process of Writing: First Draft

The finished essay is the product of the writer's work, and that work consists of interrelated and interwoven actions that are collectively called a *process*. It is a complex process whose parts are unpredictable, because writers tend to develop their own distinct processes as they grow in experience. And it is a process that shapes itself as it goes.

If you set out to make a box, you begin with a clear mental picture of what a box is and can easily follow a simple process of construction that will give you a product with a bottom, four sides, and a lid connected at right angles. But when you decide to write, your image of the product is vague or perhaps nonexistent. You might, for example, begin with the idea of saying something about air pollution and find yourself discussing alternative forms of energy production, only to discover that what you really feel strongly about is the possible danger of nuclear reactors. The process of writing is likely to produce such discoveries.

In addition, the process may loop back on itself or even change direction altogether, and so it is partly misleading to present it as a series of steps that are completed and cemented in place one on top of another. But familiarity with the various steps in the writing process will help you understand the process as a whole and give you freedom to apply it as you find best in your case. The actions most writers find necessary in the process of writing are *prewriting, drafting, revising,* and *proofreading.*

2a Prewriting

When people think about writing a paper, they usually think in terms of the finished product. They envision a paper that is correct in terms of both *form* and *content.* The truth is, however, that a successful draft stems from planning, which with writing is called **prewriting.** This stage of the writing process involves a number of activities that enable you to focus on a specific subject and generate examples, illustrations, and details to support and explain that subject. This stage also includes identifying and addressing other elements of writing that affect the effectiveness of your paper, such as its purpose, audience, and tone. But the emphasis at this point in the writing process is on content—on developing ideas—rather than on form.

On the following pages, you will find a number of suggestions for prewriting. Do not regard them as a prescription, every element of which must be used. Experiment until you find the practices that work for *you.* If some do not help, do not frustrate yourself by following them.

Freewriting

If you are at a loss for an idea, try **freewriting.** Set yourself a time limit of, say, ten minutes and write down anything that comes into your head during that time. No restrictions apply as far as content is concerned. Don't worry about misspelling words or using incorrect grammar or about your writing not sticking to one subject or even making sense. The only rule is that your pen or pencil must keep moving on the page for those ten minutes. This is a sample of one writer's freewriting:

On the mark - ten minutes. Find something to say. Find something to fix your mind on. What's on the desk here? Brother's photograph. Some sort of Middle Eastern pot with two pencils and a letter opener in it. Sundial I never fixed up in the yard. (Think my brother gave me that two years ago.) Why did I never put that thing to use? Is it something about an unwillingness to face passage of time? Timeless society. Aging without counting. How long does it take to put a sundial on a post? If I did put it up, would I look at it? What's the point of a sundial in today's world of quartz watches? A timeless way of keeping time? Why are sundials in the Northern part of U.S. different from those in the South? Something to do with the angle of the sun, I guess.

Go back to the sundial and time.

Remember verse I once saw on a sundial. Something about "I record only sunny hours." The sundial is an attractive anachronism because it is a *timeless way of telling time and counts only hours in the Sun.*

In this first freewriting, the writer reviews and examines the random articles on the desk and then fixes on one particular object, thus developing a focus and some preliminary supporting details for it. As you can see, not all the information that appears in a freewriting will be useful, of course; this excess of material is another characteristic of freewriting. Sometimes such a random examination of objects around you will lead you to a specific focus. With freewriting, however, virtually any subject will lead you in some direction. In this next freewriting, for example, the writer tries to discover some ideas by dealing with the idea of freewriting itself.

Freewriting for ten minutes! What's "free" about that? Freewriting should include freedom not to write at all. I don't intend to make my living like Hemingway, and I bet he didn't have to spend time free-algebraing. This assignment is about as fair as required military service. Do what you aren't inclined to for your own good. Develop writing habits. Develop writing rabbits! New breakthrough in veterinary medicine - or would that be behavioral psychology? See the writing rabbit autograph a lettuce leaf! This is getting nowhere.

At first glance, this freewriting might not seem to hold much promise. In fact, however, this writer has found two or three openings for an essay: the freedom exercised by saying no, the fairness of required military service, and the merit—or lack of merit—in being made to do something distasteful for one's own good.

Brainstorming

Another prewriting technique is **brainstorming.** While freewriting is a prewriting activity designed so that a writer generates much more information with the intent of discovering a specific focus in the random material, brainstorming is a far more deliberate, purposeful attempt to develop a specific list of information. A writer can undertake brainstorming alone or as part of a group. Obviously, the results of a group's brainstorming will be more diverse than the products of a single imagination, but the object in either case is the same: to generate as many topics as possible for exploration. In the first stage of brainstorming, keep the topics to simple nouns and noun phrases. Set a goal of ten different topics for a start, such as the following:

gun control	nuclear disarmament
vocational training	new roles for women
holidays	military conscription
drunken driving	drug abuse
environmental pollution	regulation of the automobile industry

Any of these topics would be worthy of your attention; sometimes you might even combine two or more of the topics. Unless for some reason you must write on a specific topic, choose one of the subjects you've developed that you already know about or are interested in pursuing. The less you know about a subject or the less interested you are in finding out about it, the more difficult you will find writing about that topic.

Once you have completed this first part of brainstorming, you move to the next step. This second part of brainstorming is similar to the first stage but the object is to write down as much as you can think of about the topic selected. Here is a sample of brainstorming on the topic "new roles for women."

Women are doing much more today than in the past--many occupations are open today that once seemed only for men--doctor, lawyer, business executive, construction worker, airline pilot, all professions and positions. It isn't always easy, of course. Wonder what the percentage of women getting into medical school is? Should be 50/50 but I don't think half the students in medical school are women. That saying says it all: "A woman must work twice as hard as a man to prove she deserves the job; fortunately, this isn't hard." Within positions more traditionally held by women, they are taking more control. In education, working as principals, superintendents, department heads--jobs were the official domain of men. In nursing, more and more women are serving as supervisors and administrators--they supervise more men working as LPNs and RNs--that's a healthy change. More women are having and keeping careers, too. Some of them put off marriage because they want a career. Many who do get married put off having children. A lot more older mothers. Returning to work presents a real problem, too: child care. Years ago child care was no problem--women traditionally stayed in the home and raised children. Now these career women want to return to their professions and therefore need someone to care for their children. With the economy, most married couples both have to work today in order to pay a mortgage or rent and to pay for a car. Even women who don't have big-time careers must work. It's a real problem. The mothers

of these women had a more defined role. They were homemakers.
Today's women are homemakers <u>and</u> workers. They have to balance
everything in their lives. If they balance everything, they're viewed
suspiciously. If a man tries hard to work himself up the ladder
somewhere, that's good. People say he's aggressive. But if a woman does
the same thing, it's bad--people say she's pushy. Some things are
resistant to change, I guess. Women's roles increase, but they don't
necessarily get easier.

If brainstorming one topic does not produce an adequate
range of thoughts, try another topic.

Clustering

A variation of brainstorming is **clustering.** Write the topic in
the middle of a piece of paper. As ideas related to the topic
occur to you, place them randomly around the topic. Let one
subject lead to another. Try to visualize your ideas as rays of
light streaming out from a central topic. Then study the related
ideas and see what kinds of connections you can find among
them. Draw lines between connected ideas. Then, on another
page, write the topic in the middle again and arrange potentially related ideas in clusters around it.

On page 12 is an example of clustering around the topic
of the changing roles of women.

Other ways of finding a topic

If freewriting and brainstorming fail to produce a workable
topic for an unspecified essay, try these other approaches.

1. If you keep a journal, page through it for a thought or
   impression you can enlarge.
2. Open a newspaper or magazine at random and read the

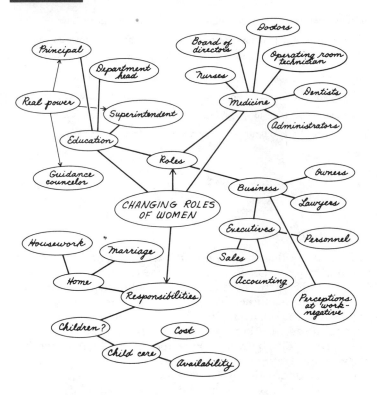

first piece or article your eye falls on. Keep trying until something inspires you to state an opinion about it.

3. Take a walk through a crowded shopping mall or sit in a busy cafeteria—anyplace where many people are congregated. Then, with a notepad in hand, simply observe and take notes about what you see. Chances are you will see something that will interest you enough for you to explore it through writing.

Finding a purpose

The purpose of an essay is not the same thing as the reason for writing an essay. An error in your telephone bill gives you a reason to write to the telephone company—the motivation—but the purpose of your letter is to *inform* the company it has made a mistake and to *persuade* it to make a correction in your favor. Once you have found a topic, a preliminary decision on your purpose in writing about that topic will help you shape your essay. You may choose to inform or to persuade or to do any of the following:

- *to record* your thoughts on a topic. Some journal entries are written to record as are your class notes.
- *to entertain* an audience. In entertaining essays the writer embellishes the topic with wit, humor, word play, and action. A writer can entertain a reader without humor, of course. A good tragedy entertains as does a good horror story or a gripping first-person presentation of a near-drowning. *Entertaining* in these cases means feeding a reader's interest.
- *to instruct,* to tell someone, for example, how to connect a printer to an Apple IIc computer. Such essays are often called process papers because they describe a process.
- *to analyze* a topic, that is, to examine the parts of the topic and the way they relate to one another. Essays about literary works are often analytical; they probe the author's performance to understand its effect.
- *to argue* a point and express an opinion. Such an essay must take both sides of an issue into account while favoring one of them.
- *to reveal* the writer. A job application letter is written not only to describe the applicant's qualifications but also to reveal the applicant's character through the manner of its describing.
- *to evaluate* a work or item. Criticism evaluates a play.

This list is not exhaustive, but it includes the primary purposes. Two or more purposes may characterize the same essay: for example, an argumentative essay may be entertaining, and an evaluative paper may include the writer's expression of opinion and an analysis of the topic. You will probably find it most helpful to decide on a single purpose and let subordinate purposes arise as you develop your thesis.

Reviewing brainstorming and clustering

As part of finding a purpose for your topic, study your brainstorming and/or clustering. You will usually find a variety of possibilities for development. The brainstorming on the changing roles of women, for instance, deals with the following:

1. Some of the professional positions that women fill today.
2. The questions of equality in society that still affect women.
3. The move of women into management positions in education, health care, and business.
4. The changing perception of marriage, child-rearing, and housework on the part of today's women.
5. The difficulty and expense of providing child care.
6. The unfair stereotype of the career woman.

All of the information concerning these subtopics is interesting and potentially useful, but the writer must identify the purpose of the writing before deciding which information to include and which to discard, at least for now.

The basic purpose formula

You may be able to establish a preliminary purpose by filling out the following formula:

In this essay I will _____ .

Fill in the blank with statements such as *record my impressions of* (the topic); *express my opinion that* (the topic) *is or is not* _____ ; *argue that* (the topic) *should or should not be approved; analyze* (the topic) *to show that* _____ ; *instruct my audience how to* _____ . You need not use exactly these phrases, but do give yourself something specific to achieve in the essay.

The journalist's formula

As a way of defining what you know about your topic (or need to know) in order to state a purpose, you can use **the journalist's formula:** Who? What? When? Where? Why? How? For example, here is how the journalist's formula might be applied to the topic of the changing roles of women.

- Who are these modern women?
- What are the problems they face?
- When do they occur?
- Where do they take place?
- Why are people concerned about them?
- How do they affect women and society at large?

The answers to these questions can actually help you focus on your purpose. If you find yourself drawn to the answer you produce to "How do they affect women and society at large?" you can use the same questions to zero in on this particular answer. The more often you follow this cycle, the more specific the information you produce will be.

Using your reader to guide you

One of the best ways to help you establish a purpose in your writing is to consider the needs and interests of your reader. Your reader is, after all, the individual for whom you are writing. Therefore, writing successfully means providing a focus and supporting information that will communicate your ideas to your reader.

The first step in communicating your ideas is to identify your reader. Sometimes doing so seems too simple; if you are writing a paper in your writing class, then the reader would logically seem to be your instructor. But it isn't always that simple. If you write your paper with the idea that your writing teacher alone will read it, then you are gearing the paper to fit the special, idiosyncratic needs of a single person whom you have gradually come to know better day by day in class. As a result, you begin to get a sense of what that instructor knows and does not know about a variety of subjects, and you begin to make subtle adjustments in your presentation. In other words, as you develop a sense of your shared information, you leave out material that you feel reasonably sure your instructor knows.

But imagine for a moment that one of the papers you prepare for this instructor is somehow sent to another instructor for evaluation. If you have written about baseball, for example, and you have talked about the infield fly rule and suicide squeeze because you knew your own instructor understands baseball, you will be in trouble if the instructor who actually does evaluate your paper does not share the same level of knowledge about baseball. Therefore, except under certain circumstances (e.g., specific directions of your instructor to do so) you should not consider your instructor as your reader.

Focusing on the general reader

Successful newspaper columnists Andy Rooney and Erma Bombeck, along with thousands of their colleagues nationwide, reach millions of readers every day. They do so by providing the types of information that most people would need to understand the points they are presenting. In writing terms, they focus on the general reader, the average individual who knows a little about many things but lacks the specific information on the subject the writer wants to present. The general reader knows what an opera generally is but not the specific details about a specific opera; the general reader knows that blood carries nourishment throughout the body but not the specific role that red blood cells, white blood cells, and platelets play in this process. And the general reader may know that more working mothers means a greater need for child care but not that there are not nearly enough reliable, inexpensive child-care centers available.

Likewise, the general reader has a variety of interests. This variety works to your benefit as the writer. As you gauge the material you have produced through your freewriting, brainstorming, or clustering and try to decide on a focus, consider the interests of the average person. Think, for example, of those specific subjects you like and of how your interests developed. Certainly, you did not awake one day with the level of enthusiasm you possess today about any subject—and you cannot expect that your reader is automatically going to have such a deep interest either. Therefore, focus on some aspect that you feel will lead that average reader to develop an interest, much as it gradually led to a greater interest on your own part. Considering the needs of the general reader will make your job of choosing a focus for your writing easier.

Of course, there will be times when you will want to write to a more expert audience. If you are preparing a lab report for chemistry, you will probably be writing to readers at least as knowledgeable about chemistry as you. If you are writing a magazine article for a running magazine, you will be writing to a group of running enthusiasts who share a great deal of technical information about running. You will not need to gear down your presentation for these audiences. Likewise, if you are preparing a pamphlet on human conception for an elementary school student audience, you would also adjust your presentation, this time to a far simpler level than you would for the general reader.

As with any writing assignment, the whole context—the subject, reader, purpose, and so on—must be considered. If you take some time to consider these elements, especially the most important element in the writing process—your reader —you will be more likely to develop an effective focus, the first step toward a successful paper.

Setting a tone

Tone cannot be determined by completing a formula; sometimes it cannot be determined until the first or even the third draft of the essay is complete. But some decision on tone before the writing begins will help you keep a consistent delivery and find the right tone for the finished essay.

Tone is the result of word choice based on attitude—on how the writer feels about the subject, on how the writer feels about the audience, and on how the writer wants the audience to feel about the writer and the subject. The writer's purpose will influence decisions on all three points, but especially on the last.

Consider the different ways two writers handled the same subject in the following sentences:

> The city planning board has apparently surpassed its usual high standard of idiocy and irresolution by willfully ignoring the menace of increased and uncontrolled heavy vehicle traffic on Prospect Avenue.

> The city planning board may have shown poor judgment in making no plans for controlling the number of trucks using Prospect Avenue.

Both sentences say essentially the same thing. The second, however, has a more neutral tone. We cannot say much about how the author sounds, except to say he sounds concerned. His audience could be anyone he does not want to offend, his subject is of minor importance to him and his audience, and his purpose is to call attention gently to a situation that may need correction at some time in the distant future.

The tone of the first sentence, on the other hand, is full of sounds. We might even call it strident. The author has loaded the statement with scorn (*apparently surpassed*), sarcasm (*high standard of idiocy*), accusation (*willfully ignoring*), foreboding (*menace*), and—overall—anger. But the author is doing more than venting wrath at the city planners. For that effect she might have written:

> Those lunkheads on the planning board really loused up when they forgot to put a "No Trucks" sign on Prospect.

But if she had written that, she would have written without considering her audience. (Are we moved by someone who writes "lunkheads"?) She would also have written without considering her purpose. (The tone calls attention to the writer, not to how the writer wants us to respond.) Instead, the writer chose an almost literary tone. She determined that this subject and her feelings called for formal language (*irresolution, vehicle, increased and uncontrolled*) and stylistic devices (scorn and sarcasm) to show that she was angry at the city planners and that her intelligent readers would agree with her. The choices may not be entirely successful, but we can see that they were made consciously.

Tone is like fire: a good servant and a bad master. To control it, the writer must have a good sense of subject and purpose and must keep a constant vision of audience in mind. To make a preliminary choice of tone, try to answer these questions:

1. What is my attitude to my topic? (Am I enthusiastic? Am I bitter? Am I cynical? Am I concerned? Many other attitudes are possible.)
2. How deeply do I feel this attitude?
3. How do I want my audience to perceive my attitude?

4. How closely do I want my audience to feel my presence as writer? (Talking directly, individual to individual? Talking from the front of the room to a group? Talking from a distance via radio?)

5. What response do I want from my audience? (Amusement? Agreement? Action?)

Remember that the audience senses the writer through tone. Writers must learn to hear themselves in their tone if they want to sound natural, for although writing and speaking differ, the essay tone of an experienced writer reflects rhythms and word choices of the writer's speaking habits. Such a tone reads more naturally than an assumed or forced one does. *As you write, ask yourself: "Would I say that if I were talking?" If, in all honesty, you doubt that you would, consider carefully whether you want to keep the construction you have used or to replace it with a more familiar expression.*

Stating a thesis

Before starting your draft, you may want to summarize your prewriting to this point by stating your thesis succinctly. The **thesis statement** is a phrase, preferably a complete sentence, composed before the draft begins. It encapsulates the point the essay will make. As you think of a thesis statement, keep two things in mind.

1. Do not try to put your thesis statement into words appropriate to the style and tone of your finished essay. Good writing does not happen on the first try. Make the plainest possible declaration of what you want to achieve. One good formula to begin with is the following:

I think _____(topic)_____ is _____

shows _____

should or should not _____

because _____

2. Do not assume your thesis statement is a fixture. If work on your essay proves that the thesis statement is indefensible or that some other aspect of your topic is more appealing, more interesting, or more controversial, restate your thesis to meet the new developments. Remember you are experimenting with an idea in the rough. You have several drafts in which to test the idea for validity.

If you use the formula recommended, take the product another step before beginning to write. *Make sure that your thesis statement does more than merely announce your topic.*

Topic:	A Brooklyn neighborhood
Formula:	I think my Brooklyn neighborhood is unique because diverse cultures form a unique identity.
Thesis statement:	My own neighborhood, Bay Ridge, shows how diverse ethnic cultures combine to give the area a unique identity.

Build on the formula to include specific words. The more specific you are, the more guidance you will have in writing your essay.

Topic:	Drivers' responsibilities
Formula:	I think young drivers are unaware of the responsibility involved in driving.
Thesis statement:	A person of seventeen seldom fully appreciates the responsibility of driving.

A thesis statement should make a *vigorous* statement; it should assert the topic in a context that demands explanation, expansion, analysis, or defense.

Bland:	Those who argue for abortion on demand sometimes also argue against capital punishment.
Vigorous:	Those who argue for abortion on demand are inconsistent when they also argue against capital punishment.

A good test of a thesis statement is to ask: Could I state the opposite and make a case for that point of view? If you can answer yes, you probably have a workable thesis statement.

The thesis statement will usually emerge in the finished essay as a thesis sentence, but let the essay's development determine how and where the thesis sentence appears.

Priming writing

Sometimes you work and work, but you simply cannot seem to develop a thesis. If you are stuck for a thesis statement, simply begin to write. This technique is called **priming writing,** and it is easy to master. First, set a goal of 150–200 words and start writing about the topic from any angle. Try to produce connected sentences, with details or subordinate points to support generalizations. The purpose of this writing is to prime the pump, to get your mind and fingers working with your topic and into the mood to write.

The following is an example of priming writing on the topic of the changing roles of women.

People say that a woman must work twice as hard as a man to prove that she deserves a job, but that, fortunately, most women do not find that hard. Maybe this is changing today, but women still face a difficult world. Their roles are changing and the result is a far more difficult time for them in the business and domestic world.

At work, women face a number of problems. If they are too ambitious or aggressive, they are distrusted. But they are now making inroads anyway. Now they are managers, supervisors, and department heads, with both men and women under their control. In schools, they are no longer just teachers; they are principals, guidance counselors, and superintendents, too. In hospitals, they are not just nurses anymore, either; they are doctors, supervisors, and administrators as well.

Working women run into many difficulties on the home front, too. Studies show that married women who work still do most of the household chores. Career women also often have to make choices between their career and having children. Many of them put off marriage and childbearing until their 30s or older. Sometimes this means more difficult pregnancies. If these women have children, they face even more problems because they must find reliable and affordable child care.

Although the priming writing contains no specific thesis statement yet, it does express some of the writer's feelings and attitudes about the changing roles of women: the roles women are playing in today's world are different and perhaps better, but they are paying an unfair price for their movement forward. As a result, the writer has a more specific direction and can develop a tentative thesis statement:

I think the roles of women today are changing and at the same time their roles are becoming more complicated.

A more explicit statement derived from the formula might be:

Today's women play many more roles than at any other time in history, and they are also paying a high price in terms of the effects such advances have on their personal, domestic, and professional lives.

Outlining

An **outline** provides a framework for a first draft and helps prevent organizational blunders. There are two main kinds of outlines. The first, and the most practical for a short essay, is the sentence outline; the second is the formal outline.

In a **sentence outline,** the writer states each subordinate topic of the thesis as a sentence and arranges the sentences in the order of development that the essay will follow. Usually, but not always, each sentence outline is the topic for a paragraph of the essay. Consider the following example of a sentence outline:

TODAY'S WOMEN: MORE ROLES, MORE RESPONSIBILITIES

1 Women have made great strides forward in terms of the roles they play in society, but the cost they must bear for such gains is high.

2 With the increasing number of women in administrative and managerial positions in business, education, and medicine, there is no doubt that the roles of women today are changing.

3 At work, women face a number of problems, especially if they are perceived as ambitious or aggressive.

4 The problems women face at home, though, are even more complicated; most married women who work are still responsible for household chores as well.

5 Career women wanting children face a great conflict as they delay childbearing until a later age and then must find adequate, affordable child care.

6 Most people would agree that the changing roles of women mean progress for all society, but women are paying a steep price for their steps forward.

The **formal outline,** by comparison, is more complicated and detailed than the sentence outline. The most common type of formal outline uses a combination of roman numerals, capital letters, arabic numbers, lowercase letters, and lowercase roman numerals to indicate the various divisions of a subject. The largest divisions are indicated by roman numerals, each of which is subdivided in sections signified by capital letters. If further subdivision of these sections is required, it is signified by arabic numbers, and so on. One traditional rule to remember with the formal topic outline is that any topic you divide must be separated into at least two portions—logically, one apple cannot be divided into one piece. In other words, there must be a subtopic B if there is a subtopic A, a subtopic 2 if there is a subtopic 1, and so on. The following example shows the arrangement of part of a typical formal outline:

TODAY'S WOMEN: MORE ROLES, MORE RESPONSIBILITIES

roman numeral	I. New Roles in Society for Women
capital letter	A. Business
arabic number	1. Owners
	2. Corporate officers
	B. Education
	1. Principals
	2. Guidance counselors
	3. Superintendents
	C. Medicine
	1. Doctors
	2. Administrators
lowercase letter	a. Full-scale executives
arabic numeral in parenthesis	(1) Presidents
	(2) Chair, board of directors
	b. Floor supervisors
	c. Personnel directors

    II. **Difficulties Women Face at Work**

        A. Reactions to perceived ambition

        B. Reactions to perceived aggressiveness

    III. **Difficulties Married Women Face at Home**

        A. Distribution of household chores

            1. Wife's responsibilities

            2. Husband's responsibilities

        B. Cooking

        C. Laundry

        D. Grocery shopping

Obviously, the writer who chooses a formal outline as a start must think the topic through completely and develop working notes *before* trying to outline. For a long essay, such as a research paper, the formal outline is valuable; for a short essay, it is probably too cumbersome. However, the formal outline can be valuable in the revising of a short paper. Once you have a suitable draft, you can plot your ideas into the framework of an outline. That way you can make sure that every part of your draft is relevant and connected.

2b Writing the First Draft

Having selected a topic; defined it, settled on purpose, audience, and tone; established a thesis sentence, and planned your essay; you are ready to write a first draft.

But take a breather for a moment. All those prewriting steps, or some of them, may well help you get started; however, there is such a thing as getting bogged down in the preliminaries. Another way of getting started is to write the first draft without making any of the preparatory efforts. It is not a crime to plunge straight in and see what happens. *What is a crime is to plunge in under the impression that the first draft will become the final draft with only a bit of light tinkering.*

Whether you make a careful prewriting preparation or let the essay happen as it may from your pen, you *must* regard your first draft as a throwaway—as something that will be only vaguely related to the finished essay. Always think of it as something to be broken down and rearranged, as prose to be thoroughly rewritten until it is right, as something far beneath your potential. In short, your first draft is a starting point *only*.

Keeping in mind that the first draft is only the first stage of an essay, follow these guidelines in writing it:

1. Write the first draft well before the finished essay is due. A week in advance is desirable; a twenty-four-hour lead is essential. *Don't wait until the last minute—ever.*

2. Write the first draft as rapidly as possible. You want to capture ideas rather than form.

3. Ignore spelling and punctuation questions as you write. If you are uncertain of one or the other at any point, mark the place and write on. Any signal will do. Use a wavy line under the doubtful place or circle it, but do not stop to look things up. Do that *after* the first draft is complete.

4. Write double or even triple space. Leave room to insert.

5. Cross out; do not erase. And when you cross out, let what you have crossed out show through. You might want to go back to that wording later.

6. Be sloppy! Discourage yourself from even *thinking* of the draft as finished work.

7. Write the draft where you are comfortable. You want a free, sequential flow of ideas.

8. Do not worry about intriguing openings and watertight conclusions. Keep your mind on your thesis, the main points supporting it, and the details that support the main points. Lay a foundation and leave architectural refinements for a later stage.

9. If you find your first draft wandering from your thesis or suggesting more interesting developments, stop. Weigh the merits of starting over to get back to the thesis against the possible value of letting the paper lead you to a thesis. *At this stage nothing is permanent.*

2c Writing with a Word Processor

If you can type at all, a word processor can be the most exciting, most valuable tool in your whole writing toolbox. A word processor enables you to type your ideas onto a piece of plastic called a disk and watch as your words appear on a visual screen where they can be manipulated—added to, erased, corrected, rearranged—and then printed out once you are pleased with them. Imagine taking your first draft and instead of crossing out, erasing, drawing arrows, writing in margins, cutting and pasting, and whiting-out as you revise, hitting a few keys here and there and then printing final copy that is neat and professional looking, with the essay stored conveniently—and permanently if you choose—on that same disk. That's what a word processor can do for you.

Many word-processing programs even check spelling, readability, and grammar. Some programs allow you to move whole portions of your writing—individual words, single sentences, whole paragraphs or more—from one place in a paper to another, a real advantage as you are revising. And no matter what program you are using, you can adjust the format all during the writing process. Some word-processing programs are harder than others to learn, but all of them have one feature in common: if you can type, they allow you to create, arrange, and edit what you write with great speed and efficiency and then store all of it, more than 100 pages in some cases, on a single disk.

Do not be surprised, however, if you find working with a word processor a bit awkward at first. Most of us are so accustomed to working with pencil and paper that we find it diffi-

cult to follow our same writing routines with a typewriter keyboard and a television screen. Stick with it, though—after a
few attempts, you will no doubt find writing with a word processor an advantage.

When you work through the prewriting stage with a word
processor, concentrate on getting ideas down without concerning yourself with errors in form. Type the information as
quickly as it comes to you; because you will easily be able to
correct any errors long before you complete your final draft,
you need not worry about the drudgery of correcting your
messy paper. To overcome the distraction that preliminary
errors might create in the early stages of writing, some researchers suggest that the brightness dial be turned so that the
screen is black. Once you complete your initial collecting of
ideas, turn the brightness back to normal and begin to turn
rough ideas into strong sentences.

Perhaps the stage during which you will find a word processor most valuable is revising. It is at this point that you have
an adequate draft that still has far greater potential. With a few
buttons, you can add or delete information on the basis of your
(or another reader's) reassessment of what you have written. A
word processor also eliminates the drudgery of having to copy
over or retype your final draft, since the changes you have
made on your draft will appear instantly. Hit the save button to
preserve your work on your disk and then the print button, and
a professional-looking final draft will be in your hands. If there
is an easier way to write, it has not yet surfaced.

3 The Process of Writing: Revision

The process of writing does not consist of a series of finite
steps, that is, of stages that have defined beginnings and ends.
When you have once stated a thesis, you are not then done

with the thesis. The first draft and subsequent revisions may substantially alter your thesis as you discover more about your relation to your topic while you write about it. You may also find that your purpose, audience, and tone change as you work. You will probably find yourself going back to the prewriting activities after a first draft—or even after a second one—because you have found a new topic or a radically different aspect of the original one during the process of writing. You must not, therefore, think that the separation of first draft and revision shown here represents a true sequence of events. It is true only insofar as revision, by definition, follows a first attempt.

3a   Revision Is Re-vision

Revising a draft is a matter of seeing again the topic, purpose, audience, and tone. To revise you must probe to discover possible new insights and overlooked opportunities, and you must test what you have written to discover whether it says what you finally want it to say. Revision requires detachment, critical and analytic attention, generating new ideas, ruthlessness, and self-discipline.

Detachment

The effort of writing leaves most of us too closely involved with what we have put on paper to judge the result immediately; therefore, put distance between you and your work. Wait several hours or a few days before revising. The difference between an impression of a draft on its completion and the impression of it a week later is often startling. You should also have someone who you feel will be honest read it; other people are generally more objective about your writing than you are.

Critical and analytic attention

Revision is not only a search for a way to express a point better, it is a search for the best possible point. The critical revision question is not "Could I have put that better?" but "Does what I say truly reflect what I feel *now* about my topic?" The analytic revision question is not "Do my sentences and paragraphs flow smoothly from my thesis to my conclusion?" but "Can I disprove or refute anything I have said?" Some other questions to ask when revising critically and analytically are the following:

- Who is my audience? How will he or she respond to my points?
- If someone else had written this, what would my impression be of that person and his or her opinions?
- Can I make a topic outline of this draft in which all the main ideas are consistent and related?
- Do the thesis statement and the conclusion match? If they do not, which should I choose as the guide to my revision?
- Does everything in the draft relate to my thesis and my conclusion? Is each point a development toward the conclusion, or is it a digression?
- Is each generalization developed with adequate specific facts, illustrations, or examples? Can I think of exceptions to my generalizations that I have not anticipated in my argument?
- If I were to start this paper over from scratch, what would I do differently?

Generating new ideas

Revision should not be restricted to what is in the draft. It should include all aspects of the topic treated—even if these aspects did not occur to you in the first trial. If review of the draft suggests new departures, explore them. Do not abandon new ideas because the first set is on paper and the new ones are not. The more you work with a topic, the more thoughts on the topic you will gather. Let those thoughts occur to you; seek them out; brainstorm again while revising.

Ruthlessness

Cross out and rewrite freely. If the change you have in mind will not fit in the space available, cut the draft apart with scissors and tape it back together with the addition inserted. *Assume from the start that the draft has promise but needs additional work to fulfill that promise.* But do not throw away what is good. Critical revision should discover merits as well as faults in a draft.

Self-discipline

Seeing yourself as others see you is part of revision. Ask someone else to read your draft and give you an opinion. If what you have written is clear to you but unintelligible to someone else, you need to express yourself better. Be careful, however, to ask someone who will be honest. A reader who tells you that your paper is good because that person does not want to offend you is not helping you.

Do not be lazy. Revision is part of the creative process. It deserves at least as much effort as a first draft—usually more. When revising, resist the temptation to focus exclusively on spelling and punctuation faults. Save that step for later. Revision is the time to test the essay for coherence and to refine your tone so that it serves the content instead of directing it. Revision is the time to suit your diction to your topic, purpose, and audience; it is not the time to be overly concerned about comma splices or pronoun reference.

3b Sample First Draft

The following is the first draft of an essay on the changing roles of women.

1   In today's society, the roles that women play are changing. Today women everywhere in business, education, and medicine are accepting the challenge to prove their equality and are moving forward. But the price they are paying for their changing roles and success may simply be too steep.

2   Women have made great strides in the world of business. The executive suite at most major corporations is no longer solely male territory; while they once were present at meetings to take notes and serve coffee, in most of today's major corporations women serve in every capacity. Today's women are entrepreneurs, too. One of America's major firms was founded by a women. Today this business is worth millions.

3   Today's women have also made great inroads in the field of education. Until the latter part of this century, the teaching profession was dominated by women. Yet the real power positions in public education--principals, guidance counselors, superintendents, and other top-level administrators--were traditionally filled by men. But in the last decade, this discrepancy has begun to change. Women are now serving at all levels of public education. A recent study reported that the numbers of women in administrative positions in education during the last quarter century has increased.

4   In the world of medicine, women usually worked as nurses. That's another barrier that today's women have broken down. Women still

serve as nurses, but they serve in various other capacities as well. The number of women applying to and completing medical and dental schools continues to increase. But women are breaking down doors in other areas of the medical world, too. In hospitals, for instance, women now serve in diverse administrative positions that used to be out of their reach.

5   At work, though, women frequently face a double standard. When men are ambitious and set their sights on moving "up the ladder," they are generally perceived in a positive light. But should a woman be ambitious and concentrate on moving up in the ranks, she often finds herself carrying a negative label. Working women still shoulder the major part of the responsibility as far as household chores are concerned, too. The average married working woman still does much more than half of the household chores.

6   But the worst problem that the changing roles of women has created for them concerns children. Many career women have put off childbearing until their 30s to concentrate on their career, and older women frequently experience more difficulties with birth than younger women. Right now, the United States is also experiencing a crisis in terms of child care. Too few decent child-care providers are currently available, so today's women are faced with this dilemma too.

7   Most people would agree that the changing roles of women mean progress for all society. But women are paying a steep price for their steps forward. No matter what their new roles are, women still often have to work twice as hard as men just to be equal, and that's not fair.

Criticizing the first draft

Returning to the draft after several days had passed, the author of the essay on the changing roles of women made the following comments:

1   I think my thesis is clear enough--that the changing roles of women cost them plenty both at work and at home. But I think my introduction is too abrupt. I'll rework it and try to ease my reader into the subject more. I have the same problem with my conclusion. The idea is there, but I need to do more to make sure that I restate the full significance of the paper. The line in the conclusion about women having to work twice as hard as men is good, though. I'll move that to the introduction to grab the reader's attention.

2   I want to make sure I'm communicating my ideas to my reader. I know all this stuff because I've been interested in the subject for a few years and I'm in a sociology course that deals with women's issues. I'd better doublecheck these examples, making sure I explain each one in enough detail and tell my reader where the information comes from. I've got to remember that not everyone knows as much or feels as strongly about this subject; if I'm going to interest somebody, I've got to make my examples complete and detailed.

3   I have to focus on my language. Some of the material flows well, but other sections sound awkward. Paragraph 2 about women and business and paragraph 4 about medicine need the most attention. I need to concentrate on making my point in simple, clear, and direct terms.

4   The fifth paragraph should really be two paragraphs. Part of it
deals with how women are perceived at work. The other part covers
women at home. I'll deal with each subject separately, giving more
detail about each. I read some statistics about household chores in
a newspaper article last week--Associated Press, I think--that said
that working women who are married do *at least* 60 percent of the
household chores in addition to their 9-to-5 jobs.

5   I think I've arranged my material pretty well. The material about
the child-care crisis is the strongest, so it definitely belongs last as
a kind of climax. I want to change some of the wording about the
child-care problem, though. I want to make sure that my reader
knows how frustrating it is for women who want to return to their
careers to be unable to get child care that they can afford and feel
comfortable with. Business, education, and medicine seem to be
about equal in impact, so I guess I'll leave them where they are.

6   The first four paragraphs show how women's roles have changed,
and the rest show how these changes have sometimes made life
harder. I think this is good, but I've got to strengthen the
connections between these two sections. If I improve this transtion,
my reader will find it easier to understand my point that women are
certainly paying for all the gains they have made in their new roles.

7   I need to reassess my tone throughout. I think I've been a strong
advocate of my position--that's what I wanted to do. I don't want to
back away from any point, but I don't want to scare anyone away or
offend anyone either. My point of view is valid--no doubt about it. I
just need to make sure that I'm letting the facts speak for
themselves.

8   I've got to turn my attention to form now. As I've reread my draft,

I've found errors in grammar and usage, some wordiness, faulty diction, and misspellings.

Avoiding sexist language

At this stage in your writing, you should also closely examine your paper for any sexist language. Basically sexist language is the use of words that inappropriately designate sex. The word *chairman,* for instance, is an example of sexist language because clearly not all people who chair something are men. In this case, you would substitute the word *chairperson.* As a writer, one of your most important jobs is to be as accurate as you can be; avoiding sexist language will enable you to fulfill this goal.

But sexist language poses a bigger threat than simply affecting your accuracy. Words have incredible power; the images they create can last a lifetime. To a world that already too often assumes that doctors are male, for instance, and nurses female, words like *foreman* suggest that only men can direct a crew of workers. What to some might seem a minor matter clearly is not; several years ago, New York City officials took this matter so seriously that they set about to revise all the job titles on their books to make them gender-neutral—that is, with references to neither sex. A foreman, for example, is now known by a title such as *supervisor* or *superintendent.* The business world has moved to make changes, too. An airline stewardess or steward, for instance, is now known as *flight attendant.*

In addition to these specific words, you need to be aware of sexist language in relation to your use of singular indefinite pronouns such as *everybody, nobody, somebody,* and so on. These words are already gender-neutral, so the pronouns themselves are not the problem. Consider these sentences for a moment, though:

Nobody wants a failing grade to be on *his* record.
Everyone can be a success if *he* is given a chance.

For many years, students were taught to write this way, to use the male pronouns *he, him,* or *his* as antecedents or referents for indefinite pronouns. In other words, in the first sentence *his* refers back to *nobody,* indirectly suggesting males only are in danger of failing. In the second, *he* refers back to *everyone,* indirectly suggesting that males only are capable of success.

You have two simple ways available to eliminate this inadvertent sexism with indefinite pronouns. One way is to make sure to use *he or she* (or *she or he*) whenever you refer back to a singular indefinite pronoun such as *everyone* or *nobody.* The second way is to use plural words rather than the singular indefinite pronouns and then use a plural pronoun to refer back to that word. Look at the same sentences, changed in these two ways:

Nobody wants a failing grade to be on *his or her* record.
No *individuals* want a failing grade on *their* record.

Everyone can be a success if *he or she* is given a chance.
People can be successes if *they* are given a chance.

Either of the two methods shown here is correct, although you will probably find it easier to make words plural whenever appropriate. Plural is neither masculine nor feminine; it refers to both collectively.

In any case, always pay attention to the language you choose. Language is powerful—it can wound by sending out a message that one sex is superior to the other. With a little extra attention, you can make sure that you communicate your ideas without offending anyone.

3c   The Intermediate Draft

Having reviewed his first draft, the author of the essay on the changing roles of women wrote additional drafts. As his view of his topic was clearer, he used these additional drafts to experiment with different phrasings. You should thus plan to write multiple drafts to express your ideas most clearly and directly in your final draft. The following excerpts from paragraphs 4–6 show the deletions and additions that occurred during the writing after several rereadings and reworkings of the work.

4 ~~In the world of medicine, women usually worked as nurses.~~ Changes have also come in the world of medicine, where women had traditionally been relegated to the position of nurse. That's another barrier that today's women have broken down. Women still serve as nurses, but they work in various other important capacities as well. ~~The number of women applying to and completing medical and dental schools continues to increase.~~ The American Medical Association reports that the number of women applying to and completing medical and dental schools continues to increase, with the gap between the percentage of male versus female doctors continuing to narrow. But women are breaking down doors in other areas of the medical world, too. ~~In hospitals, for instance, women now serve in diverse administrative positions that used to be out of their reach.~~ In hospitals, for instance, women now serve in such diverse administrative positions as floor supervisors, personnel directors, president or ~~other~~ some other executive officer, and members, sometimes even the head, of the hospital's board of directors.

5 ~~At work, though, women frequently face a double standard.~~ All these examples point to success, yet the less visible element of these examples is the toll women face to move forward. At work, for instance, women frequently face a double standard. When men are

ambitious and set their sights on moving "up the ladder," they are generally perceived in a positive light. They are dedicated, hard-working, and self-motivating. But should a woman be ambitious and concentrate on moving up in the ranks, she often finds herself carrying a negative label. She is considered hard-nosed, driven, and impatient for success.

6   Things are not much better for career women at home. ~~Working women still shoulder the major part of the responsibility as far as household chores are concerned, too.~~ Numerous studies show that working women still shoulder the major part of the responsibility as far as household chores are concerned. ~~The average married working woman still does much more than half of the household chores.~~ One estimate suggests that for such domestic duties as cooking, laundry, and grocery shopping, the average married career woman does more than 60 percent of the work in comparison to her husband doing less than 40 percent.

3d The Final Draft

Here is the final draft on the essay dealing with the changing roles of women:

TODAY'S WOMEN: MORE ROLES, MORE RESPONSIBILITIES

1   There's a saying that a woman must work twice as hard as a man to prove that she deserves a job but that, fortunately, most women do not mind working so hard. In today's society, the roles of women are changing; women everywhere in business, education, and

medicine are accepting the challenge to prove their equality and are moving forward. But as they successfully meet this challenge, they find that they are still working twice as hard as men, both at work and at home. The price they are paying for their changing roles and success, however, may simply be too steep.

2   Few people would argue that women have made great strides in the world of business. As Business Week recently noted, the executive suite at most major corporations is no longer solely the territory of men; while women were once present at business meetings to take notes and serve coffee, in most of today's major corporations they serve in every capacity, from executive officers who direct the company to the lawyers who represent its various interests. Today's women are entrepreneurs, too. One of America's major cosmetics firms was founded by a woman who developed her company to such an extent it is now a multimillion dollar business empire.

3   Today's women have also made great inroads in the field of education. Until the latter part of this century, the teaching profession, especially at the elementary school level, was dominated by women. Yet the real power positions in public education--principal, guidance counselor, superintendent, and top-level administrator--were traditionally filled by men. But during the last decade, this discrepancy has begun to change. Women are now successfully serving at all levels of public education. A recent study reported in Time magazine last month, for example, showed that the number of women in administrative positions in education during the last quarter century has quadrupled.

4   Changes have also come in the world of medicine, where women

had traditionally been relegated to the position of nurse. That's another barrier that today's women have broken down. Women still serve as nurses, but they work in various other important capacities as well. The American Medical Association reports that the number of women applying to and completing medical and dental schools continues to increase, with the gap between the percentage of male versus female doctors continuing to narrow. And women are breaking down doors in other areas of the medical world, too. In hospitals, for instance, women now serve in such diverse administrative positions as floor supervisor, personnel director, president or some other executive officer, and as members, sometimes even the head, of the hospital's board of directors.

5   All these examples point to success, yet the less visible element of these examples is the toll women face to move forward. At work, for instance, women frequently face a double standard. When men are ambitious and set their sights on moving "up the ladder," they are generally perceived in a positive light. They are dedicated, hard-working, and self-motivating. But should a woman be ambitious and concentrate on moving up in the ranks, she often finds herself carrying a negative label. She is considered hard-nosed, driven, and impatient for success.

6   Things are not much better for career women at home. Numerous studies show that working women still shoulder the major part of the responsibility of household chores. One estimate suggests that for such domestic duties as cooking, laundry, and grocery shopping, the average married career woman does more than 60 percent of the work in comparison to her husband doing less than 40 percent.

7   But the worst problem that changing roles have created for women is childbearing as related to their health. For example, many career women have put off childbearing until their 30s to concentrate on their career; statistics show that older women frequently experience more difficulties with birth than younger women. But the biggest difficulty awaits these new mothers when they try to return to their careers. Right now, the United States is experiencing a crisis in child care. For all their steps forward, today's career women now find themselves held hostage by the lack of adequate and affordable child care.

8   Most people would agree that the changing roles of women mean progress for society at large. Women represent roughly half of our population; the more women involved in business, education, and medicine, the more balanced those areas will be. But women are paying a steep price for their steps forward. They face a double standard as far as their behavior at work is concerned. Further, married career women face difficulties with domestic duties, childbearing, and childrearing. In too many cases, therefore, having to work twice as hard as men to prove their equality is not so easy for today's women after all.

3e Components of the Essay

In the process of writing, the writer should be concerned primarily with generating ideas and shaping them for expression. The "form" of the essay should develop naturally during this process, and worrying about parts of the form in isolation is often counterproductive. Toward the end of the composing process, however, an awareness of the parts of the essay may help in revising and polishing. The parts that most often come under consideration are the title, the thesis sentence, the opening, the body, and the conclusion.

Title

Wait until the essay is in almost final draft or completely finished to pick a title. When you do choose a title, search for a word or phrase—the briefer, the better is the rule—that suggests the topic, the tone, and perhaps the purpose of the essay. Alternatively, you may want to use a title that does none of these things but that challenges interpretation.

Make sure, however, that you do not rely on your title to direct your reader; your thesis should do that. Remember—a good title caps off a good paper, but it does not make a weak paper any better. Therefore, choose your title carefully, but recognize its limitations, too.

Thesis sentence

Much ink has been spilled in arguments over the importance of the thesis sentence. As a rule of thumb, the more complex the topic is and the more serious the discussion of it is, the more value a thesis sentence will have. The lighter the topic and treatment, the less significant a detailed thesis sentence is.

The most obvious place to insert your thesis sentence is in the first paragraph—your opening. In "Today's Women: More Roles, More Responsibilities," for example, the thesis is the last sentence of the first paragraph. It is a fine lead-in to the rest of the essay for the reader.

Keep in mind that, although your thesis sentence may be clearly apparent, sometimes it is suggested rather than overt. As long as your reader gets a clear direction of what is to follow, you have done a good job.

Opening

In a short essay, the opening is usually restricted to the first paragraph. The opening is important because it shapes the reader's first impression and may be a deciding factor in whether the reader goes beyond it. The opening sets the tone of the essay, establishes the writer's relation to the reader, and indicates the direction the essay will take.

Openings can take many forms to achieve a variety of effects. An opening can:

- be a straight piece of narrative that sets the scene for the reader and gives information necessary to an understanding of the essay's thesis.
- be a personal anecdote or invented piece of fiction to arouse the reader's interest or entertain as a way of leading to the thesis sentence.
- consist of a joke or an inflated treatment of a minor issue to amuse the reader.
- begin with a paradoxical statement, one that seems to contradict itself: "Most law-abiding citizens break at least three laws a day." Or the writer may use the opening to take a position toward the subject that is the opposite of the position to be developed in the paper. Such openings surprise readers or intrigue them.
- lead with a contradiction of a popular assumption as a challenge to the reader: "Cats and dogs are by nature affectionately drawn to each other. Unfortunately, dogs like playing tag and cats don't."
- employ a famous quotation or a piece of dialogue as a means of establishing the thesis.

An opening can also, of course, simply identify the topic to be addressed, as is the case with this opening for a paper on young drivers:

When we obtained our first driver's licenses at sixteen, seventeen, or eighteen, few of us paused before hitting the accelerator to think that we were about to solo in a machine with the destructive power of four sticks of dynamite and a record for manslaughter three times greater than that of the notorious handgun.

Or an opening may be a focus of inquiry. An essay on legalized abortion, for example, might begin with an explanation of the views in opposition over the topic.

Avoid attempts at that perfect opening in your first draft. You cannot expect to do your best writing the first time. Refine a draft thesis as you work through your multiple drafts. In other words, shape the final opening against the structure and tone of the essay.

Body

The body of an essay consists of everything between the opening and the conclusion. In the body, the writer develops the thesis with facts, examples, and specific points so that the reader fully understands or accepts the writer's position. Every part of the body must not only relate to the essay's thesis but also increase readers' understanding of the problem being explored or their appreciation of the thesis.

A finished essay should balance generalization and specific information. The thesis of the essay is a statement that includes all conditions or circumstances indicated by a given set of evidence. You, the writer, have arrived at your thesis by considering the evidence. In the body of your essay, you must retrace your steps to your thesis to demonstrate the truth of it to your reader. In most essays, this demonstration follows a pattern of a thesis supported by a series of narrower generalizations that are supported in turn by reference to facts, examples, specific details, or other information that confirms or strongly suggests the truth of the thesis. This pattern of generalization, narrower generalization, and specific detail need not emerge in the finished essay as a rigid A-because-B-because-C formula, but the principle of it should influence the overall content of the essay.

Consider the final draft of the sample essay "Today's Women: More Roles, More Responsibilities" (look back to section 3d, pp. 40–43). The final thesis of the essay is "The price they are paying for their changing roles and success . . . may simply be too steep." The writer's obligation to the reader is to show that women have indeed made progress but that the sacrifices they have made to move forward have brought greater responsibilities. That means the writer has two basic purposes: first to show the progress women have made in various fields and then to show some of the drawbacks that their progress has created for them.

Therefore, paragraphs 2, 3, and 4 feature examples of the progress women have made in business, education, and medicine. The references are to specific positions that today's women are currently filling: executive officer, lawyer, entrepreneur, principal, guidance counselor, superintendent, doctor, dentist, floor supervisor, personnel director, hospital president, and head or member of a hospital's board of directors. The result is that these paragraphs support and illustrate the general claim—that women today are forging new ground in their professional lives.

Then, paragraphs 5, 6, and 7 deal with the various additional responsibilities and burdens that professional women face as a result of their movement forward. The examples given in paragraph 5 show that ambition and aggressiveness are often interpreted differently for men and women. In paragraph 6, the examples illustrate that married professional women are still responsible for the majority of household duties. And in paragraph 7, the examples point out that married professional women who have children face perhaps the greatest burden of all modern women: the potential for complications with a pregnancy delayed until their 30s plus the dilemma of finding adequate, affordable child care in a society currently facing a critical shortage in this area. As a result, the thesis for the paper—that women are paying a stiff price for the progress they are making—is supported and illustrated.

Coherence

The essence of the body of the essay is **coherence,** the quality of writing concerned with the flow and connection of all the elements in any text. This quality depends not only on the relevance of detail and the transitional devices of language, but also on an agreement of tone, subject, purpose, and audience. All the parts of the essay should have meaning within the context of the essay.

Through the various drafts of "Today's Women: More Roles, More Responsibilities," the supporting examples have been revised and spelled out in much greater detail than they had been in the initial draft. As a result, the various examples are more obviously connected to each other; the result is a final draft that flows better than the earlier drafts. In a coherent essay, the reader should be able to follow the writer's thoughts without having to ask, "Why is that here?" or "How is one idea connected to the rest?" With the final draft of "Today's Women: More Roles, More Responsibilities," both the rationale behind the examples and the connections between them are obvious to the reader. In short, then, the essay is coherent.

Conclusion

The Latin word *concludere,* from which *conclusion* derives, means "to shut up closely." An essay should not just stop; it should conclude—that is, it should end by emphasizing the point the writer has made.

The thesis should therefore be reflected in some way in the conclusion. In "Today's Women: More Roles, More Responsibilities," the point is again made in the conclusion that women are paying deeply for the strides they've made forward, that they face a double standard at work, an unfair work-load at home, and incredible frustrations when it comes to bearing and rearing children. Although it is not a word-for-word repetition of the thesis, it is clearly, as it should be, a reaffirmation of that main idea.

When writing a conclusion, remember to look back. The final paragraph or final sentence should not contain arguments, perceptions, expansions, or ideas that are not already present in the essay. New ideas belong in the body of the paper where they can be explained and supported. Although a conclusion may contain a prediction for the future or a suggestion for future action, it should include such an element only if the preceding content of the essay clearly establishes the ground for it. In other words, the conclusion should refer to "what I have said" rather than to "what I can say next."

As a general rule, avoid phrases like *in sum, to conclude,* and *in conclusion* when closing your essay. A good conclusion does not need to be announced.

3f Proofreading

The last stage of writing is proofreading. Proofreading may be a noncreative, mechanical duty, but it is not an optional part of the writing process. There is no choice about proofreading. Spell *separate* as *seperate* and your paper will strike someone as flawed, however ingeniously it is constructed.

In proofreading, look up in this handbook or a dictionary every point in your essay you have marked for spelling or punctuation questions. Pay particular attention to the following matters:

- Read your final draft backward, from last to first word. You may find spelling errors you miss reading the normal way.
- Check each pronoun carefully. Can it possibly refer to the wrong antecedent?
- Read each sentence critically. Have you by chance used a singular verb form with a plural subject, or vice versa?

- Read your essay aloud. Where you make pauses to make the sense clear, have you used a punctuation mark?
- Be careful of possessives. Have you used all the apostrophes you should?

The main point to remember about proofreading is that it is vitally important. Readers generally notice mistakes in form first; therefore, if you know you are weak in punctuation or spelling, persuade someone who is strong in these niceties to proofread for you. After being corrected half a dozen times, you will learn to correct yourself.

Correct mistakes in your final draft neatly in ink, or use a correcting tape and retype the error. Check with your instructors to find out how they regard handwritten corrections in a final paper. Some require a perfect typescript; others accept neat corrections.

Also, keep essays returned to you by your instructors. Where you have made a mistake before, you are likely to make one again. Look for similar situations in your current essay and see if the same red pencil marks apply to it.

Most important of all, if an essay is returned to you with mistakes marked, go through it and correct each mistake. Look up the rule that covers the error and be sure you understand it. If you do not understand the error, ask someone to explain it until you do. Write out misspelled words twenty times, using the right spelling. Remember that coordination of language, hand, and thought builds correct habits.

4 Writing Coherent Paragraphs

A **paragraph** is a group of sentences that develops an idea about a topic. The word *paragraph* comes from an ancient Greek word referring to the short horizontal line that the

Greeks placed beneath the start of a line of prose to indicate a break in thought or a change in speaker. This convention of marking the places in a written work where the sense or the speaker changed was followed by medieval monks, who used a red or blue symbol much like our modern paragraph symbol ¶ in their manuscripts. Today, we indicate such a change in thought by indenting the first line of each new paragraph.

While a paragraph is usually self-contained, at the same time it is usually part of a larger work, such as an essay or a research paper, and depends on the paragraphs before and after it. For example, look at the following three paragraphs.

There seems to be no limit to the number of individuals a single person is capable of recognizing. An adult living in a large city probably sees millions of faces over a lifetime, and can recognize thousands of them, even if he cannot assign names to them. Not even the passage of decades clouds the memory for faces. Psychologists have shown people photographs cut out from their high school yearbooks 15 years after graduation, and they were able to match 90 percent of the faces with the correct names. Nearly fifty years after graduation the accuracy only dropped to 70 percent.

Identifying and remembering faces is a mental process that takes place in the cerebral cortex, the most highly evolved area of the brain, where thinking occurs. Neurologists in France made this discovery in the nineteenth century, when they found that injuries to certain parts of the brain could cause a total loss of the ability to recognize people visually, including family and even one's own reflection in a mirror. This rare condition, called prosopagnosia (literally, not knowing people), usually occurs when the lesion is in the right temporal lobe, the portion of the cortex behind the ear (although injuries in the left hemisphere can produce the same symptoms). To a prosopagnosic, people look like cubist Picassos, with the features in the wrong positions, or the entire face appears out of focus. Those with the condition have difficulty reading expressions as well as identifying faces.

Learning to recognize people is a process that starts at birth and isn't complete until adulthood. For the past 20 years psychologists have been trying to find out how babies first acquire this ability, but their quest hasn't been easy. They can't ask an infant, "Have you ever seen this face before?" Instead, the researchers make use of curiosity: A baby's heartbeat will often change at the sight of a new object; babies spend extra time studying new things, as well as those that are vaguely familiar (moderately discrepant stimuli, in psychology jargon), whereas they will soon turn away in boredom from anything they already know. The general procedure in recognition studies is to show a baby a photograph of a face, then sometime later show the same face alongside another, and observe which one evokes the greater response.

Shannon Brownlee
"What's in a Face"

Each of these paragraphs develops its own point. This point, which guides the paragraph, is often referred to as the **controlling idea.** The controlling idea of the first paragraph is that a human being is capable of recognizing an unlimited number of people. This idea is supported by examples of people recognizing a great number of faces. The controlling idea of the second paragraph is that the process of identifying and remembering faces takes place in the cerebral cortex. This idea is supported by an explanation of how this discovery was made by nineteenth-century French neurologists. The controlling idea of the third paragraph is that for the past twenty years, psychologists have been trying to answer a difficult question: how do babies learn to recognize people? This idea is supported by an explanation of how they have used a baby's natural curiosity to help them answer this question.

Although each of these paragraphs is controlled by its own idea, the three also work together. The second picks up the general subject discussed in the first paragraph but focuses on a single aspect of it. Whereas the first paragraph was concerned with the fact that faces are recognized, the second is concerned with the part of the brain that controls recognition. The third paragraph then picks up the general subject discussed in the first paragraph and focuses on another aspect. While the second paragraph was concerned with where the process occurs, the third paragraph is concerned with how it is developed. Therefore, we can say that although a paragraph is largely self-contained, its general subject and controlling idea must conform to the objectives of the larger work of which it is a part.

A paragraph is made up of individual sentences, but these sentences must cohere, or fit together, in order to be effective. Three interrelated qualities contribute to the coherence of a paragraph: unity, a consistent method of development, and clear transition from one idea to another.

4a Unity

Unity in a paragraph means that all the sentences in the paragraph relate to and develop the controlling idea. In other words, no sentences digress, or go off the track. Unity can be achieved through the use of a topic sentence and of relevant support.

The topic sentence

A paragraph develops a controlling, or main, idea, which is often summarized in a **topic sentence.** Functioning in a paragraph as a thesis statement functions in an essay, a topic sentence establishes the direction for the paragraph, with all the other sentences in the paragraph supporting and developing it.

Although a topic sentence often appears at the beginning of a paragraph, it may also be placed in the middle or at the end. When it is placed at the beginning of the paragraph, the rest of the sentences support the topic sentence, and the paragraph is developed deductively. In other words, the main idea is presented first, and then the information supporting this idea is given. For example, the following paragraph is about the British composer Peter Maxwell Davies. The controlling idea, or the idea to be developed, is that he had a difficult time winning recognition both at home and abroad.

> **For Davies, winning recognition wasn't easy, at home or abroad.** He was born near Manchester, a grim industrial city. The son of working-class parents, he taught himself composition by studying scores in the library. When he asked to study music at his grammar school, in preparation for the O-level exams given all British students, the headmaster scoffed. The faculty at the Royal Manchester College of Music and at Manchester University, where Davies subsequently studied, proved to be hardly more enlightened. It was the mid-fifties, and the Austrian moderns—Mahler and Bruckner—were still highly suspect. So, in fact, was anyone but such homegrown products as Sir Edward Elgar, Ralph Vaughan Williams, and Charles Villiers Stanford. Davies wanted none of it. Along with a group of other students, including Harrison Birtwistle, who were eager to hear the new European music, he began listening to Stravinsky and Schoenberg.
>
> Annalyn Swan
> "A Visionary Composer"

Sometimes the topic sentence is expressed in the form of a question. When this is the case, the rest of the paragraph answers the question. For example, the following paragraph is about the black artist's obligations to the black community. The controlling idea is that a certain kind of art fulfills these obligations. The rest of the paragraph explains what kind of art this is.

> **What kind of art meets the Black artist's obligations to the community?** First, these obligations require an art that is functional, an art that makes sense to the audience for which it was created. They also require a highly symbolic art that employs the symbols common to Black lives. Next, art by Black Americans should reflect a continuum of aesthetic principles

derived from Africa, maintained during slavery, and emergent today. The art that the Black artist produces should also be relatively inexpensive to buy. This does not mean, as one might suppose, that only drawings and prints rather than paintings and sculpture should be produced. It does, however, mean that volume production at a low cost is a primary consideration. Black art should also help enrich the physical appearance of the community. This does not mean uncontrolled graffiti and fanciful false facades on buildings. It does mean the use of legitimate opportunity to enhance the quality of the environment. Finally, the obligations of the Black artist require a diverse art: an art that explores every avenue of search and discovery, an art that exploits every possible quality of individual difference in the artist who produces it.

Samella Lewis
Art: African American

A paragraph that begins with a topic sentence sometimes ends with a concluding statement that restates the controlling idea, or summarizes or comments on the information in the paragraph. For example, the following paragraph is about wolves. The controlling idea is that they are Holarctic. The topic sentence is printed in **boldface** and the concluding statement is in *italics*.

> **Wolves, twenty or thirty subspecies of them, are Holarctic—that is, they once roamed most of the Northern Hemisphere above thirty degrees north latitude.** They were found throughout Europe, from the Zezere River Valley of Portugal north to Finland and south to the Mediterranean. They roamed eastern Europe, the Balkans, and the Near and Middle East south into Arabia. They were found in Afghanistan and northern India, throughout Russia north into Siberia, south again as far as China, and east into the islands of Japan. In North America the wolf reached a southern limit north of Mexico City and ranged north as far as Cape Morris Jesup, Greenland, less than four hundred miles from the North Pole. *Outside of Iceland and North Africa, and such places as the Gobi Desert, wolves—*

you imagine the differences in geography it seems astonishing —had adapted to virtually every habitat available to them.

Barry Holstun Lopez
Of Wolves and Men

Sometimes the topic sentence occurs at the end of the paragraph. When this is the case, the topic sentence provides the focus for the sentences that lead up to it. The paragraph is developed inductively; that is, the evidence is given first and then the conclusion derived from this evidence is given. For example, the following paragraph is about the Hill Country in Texas. The controlling idea, or the idea that the rest of the sentences lead up to, is that to the early settlers, this country seemed like a paradise.

> And the streams, these men discovered, were full of fish. The hills were full of game. There were, to their experienced eyes, all the signs of bear, and you didn't need signs to know about the deer—they were so numerous that when riders crested a hill, a whole herd might leap away in the valley below, white tails flashing. There were other white tails, too: rabbits in abundance. And as the men sat their horses, staring, flocks of wild turkeys strutted in silhouette along the ridges. Honeybees buzzed in the glades, and honey hung in the trees for the taking. Wild mustang grapes, plump and purple, hung down for making wine. **Wrote one of the first men to come to the Hill Country: "It is a Paradise."**

Robert A. Caro
The Path to Power

This type of topic sentence often appears in opening paragraphs where it acts as a lead-in to the body of the paper.

Sometimes the topic sentence is delayed until the middle or near the middle of the paragraph. When this is the case, the topic sentence serves as a bridge between the information in the first part of the paragraph and the information in the second. The following paragraph is about King Richard III of

England. The controlling idea of this paragraph is that the traditional view of Richard III has been obstinately opposed over the years.

> History is always written by the victors. The basic Tudor picture of Richard as a bloodthirsty tyrant was handed down through the standard histories of England and the school textbooks for five centuries. **There has been an obstinate opposition, however.** Beginning with Sir George Buck in the 17th century, a series of writers and historians have insisted that Richard was not getting a fair break, that the Tudor version was largely fabrication: far from being a monster Richard was a noble, upright, courageous, tenderhearted and most conscientious king. This anti-Tudor version reached its definitive statement in the work of Sir Clements Markham, a 19th-century eccentric who spent years of passionate research trying to prove that crimes attributed to Richard were either outright libels by, or the actual work of, a pack of villains, most notably including Cardinal Morton and Henry VII.
>
> Robert Wernick
> "After 500 Years, Old Crookback
> Can Still Kick Up a Fuss"

Sometimes a topic sentence is really two sentences. The first sentence states the controlling idea and the second sentence clarifies or restricts the controlling idea in some way. The controlling idea in the following paragraph is that the content of coffee-table art books is changing.

> **The topography of the coffee-table art book is changing.** *Each year, it seems, larger and more daunting mountains of text rise from the lush lowlands of visual reproduction, obliging the reader to sit up and take notice.* It used to be commonly accepted that the text of a large-format art book was a joke—a harmless effusion of bold type between the title page and the color reproductions—but these days you are likely to find yourself scaling craggy massifs of prose by some well-known scholar or art historian. My own feelings about this are ambivalent. Art

scholarship takes it out of you under the best of circumstances. It also tends to make you suspect that the reproductions in a book are a very far cry from the original paintings—which is true, of course, but not necessarily what you long to hear when you have just paid seventy-five dollars plus tax for the book in question. The fact that books of this calibre have to be read at a desk or a table—they are too cumbersome for all but world-class laps— adds to the inner conflicts that they set up. Objects that used to be associated with conspicuous display or with sybaritic leafing- through are coming to be associated increasingly with hard work.

Calvin Tompkins
"Heavyweights"

Sometimes a topic sentence is implied. This is especially the case when the paragraph elaborates on or continues a discus- sion started in a preceding paragraph. When there is no overt topic sentence, the details in the paragraph should be so clear and well organized that it is easy to state the implied main idea for yourself. The implied main idea of the following paragraph is that the population of wolves in North America has dwin- dled.

Mexico still has a small population of wolves, and large populations—perhaps twenty to twenty-five thousand—remain in Alaska and Canada. The largest concentrations of wolves in the lower forty-eight states are in northeastern Minnesota (about one thousand) and on Isle Royale in Lake Superior (about thirty). There is a very small wolf population in Glacier National Park in Montana and a few in Michigan's Upper Peninsula. Oc- casionally lone wolves show up in the western states along the Canadian border; most are young animals dispersing from packs in British Columbia, Alberta, and Saskatchewan.

Barry Holstun Lopez
Of Wolves and Men

Support

Support your controlling idea with specific information—facts, statistics, details, examples, illustrations, anecdotes—that backs it up. Consider the following paragraph.

> Oranges and orange blossoms have long been symbols of love. Boccaccio's *Decameron,* written in the fourteenth century, is redolent with the scent of oranges and orange blossoms, with lovers who wash in orange-flower water, a courtesan who sprinkles her sheets with orange perfume, and the mournful Isabella, who cuts off the head of her dead lover, buries it in an ample pot, plants basil above it, and irrigates the herbs exclusively with rosewater, orange-flower water, and tears. In the fifteenth century, the Countess Mathilda of Württemberg received from her impassioned admirer, Dr. Heinrich Steinbowel, a declaration of love in the form of a gift of two dozen oranges. Before long, titled German girls were throwing oranges down from their balconies in the way that girls in Italy or Spain were dropping handkerchiefs. After Francis I dramatically saved Marseilles from a Spanish siege, a great feast was held for him at the city's harborside, and Marseillaise ladies, in token of their love and gratitude, pelted him with oranges. Even Nostradamus was sufficiently impressed with the sensual power of oranges to publish, in 1556, a book on how to prepare various cosmetics from oranges and orange blossoms. Limes were also used cosmetically, by ladies of the French court in the seventeenth century, who kept them on their person and bit into them from time to time in order to redden their lips. In the nineteenth century, orange blossoms were regularly shipped to Paris in salted barrels from Provence, for no French bride wanted to be married without wearing or holding them.
>
> John McPhee
> "Oranges"

The controlling idea of this paragraph is contained in the first sentence. Notice all the details McPhee gives to support his controlling idea. First he tells us about oranges and orange blossoms in Boccaccio's *Decameron.* Then he tells us about Countess Mathilda in the fifteenth century and how the gift of oranges from her admirer led to the custom of German girls throwing oranges from their balconies. Next he tells us how Francis I was pelted with oranges as a token of love, and how Nostradamus published a book on how to prepare cosmetics from oranges and orange blossoms. Finally, he tells us that in the nineteenth century a French bride would not want to be married without holding or wearing orange blossoms. Notice how fully he treats these details. He tells you not only that Boccaccio wrote about oranges and orange blossoms in the *Decameron* but also what he said about them—the lovers, the courtesan, the mournful Isabella.

Notice all the supporting details Peter Steinhart uses to develop his controlling idea in the following paragraph.

> Adobe is an ancient material. Peruvians and Mesopotamians knew at least 3,000 years ago how to mix adobe—three parts sandy soil to one part clay soil—and box-mold it into bricks. The Walls of Jericho, the Tower of Babel, Egyptian pyramids, and sections of China's Great Wall are adobes. So are more modern structures like Spain's Alhambra, the great mosques of Fez and Marrakesh, and the royal palace at Riyadh.
>
> Peter Steinhart
> "Dirt Chic"

Not only must a paragraph contain support for its controlling idea, but this support must be relevant. Consider the following paragraph:

> Several writers have used San Francisco as a backdrop for their novels. Kathryn Forbes's novel *Mama's Bank Account,* on which the movie *I Remember Mama* was based, is set in San Francisco. The immigrant family lives on Steiner Street, in a big house in the middle of the city that Mama loved so well. Jack

London's novel *The Sea Wolf* is enriched by its vivid depiction of San Francisco, the city in which London grew up. London set what is perhaps his most famous novel, *The Call of the Wild,* in the Klondike, however. Dashiell Hammett's detective, Sam Spade, lives and works in San Francisco. As he solves his cases, Spade reveals to us the seamy underbelly of the city, which challenges his ideals and forces him to develop a mask of cynicism. Other writers reveal to us the corrupt side of city life, too. For example, in his short novel *Maggie: A Girl of the Streets,* Stephen Crane shows us the lower depths of New York's Bowery and the effects of this environment on the destiny of a young girl, Maggie Johnson.

This paragraph lacks unity. The controlling idea is that several writers have used San Francisco as a backdrop for their novels. However, the paragraph contains three sentences that do not relate to this main idea. The fifth sentence is a digression because it does not develop the idea of novels set in San Francisco. The last two sentences also wander off the track. The next-to-last sentence is not limited to San Francisco, and the last deals with New York City.

Digressions weaken your paragraphs. Eliminate or rewrite any sentences that do not develop the controlling idea. Notice how the sample paragraph is improved by removing the digressions.

Several writers have used San Francisco as a backdrop for their novels. Kathryn Forbes's novel *Mama's Bank Account,* on which the movie *I Remember Mama* was based, is set in San Francisco. The immigrant family lives on Steiner Street, in a big house in the middle of the city that Mama loved so well. Jack London's novel *The Sea Wolf* is enriched by its vivid depiction of San Francisco, the city in which London grew up. Dashiell Hammett's detective, Sam Spade, lives and works in San Francisco. As he solves his cases, Spade reveals to us the seamy underbelly of the city, which challenges his ideals and forces him to develop a mask of cynicism.

4b Organizational Strategies

A paragraph should be developed and organized in a purposeful way to assist the reader in following your argument or line of reasoning. The paragraph's organization should depend on your overall aim in the particular section of your essay. Sometimes a method of development will come to you naturally, without thought; at other times you will have to choose deliberately from a variety of options in order to fulfill your purpose. These options include some organization strategies as well as some more specific techniques commonly called the patterns of development.

You have a variety of organization strategies available to arrange your paragraphs. The following represent the most common types.

General to specific

Arrange your information from general to specific when you want to present a general idea first and then supply specific examples, details, or reasons to support your idea. The following paragraph is organized in a general to specific pattern. Notice how the information in it becomes more and more specific.

> As of now, the biological productivity of the lower Hudson is staggering. Fishes are there by the millions, with marine and freshwater species often side by side in the same patch of water. All told, the population of fishes utilizing the lower Hudson for spawning, nursery or feeding grounds comprises the greatest single wildlife resource in New York State. It is also the most neglected resource; at this writing, not one state conservation department biologist is to be found studying it regularly. Besides sea sturgeon, the river is aswarm year-round or seasonally with striped bass, white perch, bluefish, shad, herring, largemouth bass, carp, needlefish, yellow perch, menhaden, golden shiners, darters, tomcod, and sunfish, to cite only some. There is the

short-nosed and round-nosed sturgeon, officially classified by the Department of the Interior as "endangered," or close to extinct, in the United States. Perhaps it is extinct elsewhere along the Atlantic Coast, but not only is the fish present in the Hudson, but occasional specimens exceed the published record size in the scientific literature. The lower Hudson also receives an interesting infusion of so-called tropical or subtropic fishes, such as the jack crevalle and the mullet, both originally associated with Florida waters.

Robert H. Boyle
The Hudson River

Specific to general

Arrange your information from specific to general when you want to present specific details first and then lead up to a generalization about them. The following narrative paragraph is organized in a specific to general pattern. The paragraph starts with a specific description of the birds' behavior, which leads up to a generalization about their behavior: they were anting, or deliberately covering themselves with ants.

As he walked in an orange grove behind Trinidad's Asa Wright Nature Centre, Ray Mendez noticed a pair of birds that were behaving strangely. The birds—violaceous trogons, judging from the ring of bright orange around their eyes—were preoccupied with something, so preoccupied that they seemed to have lost their usual bird sense. They appeared fascinated, expectant, oblivious. Mendez drew close and watched. Suddenly one of the trogons broke from its perch and flew a hard flat line at an ants' nest hanging from a tree branch. The bird crashed into the nest, held on, and then shoved itself in headfirst, allowing *Azteca* ants to cover its body. It flittered its wings a moment and the *Azteca* boarded them too. Then the trogon flew back to a safe perch, and Mendez, entranced by the mystery of these events, suddenly saw the simple answer. The trogons were anting.

David Weinberg
"Ant Acid Spells Relief"

The following paragraph is also organized in a specific to general pattern. The author first gives the evidence supporting his argument and then concludes the paragraph with a general statement of his position.

> American workers understand that the manufacturers of arms have been the bulwark of the capitalist system in the United States, as well as of the communist Soviet Union. In their bones these workers sense that what financial security they have—little enough—is tied to the billions of dollars invested in the arms race. Where would America's "free enterprise" be without that ongoing safety net? Some of us—the more privileged—can afford not to wonder. But most cannot. It wouldn't hurt the peace movement if we found a better way to reach out to this less affluent majority, if we coupled our opposition to nuclear weapons with a clear and compelling program for economic reform.
>
> Robert Coles
> "The Doomsayers: Class Politics
> and the Nuclear Freeze"

Climactic order

Arrange your information in climactic order when you want to begin by supporting your generalization with the least important information and build up to the most important. The following paragraph is organized in climactic order. It starts with the least important criterion for judging a behavior as conscious and builds up to the most important.

> What criteria lead us to judge that a particular behavior is conscious? What is the difference between the eight-month baby who clumsily knocks over its milk, and the two-year-old who obviously does it on purpose? Several things incline us to judge that another being is acting consciously: if it studies its goal before acting, if it chooses one of a very flexible set of behaviors, or even a novel behavior with detours to reach the goal. Conscious purpose seems especially likely if some learned symbol

like "No! Naughty!" communicates the situation to the aggravated parents. Finally, if there is misdirection—hiding or lying —it seems likely that the creature has formed some conception of other animals' intentions and awareness.

Alison Jolly
"A New Science that Sees Animals as Conscious Beings"

Time order

Arrange your information in time order when you want to explain a sequence of events or tell a story. The details in the following expository paragraph are organized according to time order.

Jesuit missionaries stationed in China were probably the first voyagers to bring soybeans to Europe, in the seventeen-thirties, and there, like potatoes before them, the beans were considered a horticultural curiosity. Specimens were planted at the Jardin des Plantes, in Paris, in 1739, and in London's Kew Gardens—these probably from India—in 1790. (As early as 1712, a German botanist, Engelbert Kämpfer, who had visited Japan in the sixteen-nineties, published a recipe for soy sauce; that may have been the first time any Europeans were informed that the bean was in any respect edible.) Benjamin Franklin has been credited, perhaps apocryphally, with having espied soybeans at the Jardin des Plantes and bringing a few home. He would have been a logical courier, for he was acquainted with the head of the Jardin. In any event, there were soybeans in the United States—brought over from China by clipper ship—in 1804, at which time an admirer wrote, "The Soy-bean bears the climate of Pennsylvania very well. The bean ought therefore to be cultivated." Whether or not Pennsylvania farmers followed that advice is uncertain; it is known that a botanical garden in Cambridge, Massachusetts, had some soybeans on display— once more, merely as a rare exhibit—in 1829. They were written up in the *New England Farmer* that October. Soybeans enjoyed another brief flurry of notice in 1854, when Commodore Perry brought some back from Japan. In 1879, they were being grown at the Rutgers Agricultural College Farm, and ten years later at the Kansas Agricultural Experiment Station. They also began to be scrutinized by botanists at Cornell—among them Edward Lewis Sturtevant, later the author of "Sturtevant's Edible Plants of the World," who in 1882 appraised soybeans as "of excellent promise as a forage plant" but added, as he doubtless would not have when he got to know them better, that "the beans are not acceptable to the palate."

E. J. Kahn, Jr.
"Soybeans"

Spatial order

Arrange your information in spatial order when you want to explain or describe the relative physical positions of people or objects. The details in the following descriptive paragraph are organized according to spatial order.

Greenwich Village is a mass of "little twisted streets that crossed and recrossed each other and never seemed to get anywhere. . . ." In its center is Washington Square, a stretch of green, bordered by a number of park benches, where one can sit and read, talk, or do nothing at all. In the background of Washington Square looms New York University. Before Washington Square became a park in 1827, it had been "in successive decades Potter's Field, parade grounds, place of executions. . . ." During Millay's time, little delicatessens and coffee shops helped to create an old English atmosphere in the Village.

Anne Cheney
Millay in Greenwich Village

4c Patterns of Development

In addition to the general techniques for arranging your paragraphs, there are a number of other techniques available. The **patterns of development,** for instance, enable you to explain information in specific ways as dictated by your purpose. The following represent the most commonly used of the patterns of development.

Definition

Develop your paragraph through definition when you want to clarify a term, assign a particular meaning to a word, or discuss a concept from a special or unusual point of view.

> What is war? It is not weapons or warheads or even military force itself; these are only "the *means* of war." According to Clausewitz, war is simply "an act of force to compel our enemy to do our will." That is precisely what the Vietnamese are attempting to do to the Cambodians, what Iraq tried to do to Iran, what Somalia is striving to do with Ethiopia, what Israel attempted to do in Lebanon, and why Soviet troops are in Afghanistan.
>
> Colonel Harry G. Summers, Jr.
> "What Is War?"

Cause and effect

Arrange your information through cause and effect when you want to discuss the causes behind certain effects or the reasons for certain results or consequences. The following paragraph gives the result first—the tartan was transformed into an instrument of Scottish nationalistic ideology. Then it provides the reasons or causes that brought about this result.

> A cluster of events transformed the tartan into an instrument of nationalist ideology. In the wake of the great defeat of Bonnie Prince Charlie in 1745, the British banned Highland wear, including tartans and the kilt, under penalty of six months in prison for a first offense and seven years' transportation for a second. The elder Pitt simultaneously formed the Highland regiments for service abroad. They alone were permitted to wear the plaid and the kilt, both for reasons of esprit de corps and, no

doubt, to impede desertion: a man running about in a skirt south of the border or in France was a conspicuous object. This is, most likely, when tartans peculiar to certain regiments became established. Finally, Scottish nationalism, seeking to extirpate both Irish and Lowland roots of the culture, turned to the literal invention of an ancient Highland culture, kilt and all. The final triumph came when Lowland Scotland, offered this bogus tradition, eagerly accepted it.

Alexander Cockburn
"The Origin of the Kilt"

The next paragraph gives the cause first—people have a stake in seeing themselves as different from computers. Then it describes the effects brought about by this cause.

But despite these encouragements to personify computers, people have a stake in seeing themselves as different. They assert this difference, much as we saw children do. They speak of human love, sensuality, and emotion. They speak of the computer's lack of consciousness, originality, and intention. In the end, many sum up their sense of difference in the statement "Computers are programmed; people aren't," or "Computers only do what they are programmed to do, nothing more, nothing less." This last response has a history. It is associated with Lady Ada Lovelace, a friend and patroness of Charles Babbage, inventor of the "analytical engine," the first machine that deserves to be called a computer in the modern sense. In a memoir she wrote in 1842 she became the first person known to go on record with a variant of "Computers only do what you tell them to do."

Sherry Turkle
The Second Self: Computers and the Human Spirit

Comparison and contrast

Arrange your information through comparison and contrast when you want to show the similarities and/or the differences between two things. The following paragraph contrasts two things—the child of fifty years ago and the child of today—by alternating between them.

> The most disquieting aspect of the silicon chip is not that it distances us from nature; even before the Industrial Revolution, man was trying to do that. The more troubling fact is that electronic developments distance us from understanding. Any child of fifty years ago looking inside a household clock, with its escapement and weights or spring, could see in a few minutes how it worked. A child of today peering at a digital watch can learn nothing. Yesterday's children could appreciate that pushing a switch on a television set meant completing a circuit. Today's children, using remote control devices based on ultrasound or infrared radiation, can scarcely comprehend what they are doing. The real danger of the microelectronic era is posed by what was called, even in the days of macroelectronics, the black box mentality: passive acceptance of the idea that more and more areas of life will be taken over by little black boxes whose mysterious workings are beyond our comprehension.

> Bernard Dixon
> "Black Box Blues"

The following paragraph compares the National Aeronautics and Space Administration's lunar explorations to the voyages of Christopher Columbus.

> Both NASA and Columbus made not one but a series of voyages. NASA landed men on six different parts of the moon. Columbus made four voyages to different parts of what he remained convinced was the east coast of Asia. As a result both NASA and Columbus had to keep coming back to the Government with their hands out, pleading for refinancing. In each case the reply of the Government became, after a few years: "This is all very impressive, but what earthly good is it to anyone back home?"

> Tom Wolfe
> "Columbus and the Moon"

Classification

Develop your paragraph through classification when you want to group information into types in order to find patterns or similarities. The following paragraph classifies ranks within a troop of rhesus monkeys.

> The core of the troop's structure is a series of matriarchies. A mother ranks above her own daughters until she becomes very, very old. She supports them in fights, so her offspring rank just below her and thus above all the other matriarchies that she can dominate. Young males commonly migrate to other troops. A male's adult rank depends on his own fighting prowess and on his charm—much of his status depends on whether the females of his new troop back him up. A female, on the other hand, is usually locked for life into the nepotistic matrix of her kin. Her adult rank is roughly predictable the day she is born. But female status changes do occasionally happen, and it is worth a young female's while to test the system. In the wild, predation and disease knock out relatives at random, so there is more flexibility than we see in our well-tended captive colonies. Wild or captive, kinship is still the major fact of female social life. A baby learns early those situations when its relatives will come and help—and when they won't.

> Alison Jolly
> "A New Science that Sees Animals as Conscious Beings"

Process

Develop your paragraph through explanation of a process when you show how something is done or how something works. The following paragraph explains how the heart works.

> With its valves, tubing, electrical system and four chambers, the heart looks for all the world like a simple pump. First, it collects the oxygen-depleted blood from the body in its right upper chamber, or right atrium, while receiving a fresh supply of

oxygen-rich blood from the lungs in its left upper chamber, the left atrium. Then as the heart's natural pacemaker, a small lump of tissue called the sinoatrial node, fires an electrical impulse, the atria contract, the valves open, and the blood rushes into the two lower chambers, the ventricles. Another electrical signal then causes the ventricles to contract, forcing the oxygen-poor blood from the lower right ventricle into the lungs and the oxygenated blood in the lower left ventricle to all the other parts of the body. It all happens in a second, this heartbeat.

Patrick Huyghe
"Your Heart: A Survival Guide"

4d Transition

Even if all the sentences in a paragraph relate to a controlling idea and follow an organized method of development, it is often helpful to the reader's understanding to link sentences with transitional devices that provide smooth passage from one idea to the next. These devices include transitional words and expressions, pronouns, repetition of key words and phrases, and parallel grammatical structure.

Transitional words and expressions

Transitional words and expressions show the relationship of one term to another term, one sentence to another sentence, one idea to another idea, and even one paragraph to another paragraph. They serve as signposts that direct the reader through the passage.

Below are some common transitional words and expressions and the relationships they may indicate:

Addition

again, also, and, besides, equally important, finally, first (second, third, and so on), furthermore, in addition, last, likewise, moreover, next, too

Similarity

in a similar fashion, likewise, moreover, similarly, so

Contrast

although, but, even so, for all that, however, in contrast, nevertheless, on the contrary, on the other hand, still, yet

Time

afterward, at the same time, before, earlier, finally, in the past, later, meanwhile, next, now, previously, simultaneously, soon, subsequently

Place or direction

above, beyond, here, in the distance, nearby, opposite, overhead, there, to the side, underneath

Purpose

for this purpose, to this end, with this object in mind

Result

accordingly, as a result, consequently, hence, then, therefore, thus

Examples or intensification

for example, for instance, indeed, in fact, in other words, that is

Summary or conclusion

finally, in brief, in conclusion, in short, in summary, on the whole, to conclude, to sum up

In the following paragraph, the transitional words and expressions are printed in **boldface.**

There were other important applications of new technology that looked ahead to the future, **too.** Thaddeus Lowe was by no means the first to fly in lighter-than-air balloons, **but** he was the first to use these craft for doing reconnaissance work on enemy positions. **Likewise,** the telegraph had been around for some years, **but** the Civil War was the first war in which it played a crucial role. **So, too,** railroads were already enjoying a robust adolescence, **but** it was during the Civil War that they found themselves making a major contribution. Barbed wire entanglements were **also** used for the first time in the Civil War, **as** were land and water mines.

> Arthur M. Schlesinger, Jr.
> *The Almanac of American History*

Pronouns

Pronouns link sentences by referring the reader to their antecedents. In the following excerpt, notice how the pronouns in the second and third sentences link these clauses and sentences to the first sentence.

> There is always a teahouse wherever you go in the Orient. **Some** are big with red pillars and gleaming orange-yellow roofs; **many** have tables in a garden among scented flowers and lotus ponds; a **few** are huge houseboats carved to look like dragons floating on the water. But **most** of **them** are just plain, unornamented, regular restaurants.

> Maj Leung
> *The Chinese People's Cookbook*

Repetition and parallel structure

Repetition of key words and phrases and the use of parallel grammatical structure provide emphasis and clear transition from one thought to another. In the following paragraph, notice how the repetition of the word *know* drives home the author's point. Notice also that the last three sentences are in parallel form: each is made up of a clause beginning with *if* followed by a clause beginning with *you will.* This structure, along with the transitional words *then* and *Next* at the beginning of the second and third sentences, makes it easy for the reader to follow the progression of ideas from one sentence to the next.

But I am wandering from what I was intending to do; that is, make plainer than perhaps appears in the previous chapters some of the peculiar requirements of the science of piloting. First of all, there is one faculty which a pilot must incessantly cultivate until he has brought it to absolute perfection. Nothing short of perfection will do. That faculty is memory. He cannot stop with merely thinking a thing is so and so; he must **know** it; for this is eminently one of the "exact" sciences. With what scorn a pilot was looked upon in the old days, if he ever ventured to deal in that feeble phrase "I think," instead of the vigorous one "**I know!**" One cannot easily realize what a tremendous thing it is to **know** every trivial detail of twelve hundred miles of river and **know** it with absolute exactness. **If** you will take the longest street in New York, and travel up and down it, conning its features patiently until you **know** every house and window and lamp-post and big and little sign by heart, and **know** them so accurately that you can instantly name the one you are abreast of when you are set down at random in that street in the middle of an inky black night, **you will** then have a tolerable notion of the amount and the exactness of a pilot's knowledge who carries the Mississippi River in his head. And **then if** you will go on until you **know** every street crossing, the character, size, and position of the crossing-stones, and the varying depth of mud in each of these numberless places, **you will** have some idea of what the pilot must **know** in order to keep a Mississippi steamer out of trouble. **Next, if** you will take half of the signs in that long street, and *change their places* once a month, and still manage to **know** their new positions accurately on dark nights, and keep up with these repeated changes without making any mistakes, **you will** understand what is required of a pilot's peerless memory by the fickle Mississippi.

Mark Twain
Old Times on the Mississippi

4e Transitional Paragraphs

A transitional paragraph consists of one or two sentences whose purpose is to carry the reader from one paragraph to another. Usually a transitional paragraph sums up or emphasizes the thoughts in the preceding paragraph and announces the idea to be developed in the next paragraph. Notice how a quotation is used as a transitional paragraph in the following passage.

I got back into the car with my escort, a former Viet Cong captain, and we drove south, down the road that my battalion had swept for mines each morning. I pointed out a narrow gravel road and we followed it through the paddies toward the mountains. Where a refugee camp had been, there was now a cemetery for the war dead, filled with hundreds of graves, each marker bearing, in Vietnamese, the word *hero*. I stopped two old men who were walking along the road. One of them had been the president of the Viet Cong in a nearby village. "All this was a no-man's-land," he said, gesturing around the paddies and hills I knew so well. "We were very strong here. We lived underground right next to the American base on Hill 10. Our best fighters worked for the Americans; at night they joined us."

Then a woman came up the road. Her name was Dong Thi San. I asked her if she had been here during the war. "Of course," she said. "I was the wife of a guerrilla. He was killed in Bo Ban hamlet by an American Marine patrol in 1969. And he left four children." She looked at me with steady eyes. In 1969 I had commanded a platoon of young Americans, their average age less than twenty. We had been through Bo Ban hamlet and had set out ambushes there. My platoon could have—I could have—killed her husband.

"But life goes on," she said. "The war is over now."

The last Americans fled Vietnam ten years ago this April, but for us the war never really ended, not for the men who fought it, and not for America. It was longer than the Civil War, the First World War, and the Second World War put together. We spent $140 billion and suffered 58,022 Americans killed, another

303,000 wounded. Perhaps a million and a half Vietnamese died. The war shook our confidence in America as a nation with a special mission, and it left the men who fought it orphans in their own country. It divided us then, and its memory divides us now. The debate over when and how to commit American power abroad is really a debate over how to avoid, at all costs, another Vietnam.

William Broyles, Jr.
"The Road to Hill 10"

Exercise 1

The following passage actually consists of three paragraphs. Read the passage carefully and decide where each new paragraph should begin.

The next issue that confronts the Bible translator is that of the textual basis for the translation. We have no original text of any biblical book, and some books may have circulated in more than one version almost from the beginning of their existence as written documents. One theory has it that in the case of a number of Old Testament books three distinct texts emerged between the fifth and first centuries B.C., among the Jews of Palestine, Egypt, and Babylonia, respectively. Later, when ancient Jewish and Christian authorities defined the limits of the biblical canon, they did not fix the precise text of each individual book. To further complicate matters, all the books of the Bible have to some degree suffered the textual corruption that is the inevitable by-product of two to three thousand years of manuscript copying and recopying. How, then, do Bible translators establish reliable working texts of the books that they are to translate? Even the assumption that a given book had a single prototype, an *Urtext,* is itself questionable and unprovable. What scholars can do is try to reconstruct, from surviving manuscripts, the earliest stage of the text that can be established with confidence. This is an extraordinarily tangled problem, one that requires scholars to sift through a prodigious mass of data. In some instances where the text of a verse is obviously corrupt, half a dozen plausible reconstructions of the verse have been proposed. Such conjectural solutions to textual cruxes are often quite ingenious. The job of a Bible translator is—or should be—to choose the most probable reconstruction, to discriminate between what is merely ingenious and what is in fact likely. Establishing a good critical text for the New Testament is a less severe task than establishing a text for the Old. Most of the books of the New Testament were composed in the second half of the first century; a few—Jude and 2 Peter, for example—may stem from the second century. We possess complete manuscripts of the Greek New Testament that date from the fourth century, as well as copies of individual books that may be as early as the second century in origin. Therefore, the oldest surviving copies were made a maximum of three centuries after the books were originally written. Thanks to the existence of these early manuscripts, New Testament scholars, unlike their Old Testament colleagues, have been able to reach something resembling a consensus on the matter of a critical text. That something is a work entitled *The Greek New Testament,* published by the United Bible Societies. It contains a critical text of the New Testament, prepared by an international, interdenominational panel of specialists and intended especially for translators.

Barry Hoberman
"Translating the Bible"

Exercise 2

Identify the topic sentence in each of the following paragraphs. If the topic sentence is not stated, write your own sentence expressing the main idea.

1.   Dirt turns out to be a miracle roofing compound. Its natural milieu is exactly that harsh environment that wreaks such havoc with roofs. Consider: dirt is composed of small particles; it can flow. It moves when vent pipes or other obstructions expand and contract, keeping tight contact. Dirt dampens the swings in temperature that crack roof materials. Farmers well know how long dirt takes to warm up. And dirt reduces oscillations between wet and dry, maintaining a more constant moisture. A layer of dirt

protects the roof itself from wind abrasion and keeps sunlight from reaching any plastic membrane underneath.

John P. Wiley, Jr.
"Phenomena, Comment, and Notes"

2.   In the 1630s Descartes visited the royal gardens at Versailles, which were known for their intricate automata. When water was made to flow, music sounded, sea nymphs began to play, and a giant Neptune, complete with trident, advanced mechanically. Whether the idea was in his mind before this visit or not, Descartes's philosophy, which he supported with his mathematics, became that the universe and all the things in it also were automata. From Descartes's time to the beginning of this century, and perhaps because of him, our ancestors began to see the universe as a Great Machine. Over the next three hundred years they developed science specifically to discover how the Great Machine worked.

Gary Zukav
The Dancing Wu Li Masters

3.   Maya art provided more puzzles than answers. Sites were full of stone carvings—upright slabs, or stelae; door lintels; occasional wall panels—that showed elaborately dressed individuals, usually in formal poses. The carvings seemed to be full of religious symbols and sometimes included fantastic, obviously mythological animals, such as the two-headed serpent that writhes through the sky in some compositions. Were the individuals portrayed the kings, chieftains, and sages that Stephens had imagined, or were they instead priests dressed for ceremonies —or perhaps the gods themselves?

T. Patrick Culbert
"The Maya Enter History"

4.   Freud's isolation during these years is part of his legend. His colleagues, the story goes, shunned him; his revolutionary ideas fell on deaf ears. These letters suggest that this view needs some revision. While he was, indeed, isolated in these ways,

there is now evidence that this was to some degree his own doing, as Frank Sulloway, the historian, has suggested.

Daniel Goleman
"New Insights into Freud: From Letters to a Friend"

5.   What are the United States' economic interests in the region? U.S. trade with East Asia and on the Pacific is greater than U.S. trade with any other region of the world. Japan is the second most important trading partner of the United States, after Canada. More than ten percent of U.S. foreign investment goes to the region, principally to Japan and Australia, though the proportion going to the Southeast Asian nations is growing. The growth of all the East Asian nations (China excepted) has been based upon a high volume of international trade. Japan in particular is totally dependent upon imports for its raw-material resources. Thus the security of the sea-lanes of East Asia, and in particular those of Southeast Asia (through which most of Japan's energy resources pass), is vital for the economic well-being of East Asia and the Pacific.

Stephen J. Morris
"Vietnam's Vietnam"

6.   A British doctor who gave physical examinations to many of the Asians who served in France during the First World War as members of the Chinese Labor Corps was impressed by the fine condition of their teeth. He attributed the good dental health to soybeans, and later, during a visit to China, he also attributed to them the absence of rickets in Chinese children at a time when, he said, perhaps eighty per cent of the elementary-school students in London had at least a trace of it. Doctors in Moscow have prescribed soybeans as a cure for rickets. Chinese physicians, for their part, have long had a high regard for the soybean's restorative powers. They use it as a remedy for ailments of the heart, liver, stomach, lungs, kidneys, bladder, bowels, and nerves, and recommend it for improving the complexion and stimulating hair growth. Yellow soybeans are favored for overcoming underweight (to soybeans of all colors is attributed the fact that the Chinese are, on the whole, less afflicted than other races with obesity), and for cooling the blood; black soybeans were often

fed to horses before a long journey, to augment endurance. In Japan, doctors have urged soy milk—which has more iron and less fat than cow's milk—upon diabetics and arteriosclerotics; and in some circles there the ingestion of at least one bowl of miso soup every day is considered a way of averting stomach cancer and ulcers.

E. J. Kahn, Jr.
"Soybeans"

Exercise 3

Reread the paragraph by John McPhee on page 59. Can you find a statement in this paragraph that does not develop the controlling idea? Do you think the inclusion of this sentence affects the power of the paragraph? What reason might McPhee have had for including this sentence?

Exercise 4

Read the following controlling idea and the sentences that follow it. Indicate which sentences develop the controlling idea and which do not.

Controlling idea: People devised several ways of keeping track of the passage of time before the invention of the clock.

The earliest device for tracking the passage of time was the sundial, which measured the sun's shadow. Many homes today have a decorative sundial in their garden. Sundials can be found among the remains of the ancient Egyptians, Greeks, and Romans. The water clock was an improvement over the sundial, since it did not depend on the sun. I think it would be very annoying to go to bed hearing the dripping of water through a water clock. The use of water clocks was widespread in the ancient world; cultures as diverse as the Chinese and the Romans depended on them to keep track of the passage of hours. The ancient Egyptians devised their water clock at Thebes so that it divided night and day into equal units, making the hour a changeable unit dependent on the length of the day and of the night. Obviously, this type of clock would not be very useful today. The perfection of the art of glassmaking brought with it the invention of the hourglass, which marked the passage of time with sand. Today we use clocks and watches to measure time, and these have been perfected to measure not only hours and minutes, but also seconds and divisions of seconds.

Exercise 5

Discuss the method of development used for each of the following paragraphs.

1.   The new breed of training institutes offer something special: individual attention for each member. No one is admitted to the high-tech centers without first undergoing thorough testing. Based on the results, a customized exercise program is drawn up, geared to the individual's needs and goals. In effect, it is a sports training prescription. If you are overweight and in danger of a heart attack, a gradual running, biking or other cardiovascular program will be emphasized, combined with nutritional guidance; if you want to simply strengthen your upper torso, a system of weight lifting will be developed for you. And to make sure you achieve these goals—to encourage, to chastise and, above all, to explain the proper way to work out efficiently and without hurting yourself—a personal trainer (a licensed physical therapist or exercise physiologist) is assigned to accompany you as you exercise.

Robert Goldberg
"Tailor-made Fitness Training"

2.   Domestic play looks remarkably alike for both sexes at age three. Costumes representing male and female roles are casually exchanged. Everyone cooks and eats pretend food together.

Mother, father, and baby are the primary actors, but identities shift and the participants seldom keep one another informed. Policemen sweep the floor and dress the baby, and mothers put men's vests over negligees while making vague appointments on the telephone. If asked, a boy will likely say he is the father, but if he were to say mother, it would cause little concern. It can be a peaceful place, the three-year-olds' doll corner, even if monsters and superheroes enter, for the cooking and dressing and telephoning are usually private affairs.

Vivian Gussin Paley
"Superheroes in the Doll Corner"

3.   After the Prophet's death, Islam (the word is Arabic and means "submission" or "surrender") was ruled by a series of caliphs ("successors") selected by the family of Muhammad and the men around him. At the death of the fourth caliph—Ali, the Prophet's son-in-law—there was a dispute among factions, and two lines of succession were established. The Sunni line—to oversimplify—eventually petered out, ending ambivalently in the twentieth century with the end of the Ottoman Empire in Turkey. The Shia line ended, after a fashion, most Shias believe, in 873 A.D., when the Twelfth Imam ("leader") died or disappeared mysteriously. "The Hidden Imam" became an omnipresent factor in Shiism: "We are waiting for you, Twelfth Imam" was a revolutionary slogan in Iran, and Ayatollah Khomeini (or Imam Khomeini; the title applies to all Shia leaders) wore, for many, the mantle of the Hidden Imam. That connection gave Khomeini a temporal power over many people that it would be virtually impossible for any Sunni leader to accumulate.

Richard Reeves
"Journey to Pakistan"

4.   Rum found a major competitor as settlement spread to the frontiers. Both molasses and finished rum were too bulky and expensive to ship far inland, and as the eighteenth-century settlement line advanced, frontiersmen shifted their loyalties to grain whiskies. Indeed, whiskey was particularly suited to the frontier. Grain was plentiful—much more was harvested than farmers could eat or sell as food—and a single bushel of surplus

corn, for example, yielded three gallons of whiskey. This assured a plentiful liquor supply for Westerners and gave them a marketable commodity, which both kept longer and was easier to transport to market than grain. The advantages of whiskey were, therefore, such that it rapidly eclipsed rum as the staple drink in the Back Country. The arrival of the Scotch-Irish, who flocked to the frontier beginning in the 1730s, dealt rum a further blow. These immigrants had enjoyed reputations as whiskey lovers in their northern Irish homes, and they brought their distilling skills across the Atlantic with them. By the later 1700s, they had given American grain spirits a new quality in taste.

Mark Edward Lender
and James Kirby Martin
Drinking in America: A History

5.   The new research shows, for the first time in a convincing, repeatable way, that our behavior can be shaped by perceptions, experiences, and memories of which we have no conscious knowledge. In one striking example, people who had undergone surgery were found to have unconscious memories of the things they heard under anaesthesia. In another, amnesiacs and the partially blind seemed to have uncanny unconscious abilities to remember and see. The work also shows that certain apparently voluntary actions, like simple movements of the hand, may be initiated unconsciously even before we're aware of our decision to make them.

Kevin McKean
"In Search of the Unconscious Mind"

5 Crafting Sentences

Writing "correct" sentences is a mechanical process of applying rules, but writing *effective* sentences is more than making sure that your ideas are set up in correct grammatical form. To make a strong impression on the reader, you need to use your ear as much as your eye; that is, you need to listen to your sentences as well as read them. One essential tool of the sentence-writing craft is effective diction, or word choice; others include variety of structure, directness of assertion, and emphasis on important elements.

5a Variety of Sentence Structure

As a writer, you have a responsibility to hold your reader's interest. One way to do this is to vary your sentence structure. Just as the speaker who talks in a monotone will quickly lose the listener's attention, the writer who uses only one sentence structure will soon lose the reader's attention.

The following passage has been rewritten in a monotonous style. Notice that most of the sentences are short and choppy and that all begin with the word *you.*

> You see things vacationing on a motorcycle in a way that is completely different from any other. You are always in a compartment in a car. You are used to it. You don't realize that through that car window everything you see is just more TV. You are a passive observer. You are bored by everything moving by you in a frame.
>
> You lose the frame on a cycle. You are completely in contact with it all. You are *in* the scene. You are not just watching it anymore. You are overwhelmed by the sense of presence. You know that the concrete whizzing by five inches below your foot is the real thing. You know it is the same stuff you walk on. You see it is right there. You can't focus on it because it is so blurred. You can, however, put your foot down and touch it anytime. You are always immediately conscious of the whole thing. You are conscious of the whole experience.

Consider how the passage is improved by varying the sentence structure.

You see things vacationing on a motorcycle in a way that is completely different from any other. In a car you're always in a compartment, and because you're used to it you don't realize that everything you see is just more TV. You're a passive observer and it is all moving by you boringly in a frame.

On a cycle the frame is gone. You're completely in contact with it all. You're *in* the scene, not just watching it anymore, and the sense of presence is overwhelming. That concrete whizzing by five inches below your foot is the real thing, the same stuff you walk on; it's right there, so blurred you can't focus on it, yet you can put your foot down and touch it anytime, and the whole thing, the whole experience, is never removed from immediate consciousness.

Robert M. Pirsig
Zen and the Art of Motorcycle Maintenance

Do not be afraid to make your sentences long enough and complex enough to express complex ideas. When several short sentences are used to state what is really one complete thought, the effect is choppy and disjointed. Such writing gives the reader no clue to what is more important and what is relevant, but less important. For example, read the following paragraph.

Francis opened the trunk lid. An odor filled the attic air. It was the odor of lost time. The odor was a cloying reek of imprisoned flowers. It unsettled the dust. It fluttered the window shades.

Now read how the novelist William Kennedy combined the ideas in these short, choppy sentences into a single sentence.

When Francis opened the trunk lid the odor of lost time filled the attic air, a cloying reek of imprisoned flowers that unsettled the dust and fluttered the window shades.

William Kennedy
Ironweed

Notice that the ideas in the second and third sentences of the paragraph form the main clause of Kennedy's sentence (*the odor of lost time filled the attic air*), while the ideas in the other sentences are expressed as subordinate clauses and appositives. Thus the idea of the odor filling the air is given the most importance, while the other ideas are given less emphasis.

Many professional writers use short, clipped sentences to create a sense of urgency or suspense in narrative writing. In most of the writing you will do for school or other purposes, however, you will often need to use a mixture of both shorter and longer, more complex sentences to express your ideas. As you write and as you revise your earlier drafts, think about whether two or more short sentences might be more effective if they were combined into one. Some of the more common ways to combine sentences are by the use of appositives; adjective and adverb clauses; and prepositional, verbal, and absolute phrases.

Appositives

An **appositive** is a word or group of words that defines or renames the noun that precedes it. Notice how the choppy sentences in the following examples can be combined through the use of appositives.

Separate: The ailanthus was brought to America by a distinguished Philadelphia importer. His name was William Hamilton.

Combined: The ailanthus was brought to America by a distinguished Philadelphia importer, William Hamilton.

Separate: The ailanthus grows in the most meager of environments. Its name means "the tree of heaven."

Combined: The ailanthus, "the tree of heaven," grows in the most meager of environments.

| *Separate:* | Beside the river was a grove of tall, naked cotton-woods so large that they seemed to belong to a bygone age. These cottonwoods were trees of great antiquity and enormous size. |
| *Combined:* | Beside the river was a grove of tall, naked cotton-woods—trees of great antiquity and enormous size—so large that they seemed to belong to a bygone age. |

Willa Cather
Death Comes for the Archbishop

Adjective clauses

An **adjective clause** is a group of words with a subject and a predicate that modifies a noun or a pronoun. Usually, an adjective clause begins with a relative pronoun. Notice how the choppy sentences in the following examples can be combined through the use of adjective clauses.

| *Separate:* | The birthplace of Jean Rhys is Dominica. Dominica is one of the Windward Islands. |
| *Combined:* | The birthplace of Jean Rhys is Dominica, which is one of the Windward Islands. |

| *Separate:* | William W. Warner described blue crabs as "beautiful swimmers." He wrote a study of the Chesapeake Bay. The book won a Pulitzer prize. |
| *Combined:* | William W. Warner, who wrote a study of the Chesapeake Bay that won a Pulitzer prize, described blue crabs as "beautiful swimmers." |

| *Separate:* | Holmes had been seated for some hours in silence with his long, thin back curved over a chemical vessel. In this vessel he was brewing a particularly malodorous product. |
| *Combined:* | Holmes had been seated for some hours in silence with his long, thin back curved over a chemical |

vessel in which he was brewing a particularly mal-
odorous product.

Sir Arthur Conan Doyle
"The Adventure of the Dancing Men"

Adverb clauses

An **adverb clause** is a group of words with a subject and a
predicate that functions as an adverb in a sentence. Usually, an
adverb clause begins with a subordinating conjunction (such
as *because, after,* or *so that*) that shows the relation of the
adverb clause to the word or words it modifies. Notice how the
choppy sentences in the following examples can be combined
through the use of adverb clauses.

Separate: He was never in a battle. Nevertheless, he wrote
movingly about war.

Combined: Although he was never in a battle, he wrote movingly about war.

Separate: My wife and I both work at home. Quintana therefore has never had any confusion about how we
make our living.

Combined: Because my wife and I both work at home, Quintana has never had any confusion about how we
make our living.

John Gregory Dunne
"Quintana"

Separate: The purple and red jukebox belted accommodat-
ing rhythms. A couple slow-dragged. Billy spun
yarns about his adventures.

Combined: While the purple and red jukebox belted accom-
modating rhythms, and while a couple slow-
dragged, Billy spun yarns about his adventures.

James Alan McPherson
"The Story of a Dead Man"

Prepositional phrases

A **prepositional phrase** consists of a preposition, a noun or pronoun called the object of the preposition, and all the words modifying this object. Notice how the choppy sentences in the following examples can be combined through the use of prepositional phrases.

> *Separate:* Jack London died at the age of forty. He had become an extremely popular writer.
>
> *Combined:* Before his death at the age of forty, Jack London had become an extremely popular writer.

> *Separate:* She had a genius for painting. She also had a talent for writing.
>
> *Combined:* In addition to her genius for painting, she had a talent for writing.

> *Separate:* His Royal Highness Prince Philippe gave me an audience. He was prince of Araucania and Patagonia. The audience was on a drizzling November afternoon. It was at his public relations firm. The firm was on the Faubourg Poissonière.
>
> *Combined:* On a drizzling November afternoon, His Royal Highness Prince Philippe of Araucania and Patagonia gave me an audience at his public relations firm on the Faubourg Poissonière.

> Bruce Chatwin
> *In Patagonia*

Participial phrases

A **participial phrase** consists of a participle and all its modifiers and complements. Notice how the choppy sentences in the following examples can be combined through the use of participial phrases.

Separate: Washington resigned as general. He then returned to his plantation.

Combined: Having resigned as general, Washington returned to his plantation.

Separate: The producers planned a two-part miniseries. This miniseries would tell the story of the native American experience from the native American point of view.

Combined: The producers planned a two-part miniseries telling the story of the native American experience from the native American point of view.

Or: The two-part miniseries planned by the producers would tell the story of the native American experience from the native American point of view.

Separate: We are given a thimbleful of facts. We rush to make generalizations as large as a tub.

Combined: Given a thimbleful of facts, we rush to make generalizations as large as a tub.

Gordon W. Allport

Absolute phrases

An **absolute phrase** is a group of words with a subject and a nonfinite verb (a verb form that cannot function as a sentence verb). When the verb is a form of *be,* it is sometimes omitted but understood. Notice how the choppy sentences in the following examples can be combined through the use of absolute phrases.

Separate: The war was over. The nation turned its attention to reconstruction of the Union.

Combined: The war being over, the nation turned its attention to reconstruction of the Union.

Or: The war over, the nation turned its attention to reconstruction of the Union.

Separate: The plane finally came to a stop. The passengers were breathing sighs of relief.

Combined: The plane finally came to a stop, the passengers breathing sighs of relief.

Separate: Breakfast had been eaten. The slim camp outfit had been lashed to the sled. The men turned their backs on the cheery fire and launched out into the darkness.

Combined: Breakfast eaten and the slim camp outfit lashed to the sled, the men turned their backs on the cheery fire and launched out into the darkness.

Jack London
White Fang

Exercise 1

Use appositives, adjective clauses, or adverb clauses to form one sentence from each of the following groups of sentences.

1. Three religions venerate Moses. The three are Christianity, Judaism, and Islam.

2. The English writer's name is Alexander Pope. He wrote "The Rape of the Lock." It is a mock epic.

3. Biblical Hebrew became modern Hebrew in the 1920s. Eliezer Ben Yehuda wrote the first modern Hebrew dictionary.

4. University researchers in California have developed a new kind of tomato. It is easy to process. It is square and has a thick skin.

5. Ancient Egyptians played a game. It was called *senet.* Archaeologists have found a number of playing boards. No one has found the rules for the game.

6. The Widener family endowed Harvard University's library in memory of their son. Henry Widener went down with the *Titanic*.

7. Edwin H. Land invented the Polaroid filter. It separated light rays and cut out glare. It was ideal for sunglasses. Then he invented a new kind of camera. It could produce an instant snapshot.

8. A massive ramp was built along with the pyramids. Its surface was of slick mud. Then the blocks for building the pyramid could be hauled upward by the workers.

9. El Niño is a climatic disturbance. It usually lasts for about eighteen months. It can do much damage to Pacific Coast states. It keeps seasonal rains from reaching them.

10. In the early decades of this century, the foremost American black painter was Henry Ossawa Tanner. He left the United States in 1891. He lived in France for the rest of his life. He died in 1937.

Exercise 2

Use prepositional phrases, participial phrases, or absolute phrases to form one sentence from each of the following groups of sentences.

1. The state of Maine manages its moose population. It forbids moose hunting almost all year. It allows moose to be hunted for only one week.

2. Outward Bound is a nonprofit organization. It teaches skills for coping with the environment. It was established at Yale in 1962.

3. The year was 1880. A diamond was discovered in South Africa. It weighed almost 60 carats.

4. The newspaper reported the event. The mayor rose to her feet. Her face was flushed. Her eyes flashed. She pointed to the councilman. She called him a snake.

5. Some famous people become equally famous recluses. Some examples are Greta Garbo, Howard Hughes, J. D. Salinger.

6. The car could not move. The mud was up to its hubcaps.

7. He sliced his first shot. He hooked the second. The third rolled down the fairway.

8. Waist-deep we pushed through the swamp. Its surface was like a buckling rug.

9. October 24, 1929, was the date of a stock market crash. This may have triggered the one hundred suicides or attempted suicides that the *New York Times* noted through January 1, 1930.

10. King Kong abducted an attractive young woman. Then he carried her to the top of the Empire State Building.

Exercise 3

Revise the following passage by combining short, choppy sentences to form strong, effective sentences.

"Blind Girls" is a short story. It is in the collection *Black Tickets*. This collection is by Jayne Anne Phillips. In this story, the author creates a picture of two teenagers. They are named Jessie and Sally. These teenagers are drunk on their first wine. They are also drunk on their awakened desire. As they drink, they tell pornographic stories. They scare themselves with tales of lonely adults. These adults are attracted to the young. These tales are also of amputees. These maimed bodies lurk in the grass around parked cars. The passion of their fantasies and the intensity of their sexual fears finally overwhelm the teenagers. They know full well that the sounds outside their shack are simply from neighborhood boys. These boys have come to spy on them. They also want to scare them. However, knowing this, Sally whines when she hears them. She has to be led blindfolded through the field. She is led to her house.

These characters are unable to connect or to confront their own desires. This is characteristic of the stories of Jayne Anne Phillips. Another of her stories is called "Heavenly Bodies." In it, a father is unable to express his concern for his daughter directly. He can ask only about her car. The daughter's name is Jancy. Jancy can complain about her mother's emotional distance only by expressing concern about the distance the mother drives. These characters reach out. Their attempt is always incomplete. The father telephones. He wants to find out if Jancy is home. He doesn't speak. He only listens for her voice. Jancy telephones Michael. She wants to rekindle their romance. She cannot speak.

Like Sally who travels the path blindfolded, the father who once built roads, and the daughter who constantly travels on them, Jayne Anne Phillips's characters are always moving. They always move blindly. They have no place to go. Their loneliness and desperation reflect the alienation of modern American society.

5b Directness of Assertion

In general, try to construct your sentences so that your ideas are expressed as forcefully and directly as possible. You can achieve force and directness by using action verbs and by writing in the active voice.

Action verbs

Action verbs give power and precision to your writing, whereas the overuse of the verb *be* weakens your writing. Note how the sentences in the following examples are strengthened when the verb *be* is replaced with an action verb.

Weak: Her face **was** a wall of brown fire.
Strong: Her face **flashed** a wall of brown fire.

James Alan McPherson
"The Story of a Scar"

Weak: Everywhere, in the bathroom too, there were prints of Roman ruins that **were** brown with age.
Strong: Everywhere, in the bathroom too, there were prints of Roman ruins **freckled** brown with age.

Truman Capote
Breakfast at Tiffany's

Weak: Their feet **were** no longer on firm sand but **were** on slippery slime and painful barnacled rock.
Strong: Their feet **lost** the firm sand and **slipped** on slime, **trod** painfully on barnacled rock.

Michael Innes
The Man from the Sea

The active voice

As its name suggests, the active voice is usually more direct and forceful than the passive voice.

Unemphatic: Kronos **was overthrown** by Zeus, his son.
Emphatic: Zeus **overthrew** Kronos, his father.

Unemphatic: At the Rubicon a decision **was made** by Caesar.
Emphatic: At the Rubicon, Caesar **made** a decision.

Unemphatic:	Infinitely less **is demanded** by love than by friendship.
Emphatic:	Love **demands** infinitely less than friendship.

George Jean Nathan

If you wish to emphasize the receiver of the action instead of the agent, use the passive voice.

The father **was granted** custody of the child by the court.
The schools **were consolidated** in 1953.

5c Emphasizing Important Elements of a Sentence

Construct your sentences to emphasize the important elements. You can achieve emphasis through careful choice of words, through proper subordination, and through any one of the following methods.

1. Achieve emphasis by placing important elements at the beginning or at the end of a sentence, particularly at the end.

Unemphatic:	It is not known why more boys than girls are autistic.
Emphatic:	Why more boys than girls are autistic is unknown.
Unemphatic:	The trip was not as bad as, but worse than, I feared it would be.
Emphatic:	The trip was not as bad as I feared it would be—it was worse.
Unemphatic:	A bore is a man who tells you how he is when you ask him.

Emphatic: A bore is a man who, when you ask him how he is, tells you.

                                        Bert Leston Taylor

2. Achieve emphasis by changing loose sentences into periodic sentences. In a loose sentence, the main clause comes first; modifying phrases, dependent clauses, and other amplification follow the main clause.

> Jane Eyre would not declare her love for Mr. Rochester, although the fortune-teller pressed her for the information when they were alone together on that dark and mysterious night.

In a periodic sentence, the main clause comes last.

> Although the fortune-teller pressed her for the information when they were alone together on that dark and mysterious night, Jane Eyre would not declare her love for Mr. Rochester.

Periodic sentences are less commonly used than loose sentences and therefore are more emphatic. They give emphasis to the idea in the main clause by saving this idea for last.

Loose: The fortune-teller was really Mr. Rochester, although she claimed to be a gypsy from a nearby camp who had come simply to tell the ladies' futures.

Periodic: Although she claimed to be a gypsy from a nearby camp who had come simply to tell the ladies' futures, the fortune-teller was really Mr. Rochester.

Loose: It's easy to choose between love and duty if you are willing to forget that there is an element of duty in love and of love in duty.

Periodic: If you are willing to forget that there is an element of duty in love and of love in duty, then it's easy to choose between the two.

Jean Giraudoux

Loose: Emancipation will be a proclamation but not a fact until justice is blind to color, until education is unaware of race, until opportunity is unconcerned with the color of men's skins.

Periodic: Until justice is blind to color, until education is unaware of race, until opportunity is unconcerned with the color of men's skins, emancipation will be a proclamation but not a fact.

Lyndon B. Johnson

3. Achieve emphasis by writing balanced sentences. A balanced sentence presents ideas of equal weight in the same grammatical form, thus emphasizing the similarity or disparity between the ideas.

Unbalanced: Generally the theories we believe we call facts, and the facts that we disbelieve are known as theories.

Balanced: Generally, the theories we believe we call facts, and the facts we disbelieve we call theories.

Felix Cohen

Unbalanced: Money—in its absence we are coarse; when it is present we tend to be vulgar.

Balanced: Money—in its absence we are coarse; in its presence we are vulgar.

Mignon McLaughlin

4. Achieve emphasis by inverting normal word order. In most English sentences, the word order is subject-verb-

complement. Changing this order makes a sentence stand out.

Unemphatic:	He gave his property to the poor.
Emphatic:	His property he gave to the poor.
Unemphatic:	Indiana Jones walked into the Temple of Doom.
Emphatic:	Into the Temple of Doom walked Indiana Jones.
Unemphatic:	Long hours of hard work lie behind every successful endeavor.
Emphatic:	Behind every successful endeavor lie long hours of hard work.
Unemphatic:	The lens, which helps to focus the image, is in the front of the eye.
Emphatic:	In the front of the eye is the lens, which helps to focus the image.

Exercise

Revise each of the following sentences to make it more forceful or to emphasize important elements. Where appropriate, change the verb *be* to an action verb, change the passive voice to the active voice, place important words at the beginning or the end of the sentence, turn a loose sentence into a periodic sentence, turn an unbalanced sentence into a balanced sentence, and invert word order.

1. Some researchers say that heart attacks are caused by unchecked cholesterol levels reaching a danger point above 200 milligrams.

2. Most Outward Bound students are between 14 and 21 years of age, but there are also people in their 70s and 80s in the program.

3. In the 1920s, Harold "Red" Grange, a professional football player called the "Galloping Ghost," played both offense and defense for the Chicago Bears.

4. Seventy inches or more can be the length of the antlers of moose and Longhorn cattle.

5. Black-tie supper clubs, small-town dance halls, and even Carnegie Hall had many "Big Bands" playing in them in the 1940s and 1950s.

6. To talk to the old woman is learning history first-hand.

7. The goal of the park service is to preserve the plant life of the island in a pristine state.

8. A diamond necklace of light is around the moon.

9. As usual, Jeeves, the soul of reason, steps into the confusion.

10. The young man rejects his community, since he feels it has rejected him.

6 Critical Thinking

To write effectively, you need to think clearly and critically. Since the effectiveness of any assertion depends on the validity of the reasoning behind it, a well-written paper must of necessity be a well-reasoned one.

6a Inductive and Deductive Reasoning

The two major kinds of sound reasoning are inductive and deductive reasoning. **Inductive reasoning** is reasoning from the specific to the general. The word *inductive* comes from a Latin word that means "to lead into." In the inductive method, you observe a number of particulars or specifics, and these particulars lead you to a general principle or conclusion. For example, imagine you are studying folk medicine. For a year you live in a society that practices folk medicine, and you carefully observe the practices of the healers. You observe that they use a preparation made from a particular plant to treat boils. In all cases, the boil disappears within two days of the application of the plant. On the basis of your observations of these particular cases, you reason that this plant helps cure boils.

Deductive reasoning is reasoning from the general to the specific. The word *deductive* comes from a Latin word that means "to lead from." In the deductive method, you start with a general principle and apply it to specific instances. For example, imagine you are a doctor. As a general principle, you accept that penicillin is effective against the bacteria causing strep throat. When a patient with strep throat comes to you, you apply the general principle to this specific case and prescribe penicillin.

The deductive method can be expressed as a three-step process, called a **syllogism.** The first step, the general principle, is called the **major premise;** the second step, the specific instance, is called the **minor premise;** and the third step, the application of the general principle to the specific instance, is called the **conclusion.**

Major premise:	Penicillin cures strep throat.
Minor premise:	This patient has strep throat.
Conclusion:	(Therefore) This patient will be cured by using penicillin.

Although inductive and deductive reasoning are powerful tools in writing, their misuse can lead to errors. To make effective use of the inductive method, make sure that you have made enough observations, that your observations are accurate and representational, that you have noted and accounted for any exceptions, and that your conclusion is derived from these observations. For example, suppose the plant mentioned earlier did not cure three cases of boils. If your conclusion is to be valid, you must note these exceptions and explain them in terms of the conclusion. Perhaps this plant will not cure boils in people who have been treated with it previously, or whose boils are especially severe. The more observations and information you accumulate, the more likely that your conclusion will be accurate.

To make effective use of the deductive method, make sure that the general principle you start with is true and that the situation to which you apply it is relevant. Note and account for any exceptions. For example, imagine that the bacteria in the strep throat patient mentioned earlier have developed an immunity to penicillin. Then the principle would not be applicable to this patient's case. The more information you have about the specific situation, the more likely you will be to apply the relevant principle.

6b Logical Fallacies

All thinking is subject to **logical fallacies,** or errors in reasoning. Test your own writing to make sure you have avoided false analogies, overgeneralizations and stereotyping, unstated assumptions, appeals to the emotions, confusion of cause and effect, improper either-or thinking, non sequiturs, and circular reasoning.

False analogies

Analogies, which are used often in inductive reasoning, are comparisons. For an analogy to be sound, or true, the comparison must make sense; that is, the things being compared must correspond in essential ways, and the ways in which they do not correspond must be unimportant in terms of the argument or conclusion. Consider the following analogies:

These are not books, lumps of lifeless paper, but *minds* alive on the shelves. From each of them goes out its own voice . . . and just as the touch of a button on our set will fill the room with music, so by taking down one of these volumes and open-ing it, one can call into range the voice of a man far distant in time and space, and hear him speak to us, mind to mind, heart to heart.

Gilbert Highet

First the writer compares books with minds. These two things are alike in essential ways. Both contain the thoughts of a person, and from both these thoughts are communicated. Then the writer compares pushing the button on a radio with taking down a book from a shelf and opening it. These acts are alike, since both call into range the voice of a person who is not present.

Here are some other sound analogies:

News is the first rough draft of history.

Ben Bradlee

The individual who pollutes the air with his factory and the ghetto kid who breaks store windows both represent the same thing. They don't care about each other—or what they do to each other.

Daniel Patrick Moynihan

If a State can prescribe, as a rule of civil conduct, that whites and blacks shall not travel as passengers in the same railroad coach, why may it not so regulate the use of the streets of its cities and towns as to compel white citizens to keep to one side of the street and black citizens to keep to the other?

Justice John Marshall Harlan

Although analogies help readers to understand a point, they are not proofs of a conclusion. In fact, many analogies that appear in writing are misleading, or false. A **false analogy** does not make sense. Although the things being compared may correspond in some ways, they are dissimilar in other ways that are crucial to the argument or conclusion, or their similarities are blown out of proportion. Consider the following false analogy.

> Buying a car is like buying a steak. You can't be sure how good the product is until you've bought it and used it.

This analogy is false because you can test-drive the car, but you cannot test-eat the steak; moreover, the economic difference between the items is so great that a comparison between the purchase of one and the purchase of the other has little meaning.

Exercise

Explain why the following analogies are false.

1. A nation's full use of its natural resources is as proper as an individual's full use of his or her talents. *don't relate*

2. A nation that can put a man on the moon can eliminate poverty. *2 different issues*

3. Think of a job interview as a first date, where you're trying to make a good impression on someone. *most similar*

Overgeneralizations and stereotyping

An **overgeneralization** is a conclusion based on too little evidence or on evidence that is unrepresentative or biased. For example, imagine you go to a major-league baseball game with your friends. You observe that attendance at this game is very low. On the basis of this observation, you conclude that attendance at major-league baseball games has fallen off drastically. This is an overgeneralization, since one observation—or even two or three—are not a sufficient number from which to draw a conclusion.

Now imagine that while you are visiting a large city for a week, you ride the subway every evening at nine. You find the ride quick and comfortable, since there are never any crowds and you always get a seat. On the basis of your observations, you conclude that the subway provides pleasant and reliable transportation. This is an overgeneralization, since your evidence is not typical of a commuter's ride on the subway during rush hour.

Here are some other examples of overgeneralization:

Since neither of my parents smokes, the number of adults who smoke must be rapidly diminishing.

Melinda and her friend had dinner at a new local restaurant. Melinda's steak was undercooked and her friend's chicken was cold. They concluded that the restaurant was poor.

A candidate for mayor makes a door-to-door survey of all the houses in the neighborhood to find out whether voters are willing to pay higher taxes to improve the public schools. Most of them express enthusiasm for the idea, and the candidate decides to campaign on this platform.

Stereotyping is overgeneralization about groups of people. **Stereotypes** are the standardized mental images that are the result of such overgeneralization. Almost everyone holds stereotypes about one group or another, and we encounter them every day in advertising, television programs, and other media. For example, we are all familiar with stereotypes like these:

Stereotype

the absentminded professor	the passionate French lover
the dumb blonde	the stoical male
the genius with glasses	the man-hunting female

Because stereotypes of this kind are so widely recognized as such, you can easily avoid them in your writing. A greater danger is that you will develop your own stereotypes by treating an individual as representative of a group to which the individual belongs. Try to eliminate stereotyping not only from your writing but also from your thinking.

Unstated assumptions

An **assumption** is an idea that we accept as true without any proof. Sometimes **unstated assumptions** enter into our reasoning and confuse our thinking. Many of these assumptions are really stereotypes. For example, consider the following statement:

> His autobiography must be fascinating because he is such a famous actor.

This reasoning does not make sense. It is based on the unstated assumption that someone who has had a glamorous or exciting career will be able to write about it in an interesting way. That may be true in this particular case, but it cannot be assumed as a general principle.

Exercise

Identify the unstated assumption in each of the following statements.

a child will always be delinquent from

1. A delinquent child comes from a delinquent family.

2. They will need to take the elevator to the top of the monument;

   they have both recently retired from the university.

   they are old.

3. Harry is so good in math, it is no wonder he is having trouble in

English. *His good in math & can't be good in English*

Appeals to the emotions

Do not draw a conclusion for yourself or tempt others into drawing a conclusion on the basis of an appeal to the emotions instead of reason. Writers use various techniques to arouse an emotional rather than a rational response. Among these are name-calling, using loaded words, creating a bandwagon effect, using flattery, and creating false associations.

Name-calling

Name-calling, which is sometimes referred to as the **ad hominem fallacy,** is an attempt to discredit an idea or conclusion by attacking not the idea or conclusion but the person presenting it.

Griffin claims that the legal drinking age should be raised in order to reduce the incidence of drunk driving. Are you going to let someone who was once himself convicted of drunk driving tell you when you can take an innocent drink?

Gardner claims that teaching is attracting mediocre people. Yet she herself is a hick from a backwater town. What can she know of quality?

So what if Mr. Klein told you you shouldn't drop out of school? He's only an old man with old ideas. What does he know about youth and adventure?

If the nature kooks had their way, America would still be a wilderness from coast to coast.

Harley G. Waller

Loaded words

Loaded words are highly charged emotional words that appeal to readers' prejudices. Readers who do not already share these prejudices are as likely to be irritated as to be convinced by the use of loaded words.

> Because of this nation's **giveaway** policies, the **hardworking** man or woman lives in squalor while the **lazy bum** drives a Cadillac.
>
> Democracy is a system in which the **screeching** and **caterwauling** of the **vulgar masses** drown the pronouncements of the **enlightened** few.
>
> Our library shelves are **infested** by the **filth** of **effete intellectuals** who crave the **corruption** of the **innocent youth** of this country.

Bandwagon effect

The **bandwagon technique** attempts to influence people by encouraging them to put aside their own powers of reasoning and simply join the crowd.

> Don't be left out—see the film that all America has been waiting for.
>
> Everyone in the neighborhood is signing the petition. You're going to sign it, aren't you?
>
> ColaRite is the most popular soft drink in the country. Buy some and join the fun!

Flattery

Flattery is often used to try to persuade a reader or listener to do something or to accept the validity of a conclusion.

> The voters of this city are too intelligent to be taken in by my opponent's promises.

You're young. You're on top of things. And you want to stay on top. That's why you need *Lifestyle,* the magazine that helps you be what you want to be.

A person of your sensitivity could not help being moved by the plight of these unfortunate victims.

False association

False association, sometimes called the **association fallacy,** attempts to convince people of the strength or weakness of a conclusion by suggesting that by agreeing or disagreeing with it, they will become associated with other people doing the same.

Many people active in the movie and theater world belong to this health club. Since you are young and talented, you should join it, too.

All of the best people in town support this proposal. Of course, you must support it, too.

Only eggheads and clods belong to that fraternity. You're not planning to pledge it, are you?

Exercise

Each of the following statements contains a logical fallacy. For each statement, indicate whether this fallacy is a false analogy, an overgeneralization, an unstated assumption, or an appeal to the emotions.

1. I won't vote for him for governor because I saw a picture of him riding a bicycle backward. *name calling*

2. The fact that half the class failed the test proves that the teacher grades unfairly. *false assot or bandwagon*

3. I am sure that he will have to buy the party food at the deli since his wife won't be home in time to cook any. *name calling*

4. After reading the first chapter of a long book, you conclude it is boring, put it down, and never open it again.

5. The federal government should live within its income just as a family must.

6. The food at Joe's Diner must be wonderful because all the football players eat there. *flattery*

7. Gun purchasers should not have to answer questions or delay their purchases any more than any other buyer. *bandwagon*

8. I wouldn't think you'd want to live on a street where every other house has a pick-up truck in its driveway. *name calling*

9. The camel is called the ship of the desert, so riding one must be like riding in a boat. *false association*

10. He has only a technical degree from some small school somewhere. *name calling*

Faulty cause and effect

Do not assume that one event causes another event simply because it precedes the second event. Many superstitions are based on this error in reasoning.

> It didn't rain today because, for once, I brought my umbrella.
>
> He won the game because he was wearing his lucky T-shirt.
>
> I now have a cold because I forgot to take my vitamin pill this morning.

Either-or thinking

Either-or thinking is a type of oversimplification that assumes that there are only two alternatives in a situation when usually there are many possibilities in between.

> You are either with us or against us.

> We have to decide: do we want clean air and water or do we want a higher standard of living?

> Every woman today must make a choice. She can have a family or she can have a career.

Non sequiturs

The Latin words *non sequitur* mean "it does not follow." A **non sequitur** is a logical fallacy in which the conclusion does not follow from the premise.

> Many wild animals live longer in zoos than in the wild. Therefore, all wild animals should be placed in zoos.

> Since Henderson does not beat his children, he is a good father.

> It is important to honor our parents, and so we should actively participate in the celebration of Mother's Day and Father's Day.

Circular reasoning

Do not try to prove that something is true by merely restating it in other words. This error is called **circular reasoning** or **begging the question.**

> Public transportation is necessary because everyone needs it.

> The play is unsophisticated because it displays a naive simplicity.

> The vest will protect an officer against a person with a gun because it is bulletproof.

ct
6b

Exercise

Each of the following statements contains a logical fallacy. For each statement, indicate whether this fallacy is faulty cause and effect, either-or thinking, a non sequitur, or circular reasoning.

1. Today I met a handsome stranger because my horoscope said I would.

2. I love mysteries; therefore, I love Sherlock Holmes' stories.

3. He is six foot, seven inches tall; he must be a basketball player.

4. Either we vote to build the nuclear power plant, or we resign ourselves to insufficient power forever.

5. The marriage is doomed; it rained for the wedding.

6. Since he washes his car every Saturday, he must be a careful driver.

7. Since she is divorced, she will not be interested in an exercise class.

8. If bars stay open until 1 A.M., church attendance will decline.

9. The company trades internationally because it sells its goods in several foreign countries.

10. Keep our city solvent; vote "yes" to a lottery.

Part II

Grammar

Grammar is the formal study of the features and constructions of language. The word *grammar* comes from the ancient Greek word *grammatiké,* which meant the study of literature, in the broad sense of "the way written language is put together." The purpose of studying grammar is to gain an understanding of language so that you can use it effectively.

The basic pattern for writing is the sentence. A useful definition of a *sentence* is "a word or group of words that expresses a complete thought." A sentence may be as short as one word or as long as fifty words or more.

Here are five sentences. Notice that each begins with a capital letter and ends with an end punctuation mark (a period, a question mark, or an exclamation point).

> Frank Lloyd Wright, considered by many to be the founder of modern architecture, profoundly influenced American life.
> Did you know that sharks, unlike human beings, grow set after set of teeth?
> Alcoholism is a disease, not an indulgence!
> Snow fell.
> Stop!

7 The Parts of a Sentence ▬▬▬

Regardless of its length, a sentence always contains at least one **clause,** consisting of a subject and its verb. (Sometimes the subject is implied rather than stated.) Study the parts of the sentences that follow.

implied subject   predicate
↓   ↓
(You) Consider the situation.

subject   predicate
↓   ↓
The scientist's research won.

direct object
↓
The scientist's research won recognition.

indirect object
↓
The scientist's research won her recognition.

objective complement
↓
Research made the scientist famous.

subject   predicate   predicate nominative
↓   ↓   ↓
The scientist is Barbara McClintock.

predicate adjective
↓
Her research is remarkable.

These are the seven basic sentence patterns—all the patterns possible. Notice how the following sentences grow by the addition of modifiers to the basic *subject-verb patterns.*

The scientist investigated.

In her laboratory, the scientist investigated.

In her laboratory at Cold Spring Harbor, the scientist investigated.

In her laboratory at Cold Spring Harbor, the scientist investigated gene development.

In her laboratory at Cold Spring Harbor, the scientist investigated gene development in maize.

In her laboratory at Cold Spring Harbor, the scientist investigated gene development in maize, and her discovery won.

In her laboratory at Cold Spring Harbor, the scientist investigated gene development in maize, and her discovery of jumping genes won.

In her laboratory at Cold Spring Harbor, the scientist investigated gene development in maize, and her discovery of jumping genes won recognition.

In her laboratory at Cold Spring Harbor, the scientist investigated gene development in maize, and her discovery of
jumping genes won her recognition.

In her laboratory at Cold Spring Harbor, the scientist investigated gene development in maize, and her discovery of
jumping genes won her recognition by the scientific community.

The award was the Nobel Prize.

The award won by Barbara McClintock was the Nobel Prize.

The award won by Barbara McClintock, who is a distinguished
cytogeneticist, was the Nobel Prize.

The award won in 1983 by Barbara McClintock, who is a distinguished cytogeneticist, was the Nobel Prize.

7a Subjects

The **subject** of the sentence answers the question "who?" or
"what?" about the predicate, or verb. The subject is the part of
the sentence about which something is being said.

How can you identify the subject of a sentence? Form a
question by putting "who" or "what" before the verb. In some
sentences, the subject *performs* the action expressed by the
verb.

Halfway through her performance, the **soprano** *hit* a flat note.

Captain Cook *searched* for a northwest passage to China.

Mass extinctions *mark* the boundaries between eras on the
geological time scale.

Who hit a flat note? The *soprano*. Who searched for a northwest passage to China? *Captain Cook*. What marks the boundaries between eras? *Mass extinctions*.

In other sentences, the subject *receives* the action of the verb; that is, it is acted upon.

The deer *was wounded* by the hunters.

Lyndon Johnson *was educated* at Southwest Texas State Teachers College.

The first modern bank in the United States *was established* by Robert Morris, a Philadelphia financier.

What was wounded by the hunters? *The deer.* Who was educated at Southwest Texas State Teachers College? *Lyndon Johnson.* What was established by Robert Morris? *The first modern bank in the United States.*

If the verb is a linking verb, such as *be* or *seem,* the subject is the person or thing identified or described.

James Boswell was both the friend and the biographer of Samuel Johnson.
George Eliot was the pseudonym of Mary Anne Evans.
Aaron Burr's reputation as a traitor seems unjustified.

Who was both the friend and the biographer of Samuel Johnson? *James Boswell.* What was the pseudonym of Mary Anne Evans? *George Eliot.* What seems unjustified? *Aaron Burr's reputation as a traitor.*

The second way to identify the subject of a sentence is to pay attention to word order. In most English sentences, the subject appears before the predicate (the verb). However, there are exceptions. Sometimes word order is reversed for effect.

On his head sits **a crown.**
Through the ice-covered streets walked **the funeral cortege.**
From these schools will come **tomorrow's leaders.**

Sometimes word order is altered to ask a question.

> Did **Miró's art** influence Pollock and Motherwell?
> Should **reporters** be required to disclose their sources?
> Does **classical music** have an audience among the young?

Sometimes one of the expletives *there* and *here* appears at the beginning of the sentence. These words are never the subject but simply serve to postpone the appearance of the subject. The word *it* is also sometimes used as an expletive. In each of the following sentences, the subject is printed in **boldface.**

> There are **six books** in this series.
> Here are **four ways to increase productivity at this plant.**
> It is necessary **to read the instructions before starting.**

Sometimes the sentence is a command. In a command, the subject *you* is implied rather than stated.

> Help me with this word-processing program.
> Please read this chapter before the next class.
> List five twentieth-century American composers.

Since a prepositional phrase ends with a noun or noun substitute, people sometimes look to it for the subject of the sentence. However, the simple subject is never found in a prepositional phrase. In each of the following sentences, the simple subject is printed in **boldface** and the prepositional phrase is in *italics*.

> **Each** *of the states* chooses delegates to the convention.
> **Neither** *of the pandas* is female.
> **One** *of Charlemagne's achievements* was the development of an effective administrative system.

The simple subject

The **simple subject** is the main noun or noun substitute in the subject.

1. Are the wives of the early presidents too often overlooked and underrated?

2. The unpretentious Martha Washington undoubtedly had a humanizing effect on her more austere husband.

3. The gifted Abigail Adams should receive recognition for the breadth of her intellectual interests rather than for her hanging of the presidential laundry in the White House.

4. The detailed letters and memoirs of Dolley Madison provide an excellent source of information about the time.

5. Through the efforts of Abigail Fillmore, congressional funds set up a small library in the White House.

7b Predicates

The **predicate** of a sentence tells what the subject does or is. It is the part of the sentence that comprises what is said about the subject. The predicate consists of a verb (a word that expresses action or a state of being) and all the words that complete the meaning of the verb.

How can you identify the predicate of a sentence? Form a question by putting "does what?" or "is what?" after the subject.

> The pianist **played a complicated piece.**
> The amateur treasure hunters **found a few valuable pieces.**
> The bald eagle **is the symbol of the United States.**

The pianist did what? *Played a complicated piece.* The amateur treasure hunters did what? *Found a few valuable pieces.* The bald eagle is what? *Is the symbol of the United States.*

A New Jersey **farmer** won a prize in London in 1986 for a 671-
pound pumpkin.
Growing **conditions** in 1987 made the pumpkins smaller.
That year a **Canadian** took first place with a 408-pound entry.
It won its grower a cash prize and a trip to San Francisco.
There are **competitions** for other vegetables—giant carrots,
radishes, onions.
Growing monstrous vegetables can be a profitable hobby.

A simple subject may consist of two or more nouns or noun
substitutes that take the same predicate.

Nicaragua and El Salvador are much in the news today.
In ancient Greece, **war and athletics** were believed to be in-
fluenced by Nike, the winged goddess of victory.
Desire, anger, and pain must be annihilated in order to reach
Nirvana.

The complete subject

The **complete subject** consists of the simple subject and all
the words that modify it. In each of the following sentences,
the simple subject is printed in **boldface** and the complete
subject is in *italics*.

Wide-visioned, closefisted **George Halas,** *originator of the Chicago Bears,* can be described as the George Washington of
pro-football.
A hot **bath and** *a vigorous* **massage** are good remedies for
aching muscles.

Note: Throughout this book, we use the term *subject* to mean
the simple subject.

Exercise

First circle the simple subject in each of the following sentences.
Then underline the complete subject.

The simple predicate

The **simple predicate** is the verb, which may consist of more than one word.

> The town meeting **is** the epitome of a democratic society in action.
> Early in her reign Elizabeth **had reestablished** the Church of England.
> The Cultural Revolution in China **was headed** by Mao Zedong.
> Many accidents **could have been prevented.**

A simple predicate may include two or more verbs that take the same subject.

> The small group of colonists **boarded** the British ships and **threw** their cargoes of tea overboard.
> Poe **fell** in love with his cousin Virginia and **married** the thirteen-year-old child.
> Thoreau **opposed** the poll tax and **had been speaking** against it for years but **had** never before **broken** the law.

The complete predicate

The **complete predicate** consists of the simple predicate and all the words that modify it and complete its meaning. In each of the following sentences, the simple predicate is printed in **boldface** and the complete predicate is in *italics.*

> A jet flying overhead **broke** *the stillness of the night.*
> The Connecticut River **divides** *the state into two almost equal regions.*
> The goal of landing Americans on the moon and returning them to Earth **was accomplished** *by Apollo 11.*

7c Complements

A **complement** completes the meaning of a verb. The five major types of complements are the direct object, the indirect object, the objective complement, the predicate nominative, and the predicate adjective.

Direct objects

A **direct object** is a noun or noun substitute that specifies the person or thing directly *receiving* the action of a transitive verb. A verb becomes transitive when it gives its action to that object (see page 129).

To identify the direct object, form a question by putting "whom?" or "what?" after the verb.

> Darwin accepted a **position** aboard H.M.S. *Beagle.*
> In addition to his other accomplishments, William James achieved a **reputation** as a literary figure.
> The congresswoman greets **us** warmly and then opens the **discussion.**

Darwin accepted what? A *position.* William James achieved what? A *reputation.* The congresswoman greets whom? *Us.* She opens what? *The discussion.*

Indirect objects

An **indirect object** is a noun or noun substitute that tells to whom or what or for whom or what the action of the verb is performed. A sentence can have an indirect object only if it has a direct object; the indirect object always comes just before the direct object. Further, indirect objects follow only those verbs that describe a "giving" action of some kind.

> The director gave the **plans** her approval.
> He wrote **her** a poem expressing his admiration.
> In one of Aesop's fables, a mouse does a **lion** a favor.

Usually, sentences containing indirect objects can be rewritten by putting *to* or *for* before the indirect object.

The director gave her approval **to the plans.**
He wrote a poem **for her** expressing his admiration.
In one of Aesop's fables, a mouse does a favor **for a lion.**

Objective complements

An **objective complement** is a noun or an adjective that completes the action of the transitive verb in relation to its object. A sentence can have an objective complement only if it has an object. Further, the action of the verb must produce a "change" of some kind in that object.

The storm made the bridge **unsafe.**
The news report declared it a **hazard.**

You can recognize objective complements by inserting a form of the verb *be* before the objective complement.

The storm made the bridge *to be* **unsafe.**
The news report declared it *to be* a **hazard.**

The noun objective complement always follows the object. Occasionally, the adjective objective complement may precede the object.

The judge ruled **impossible** the impartiality of a trial held in the victims' community.

Predicate nominatives

A **predicate nominative** is a noun or noun substitute that follows an intransitive linking verb and renames the subject (see page 131).

The culprit is **he.**
Martha Graham became **one** of the principal innovators of modern dance.
E. B. White's closest companion at the *New Yorker* was **James Thurber.**

The pronoun *he* renames *culprit*. The pronoun *one* renames *Martha Graham*. The noun *James Thurber* renames *companion*.

In a construction of this type, the linking verb serves as an equal sign. The noun on the left-hand side of the linking verb equals the noun on the right-hand side.

Predicate adjectives

A **predicate adjective** is an adjective that follows an intransitive linking verb and describes the subject (see page 131).

> Isadora Duncan's style of dancing seemed **revolutionary** to her contemporaries.
> The drama critic's review was especially **acrimonious.**
> Halfway through their journey over the mountains, the pioneers felt too **weary** to travel on.

Exercise

First circle the simple subject and the simple predicate in each of the following sentences. Then identify any complements. Underline each complement and classify it as a direct object, an indirect object, an objective complement, a predicate nominative, or a predicate adjective.

1. Saint Columba came to Britain in 565 A.D. and brought the Picts the message of Christianity.

2. Travelers have circulated the legend of the Loch Ness monster since that time.

3. Over the past fifty years three thousand people have offered the press proof of Nessie's existence.

4. Photographs and sonar contacts appear plausible, but the London Zoo declares belief in Nessie "mass hallucination."

5. Nessie, fact or fiction, is a plesiosaur, a long-necked reptile or serpent.

8 The Parts of Speech

Words have traditionally been classified into eight categories, called **parts of speech**—noun, verb, adjective, adverb, pronoun, preposition, conjunction, and interjection. The function a word performs in a sentence determines which part of speech it is. A word may function as more than one part of speech, as shown in the following examples.

> The committee is seeking ways to make a **ride** on the bus more comfortable. (*noun*)
> Thousands of commuters **ride** the bus to work every day. (*verb*)
> For many years **New England** dominated literary life in America. (*noun*)
> Emily Dickinson's poems carry traces of other **New England** writers. (*adjective*)
> Some scholars feel that the story of Jason and the Argonauts reflects trading expeditions that occurred **before** the Trojan War. (*preposition*)
> **Before** Schliemann excavated the ruins of ancient Troy, most people believed that the story of the Trojan War was pure myth. (*conjunction*)
> Any civilization is the product of those who came **before.** (*adverb*)

8a Nouns

A **noun** is a word that names. Nouns may name persons.

Shakespeare	actor	women
Margaret Mead	citizen	scholars

Nouns may name places.

Pittsburgh	prairie	suburbs
Pacific Ocean	camp	Great Lakes

Nouns may name animate or inanimate objects.

reindeer	Bunsen burner	cassettes
baboon	veranda	word processors

Nouns may name events, ideas, or concepts.

meeting	freedom	frustration
French Revolution	honor	philanthropy

In the following sentences, the nouns are printed in **boldface.**

> While in his **bath, Archimedes,** a Greek **mathematician** and **inventor,** worked out the **principle** of **buoyancy.**
> **Barbara Tuchman** argues that the **acceptance** of the **Wooden Horse** by the **Trojans** was the **epitome** of **folly.**
> The **discovery** of the **Rosetta stone** led to an **increase** in **knowledge** of the ancient **world.**

Proper, common, concrete, and abstract nouns

Nouns can be classified in other ways: as proper or common nouns, and as concrete or abstract nouns. **Proper nouns** name particular persons, places, objects, or ideas. Proper nouns are capitalized.

Milton	Honda	Martin Luther King, Jr.
San Francisco	Hinduism	West Germany

Common nouns are less specific. They name people, places, objects, and ideas in general, not in particular. Common nouns are not capitalized.

| poet-dramatist | motorcycle | preacher |
| port city | religion | democracy |

Concrete nouns name things that can be seen, touched, heard, smelled, tasted, or felt.

| horizon | marble | music |
| peanut butter | garbage | heat |

Abstract nouns name concepts, ideas, beliefs, and qualities. Unlike concrete nouns, abstract nouns name things that cannot be perceived by the five senses.

| love | justice | creativity |
| inspiration | kindness | monotheism |

Compound nouns

As you read the preceding lists, you probably noticed that some nouns are made up of more than one word. Nouns that consist of more than one word are called **compound nouns.** Some compound nouns are written as one word, some are hyphenated, and some are written as two or more separate words. (When in doubt, check your dictionary.)

| bedroom | tomato plant | cathode-ray tube |
| heartland | fire insurance | father-in-law |

Nouns are characterized by several features.

1. Nouns show **number.** Most nouns can be either singular or plural. (For guidelines on forming the plural of nouns, see pages 331–334.)

| *Singular:* | computer | success | criterion | woman | sheep |
| *Plural:* | computers | successes | criteria | women | sheep |

2. Nouns have **gender.** They are either masculine, feminine, or neuter (sometimes called "indeterminate").

Masculine:	Abraham Lincoln	waiter	boy
Feminine:	Harriet Tubman	waitress	girl
Neuter:	human being	attendant	child
	Eiffel Tower	chair	justice

3. Nouns have **case.** Case refers to the structural function of a noun in a sentence. English has three cases—subjective (nominative), objective, and possessive—obvious in pronouns (see pages 144, 217–223). The form of the noun changes only when it is used in the possessive case. (For more information on forming the possessive case, see pages 348–351.)

The subjective case is used for subjects and predicate nominatives. The objective case is used for direct and indirect objects and for objects of prepositions. The possessive case is used to show possession.

Subjective:	**Harrison** worked late.	**He** worked late.
Objective:	The boss trained **Harrison.**	The boss trained **him.**
Possessive:	**Harrison's** proposal was accepted.	**His** proposal was accepted.

8b Verbs

A **verb** is a word that expresses action—physical or mental—or a state of being. In the following sentences, the verbs are printed in **boldface.**

Isaac Bashevis Singer **writes** his stories and novels in Yiddish. (*physical action*)
Puritans **valued** industry and thrift. (*mental action*)
The Constitution **is** the keystone of our democracy. (*state of being*)

Action verbs

An **action verb** may be *transitive* or *intransitive*. An action verb that takes an object is **transitive**. An **object** is a word (a noun or noun substitute) that completes the idea expressed by the verb.

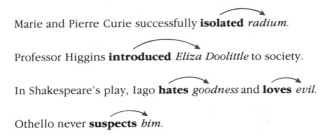

Marie and Pierre Curie successfully **isolated** *radium*.

Professor Higgins **introduced** *Eliza Doolittle* to society.

In Shakespeare's play, Iago **hates** *goodness* and **loves** *evil*.

Othello never **suspects** *him*.

When the subject of a transitive verb performs the action received by the object, the verb is said to be in the **active voice.** The verbs in the preceding sentences are **transitive active.** A transitive verb is in the **passive voice** when the active voice object has become subject of that verb.

Radium **was** successfully **isolated** by Marie and Pierre Curie.

Eliza Doolittle **was introduced** to society.

In Shakespeare's play, *goodness* **is hated** by Iago and *evil* **is loved.**

He **is suspected** by Othello.

Only transitive verbs can be described as having voice. (For more about voice, see pages 95–96 and 139–140.) An action verb that has no object is **intransitive.**

Sometimes even good old Homer **nods.**

Horace

Consider the lilies of the field, how they **grow; they toil** not, neither **do** they **spin.**

Matthew 6:28

People **hate,** as they **love,** unreasonably.

William Thackery

An action verb may be transitive in one sentence and intransitive in another.

The narrator **mourned** the *loss* of his beautiful Annabel Lee. (*transitive*)

After the death of the President, the nation **mourned.** (*intransitive*)

The audience **howled** its *derision* at the speaker. (*transitive*)

Out on the tundra, the wolves **howled.** (*intransitive*)

Queen Victoria **ruled** *Great Britain, Ireland, and India.* (*transitive*)

In the midst of battle, death **ruled.** (*intransitive*)

Some action verbs are always **intransitive**—for example, *sit, lie, rise, die, reminisce.*

State-of-being verbs

State-of-being verbs may be *linking* or *nonlinking.* They are, however, always **intransitive** because they never take objects.

Linking verbs

A **linking** verb expresses a state of being or condition and connects its subject to a word that describes or identifies that subject. The most common linking verb is *be* and its forms— *am, is, are, was, were, will be, have been,* and so on.

Radiotherapy **is** the treatment of disease with radiation.
Woody Guthrie **was** a popular folksinger.
Americans **were** aghast at the sinking of the *Lusitania.*

Other common linking verbs are *appear, become, feel, grow, look, remain, seem, smell, sound,* and *taste.*

Compared to other warm-blooded animals, hummingbirds **appear** extravagant in their use of energy.
Houdini **became** world-famous for his daring escapes.
The fate of Amelia Earhart **remains** a mystery.

A linking verb connects the subject to a predicate nominative or to a predicate adjective. A predicate nominative identifies the subject, whereas a predicate adjective describes the subject.

Napoleon was a brilliant **general.** (*predicate nominative*)

After his defeat at Waterloo, **Napoleon** was *disconsolate.* (*predicate adjective*)

The *macadamia* is Australia's only edible **nut.** (*predicate nominative*)

The macadamia's *shell* is nearly **impregnable.** (*predicate adjective*)

The *bobcat* remains North America's most common native **cat.** (*predicate nominative*)

Despite the trainer's efforts, the *bobcat* remains **wild.** (*predicate adjective*)

Nonlinking verbs

A **nonlinking,** state-of-being verb is not followed and completed by a predicate noun or adjective, but may be followed by an adverb modifier.

We were *upstream* from their camp.
The plane was directly *overhead* when it burst into flames.
Unfortunately, they were *downwind* of the skunk when it sprayed.
It seems *so.*

Note: A verb earns its label only as it operates with its subject plus object or complement if it has either.

Gregor Mendel **grew** his *plants* in the monastery garden. (*action verb, transitive*)
The plants **grew** vigorously. (*action verb, intransitive*)
During the campaign, the arguments **grew** *heated.* (*state-of-being verb, linking*)

Exercise*

Underline the simple components of the following sentences using these abbreviated labels: *S* = subject; *TV* = transitive verb; *IV* = intransitive verb; *LV* = linking verb; *PV* = passive voice verb; *O* = object; *PN* = predicate noun; *PA* = predicate adjective.

* Adapted from "Research Briefs," *The University of Georgia Research Reporter* 18:4, 1987, p. 4.

Examples:

```
         S        TV       O
```
Vandals destroyed Rome during Nero's reign.

```
         S           PV
```
Rome was destroyed.

```
         S      IV
```
Rome burned furiously.

```
         S      IV
```
Nero remained in his palace.

```
         S   LV         PN
```
Nero was an evil emperor.

```
         S     LV        PA
```
Nero remained indifferent to the fate of the city.

1. A team of archaeologists from the Universities of Colorado, Georgia, and Michigan have excavated the site of the ancient circus in Carthage.

2. From the second through the fifth centuries A.D., the circus remained a huge and magnificent building.

3. It could seat as many as 75,000 people.

4. The rear of the building was decorated with a colonnade of fine white marble.

5. Spectators sat behind a thick wall of stuccoed limestone, crowned with dark green stone flecked with mica.

6. Chariots raced on a firmly compacted, hard, flat track.

7. Excavators have found an interesting group of artifacts: curse tablets.

8. A curse tablet is a sheet of lead, bearing pictures, inscriptions, and magic symbols.

9. The sheet would be rolled and thrown onto the track to bring bad luck to a charioteer.

10. Chariot racing in ancient Carthage must have been dangerous and violent.

Auxiliary verbs and modals

A verb has four basic forms, called **principal parts;** the present infinitive, the past tense, the past participle, and the present participle.

Present infinitive	*Past tense*	*Past participle*	*Present participle*
compute	computed	computed	computing
analyze	analyzed	analyzed	analyzing
fall	fell	fallen	falling
bring	brought	brought	bringing

The **present infinitive** is the dictionary form of the verb. For example, if you wanted to know the meaning of the first verb in the chart above, you would look up *compute,* the present infinitive form, in your dictionary. The **present participle** of all verbs is formed by adding *-ing* to the present infinitive. The **past tense** and **past participle** of most verbs, called **regular verbs,** are formed by adding *-d* or *-ed* to the present infinitive. Verbs like *fall* and *bring* are **irregular verbs;** their past tense and past participle are formed in some other way. (For more information on irregular verbs, see pages 189–191.)

A **verb phrase** is made up of the present infinitive, the present participle, or the past participle preceded by one or more auxiliary verbs or modals. As discussed in the following pages, the **auxiliary** verb *have* is used to form the perfect tense; the auxiliary verb *be* is used to form progressive tenses and the passive voice. In the following sentences, the verb phrase is printed in *italics* and the auxiliary in **boldface.**

> Several movies **are** *popularizing* a street form of dance called break dancing. (*progressive present tense*)
> Edna St. Vincent Millay's first book of poems **was** *published* in 1917. (*passive voice, past tense*)
> Jacobo Timerman **has** *called* attention to the violation of human rights in Argentina. (*present perfect tense*)

Modals are used to form questions, to help express a negative, to emphasize, to show future time, and to express such conditions as possibility, certainty, or obligation. The words *do, does, did; can, could; may, might, must; will, shall; would, should;* and *ought to* are modals. A verb phrase may include both auxiliaries and modals. In each of the following sentences, the verb phrase is printed in *italics* and the modal in **boldface.**

> For a democracy to work, its citizens **must** *participate.*
> You **should** *practice* at least an hour a day.
> The election **may** *be decided* on the basis of personality.

Sometimes an auxiliary or modal is separated from the main part of the verb.

> **Do** you *know* the full name of the Imagist poet H. D.?
> The price of gold **has** not *been falling.*
> The teacher **is** now *computing* students' grade-point averages.

Verbs display three characteristics: *tense, voice,* and *mood.*

Tense

Tense is the time expressed by the form of the verb. The six tenses are the *simple present, present perfect, simple past, past perfect, simple future,* and *future perfect.* Each of these tenses has a progressive form that indicates continuing action.

	Basic form	*Progressive form*
Simple present:	compose(s)	is (are) composing
Present perfect:	has (have) composed	has (have) been composing
Simple past:	composed	was (were) composing
Past perfect:	had composed	had been composing
Simple future:	will (shall) compose	will (shall) be composing
Future perfect:	will (shall) have composed	will (shall) have been composing

Usually, the simple present, the simple past, and the simple future are referred to as the present, the past, and the future tense, respectively.

The time of an action does not always correspond exactly with the name of the tense used to write about the action. For example, in special situations the present tense can be used to write about events that occurred in the past or will occur in the future as well as events that are occurring in the present.

Present tense

In general, the **present tense** is used to write about events or conditions that are happening or existing now.

She **lives** in Austin, Texas.
An accountant **is preparing** our tax returns.
They **are** dissatisfied with their grades.

The present tense is also used to write about natural or scientific laws or timeless truths, events in literature, and habitual action.

> Some bacteria **are** beneficial, while others **cause** disease.
> No one **lives** forever.
> Sherlock Holmes and his archenemy, Dr. Moriarty, apparently **perish** together.
> He always **begins** his speeches with an anecdote.
> She **goes** to work every day at eight.

The past tense can also be used to write about events in literature. Whichever tense you choose, be consistent.

The present tense can be used with an adverbial word or phrase to indicate future time. In the following sentences, the adverbs that indicate time are *italicized*.

> This flight **arrives** in Chicago *at 7:30 P.M.*
> *Next week* the class **meets** in the conference room.
> She **begins** her campaign *tomorrow.*

The verb *do* is used with the present infinitive to create an emphatic form of the present tense.

> You **do know** your facts, but your presentation of them is not always clear.
> He certainly **does cover** his topic thoroughly.
> After six weeks of training, they **do look** fit.

Present perfect tense

The **present perfect tense** is used to write about events that occurred at some unspecified time in the past and about events and conditions that began in the past and may still be continuing in the present.

> The novelist **has incorporated** theories of psycholinguistics into his mysteries.

Their new line of greeting cards **has been selling** well.
The two performers **have donated** the profits from their concert
to charity.

Past tense

The **past tense** is used to write about events that occurred and
conditions that existed at a definite time in the past and do not
extend into the present.

The study **explored** the dolphin's ability to communicate.
The researchers **were studying** the effects of fluoridation on
tooth decay.
The patient **was relieved** when the doctor **told** him the results
of the tests.

The word *did* (the past tense of *do*) is used with the present
infinitive to create an emphatic form of the past tense.

In the end he **did vote** against the bill.
Despite opposition, she **did make** her opinions heard.
They **did increase** voter registration, but they lost the election.

Past perfect tense

The **past perfect tense** is used to write about a past event or
condition that ended before another past event or condition
began.

She voted for passage of the bill because she **had seen** the
effects of poverty on the young.
The researchers **had tried** several drugs on the microorganism
before they found the right one.
He **had been painting** for ten years before he sold his first
canvas.

Future tense

The **future tense** is used to write about events or conditions that have not yet begun.

Her next book **will continue** the saga of the Anderson family.
The voters **will be deciding** the role of religion in the schools.
We **shall stay** in London for two weeks.

Future perfect tense

The **future perfect tense** is used to write about a future event or condition that will end before another future event or condition begins or before a specified time in the future.

Before I see him again, the editor **will have read** my short story.
If he keeps to this regimen, by the end of the month the boxer **will have lost** the necessary ten pounds.
By October, she **will have been singing** with the City Opera five years.

For more information on the use of tenses, see pages 243–246.

Voice

Active and passive voice

Voice indicates whether the subject performs or receives the action of the transitive verb. If the subject performs the action completed by an object, the verb and the clause are in the **active voice.** (See also pages 95–96, 129.)

The President **announced** his decision.
The journal **offers** insights into contemporary poetry.
Anxiety **can cause** a rise in blood pressure.

If the subject receives the action of the verb, that is, if the subject is acted upon, the verb and the clause are in the **passive voice.** The passive voice of a verb consists of a form of *be* followed by the past participle of the verb.

> The decision **was announced** by the President.
> Insights into contemporary poetry **are offered** by the journal.
> A rise in blood pressure **can be caused** by anxiety.
> The money **has been stolen** from the safe.

Many sentences written in the passive voice, like the first three preceding examples, contain a phrase beginning with the word *by.* This phrase usually tells who or what actually performed the action.

Mood

Mood refers to whether a verb expresses a statement, a command, a wish, an assumption, a recommendation, or a condition contrary to fact. In English there are three moods: the *indicative,* the *imperative,* and the *subjunctive.*

Indicative mood

The **indicative mood** is used to make a factual statement or to ask a question.

> William Carlos Williams **lived** in Paterson, New Jersey.
> **Did** William Carlos Williams **live** in Paterson, New Jersey?

> Kublai Khan **was** the grandson of Genghis Khan.
> **Was** Kublai Khan the grandson of Genghis Khan?

> Forced from their land, the Cherokees **embarked** on the Trail of Tears.

Imperative mood

The **imperative mood** is used to express a command or a request. In a command, the subject *you* is often not stated, but understood.

> **Bring** me the newspaper.
> **Come** here!
> **Would** you please **close** that door.

Subjunctive mood

The **subjunctive mood** is used to indicate a wish, an assumption, a recommendation, or a condition contrary to fact.

> He wished he **were** rich. (*wish*)
> If this **be** true, the validity of the collection is in doubt. (*assumption*)
> It is mandatory that he **dress** appropriately. (*recommendation*)
> If I **were** mayor, I would solve the problems of this city. (*condition contrary to fact*)

As you can see from these examples, the form of a verb in the subjunctive is often different from the indicative form. With most verbs the only difference is in the third-person singular form in the present tense, where the subjunctive does not have the final *s* of the indicative form.

Indicative	*Subjunctive*
he speaks	he speak
she manages	she manage
it works	it work

The subjunctive of the verb *to be* differs from the indicative in both the present and the past tenses.

Present Tense

Indicative		*Subjunctive*	
I am	we are	(if) I be	(if) we be
you are	you are	(if) you be	(if) you be
he/she/it is	they are	(if) he/she/it be	(if) they be

Past Tense

Indicative		*Subjunctive*	
I was	we were	(if) I were	(if) we were
you were	you were	(if) you were	(if) you were
he/she/it was	they were	(if) he/she/it were	(if) they were

The subjunctive is falling into disuse. However, it is still preferred for expressing a condition contrary to fact, and it is required in *that* clauses of recommendation, wish, or command and in a few idiomatic phrases.

> If she **were** in command, we wouldn't be having this problem.
> In Kipling's tale, Danny wished that he **were** king.
> He resolved that if need **be,** he would study night and day.

Exercise

Underline the verbs in the following sentences, circle their subjects, and name their tenses.

1. Although people think of apples whenever the story of Adam and Eve is read, the apple is not mentioned in Genesis.

2. According to the Bible, the first man and woman ate the fruit of the tree of knowledge of good and evil, but this fruit is never identified.

3. Storytellers and writers have often used the apple as a symbol of all fruits, and the apple has figured prominently in mythology and folklore.

4. An ancient Greek myth tells how Paris, a Trojan prince, judged a beauty contest among three goddesses and gave the prize, a golden apple, to Aphrodite; this decision led to the Trojan War.

5. Most Americans know the tale of Johnny Appleseed, but many people do not know that this legend is based on the life of a real person, John Chapman.

8c Pronouns

A **pronoun** is a word that stands for or takes the place of one or more nouns. When a pronoun refers to a specific noun, that noun is called the **antecedent** of the pronoun. In the following sentences, the arrows indicate the *italicized* antecedents of the pronouns in **boldface** type.

> Because *vitamins* can have toxic side effects, **they** should be administered with care.

> Megadoses of *niacin,* **which** is a B vitamin, can cause nausea and vomiting.

A pronoun may also have another pronoun as an antecedent.

> **Most** of the records are scratched. **They** will have to be replaced.

Each of the mothers thought **her** child should receive the award.

A pronoun may lack a specific antecedent.

Who can understand the demands made upon a child prodigy?
Everyone knew that **something** was wrong.

There are seven categories of pronouns: *personal, demonstrative, indefinite, interrogative, relative, intensive,* and *reflexive.*

Personal pronouns

Personal pronouns take the place of a noun that names a person or a thing. Like nouns, personal pronouns have number, gender, and case. This means that they can be singular or plural; that they can be masculine, feminine, or neuter; and that they can function in the subjective, the objective, or the possessive case. (For more information about pronoun case, see pages 217–223.) In addition, personal pronouns are divided into three "persons": **first-person pronouns** refer to the person(s) speaking or writing, **second-person pronouns** refer to the person(s) being spoken or written *to,* and **third-person pronouns** refer to the person(s) or thing(s) being spoken or written *about.* The following is a list of all the personal pronouns.

	Singular	*Plural*
First person:	I, me, my, mine	we, us, our, ours
Second person:	you, your, yours	you, your, yours
Third person:	he, him, his	they, them, their, theirs
	she, her, hers	
	it, its	

Demonstrative pronouns

Demonstrative pronouns point to someone or something. The demonstrative pronouns are *this* and *that* and their plural forms *these* and *those*.

Demonstrative pronouns are usually used in place of a specific noun or noun phrase.

> The sandwiches I ate yesterday were stale, but **these** are fresh.
>
> The goddess of retributive justice was called Nemesis, and **this** is the word we use today to refer to an avenger or an unbeatable rival.
>
> James named the character Mrs. Headway, for **that** was her chief characteristic, her ability to make headway.

In addition, demonstrative pronouns are sometimes used to refer to a whole idea.

> Should we welcome the electronic age? **That** is a good question.
>
> **This** is the challenge new sergeants face: finding ways to make recruits respect you, not just fear you.

If you use a demonstrative pronoun in this way, be sure that the idea it refers to is clearly stated and not just vaguely suggested (see pages 211–212).

Indefinite pronouns

Indefinite pronouns do not take the place of a particular noun, although sometimes they have an implied antecedent. Indefinite pronouns carry the idea of "all," "some," "any," or "none." Some common indefinite pronouns are listed below.

everyone	somebody	anyone	no one
everything	many	anything	nobody

Some indefinite pronouns are plural, some are singular, and some can be either singular or plural.

Everything *is* going according to plan. (*singular*)
Many *were* certain that the war which officially started on July 28, 1914, would be over before autumn. (*plural*)
Some of the material *was* useful. (*singular*)
Some of the legislators *were* afraid to oppose the bill publicly. (*plural*)

For more information on the number of indefinite pronouns, see pages 201–202.

Interrogative pronouns

Interrogative pronouns are used to ask a question.

who   whom   whose   what   which

Who, whom, and *whose* refer to people. *What* and *which* refer to things.

What were the effects of the Industrial Revolution on Europe during the first decade of the twentieth century?
Who is Barbara McClintock, and for **what** is she best known?
Which of the economic depressions have been most damaging?

Relative pronouns

Relative pronouns are used to form adjective clauses and noun clauses (see pages 167–170).

who	which	whoever	whatever
whose	that	whomever	
whom	what	whichever	

Who, whom, whoever, and *whomever* refer to people. *Which, what, that, whichever,* and *whatever* refer to things. *Whose* usually refers to people but can also refer to things.

The Black Emergency Cultural Coalition is an organization **whose** members have dedicated themselves to the elimination of racism in the arts.

Betye Saar's *The Liberation of Aunt Jemima,* **which** was purchased by the University Art Museum at Berkeley, is a multidimensional work **that** uses a collage of labels from pancake-mix boxes.

The food was given away to **whoever** wanted it.

For more information about relative pronouns, see pages 202–203, 208–209, 221–223.

Intensive pronouns

Intensive pronouns are used to emphasize their antecedents. They are formed by adding *-self* or *-selves* to the end of a personal pronoun.

The detectives **themselves** didn't know the solution.
The producer wasn't sure **herself** why the show was a success.

Reflexive pronouns

Reflexive pronouns are used to refer back to the subject of the clause or verbal phrase in which they appear. They have the same form as intensive pronouns.

During her illness Marjorie did not seem like **herself.**
If you have young children in the house, take precautions to prevent them from electrocuting **themselves** accidentally.
This plant can fertilize **itself.**

8d Adjectives

An **adjective** is a word that modifies, or describes, a noun or pronoun. It limits or makes clearer the meaning of the noun or pronoun.

The **efficient** *secretary* organized the schedule. (*modifies a noun*)

He is **efficient.** (*modifies a pronoun*)

The songs of George Gershwin were antidotes to the **psychological** and **financial** *depression* of the 1930s. (*modify a noun*)

They are still **popular** though **their** *composer* died in 1937.

(*modifies a pronoun*)   (*modifies a noun*)

An adjective modifies by answering one of three questions about the noun or pronoun. These questions are (1) "what kind?" (2) "how many?" and (3) "which one?"

By describing a quality or a condition, an adjective answers the question "what kind?"

The England of the Anglo-Saxons was not a **unified** *country,* but a land divided into **separate** *kingdoms.*

Much of the poetry of the Anglo-Saxons was in the **heroic** *tradition.*

The *riddles* in **Anglo-Saxon** *poetry* were **clever** and **humorous.**

By telling quantity, an adjective answers the question "how many?" This quantity may be definite (*one, twenty*) or indefinite (*several, few*).

When writing about literature, keep in mind **six** *features:* plot, characterization, setting, theme, point of view, and style.

The report listed **several** *reasons* for the decline of literacy.

He has **many** *questions* but **no** *answers.*

An adjective answers the question "which one?" by showing possession or by pointing out people or objects. Possessive forms of both nouns and pronouns may be considered adjectives (*girl's, his*), as may the demonstratives *this, these, that,* and *those* and the articles *a, an,* and *the.*

Bauhaus sought to correct **the** *alienation* of factory workers from **their** *products.*

Asplund's *buildings* vividly revealed **the** *possibilities* of steel and glass.

These *artists* were interested in everything from designing glassware to planning factories.

Adjectives are characterized by several features.

1. Most adjectives have a comparative form to compare two things and a superlative form to compare three or more.

	Comparative	*Superlative*
rich	richer	richest
beautiful	more beautiful	most beautiful
bad	worse	worst

Chocolate mousse is a **rich** dessert.
Chocolate mousse is a **richer** dessert than apple pie.
Chocolate mousse is the **richest** of the three desserts.

The roses are **beautiful.**
The roses are **more beautiful** than the hyacinths.
The roses are the **most beautiful** flowers in the garden.

(For information about the comparative and superlative forms of adjectives, see pages 229–232.)

2. Adjectives can usually be identified by their position in a sentence. For example, an adjective will fit sensibly into one of the following blanks.

The _____ object was removed.
It seems _____ .
The woman, _____ and _____ , left early.

3. Usually, the adverb *very* can be placed before an adjective.

The **very large** object was removed.
It seems **very odd.**
The woman, **very tired** and **very cold,** left early.

8e Adverbs

An **adverb** is a word that modifies, or limits the meaning of, a verb, an adjective, or another adverb.

During the Harbor Festival, the tall ships *sailed* **gracefully** into the bay. (*modifies a verb*)

The exhibition of art from Pompeii drew **extremely** *large* crowds. (*modifies an adjective*)

The accident at Chernobyl demonstrated **very** *powerfully* the hazards of nuclear energy. (*modifies an adverb*)

An adverb modifies by answering one of the following questions: (1) "when?" (2) "where?" (3) "to what extent?" (4) "how?"

Adverbs of time

Adverbs of time answer the question "when?"

We *will discuss* the matter **then.**

Environmentalists warn that we *must* **eventually** *reach* an equilibrium with nature.

Photography *is* **now** *accorded* equal status with painting and sculpture.

Adverbs of place

Adverbs of place answer the question "where?"

As the ambassador traveled through the Middle East and North Africa, he *encountered* an Islamic revival **everywhere.**

Faith healers *look* **upward** and **inward** for cures for disease.

The ceremony *was held* **outdoors** to accommodate the large crowd.

Note that nouns can function as adverbs of time and place.

The symposium *was held* **yesterday.**

Registration *began* last **week.**

Some students *go* **home** nearly every **weekend.**

Adverbs of degree

Adverbs of degree answer the question "to what extent?" In addition, they are used to heighten, or intensify, the meaning of a verb, adjective, or adverb.

The Empire State Building is **far more** *beautiful* than the World Trade Center.

After paying her medical bills, she was left **almost** *destitute.*

In his films the **very** *talented* Charlie Chaplin was able to make people laugh at the absurdities of life.

Adverbs of manner

Adverbs of manner answer the question "how?" They tell in what manner or by what means an action was done.

Disaster films *were* **enthusiastically** *embraced* by the movie-going public.

The Beatles proved that rock music *had to be taken* **seriously.**

People *are* **strenuously** *debating* whether the lives of comatose patients *should be maintained* **artificially.**

Characterizing adverbs

Adverbs are characterized by two features.

1. Adverbs can be formed from many adjectives by adding the suffix *-ly* to the adjective. An additional spelling change is sometimes required.

The artist's style was **delicate.** (*adjective*)
The artist painted **delicately.** (*adverb*)

Lech Walesa's actions seemed **heroic.** (*adjective*)
Lech Walesa acted **heroically.** (*adverb*)

2. Most adverbs have comparative and superlative forms.

	Comparative	*Superlative*
profoundly	more profoundly	most profoundly
fast	faster	fastest
well	better	best

The soprano is singing **well** today.
The soprano is singing **better** than she sang yesterday.
The soprano is singing the **best** she has in days.

The plight of the homeless is **profoundly** moving.
The plight of the homeless is **more profoundly** moving than I had imagined.
The plight of the homeless is the **most profoundly** moving story in the paper today.

(For more information about the comparative and superlative forms of adverbs, see pages 229–232.)

Exercise

Identify, underline, and label the adjectives, adverbs, and pronouns in each of the following sentences.

1. What do you know about train travel, which is becoming again popular in America?

2. Passenger trains almost disappeared with the advent of faster, more convenient, though more expensive air travel.

3. No airplane, however, can offer a view except for the tops of clouds and an occasional, brief glimpse of a distant terrain.

4. Today, refurbished passenger cars are comfortable; they have reliable heating and cooling systems; moreover, their wide windows offer spectacular views.

5. Unfortunately, those who travel on business must usually forego the leisurely, scenic, romantic rail ride for the sake of getting somewhere in the shortest time possible.

8f Prepositions

across	during	near	toward
below	from	on	with

The preceding words are **prepositions,** which are words used to show the relationship of a noun or a pronoun, called the *object of the preposition,* to another part of the sentence. The preposition and its object and any modifiers of the object (*the prepositional phrase*) then function in the sentence as adjective, adverb, or, occasionally, noun. Prepositions are among the most familiar and frequently used words in the language. Some common ones are listed here.

about	concerning	past
above	despite	save (meaning
across	down	"except")
after	during	since
against	except	through
along	for	throughout
among	from	till
around	in	to
at	inside	toward(s)
before	into	under
behind	like	underneath
below	near	until
beneath	of	unto
beside	off	up
between	on	upon
beyond	onto	with
but (meaning	out	within
"except")	over	without

A **compound preposition** is made up of more than one word. Some commonly used compound prepositions are listed here.

ahead of	in addition to	on account of
as for	in back of	on top of
as well as	in case of	out of
because of	in front of	together with
by means of	instead of	with regard to

Prepositions appear only in and at the beginning of prepositional phrases. In the following sentences, the prepositions are printed in **boldface** and the prepositional phrases in *italics*.

The term "metaphysical poets" was coined **by** *Samuel Johnson* **in** *the eighteenth century.*

Metaphysical poets wrote **about** *human love* **in addition to** *religious love.*

Often they used language normally associated **with** *human love* to describe their love **of** *God* and religious images to explain their love **for** *other human beings.*

Note: The *to* in the infinitive form of the verb (such as *to describe*) is not a preposition. (For more information on prepositional phrases, see pages 89, 163–164, 271.)

Exercise

Identify the prepositions in each of the following sentences.

1. The word *library* comes from *liber,* the Latin word for book.

2. Aristotle had an excellent private library, and upon his death this library was given to one of his students.

3. However, the greatest library of the ancient world was established around 300 B.C. by Ptolemy I at Alexandria, which was located at the mouth of the Nile in Egypt.

4. Within this library were manuscripts from every part of the then known world.

5. Throughout the reign of the Caesars, libraries flourished in Rome, but with the rise of Christianity libraries declined in Western Europe, until the founding of the great monastic libraries during the sixth and the seventh centuries.

8g Conjunctions

and   if   until   but   or   when

The preceding words are **conjunctions,** which are words used to join other words, phrases, clauses, or sentences. There are three types of conjunctions: *coordinating conjunctions, correlative conjunctions,* and *subordinating conjunctions.*

Coordinating conjunctions

A **coordinating conjunction** joins elements that have equal grammatical rank. These elements may be single words, phrases, or clauses. The common coordinating conjunctions are these:

and	or	for	yet
but	so	nor	

In the following sentences, the coordinating conjunctions are printed in **boldface** and the elements being joined in *italics.*

> The children of *Queen Victoria* **and** *Prince Albert* married into many of the other ruling houses of Europe.
> *Some enjoy Matthew Arnold primarily for his poetry,* **but** *others respect him more for his criticism.*
> The flax is then soaked *in tanks, in streams,* **or** *in pools.*

Conjunctive adverbs

Words like the following, called **conjunctive adverbs,** may make clear the connection between *independent clauses* (clauses that can stand by themselves as sentences), but they cannot—as conjunctions can—join the clauses.

accordingly	hence	otherwise
also	however	still
besides	moreover	therefore
consequently	nevertheless	thus
furthermore		

In the following sentences, the conjunctive adverbs are in **boldface** and the independent clauses in *italics.* Notice that a semicolon precedes a conjunctive adverb that appears between independent clauses.

She wanted to photograph the building in the early morning light; **therefore,** *she got up at dawn on Saturday.*

For years the elderly have moved from the North to Florida to retire; **however,** *today many are returning to the North to be near their children.*

William Morris was a noted painter, weaver, and pattern maker; **moreover,** *he was a respected poet, novelist, and critic.*

Correlative conjunctions

Correlative conjunctions are coordinating conjunctions that are used in pairs. The most common correlative conjunctions are these:

both . . . and	not only . . . but also
either . . . or	whether . . . or
neither . . . nor	

In the following sentences, the correlative conjunctions are in **boldface.**

Whether you go **or** stay makes no difference to us.

Both diet **and** exercise are necessary for losing weight.

Either the festival will be a success, **or** the city will have wasted taxpayers' money.

Subordinating conjunctions

Subordinating conjunctions join subordinate, or dependent, clauses to main, or independent, clauses. The following are some common subordinating conjunctions:

after	if	than
although, though	in order that	that
as	in that	unless
as if	inasmuch as	until
as long as	now that	when

as much as	once	where
because	provided that	whereas
before	since	wherever
even though	so long as	while
how	so that	whether

A clause that is structurally independent, that can stand by itself, is called an *independent clause*. A clause that is structurally dependent, that cannot stand by itself, is called a *dependent clause*. A subordinating conjunction is used at the beginning of a dependent clause to show the relation between this clause and the independent clause to which it is attached. In the following sentences, the subordinating conjunction is printed in **boldface** and the dependent clause in *italics*.

> The tepee was an improvement over the traditional tent, **since** *it had a smoke hole at the top.*
> **When** *a chief died,* his heir erected a totem pole to honor him.
> **Although** *the Japan Current makes winters in the Pacific Northwest fairly easy,* it brings with it much rain.

(For more information on clauses, see pages 87–88, 166–170, 267–282.)

Exercise

First underline the conjunctions in each of the following sentences. Then decide whether each is a coordinating, a correlative, or a subordinating conjunction.

1. Neither the hippopotamus nor the rhinoceros is as large as is the elephant; however, the blue whale is larger than all three.

2. Since the Asiatic elephant and the African elephant have distinctive features, they are easy to tell apart.

3. Have you noticed that Asiatic elephants have small ears and high foreheads, while African elephants have large ears and low foreheads?

4. The average African male elephant weighs about 12,000 pounds, but the average Asiatic male weighs only 10,000 pounds; furthermore, both male and female African elephants have tusks, whereas only male Asiatic elephants do.

5. Although elephants are huge, they can walk very quietly when they want, because the soles of their feet are covered with thick elastic pads.

8h   Interjections

Oh!   Wow!   Great!   Ouch!   Drat!   Whew!

The preceding words are **interjections,** words that express emotion. Grammatically, an interjection has no connection to the rest of the sentence or fragment in which it appears. In the following sentences, the interjections are in **boldface.**

Ouch! I burned my finger.	The rescuers, **alas,** arrived too late.
Well, there it is.	**What,** no kosher pizza?
Curses! Foiled again!	**Ah,** what a life!

Interjections are used much more in speech than in writing, where they are used mostly in dialogue. An interjection may be followed by an exclamation mark or by a comma. An exclamation mark indicates a strong emotional response. A comma indicates a milder response.

8i   Verbals

A **verbal** is not a "part of speech." Rather it is a grammatical form that is derived from a verb but does not function as a verb in a sentence. A verbal functions as a noun, an adjective, or an adverb. There are three types of verbals: *participles, gerunds,* and *infinitives.*

Participles

The **present participle** and the **past participle** of most verbs can be used as adjectives. (For more information about parti ciples, see page 134.)

> A **dancing** bear is an image associated with Theodore Roethke.
> The peace between the two wars has been compared to a **held** breath.
> Countee Cullen used the image of **bursting** fruit as a symbol of abundance and fecundity.

Gerunds

A **gerund** is a verb form spelled in the same way as the present participle and used as a noun in a sentence.

> The problems of **parenting** were discussed at the symposium.
> The school taught **reading** and **writing** but little else.
> **Exercising** can help relieve stress.

Infinitives

The present infinitive and the present perfect infinitive of a verb can be used as a noun, an adjective, or an adverb. The **present infinitive** is the *to* form of the verb (e.g., *to go*); the **present perfect infinitive** is the *to have* form (e.g., *to have gone*).

> She wanted **to resign** at first but finally decided **to stay.**
> (*nouns*)
> *King Lear* is considered a difficult play **to stage.** (*adjective*)
> What he wanted most was someone **to love.** (*adjective*)
> By the end of the day I was ready **to scream.** (*adverb*)
> They were sorry **to have left** before you arrived. (*adverb*)

Sometimes the word *to* in the infinitive is understood rather than stated.

> Therapists must help their patients cope with life's problems.
> Therapists must help their patients **to** cope with life's problems.

Exercise

Circle the verbals in the following sentences. Decide whether each verbal is a participle, a gerund, or an infinitive.

1. Many people agree with the often repeated adage that seeing is believing.

2. Some agree with the statement that to see is to understand.

3. Seeking to gain insight into the ways of gorillas in the wild, Dian Fossey traveled to Africa at the request of the acclaimed scientist Louis Leakey.

4. Living among the wild gorillas and imitating their behavior, Fossey became a partially accepted member of a band of mountain apes who allowed her to sit and to eat with them.

5. Fossey's most thrilling moment occurred when a 450-pound gorilla touched her hand and then ran off, beating his chest excitedly.

9 Phrases

A **phrase** is a group of words lacking a subject and a predicate that functions as a single part of speech. There are several types of phrases. This section discusses *prepositional phrases* and *verbal phrases*.

9a Prepositional Phrases

A **prepositional phrase** consists of a preposition, the object of the preposition, and all the words modifying this object. In the following sentences, the prepositional phrases are in **boldface** and the prepositions and their objects in *italics*.

> *In* **many** *cultures* whale meat has been an essential source *of* **protein.**
>
> Some *of* **these cultural** *groups* resent efforts *by* **conserva-** *tionists* to protect the whale, since these efforts would restrict the group's ability to obtain food and would conflict *with* **its** *traditions.*
>
> Conservationists, however, argue that the whale is an intelligent creature *about* **which** we know far too little and that if these creatures are not protected, they will disappear *from* **the** *earth.*

Note: The word *to* with the infinitive (e.g., *to obtain*) is not a preposition and does not introduce a prepositional phrase.

Usually a prepositional phrase functions as an adjective or an adverb. Occasionally it may act as a noun.

> The *computer* **for the home** may become as ubiquitous as the typewriter. (*adjective*)

> The phrase "fruit *fresh* **from the farm**" has become quite *popular* **in merchandising circles.** (*adverbs*)

The only reason that she wrote the book was **for the money.**
(*noun*)

9b   Verbal Phrases

A **verbal phrase** consists of a verbal and all its complements and modifiers. (To review verbals, see pages 89–91 and 161–162.) There are three types of verbal phrases: *participial phrases, gerund phrases,* and *infinitive phrases.*

Participial phrases

A **participial phrase** consists of a participle and all its modifiers and complements. It acts as an adjective in a sentence. In the following sentences, the participial phrases are in **boldface** with the participles in ***boldface italics.***

> Throughout his life, Whitman adhered to the beliefs ***summarized* in the preface of the work.**
> A man ***curled* in the fetal position** with his arm ***covering* his head** is the subject of one of Rodin's most moving sculptures.
> Serenity is the chief quality ***embodied* in the pottery of Jade Snow Wong.**

Absolute phrases

A participle modifying its own subject instead of a noun or noun substitute in the sentence creates an **absolute phrase.** An absolute phrase must be set off from its sentence by a comma.

> **Their voices *raised* in song,** the settlers rode out of sight.
> **The wind *having disappeared,*** the boat drifted idly with the current, **sails *banging* limp, the passengers *complaining* but *refusing* to touch the oars.**

Gerund phrases

A **gerund phrase** consists of a gerund and all its modifiers and complements. A gerund phrase acts as a noun in a sentence. In the following sentences, the gerund phrases are in **boldface** with the gerunds in ***boldface italics.***

> For Freud, ***remaining* in Vienna** became impossible once the Nazi forces invaded Austria in 1938.
> Today we use the term loosely to mean any person who enjoys ***inflicting* pain.**
> ***Running* five miles a day** keeps a person in good condition.

Infinitive phrases

An **infinitive phrase** consists of the present infinitive or the present perfect infinitive form of the verb and all its modifiers and complements. It acts as a noun, an adjective, or an adverb. In the following sentences, the infinitive phrases are in **boldface** with the infinitives in ***boldface italics.***

> ***To be* a pilot on the Mississippi** was young Sam Clemens's dream. (*noun*)
> ***To know* him** is ***to love* him.** (*nouns*)
> Hard work is one way ***to gain* success in business.** (*adjective*)
> She is proud ***to have dedicated* her life to music.** (*adverb*)

Exercise

Underline all the prepositional phrases in the following sentences. Bracket each verbal phrase.

1. The Clown College, in Venice, Florida, has trained hundreds of clowns since its founding in 1967 by Ringling Brothers and Barnum & Bailey.

2. Some of the subjects studied during the ten-week course include walking on stilts, juggling china plates, and throwing custard pies.

3. After completing the course, not all graduates decide to become full-time clowns; only one-third get contracts to perform with the Ringling circus.

4. A famous graduate is Lou Jacobs, his face having appeared on a U.S. postage stamp.

5. A woman's becoming a clown was unlikely before the founding of Clown College; now women are welcome to come to Venice to learn the art of clowning professionally.

10 Clauses

A **clause** is a group of words with a subject and a predicate. A clause may be independent or dependent.

10a Independent Clauses

An **independent clause** is a group of words with a subject and a predicate that expresses a complete thought. In other words, an independent clause is structurally independent and can stand by itself as a simple sentence.

The Spanish conquistadors heard the legend of El Dorado, the Man of Gold.
The bottom of the lake was encrusted with gold.
Some soldiers of fortune traveled down the Amazon.

10b Dependent Clauses

A **dependent clause** is a group of words with a subject and a predicate. Dependent clauses cannot stand by themselves as sentences; they must be attached to or be part of an independent clause. They are often called *subordinate* clauses because they are structurally subordinate to the independent clause. Usually, a dependent clause begins with a subordinating word, which may be a subordinating conjunction or a relative pronoun. There are three types of dependent clauses—*adjective, adverb,* and *noun clauses.*

Adjective clauses

An **adjective clause,** or **relative clause,** acts as an adjective and modifies a noun or pronoun. Usually, an adjective clause begins with a relative pronoun: *who, whose, whom, that,* or *which.*

Jazz is a musical *form* **that originated among black Americans.**

Charlie Parker, **who was known as Bird,** played for a while with the Billy Eckstine band.

Jazz critics have extolled *John Coltrane,* **whose penetrating, raspy sound has been imitated by many other players.**

> *Jazz,* **which began as an American art form,** is being interna-
> tionalized by players such as the Argentinean Gato Bar-
> bieri.

In the first sentence above, the subject of the adjective clause
is *that* and the simple predicate is *originated.* In the second
sentence, the subject of the adjective clause is *who* and the
simple predicate is *was known.* In the third sentence, the
subject of the adjective clause is *sound* and the simple predicate is *has been imitated.* In the fourth sentence, the subject of
the adjective clause is *which* and the simple predicate is
began.

An adjective clause also can begin with a relative adverb
—*when, where, why.*

> The *shop* **where I bought the bracelet** is near here.

> The old man told of a *time* **when the stars fell.**

> The *reason* **why he acted** is unclear.

Sometimes an adjective clause modifies the entire idea expressed in the preceding clause.

> On her birthday, John asked Susan to marry him, **which made
> her very happy.**

Adverb clauses

An **adverb clause** acts as an adverb in a sentence. Usually, an
adverb clause modifies the verb in another clause. Sometimes,
though, it modifies an adjective or an adverb. An adverb clause

usually begins with a subordinating conjunction that shows the relation of the adverb clause to the word or words it modifies. (To review subordinating conjunctions, turn to pages 158–159.)

> The grandfather clock *experienced* renewed popularity **after Henry Clay Works published his song "My Grandfather's Clock."** (*modifies the verb* experienced)

> **Since hash is an inexpensive meal,** Americans *call* any cheap restaurant a hash house. (*modifies the verb* call)

> Is the Golden Gate Bridge as *long* **as the Verrazano Bridge is?** (*modifies the adjective* long)

> She speaks *more persuasively* **than I do.** (*modifies the comparative adverb* more persuasively)

Sometimes an adverb clause is elliptical, or incomplete, with the verb omitted but understood.

> Is the Golden Gate Bridge **as long as the Verrazano Bridge** (is)?
> She speaks more persuasively **than I** (speak).

(For information on using commas with adverb clauses, see pages 271–274, 277, 281.)

Noun clauses

A **noun clause** acts as a noun in a sentence. This means that it can function as a subject, an object, or a predicate nominative. Usually, a noun clause begins with one of the following subordinating words: *that, how, what, whatever, whenever, wherever, whichever, who, whoever, whose, why.*

> **That she would run for President** seemed a certainty. (*subject*)

The book explains **why the United States refused to join the League of Nations.** (*direct object*)

His home is **wherever he stops his car for the night.** (*predicate nominative*)

Exercise

Bracket each dependent clause in the following sentences. For each dependent clause, be prepared to tell whether it is an adjective clause, an adverb clause, or a noun clause.

1. If some joker yells "Shark!" at the beach, all the swimmers will run to their cars and light up cigarettes.

2. While sharks kill two persons a year, cigarettes kill 500,000, and traffic accidents kill 250,000, says the Surgeon General.

3. What should be a dying industry, cigarette manufacturing, is actually thriving because the tobacco companies are acquiring companies selling such diverse products as beer, fish, and insurance.

4. About 30 percent of the infants who get whooping cough vaccine respond with fairly severe reactions.

5. About 1 percent of the babies experience a reaction that could be life threatening.

6. Nevertheless, that the disease is worse than the dangers of the vaccine is the conclusion reached by most experts.

11 Kinds of Sentences ▬▬▬

Sentences can be classified into four basic groups according to the number and kinds of clauses they contain. These four basic types are *simple, compound, complex,* and *compound-complex sentences.*

11a Simple Sentences

A **simple sentence** contains only one independent clause and no dependent clause.

> Hokusai and Kunisada are two important Japanese artists.
> Sacajawea, a Shoshone Indian, worked as a guide and an interpreter on the Lewis and Clark expedition.
> According to most authorities, Tutankhamen became pharaoh in 1361 B.C. and died in 1352 B.C.

11b Compound Sentences

A **compound sentence** contains two or more independent clauses and no dependent clause.

> The goddess Eos granted Tithonus his request for immortality, but he forgot to ask for eternal youth.
> During the Crimean War, Florence Nightingale was appalled by the unsanitary conditions in British army hospitals; therefore, she introduced strict standards of cleanliness.
> First dice the celery; then peel and chop the onion; next brown the meat in a frying pan.

11c Complex Sentences

A **complex sentence** contains one independent clause and one or more dependent clauses.

> Nihilists advocated the violent overthrow of all existing governments, while anarchists originally advocated freedom from governmental control through nonviolent evolution.
>
> After the museum bought one of his paintings, Cortez was interviewed on a local cable program.
>
> Because it is noted for its ability to weave intricate webs, the spider is a fitting symbol for the storyteller, or spinner of tales.

11d Compound-Complex Sentences

A **compound-complex sentence** contains two or more independent clauses and one or more dependent clauses.

> Unfortunately, the danger of crime in the cities is a bleak reality; therefore, some couples with small children choose to move to the suburbs, where they feel they can raise their children in safety.
>
> A group of painters called "neorealists" is turning back to representational styles, and the mass public, which never quite embraced abstract art, is responding enthusiastically to their work.
>
> In the last twenty years, medicine has made major advances; doctors, for example, now perform bone-marrow transplants, procedures which, though risky, offer new hope to patients whose diseases were once considered terminal.

Exercise

Identify each of the following sentences as simple, compound, complex, or compound-complex.

1. Originating in the Himalayas and terminating in the Bay of Bengal, the Ganges, the holiest of all Hindu rivers, flows for 1,560 miles and drains eight Indian states.

2. The Yangtze flows from Northeast Tibet to the East China Sea, a distance of 3,600 miles, which makes it the world's fourth longest river; it is also remarkable for the fact that it is navigable for more than a thousand of those miles.

3. The Nile is like a long oasis that cuts Egypt from south to north for a distance of almost 900 miles from the Sudan to Cairo, where it divides into two branches, each 150 miles long, forming the great Delta.

4. The Rhine rises in East Switzerland and flows north into the North Sea; the Rhone rises in Southwest Switzerland, then flows south to the Mediterranean.

5. The Mississippi and the Missouri flow side by side for miles south of St. Louis, their waters scarcely mingling, the red waters of the Missouri in sharp contrast to the clear currents of the Mississippi.

■ Part III ■

Sentence
Form

To write a good sentence, it is not enough to have a good idea. You have to express your idea in a form that your readers will understand. The form of a sentence has to follow certain conventions, traditional guidelines that are generally understood and accepted. The conventions of written English are much like rules of etiquette; they are essential for helping people to communicate clearly and effectively with one another. In fact, you know most of these conventions so well that you follow them without even thinking about them. Some, however, you may need to review.

12 Sentence Fragments

Use sentence fragments judiciously. For formal writing avoid their use except in special situations.

A **sentence fragment** is an incomplete sentence punctuated as if it were a complete sentence. A sentence fragment lacks a subject, a predicate, or both.

12a Fragments Lacking a Subject

Do not punctuate as a sentence a group of words that lacks a subject.

To eliminate a sentence fragment lacking a subject, simply add a subject to this group of words or connect it to another sentence containing its subject.

> *Not:* Went dancing last night.
> *But:* I went dancing last night.

Not: Jean Rhys was born in the West Indies. And evoked the magic of these islands in *Wild Sargasso Sea.*

But: Jean Rhys was born in the West Indies and evoked the magic of these islands in *Wild Sargasso Sea.*

Not: American public opinion became sharply divided. Most Americans had considered World War II a just war. Were willing to give their lives for their country. But many came to think Vietnam was an unjust war. And were repelled by the slaughter of their sons.

But: American public opinion became sharply divided. Most Americans had considered World War II a just war and were willing to give their lives for their country. But many came to think Vietnam was an unjust war and were repelled by the slaughter of their sons.

12b Fragments Lacking a Predicate

Do not punctuate as a sentence a group of words that lacks a predicate.

A predicate must be a finite, or complete, verb. Some verb forms require an auxiliary verb or a modal in order to be finite. (To review auxiliary words and modals, see pages 134–135.)

To eliminate a sentence fragment that lacks a predicate, simply add a finite verb or an auxiliary verb or modal to make the verb finite, or connect the fragment to another sentence that contains its verb.

Not: People of many different nationalities together on the same block.

But: People of many different nationalities live together on the same block.

Not: The sun rising over the rooftops.

But: The sun was rising over the rooftops.

Not: The alumni already given millions of dollars for the new library.

But: The alumni have already given millions of dollars for the new library.

Not: In the early twentieth century, Paris was the undisputed cultural capital of the Western world. At one point, for example, Aaron Copland, one of the foremost composers of our age, Tristan Tzara, a leading Dadaist, and James Joyce, the author of *Ulysses,* all living in Paris at the same time.

But: In the early twentieth century, Paris was the undisputed cultural capital of the Western world. At one point, for example, Aaron Copland, one of the foremost composers of our age, Tristan Tzara, a leading Dadaist, and James Joyce, the author of *Ulysses,* were all living in Paris at the same time.

Not: In the back of the theater were standing-room-only ticket holders. And latecomers impatient for their seats.

But: In the back of the theater were standing-room-only ticket holders and latecomers impatient for their seats.

12c Phrase Fragments

Do not punctuate a phrase as a sentence.

To eliminate a phrase fragment, simply add it to or make it part of an independent clause.

Not: We swerved when we saw the deer. Running across the highway.

But: We swerved when we saw the deer running across the highway.

Not: The professor rode with two officers in their squad car for six weeks. To learn about police work firsthand.

But: To learn about police work firsthand, the professor rode with two officers in their squad car for six weeks.

Not: The highlight of the show was appearances by several guest stars. Cynthia Gregory, for example, one of the country's finest ballerinas.

But: The highlight of the show was appearances by several guest stars—Cynthia Gregory, for example, one of the country's finest ballerinas.

Not: Because of public opposition. The city refused to grant permission. For a skyscraper to be built on the site of the church.

But: Because of public opposition, the city refused to grant permission for a skyscraper to be built on the site of the church.

Not: Computer manufacturers use various gimmicks to attract users. In order to appeal to children. This writing program features a turtle. Instead of the ordinary cursor.

But: Computer manufacturers use various gimmicks to attract users. In order to appeal to children, this writing program features a turtle instead of the ordinary cursor.

12d Dependent Clause Fragments

Do not punctuate a dependent clause as a sentence.

Usually, a dependent clause begins with a subordinating word, which may be a subordinating conjunction or a relative pronoun. (To review dependent clauses, see pages 167–170.)

One way to eliminate a dependent clause fragment is to remove the subordinating word. Another way is to connect the dependent clause to an independent clause.

Not: Because Charlene was fluent in French.

But: Charlene was fluent in French.

Not: Before Harrison wrote his term paper. He prepared an outline.

But: Before Harrison wrote his term paper, he prepared an outline.

Not: Harold Macmillan felt it imperative for Britain to develop a firm relationship with de Gaulle. Even though the United States opposed official recognition of him.

But: Harold Macmillan felt it imperative for Britain to develop a firm relationship with de Gaulle, even though the United States opposed official recognition of him.

Not: Although John Muir is often pictured as a genial and perhaps somewhat innocent nature guide. He was actually a shrewd, strong-willed, thoughtful man. Who was an effective political lobbyist for conservation.

But: Although John Muir is often pictured as a genial and perhaps somewhat innocent nature guide, he was actually a shrewd, strong-willed, thoughtful man who was an effective political lobbyist for conservation.

Not: Since he was avidly interested in Holmesiana. He decided to apply for membership in the Baker Street Irregulars. Where he would be able to enjoy the company of other Sherlock Holmes enthusiasts.

But: Since he was avidly interested in Holmesiana, he decided to apply for membership in the Baker Street Irregulars, where he would be able to enjoy the company of other Sherlock Holmes enthusiasts.

Exercise

Revise the following items to eliminate any sentence fragments. Two of the items contain no fragments.

1. Walter having had his car repaired.

2. Americans love fast food. Pizza, for example, and french fries. Also hamburgers and cola drinks.

3. Wrote novels, poems, and short stories which focus on themes of alienation and guilt.

4. James is the best person for the job. And the one with the best chance of being chosen.

5. The bus was turning the corner. And the car was following too closely.

6. The hotel built on top of the cliff, offering from its balconies an unparalleled view of the harbor.

7. As the settlers pushed their way west of the Appalachians, tribes living in the Great Lakes region became alarmed.

8. When we think of the enchantment of music, we often think of Orpheus. Whose music charmed even the ruler of Hades.

9. The Constitution is often described as a living document. Since it is capable of growing and changing with the times.

10. Many Westerners see only harmony and tranquility when they view Japanese art. Although there is sometimes underlying violence.

12e Intentional Fragments

We use fragments all the time, especially in speech. We see them in advertising and in newspapers and magazines. In formal writing, they can be used appropriately to ask and answer questions and to emphasize a point, to record exclamations in dialogue, and to provide transition between ideas. Note the use of fragments in the following passages by professional writers. (The fragments are printed in *italics*.)

There has been a flood of new studies of the Wild Child: historical, literary, psychological. The story is still evocative, "good to
think with." But there is something new. There is a new focus for
a forbidden experiment. *A new mind that is not yet a mind. A
new object, betwixt and between, equally shrouded in supersti-
tion as well as science.* This is the computer.

Sherry Turkle

Hating to ask questions and never trusting the answers has defined the type of reporting I do. What I do is hang around.
Become part of the furniture. An end table in someone's life. It is
the art of the scavenger: set a scene, establish a mood, get the
speech patterns right. What matters is that the subject bites his
nails, what matters is that he wears brown shoes with a blue suit,
what matters is the egg stain on his tie, the Reader's Digest
Condensed Books on the shelves, the copy of *Playboy* with the
centerfold torn out.

John Gregory Dunne

As you can see from these passages, fragments can be used
effectively in formal writing. However, unless you have a
well-thought-out reason for using fragments, avoid them in
formal writing.

13 Run-on Sentences

Separate sentences correctly from one another.

A **run-on sentence** occurs when two or more complete sentences are written as though they were one sentence. Two
types of errors result in a run-on sentence: *comma splices* and
fused sentences.

13a Comma Splices

Do not separate two independent clauses with only a comma, unless the clauses are very short and closely related.

A comma is sometimes used between clauses of two or three words, especially if the clauses are in parallel grammatical form.

> One sings, the other dances.
> The grass withers, the flowers fade.

In general, however, using only a comma between two independent clauses is considered a serious grammatical error, called a **comma splice.**

Not: Researchers are attempting to program robots to see, this procedure is much more complicated than you might expect.

But: Researchers are attempting to program robots to see. This procedure is much more complicated than you might expect.

Or: Researchers are attempting to program robots to see, but this procedure is much more complicated than you might expect.

Not: Some monasteries during the Middle Ages had fine libraries, in these libraries monks copied and illuminated manuscripts.

But: Some monasteries during the Middle Ages had fine libraries; in these libraries monks copied and illuminated manuscripts.

Or: Some monasteries during the Middle Ages had fine libraries, in which monks copied and illuminated manuscripts.

A comma splice also occurs when a comma (instead of a semicolon) is used between two independent clauses joined by a transitional phrase or adverb (in **boldface**).

Not: The exhibit at the museum was well reviewed and well promoted, **consequently,** there were long lines for tickets.

But: The exhibit at the museum was well reviewed and well promoted; **consequently,** there were long lines for tickets.

Not: When the smoke alarm sounded in the middle of the night, Melissa jumped out of bed and rushed to get her family out of the house, **in the meantime,** her neighbor called the fire department.

But: When the smoke alarm sounded in the middle of the night, Melissa jumped out of bed and rushed to get her family out of the house; **in the meantime,** her neighbor called the fire department.

13b   Fused Sentences

Do not write two independent clauses without any punctuation between them.

This error is called a **fused sentence.**

Not: The school was closed because of the snowstorm not knowing this, some students showed up for classes.

But: The school was closed because of the snowstorm. Not knowing this, some students showed up for classes.

Or: Not knowing that the school was closed because of the snowstorm, some students showed up for classes.

Not: First boil the squash until it is tender then cut it open and scoop out its insides.

But: First boil the squash until it is tender; then cut it open and scoop out its insides.

Or: First boil the squash until it is tender, and then cut it open and scoop out its insides.

Although there are many ways of correcting run-on sentences, these are the four most common:

1. Make two sentences by adding a period at the end of the first clause and capitalizing the first word of the second clause.

   Not: Doctors are again using leeches these creatures can prevent the problem of clotting that occurs after reattachment surgery.

   But: Doctors are again using leeches● These creatures can prevent the problem of clotting that occurs after reattachment surgery.

2. Add a coordinating conjunction between the two clauses. Place a comma before the coordinating conjunction, unless the two clauses are very short.

   Not: Maria washed the car, Carol mowed the lawn.
   But: Maria washed the car, **and** Carol mowed the lawn.

3. Rewrite one of the independent clauses as a dependent clause.

   Not: The cat wanted her breakfast, she mewed loudly at the foot of the bed.

   But: **When** the cat wanted her breakfast, she mewed loudly at the foot of the bed.

4. If the two clauses are closely related, place a semicolon between them.

   Not: Cindy found the movie disappointing, Jayne thought it was wonderful.

   But: Cindy found the movie disappointing**;** Jayne thought it was wonderful.

Exercise 1

Eliminate the run-on sentence in each of the following items. Identify the error as a comma splice or fused sentence.

1. Years ago, all movie animation was done by hand, today, much of it is done by computer.

2. Some people consider Satchel Paige the greatest baseball player who ever lived others point to Lou Gehrig.

3. When ancient Aztec astronomers constructed their calendar, they calculated their year as having 365 days, however, each year had a few hours left over.

4. Daredevils will ride Niagara Falls in a barrel although the drop is 176 feet, some will survive while some will perish.

5. Noah Webster changed the spelling of many words he thought they should be spelled as they are pronounced.

Exercise 2

Eliminate the fragments and run-on sentences in each of the following items.

1. Have you heard the story of Casey Jones? A brave engineer who died in a terrible railroad accident in 1900.

2. Casey Jones's real name was John Luther Jones, his story has been recounted in folk songs.

3. The original version of the folk song was composed by Wallace Saunders. A man who worked in the railroad roundhouse near the site of Casey's terrible accident.

4. Saunders put together a blues ballad that spoke not only of the tragedy of Casey Jones. But also of the pain and suffering of the many people who were injured or killed during the early, dangerous days of railroading.

5. Saunders sang about that fateful night of April 29, 1900. When Casey Jones, an engineer for the Illinois Central Railroad, drove the *Cannonball* into immortality.

6. Since the *Cannonball* was already 96 minutes late when Casey pulled out of the station at Memphis. He knew he would have to make up time to get to Canton, Mississippi, on time at first it looked as though luck was on Casey's side.

7. While his friend Sim Webb fed the fire, Casey raced the clock, pushing the *Cannonball* to do more than seventy on the straight stretches of track, Casey was unaware that disaster awaited four freight cars were stuck on the track ahead.

8. By the time Casey saw the freight cars ahead of him, it was too late to stop, however, it was not too late to save his friend Casey forced Sim to jump from the train.

9. Casey stayed with the *Cannonball*. Pulling on the brakes and jamming the engine into reverse. He cut the *Cannonball*'s speed in half.

10. Only Casey died in the terrible crash he was found with one hand on the brake and the other hand on the throttle.

14 Verb Forms

14a Present Infinitive, Past Tense, Past Participle, and Present Participle

Use the appropriate form of the verb.

English verbs have four principal parts, or forms: present in-finitive, past tense form, past participle, and present participle. The **infinitive** is the base form of the verb, the form that appears in the dictionary. Regular verbs add *-ed* or *-d* to their present infinitive to form the **past tense** and **past participle.**

| paint | painted | cook | cooked |
| dance | danced | slice | sliced |

Irregular verbs form their past tense and past participle in a variety of other ways.

Present infinitive	*Past tense*	*Past participle*
begin	began	begun
catch	caught	caught
draw	drew	drawn
put	put	put

You can use a dictionary to find the principal parts of a verb. In most dictionaries, after the abbreviation *v.* or at the end of the definitions for the verb, the entry gives the principal parts and the third-person singular present-tense form of the verb. When the past tense and past participle are the same, the entry lists only three forms of the verb. When the past tense and past participle are different, the entry lists four forms.

The fourth form is called the **present participle,** always formed by adding *-ing* to the infinitive (see p. 134.)

dance (dăns) *v.:* **danced, dancing, dances**
be·gin (bĭ-gĭn′) *v.:* **began, begun, beginning, begins**
draw (drô) *v.:* **drew, drawn, drawing, draws**

Most people have few problems using the proper forms of regular verbs. Many, however, do have problems with the past tense and past participle of irregular verbs. Here is a list of common irregular verbs.

Irregular Verbs

Present infinitive	*Past tense*	*Past participle*
arise	arose	arisen
awake	awoke	awaked
be	was, were	been
bear	bore	borne
		born
become	became	become
begin	began	begun
bind	bound	bound
bite	bit	bitten
blow	blew	blown
break	broke	broken
bring	brought	brought
build	built	built
burst	burst	burst
cast	cast	cast
catch	caught	caught
choose	chose	chosen
cling	clung	clung
come	came	come
creep	crept	crept
deal	dealt	dealt
dig	dug	dug
dive	dived, dove	dived
do	did	done
draw	drew	drawn
drink	drank	drunk
drive	drove	driven

Present infinitive	*Past tense*	*Past participle*
eat	ate	eaten
fall	fell	fallen
feel	felt	felt
flee	fled	fled
fling	flung	flung
fly	flew	flown
forbid	forbade, forbad	forbidden
forget	forgot	forgotten, forgot
forgive	forgave	forgiven
freeze	froze	frozen
get	got	got, gotten
give	gave	given
go	went	gone
grow	grew	grown
hang (objects)	hung	hung
hang (people)	hanged	hanged
have	had	had
hit	hit	hit
know	knew	known
lay	laid	laid
lead	led	led
lend	lent	lent
lie	lay	lain
lose	lost	lost
mean	meant	meant
pay	paid	paid
prove	proved	proved, proven
put	put	put
ride	rode	ridden
ring	rang	rung
rise	rose	risen
run	ran	run
say	said	said
see	saw	seen
seek	sought	sought
send	sent	sent
set	set	set
shake	shook	shaken

Present infinitive	*Past tense*	*Past participle*
shine (give light)	shone	shone
shine (polish)	shined	shined
shrink	shrank	shrunk
sing	sang	sung
sink	sank, sunk	sunk, sunken
sit	sat	sat
slay	slew	slain
speak	spoke	spoken
spin	spun	spun
spit	spit, spat	spit, spat
spread	spread	spread
spring	sprang, sprung	sprung
steal	stole	stolen
sting	stung	stung
stink	stank	stunk
swear	swore	sworn
swim	swam	swum
swing	swung	swung
take	took	taken
teach	taught	taught
tear	tore	torn
think	thought	thought
thrive	throve, thrived	thriven, thrived
throw	threw	thrown
wear	wore	worn
weep	wept	wept
win	won	won

Over the years some irregular forms have been eliminated from the language, while others are in the process of changing. As you can see from the preceding list, the preferred past tense form of *dive* is now *dived,* not *dove.* The preferred past participle form of *prove* is *proved,* not *proven.*

The following rules will help you select the appropriate verb form.

Use the past tense form to indicate simple past time.

Not: We **seen** him in the library yesterday.
But: We **saw** him in the library yesterday.

Not: Rhonda **swum** fifteen laps.
But: Rhonda **swam** fifteen laps.

Not: His clothing **stunk** from the skunk's spray.
But: His clothing **stank** from the skunk's spray.

Use the past-participle form with auxiliary verbs *have* and *be*.

Not: **Have** you **chose** a major?
But: **Have** you **chosen** a major?

Not: If you don't lock up your bike, it **will be took.**
But: If you don't lock up your bike, it **will be taken.**

Not: Lenny **has wrote** home to his parents, asking for money.
But: Lenny **has written** home to his parents, asking for money.

Use the past-participle form with a contraction containing an auxiliary verb.

Not: **He's drove** all the way from Miami.
But: **He's driven** all the way from Miami.

Not: **She'd** never **flew** in an airplane before.
But: **She'd** never **flown** in an airplane before.

Not: **They've sang** in the choir for many years.
But: **They've sung** in the choir for many years.

14b Troublesome Verbs

Master troublesome pairs of words.

The following pairs of words often give people trouble: *lie* and *lay; sit* and *set; rise* and *raise.*

Lie and *lay*

The verb *lie* means "recline." The verb *lay* means "put" or "place." Do not confuse the principal parts of these verbs.

Present infinitive	Past tense	Past participle	Present participle
lie	lay	lain	lying
lay	laid	laid	laying

The problem most people have with these verbs is using a form of *lay* when they mean *lie*. *Lie* is intransitive; it does not take an object. *Lay* is transitive; it does take an object.

Lie on the floor. (*no object*)

Lay the *book* on the table. (*object*)

Not: Why is Millie **laying** on the couch in the nurse's office?
But: Why is Millie **lying** on the couch in the nurse's office?

Not: Peter **laid** in the sun too long yesterday.
But: Peter **lay** in the sun too long yesterday.

Not: She had just **laid** down when the telephone rang.
But: She had just **lain** down when the telephone rang.

Sit and *set*

The verb *sit* means "be seated." The verb *set* usually means "place" or "put in a certain position." Do not confuse the principal parts of these verbs.

Present infinitive	Past tense	Past participle	Present participle
sit	sat	sat	sitting
set	set	set	setting

The problem most people have with these verbs is using a form of *set* when they mean *sit*. *Sit* is intransitive; it does not take an object. *Set* is usually transitive; it does take an object.

Sit in the chair by the fireplace. (*no object*)

Please **set** the *table* for me. (*object*)

Note: Set is sometimes intransitive: *The sun sets.*

Not: Some people **set** in front of the television far too much.
But: Some people **sit** in front of the television far too much.

Not: He **set** up until two in the morning, waiting for his daughter to come home from her date.
But: He **sat** up until two in the morning, waiting for his daughter to come home from her date.

Not: After **setting** in the sun for five hours, Don was burned bright red.
But: After **sitting** in the sun for five hours, Don was burned bright red.

Rise and *raise*

The verb *rise* means "go up" or "get into a standing position." The verb *raise* means "lift." Do not confuse the principal parts of these verbs.

Present infinitive	Past tense	Past participle	Present participle
rise	rose	risen	rising
raise	raised	raised	raising

Rise is intransitive; it does not take an object. *Raise* is transitive; it does take an object.

Without yeast, the bread will not **rise.** (*no object*)

After they won the game, they **raised** the school *banner*. (*object*)

Not: They **rose** the curtain before the cast was fully assembled on stage.

But: They **raised** the curtain before the cast was fully assembled on stage.

Not: Every morning they **rise** the blinds before leaving for work.

But: Every morning they **raise** the blinds before leaving for work.

Not: He **rose** his voice in order to be heard.

But: He **raised** his voice in order to be heard.

Exercise

Identify the inappropriate verb form in each of the following sentences. Replace it with the appropriate form.

1. During spring holidays we will go to the lake and lay out in the sun.

2. I am sorry I breaked your china cup.

3. In the Old West posses often hung horse thieves.

4. The campers were awoke by the sound of the crash.

5. The light in the sky could of been a UFO.

6. I seen UFOs many times.

7. We eaten dinner often together.

8. He shone his shoes almost every time he weared them.

9. Few Americans have rode on a camel.

10. We have ran two miles daily since we begun the exercise program.

11. The house sets on a hill with a view of the river.

12. Yesterday I ask my friend what he knowed about the plans.

13. The bus past the bus stop and never slowed down.

14. When I live near Savannah, we use to go to the beach often.

15. I wished I had wrote the letter earlier.

16. The assignment was suppose to be posted yesterday.

17. Before the game started, the color guard rose the flag.

18. I known him since we been in high school together.

19. Someone's stole my class notes.

20. We were all shook up by what we saw.

15 Subject-Verb Agreement

Make a verb agree with its subject in number.

For most verbs the only form change to indicate number occurs in the present tense and with a third-person singular subject. The change is the addition of -*s* or -*es* to the basic present-tense form.

The cushion **feels** soft.	The tomato **tastes** ripe.
The goose **flies** south.	He **brushes** his hair.

No change occurs with other singular subjects nor with all plural ones.

	Singular	*Plural*
First person:	I **feel**	We **brush**
Second person:	You **fly**	—
Third person:	It **tastes**	They **taste**

Except for the verb *do*, modal auxiliaries (*may, can, will,* and so on) do not add *s* or *es* in third-person singular present tense. The auxiliary *have* changes form to *has*.

The verb *be* changes to indicate number in both the present tense and the past tense and in both the first person and the third person.

Present tense		*Past tense*	
I am	we are	I was	we were
you are	you are	you were	you were
he/she/it is	they are	he/she/it was	they were

Some kinds of subjects present special problems with subject-verb agreement. The following rules will help you choose the appropriate verb form.

15a Compound Subjects

Compound subject with *and*

In general, use a plural verb form with a compound subject joined by the word *and*.

A **compound subject** consists of two or more nouns that take the same predicate.

> *Crystal and Sal* **make** films for a living.
> *History and biology* **were** his best subjects.
> *Ted and his friends* **are supporting** Greene for mayor.

Use a singular verb form with a compound subject joined by *and* if the compound is considered a single unit.

> *Pork and beans* **is** a popular dish.
> The *bow and arrow* **is** still regarded as a useful weapon.

Use a singular verb form with a compound subject joined by *and* if the parts of the compound refer to the same person or thing.

> My *friend and guest* **is** the artist Laura Anderson.
> His *pride and joy* **was** his 1962 convertible.

Compound subject with *or* or *nor*

With a compound subject joined by *or* or *nor* or by *either . . . or* or *neither . . . nor,* make the verb agree with the subject closer to it.

> The *cat or her kittens* **have pushed** the vase off the table.

> *Either the employees or their supervisor* **is** responsible.

> *Neither the camera nor the lenses* **were broken.**

15b Intervening Phrases or Clauses

Make the verb agree with its subject, not with a word in an intervening phrase or clause.

Intervening Phrases

> Several *people* in my club **subscribe** to that magazine.
> The *books* by that writer **are** very popular.
> The *picture* hanging between the windows at the top of the stairs **is** a portrait of the artist's mother.

Phrases introduced by *together with, as well as, in addition to, accompanied by,* and similar expressions do not affect the number of the verb.

> The emerald *bracelet,* as well as her other jewels, **is** in the safe.
> The *novel,* together with the plays that she wrote when she was much younger, **establishes** her reputation.
> His *wit,* accompanied by his excellent grasp of the facts, **makes** him a sharp interviewer.

Intervening Clauses

> The *books* that are in my briefcase **are** about Russian history.
> The *people* who came to the concert that was canceled **are receiving** rain checks.
> The *doctor* who is attending these patients **is** Ellen Okida.

15c Collective Nouns

A collective noun may take either a singular or a plural verb form.

Usually a collective noun refers to a group of people or things as a single unit. When this is the case, the collective noun is singular and the verb form should be singular.

> The *army* **needs** the support of the civilian population.
> The *flock* **is heading** toward the west end of the lake.
> The *group* **is selling** tickets to raise money for charity.

Sometimes a collective noun refers to a group of things or people as individuals. When this is the case, the collective noun is plural and the verb form should be plural.

> The *jury* **are arguing** among themselves; six feel the defendant is guilty, two feel he is innocent, and four are undecided.
> The *congregation* **disagree** about whether to keep the church open during the week.

Some people feel that using a plural verb form with a collective noun sounds awkward. You can avoid this problem by inserting "the members of" or a similar expression before the collective noun.

> The *members* of the jury **are arguing** among themselves; six feel the defendant is guilty, two feel he is innocent, and four are undecided.
> The *members* of the congregation **disagree** about whether to keep the church open during the week.

15d Nouns Plural in Form but Singular in Meaning

Use a singular verb form with nouns plural in form but singular in meaning.

The following are some common words that are plural in form but singular in meaning.

checkers	molasses
civics	mumps
economics	news
mathematics	physics
measles	statistics

> *Checkers* **is called** draughts in Great Britain.
> *Measles* **is** a contagious childhood disease.
> The *news* **is broadcast** around the clock on some radio stations.

The words *pants, trousers,* and *scissors* are considered plural and take a plural verb form. However, if they are preceded by the words *pair of,* the verb form is singular, since *pair* is the subject.

> The *scissors* **need** to be sharpened.
> The *pair* of scissors **needs** to be sharpened.

The *pants* **match** the jacket.
The *pair* of pants **matches** the jacket.

15e Indefinite and Relative Pronoun Subjects

Indefinite pronoun subjects

The following indefinite pronouns are considered singular. Use a singular verb form with them.

anybody	either	neither	one
anyone	everybody	nobody	somebody
each	everyone	no one	someone

Neither **is** the best pizza parlor in town.
Everybody **is going to vote** on Tuesday.

Do not be confused by prepositional phrases that follow the indefinite pronoun. The verb must agree with its subject, not with the object of a preposition.

Each of the apartments in the north wing of the building **has** a fireplace.
Either of those methods **is** feasible.

The following indefinite pronouns are considered plural. Use a plural verb form with them.

both	few	many	several

Few **are** certain enough of their beliefs to take a stand.
Several **are** riding their bicycles to school.
Both of the paintings **were** sold at the auction.

The following indefinite pronouns·may be singular or plural. If the noun to which the pronoun refers is singular, use a singular verb form. If the noun is plural, use a plural verb form.

all   any   enough   more   most   some

All of the *money* **was** recovered. (*singular*)

All **was** recovered. (*singular*)

All of these *records* **are** scratched. (*plural*)

All **are** scratched. (*plural*)

Most of the *cake* **was** eaten. (*singular*)

Most **was** eaten. (*singular*)

Most of the *guests* **were** hungry. (*plural*)

Most **were** hungry. (*plural*)

The indefinite pronoun *none* can be used with either a singular or a plural verb form when it refers to a plural noun. For example, both of the following sentences are acceptable.

None of the books **was** missing.
None of the books **were** missing.

Relative pronoun subjects

A verb whose subject is a relative pronoun should agree with the antecedent of the pronoun.

The man *who* **narrates** the film has a raspy voice. (*singular antecedent*)

The radios *that* **were made** in Japan are selling well. (*plural antecedent*)

The newspaper, *which* **was founded** in 1893, is closing. (*singular antecedent*)

The phrase *one of* is worth mentioning. Usually, the relative pronoun that follows this phrase is plural because its antecedent is a plural noun or pronoun. Therefore, the relative pronoun takes a plural verb form.

That man is one of the hostages *who* **are** in most danger.

Ralph is one of those *who* never **gain** weight.

However, when the words *the only* come before this phrase, the relative pronoun is singular because its antecedent is *one*. Therefore, it takes a singular verb form.

This is the only one of Mark's songs *that* **has been published.**

Mitch is the only one of those men *who* **is** athletic.

15f Titles

Use a singular verb form with a title, even if the title contains plural words.

Guys and Dolls **was** a popular Broadway musical.
Sixty Minutes **is** on television tonight.
Wuthering Heights **tells** the story of a doomed love.

15g Units of Measurement, Time, and Money

Use a singular verb form with a plural noun phrase that names a unit of measurement, a period of time, or an amount of money.

> *Five miles* **is** too far to walk to school.
> *One hundred years* **is** the usual life span for the crocodile.
> *Twenty-five thousand dollars* **is** a good salary for this job.

15h Inverted Sentence Order

Use a verb that agrees with its subject, even when the subject follows the verb.

> Outside the building **were** *crowds of spectators.*
> From the chimneys **rises** thick black *smoke.*
> On the wall **are** *portraits* of her ancestors.

Do not be confused by sentences beginning with the expletives *there* and *here*. These words are never the subject.

> There **is** a *chicken* roasting in the oven.
> Here **are** the *groceries* you asked me to pick up.

15i Agreement with Subject Not Predicate Nominative

Use a verb that agrees with the subject, not with the predicate nominative.

> A firm *moral sense* and a *belief* in the goodness of human beings **were** his inheritance.

His *inheritance* **was** a firm moral sense and a belief in the goodness of human beings.

Exercise

Revise any of the following sentences in which a verb does not agree with its subject. Some of the sentences are correct as written.

1. Neither of us know the time of the movie.

2. A hamburger, fries, and a milkshake is not my idea of a good dinner.

3. A pair of scissors are in the drawer.

4. Either the coach or the team is responsible for the error.

5. The charge for the tour guide and the taxi are included in the fee.

6. The person who borrowed my notes certainly know how much I need them.

7. Does the government or the airlines control ticket prices?

8. Skillful use of light and shadow characterize the painter's work.

9. A jacket along with gloves and a hat seem sensible for the trip.

10. Her husband's mother along with a cousin is coming for dinner.

11. The colonel is the only one of the officers who have served overseas.

12. There is a large sapphire and two diamonds in the ring.

13. The choir stand behind each other, shortest members in front.

14. Each of the roses and daisies in the bouquets were wired to stand straight.

15. My friend is one of those sculptors who welds metal.

16. The salesperson will invite to the seminar each of the prospects who respond to the questionnaire.

17. Eighty-five dollars are more than I want to pay for shoes.

18. How many of you present today has heard of the problem?

19. *The Grapes of Wrath* are considered one of John Steinbeck's finest novels.

20. The pyramids with the desert behind are an impressive sight.

16 Pronouns: Agreement, Reference, and Usage

By themselves, most pronouns have little meaning. For a pronoun's meaning to be clear, it usually must have a clear antecedent, and it must agree with its antecedent in number and gender.

> After the *pilot* checked **her** instruments, **she** prepared for takeoff.

> After the *pilots* checked **their** instruments, **they** prepared for takeoff.

16a Pronoun-Antecedent Agreement

Indefinite pronouns as antecedents

Use a pronoun that agrees in gender and number with an indefinite pronoun antecedent.

Use a masculine pronoun with an indefinite pronoun that refers to a masculine noun. Use a feminine pronoun with an indefinite pronoun that refers to a feminine noun. Use a neuter, or indeterminate, pronoun with an indefinite pronoun that refers to a neuter noun.

> There are twenty men in the training program. *Each* is a unique individual with **his** own goals and ideals.

Many times, however, a singular indefinite pronoun refers to a group consisting of both males and females, as in the following sentence:

> Everyone should cast _____ vote in the next election.

What should the pronoun in the blank be? Traditionally, a masculine pronoun (*his*) was used in such constructions to refer to an antecedent that included both men and women. Today, most people consider this usage sexist and prefer to use *his or her.* However, a paragraph or a paper can become tedious and hard to read if it is filled with too many pairs of *his or her, he or she, him or her,* and so on. Here are three suggestions for rewriting sentences like this to avoid the problem of pronoun choice.

1. Make the pronouns plural.

> **All** should cast **their** votes in the next election.

2. Use an article (*a, an,* or *the*) in place of the possessive pronoun.

> Everyone should cast **a** vote in the next election.

3. Rewrite the sentence more extensively.

> Everyone should vote in the next election.

Although *everyone* and *everybody* are considered grammatically singular, they obviously refer to more than one person. Therefore, logic can lead to and legitimatize the use of a plural pronoun with these antecedents, particularly when the pronoun is not in the same clause as the antecedent.

> Although *everyone* made enthusiastic noises about the project, **they** fell silent when asked to contribute money.

The "correct" singular pronoun would, in fact, sound most illogical!

> Although *everyone* made enthusiastic noises about the project, **he or she** fell silent. . . .

In such a case, *everyone* or *everybody* would be treated as a collective word. However, these two pronouns are different from other collectives in that usage still requires that they be considered singular in relation to their verbs. So with a present-tense verb and a pronoun in the same clause, logic of agreement still requires a singular pronoun or a recasting of the sentence in one of the ways suggested earlier.

Relative pronouns

Use the appropriate relative pronoun.

The pronouns *who, whom,* and *whose* refer to people. They also refer to animals thought of in human terms and called by name. The pronoun *that* usually refers to animals and things, but it is sometimes used to refer to people. The pronoun *which* refers to animals and things.

The *ballplayer* **who** broke Babe Ruth's career home run record is Hank Aaron.

The *movie* **that** Gene saw last night was *Terms of Endearment.*

Orwell's *1984,* **which** was published in 1949, is still in print.

Someone **whom** voters can trust will win the election.

Do not use *what* as a relative pronoun.

Not: The stereo **what** I want costs three hundred dollars.
But: The stereo **that** I want costs three hundred dollars.

To avoid an awkward sentence, use the possessive pronoun *whose* to mean "of which."

Not: The car the windshield wipers **of which** are not working failed to pass inspection.
But: The car **whose** windshield wipers are not working failed to pass inspection.

A relative pronoun takes its number from its antecedent. The number of the relative pronoun determines the number of any other pronouns used with it.

Students **who** show **their** identification cards will get a discount.

A *man* **who** cannot make up **his** mind is of no use to this company.

Compound antecedent

Use a plural pronoun to refer to a compound antecedent joined by *and.*

Grant and Howard have finished **their** assignments.

The judge and the district attorney have completed **their** terms of office.

When the antecedent is a compound joined by *or* or *nor* or by *either . . . or, neither . . . nor,* or *not only . . . but also,* make the pronoun agree with the part of the compound that is closer to it.

Neither the district attorney nor the defense *lawyers* stated **their** cases clearly.

Not only the jurors but also the *judge* found **his** attention wandering.

Collective nouns as antecedents

Use a singular pronoun with a collective noun antecedent if the members of the group are thought of as one unit. Use a plural pronoun if the members are thought of as individuals.

After winning the race, the *crew* placed **its** trophy on the mantelpiece.

The leader asked the *group* to lower **their** voices.

16b   Pronoun Reference

Vague reference

Provide a clear antecedent for each pronoun that needs one.

In general, do not use a pronoun to refer to the entire idea in a previous sentence or clause or to an antecedent that has not been clearly stated.

> *Vague:*   Harry usually taps his feet, rolls his eyes, and fidgets when he is nervous, **which** annoys his girlfriend.

The pronoun *which* refers vaguely to the entire idea of Harry's behavior when he is nervous.

> *Clear:*   Harry's habit of tapping his feet, rolling his eyes, and fidgeting when he is nervous annoys his girlfriend.

> *Vague:*   Lou is an excellent mechanic, and she uses **this** to earn money for college.

The pronoun *this* refers vaguely to the idea of Lou's skill as a mechanic.

> *Clear:*   Lou is an excellent mechanic, and she uses her skill to earn money for college.

> *Vague:*   The tourists stared in awe as the great Christmas tree in Rockefeller Center was lit. They listened in rapt attention to the speeches and sang along with the carolers. **It** was something they would tell their friends about back home.

> *Clear:*   The tourists stared in awe as the great Christmas tree in Rockefeller Center was lit. They listened in rapt attention to the speeches and sang along with the carolers. The spectacle was something they would tell their friends about back home.

> *Vague:* Now that her children·were away at school, she felt free to pursue her own interests for the first time in years. Perhaps she would get a job. Perhaps she would go back to school. Suddenly she felt alive again. Until this moment, she hadn't realized how badly she had needed **this.**
>
> *Clear:* Now that her children were away at school, she felt free to pursue her own interests for the first time in years. Perhaps she would get a job. Perhaps she would go back to school. Suddenly she felt alive again. Until this moment, she hadn't realized how badly she had needed a change in her life.

> *Vague:* In the novel Christophine tries to discourage Antoinette from going to England. She says England is a cold place with bad weather and bad people, and she cautions Antoinette not to do **it.**
>
> *Clear:* In the novel Christophine tries to discourage Antoinette from going to England. She says England is a cold place with bad weather and bad people, and she cautions Antoinette not to go there.

Ambiguous reference

Do not use a pronoun that could refer to either of two or more antecedents.

> *Ambiguous:* Malcolm told Henry that **he** had won a trip to France.

The pronoun *he* could refer to either Malcolm or Henry. If it refers to Malcolm, rewrite the sentence to make this reference clear.

> *Clear:* Malcolm told Henry, "I have won a trip to France."
>
> *Or:* Malcolm, who had won a trip to France, told Henry the news.

If the pronoun refers to Henry, rewrite the sentence a different way.

Clear: Malcolm told Henry, "You have won a trip to France."

Or: Malcolm knew that Henry had won a trip to France and told him so.

Ambiguous: Darlene met Dr. McCluskey when **she** visited the lab last week.

The pronoun *she* could refer to either Darlene or Dr. McCluskey.

Clear: When Darlene visited the lab last week, she met Dr. McCluskey.

Clear: When Dr. McCluskey visited the lab last week, Darlene met her.

Ambiguous: In the saga Luke Skywalker and Han Solo are at first rivals. Both want to win the affection of the princess. As the saga progresses, however, the two young men gain respect for each other, until finally the rivalry ends when **he** discovers he is Leia's brother.

The pronoun *he* could refer to either Luke or Han.

Clear: In the saga Luke Skywalker and Han Solo are at first rivals. Both want to win the affection of the princess. As the saga progresses, however, the two young men gain respect for each other, until finally the rivalry ends when **Luke** discovers he is Leia's brother.

Ambiguous: Fourteenth-century Europe was scarred by war and plague. It is hard to tell which was worse. The figures given by the chroniclers differ, but according to some accounts, **it** reduced the population by a third.

Clear: Fourteenth-century Europe was scarred by war and plague. It is hard to tell which was worse. The figures given by the chroniclers differ, but according to some accounts, **plague alone** reduced the population by a third.

16c Pronoun Usage

Do not use a personal pronoun immediately following its antecedent.

Pronouns are often used this way in conversation to emphasize the antecedent, but this construction is inappropriate in writing.

Not: The dictator **he** would not give up any of his power.
But: The dictator would not give up any of his power.

Not: Cuckoos **they** lay their eggs in other birds' nests.
But: Cuckoos lay their eggs in other birds' nests.

Use a pronoun ending in *-self* or *-selves* only when an antecedent for this pronoun appears in the sentence.

I bought the tickets for Doris and **myself.**

Not: Give the tickets to Doris and **myself.**
But: Give the tickets to Doris and **me.**

Not: The invitation was addressed to his wife and **himself.**
But: The invitation was addressed to his wife and **him.**

Exercise 1

Rephrase any of the following sentences in which a pronoun does not agree with its antecedent. Some of the sentences are correct as written.

1. Everyone brought to the bake sale the most delicious cake they could bake.

2. Neither of the boys had his license when they were stopped by the patrol.

3. The child with the blonde hair, which is my niece, will be performing next.

4. She had her eyes checked, hoping it would uncover the cause of her headaches.

5. Each of the girls took their book to the beach.

6. As the travelers climbed on the donkeys, they started down the ravine; then they turned around to wave.

7. Both of the boys handed their papers in on time.

8. If the store runs out of an advertised item, it gives its customers "rain checks."

9. A person who hopes to make their home in New York may be discouraged at the lack of available apartments.

10. It was time for the group to take their seats on the bus.

Exercise 2

Rephrase each of the following sentences to eliminate the vague or ambiguous pronoun antecedent.

1. On the way to the restaurant, Marge told Kate that she had received a telegram that morning.

2. The chef hired Ed as a cook because he appreciated good food.

3. The baby started to cry whenever company came, which embarrassed her parents.

4. Jenkins broke up with Mullagan when he got an offer from a club in Las Vegas to do a solo act.

5. The man on the bus was sneezing and coughing. It made the person sitting next to him uncomfortable.

6. Many people crowded around the woman and asked for her autograph. It was because she was a movie star.

7. Shortly after Don opened a restaurant at the shopping mall, it closed.

8. He has dinner and plays squash with his friends every Friday night, and this is excellent exercise.

9. When the stockholders met with the company's directors and the reporters, they started to ask questions.

10. Roy was playing pool with Larry, and he looked as if he were losing.

Exercise 3

Rephrase any of the following sentences that contain pronoun usage problems.

1. No one told Mary and myself about the change in plans.

2. The house, although it was overpriced, it met our needs and matched our dreams.

3. Abigail reminded Rebecca that she had accused her of being a witch and she would never forget it.

4. Some of the critics, they were very cruel in their comments.

5. He trained wild horses with a combination of firmness and kindness, which brought him a good income and some fame.

17 Pronoun Case

17a Subjective, Possessive, and Objective

Personal pronouns take the form of the *subjective,* the *possessive,* or the *objective case,* depending on their use in the sentence. The pronouns *who* and *whoever* also have different forms to indicate case.

Subjective:	I, you, he, she, it, we, they, who, whoever
Possessive:	my, mine, your, yours, his, her, hers, its, our, ours, their, theirs, whose
Objective:	me, you, him, her, it, us, them, whom, whomever

He wrote *The Way to Rainy Mountain.* (*subjective*)
Scott Momaday has increased **our** awareness of the daily struggle of American Indians. (*possessive*)
Many awards have been given to **him.** (*objective*)
The author is **he.** (*subjective*)

Most people have little trouble choosing the appropriate case when a personal pronoun is used by itself. Many do have trouble, though, when the pronoun is part of a compound structure. Almost everyone has trouble at times with *who* and *whom* and with *whoever* and *whomever*.

In compound subjects and objects

Place a pronoun that is part of a compound subject in the subjective case.

> *Not:* Fanny and **me** have tickets for the football game.
> *But:* Fanny and **I** have tickets for the football game.
>
> *Not:* Neither Wally nor **him** is on the wrestling team.
> *But:* Neither Wally nor **he** is on the wrestling team.

Place a pronoun that is part of a compound direct object or a compound indirect object in the objective case.

> *Not:* The fly ball bounced off the fence and then hit Christine and **I.**
> *But:* The fly ball bounced off the fence and then hit Christine and **me.** (hit . . . me)
>
> *Not:* Give Mel and **she** the blueprints so that they can check the measurements.
> *But:* Give Mel and **her** the blueprints so that they can check the measurements. (Give . . . her)

Place a pronoun that is part of a compound object of a preposition in the objective case.

> *Not:* Although there are thirty people competing, everyone knows the race is really between you and **I.**
> *But:* Although there are thirty people competing, everyone knows the race is really between you and **me.**
>
> *Not:* The symposium is being conducted by Dr. Fell and **she.**
> *But:* The symposium is being conducted by Dr. Fell and **her.** (by . . . her)
>
> *Not:* Several of **we** amateurs were allowed to play in the pro tournament.
> *But:* Several of **us** amateurs were allowed to play in the pro tournament. (of us, *not* of we)

In predicate nominatives

Place a pronoun that is part of a predicate nominative in the subjective case.

> *Not:* The people to see for tickets are Blake and **him.**
> *But:* The people to see for tickets are Blake and **he.**
>
> *Not:* The winners are Sharon and **her.**
> *But:* The winners are Sharon and **she.**

In speech, many people accept the informal use of the objective case of the pronoun following the verb *be.* In formal writing, however, the subjective case is still required in this construction.

> *Informal:* It is **me.**
> *Formal:* It is **I.**
>
> *Informal:* Was it **him** who asked you to the dance?
> *Formal:* Was it **he** who asked you to the dance?

After *than* or *as*

In an elliptical, or incomplete, clause, place the pronoun in the case it would be in if the clause were complete.

> *Not:* Kenneth is stronger than **him.**
> *But:* Kenneth is stronger than **he.** (than he is)
>
> *Not:* No one could have worked more skillfully than **her.**
> *But:* No one could have worked more skillfully than **she.** (than she did)
>
> *Not:* Martha knew she could love no one as much as **he.**
> *But:* Martha knew she could love no one as much as **him.** (as she loved him)

In appositives

Place a pronoun that is part of a compound appositive in the same case as the noun to which the appositive refers.

An **appositive** is a noun or noun substitute that renames or identifies the noun or noun substitute preceding it.

> *Not:* The partners—Fran, Scott, and **me**—plan to open a bicycle repair shop in July.
> *But:* The partners—Fran, Scott, and **I**—plan to open a bicycle repair shop in July.
>
> *Not:* Only two people, the manager and **him,** knew the combination of the safe.
> *But:* Only two people, the manager and **he,** knew the combination of the safe.

Before verbals or verbal phrases

Place a pronoun that precedes a gerund or gerund phrase in the possessive case. A noun follows this rule also.

> *Not:* The audience applauded **them** dancing.
> *But:* The audience applauded **their** dancing. (the Castles')
>
> *Not:* I resented **him** criticizing me in front of my friends.
> *But:* I resented **his** criticizing me in front of my friends. (my dad's)
>
> *Not:* Pauline liked everything about Ron but **him** singing first thing in the morning.
> *But:* Pauline liked everything about Ron but **his** singing first thing in the morning. (Ron's)

Place a pronoun that precedes a participle or participial phrase in the objective case.

> *Not:* When Penny recalled her grandfather, she pictured **his** smiling.
> *But:* When Penny recalled her grandfather, she pictured **him** smiling.
>
> *Not:* I heard **his** starting the car.
> *But:* I heard **him** starting the car.
>
> *Not:* Phil had seen **their** racing to class.
> *But:* Phil had seen **them** racing to class.

To decide which case of the pronoun to use, you have to decide whether the verbal following it is a gerund or a participle. Look at the next two sentences.

> I can hear your singing.
> I can hear you singing.

Both of these sentences are grammatically correct, but they have slightly different meanings. In the first sentence, *singing* is a gerund modified by the possessive pronoun *your;* in the second sentence, *singing* is a participle that modifies the objective pronoun *you.* The first sentence emphasizes an action, *singing,* while the second sentence emphasizes the performer of the action, *you.* Thus, in writing sentences like these, you can often convey different shades of meaning by using the possessive or the objective case of the pronoun.

Who and *whom; whoever* and *whomever*

In conversation, many people no longer use *whom* or *whomever* except directly after a preposition. In writing, however, you should always be careful to distinguish between *who* and *whom* and between *whoever* and *whomever.*

Use *who* and *whoever* as the subject of a sentence or clause.

> **Who** founded the American Red Cross? (*subject of sentence*)
> The book is about Clara Barton, **who** founded the American Red Cross. (*subject of clause*)
> **Whoever** lost the book will have to pay for it. (*subject of clause*)

Use *whom* and *whomever* as the direct object or the object of a preposition.

> **Whom** shall I call? (*direct object*)
> **Whomever** the *Union Leader* endorsed enjoyed a substantial advantage. (*direct object*)

The person to **whom** I gave the packages was Pete. (*object of preposition*)

How can you tell whether the pronoun should be *who* or *whom?* For sentences, mentally rephrase the question as a declarative statement. Then substitute *who* for *he, she,* or *they,* or *whom* for *him, her,* or *them.*

(*Who/Whom*) founded the American Red Cross?
She founded the American Red Cross.
Who founded the American Red Cross?

(*Who/Whom*) shall I call?
I shall call **him.**
Whom shall I call?

For clauses, follow the same process. Rephrase the clause as a statement and substitute *who* for *he, she,* or *they,* or *whom* for *him, her,* or *them.*

The person (*who/whom*) founded the American Red Cross was Clara Barton.
She founded the American Red Cross.
The person **who** founded the American Red Cross was Clara Barton.

The writer (*who/whom*) she enjoyed most was Dickens.
She enjoyed **him** most.
The writer **whom** she enjoyed most was Dickens.

(*Whoever/Whomever*) the *Union Leader* endorsed enjoyed a substantial advantage.
The *Union Leader* endorsed **him.**
Whomever the *Union Leader* endorsed enjoyed a substantial advantage.

If words intervene between the pronoun and the main verb of the sentence or clause, mentally delete them as you rephrase.

(*Who/Whom*) <u>did he think</u> he had offended?
He had offended **them.**

Whom did he think he had offended?

One person (*who/whom*) <u>the newspaper said</u> was killed was
actually unhurt.
She was killed.
One person **who** the newspaper said was killed was actually
unhurt.

The stores gave away the food to (*whoever/whomever*) <u>they
knew</u> could use it.
They could use it.
The stores gave away the food to **whoever** they knew could
use it.

Exercise 1

Select the appropriate form of the pronoun in each of the following
sentences.

1. The art appreciation class and (*we/us*) joined for a trip to the
   museum.

2. Arrangements were made by the teacher and (*I/me*).

3. Three of us—Alex, Jose, and (*I/me*)—prepared background material on the artist, Zurbarán.

4. The Golden Age of Spanish painting produced Velasquez, El
   Greco, Ribera, and (*he/him*).

5. Although Velasquez is better known than (*he/him*), Zurbarán is a
   painter of some importance.

6. The two of them—Velasquez and (*he/him*)—studied together.

7. Some think that Velasquez makes (*he/him*) look primitive.

8. Traditionalists object to (*his/him*) portraying St. Francis as a gaunt, gloomy man.

9. Yet, it is (*he/him*) (*who/whom*) surrealists have admired for his primitiveness.

10. Critics acknowledge Zurbarán's powerful realism, but they praise Velasquez far more than (*he/him*).

Exercise 2

Select the appropriate form of the pronoun in each of the following sentences.

1. (*Who/whom*) do you intend to nominate?

2. (*Who/whom*) do you think will win the election?

3. The generosity of Alfred Nobel, (*who/whom*) invented dynamite, created the Nobel Prize for Peace.

4. (*Whoever/whomever*) can devise a plan for peace in the Near East will be a genius.

5. If you are persistent, you will find the person (*who/whom*) you are looking for.

6. The person (*who/whom*) you must consult has gone to lunch.

7. The economist, (*who/whom*) neither drinks nor smokes, planned the merger of the tobacco company and the distillery.

8. Harry's wife, (*who/whom*) he admits has been his "right hand," will manage his campaign.

9. I will hire (*whoever/whomever*) I can find to stop the leaks in the roof.

10. I will hire (*whoever/whomever*) I can find (*who/whom*) will be able to mend the roof.

18 Adjectives and Adverbs

An **adjective** is a word that modifies a noun or a pronoun. An **adverb** is a word that modifies a verb, an adjective, or another adverb.

Do not confuse these two parts of speech.

Adjective	*Adverb*
happy	happily
graceful	gracefully
most	almost

Although most adjectives and adverbs have different forms, a few words can function as both. Among them are the following:

deep	hard	late	loud	slow	very
far	high	little	low	straight	well
fast	kindly	long	parallel	tight	wild

18a Misused Adjective Forms

Do not use an adjective to modify a verb, an adjective, or an adverb. Use an adverb instead.

Not: The lawyer answered very **quick.**

But: The lawyer *answered* very **quickly.**

Not: The director thought Marie's reading was **near** perfect.

But: The director thought Marie's reading was **nearly** *perfect.*

Not: The group performing at the club plays **real** well.

But: The group performing at the club plays **really** *well.*

Do not be confused by words separating the adverb from the word it modifies. For example:

The lawyer *answered* each of her client's questions very **quickly.**

Do not use an adjective ending in *-ly* in place of an adverb or an adverb phrase.

Although the suffix *-ly* usually signals an adverb, a few adjectives end in *-ly* too. For example:

earthly	ghostly	holy	lovely
friendly	heavenly	homely	manly

Do not mistake these adjectives for adverbs or try to use them as adverbs. Either use another word or express your idea as a phrase.

Not: A figure was moving **ghostly** through the darkened room.

But: A figure was moving **like a ghost** through the darkened room.

Or: A figure was moving **ghostlike** through the darkened room.

Not: They do not generally answer the questions of American tourists **very friendly.**

But: They do not generally answer the questions of American tourists **in a very friendly way.**

Or: They do not generally answer the questions of American tourists **very pleasantly.**

18b Misused Adverb Forms

Do not use an adverb to modify a direct object. Use an adjective instead for this as objective complement. (See page 123.)

Think about the difference in meaning between the following two sentences.

The instructor considered the student's paper careful.
The instructor considered the student's paper carefully.

In the first sentence, the adjective *careful* modifies the direct object *paper.* It tells what opinion the professor held of the paper. In the second sentence, the adverb *carefully* modifies the verb *considered.* It tells in what manner the professor considered the paper.

Not: He keeps his work station **tidily.**

But: He keeps his *work station* **tidy.**

Not: She considers her grades **excellently.**

But: She considers her *grades* **excellent.**

Not: The jury found the defendant **guiltily.**

But: The jury found the *defendant* **guilty.**

Do not use an adverb after a linking verb. Use the corresponding adjective instead for this as a predicate adjective. (See pages 124, 131.)

Not: After the operation, the patient felt **badly.**

But: After the operation, the *patient* felt **bad.**

Not: This proposal sounds **sensibly** enough.

But: This *proposal* sounds **sensible** enough.

Not: After he took that cooking course, his meals tasted **differently.**

But: After he took that cooking course, his *meals* tasted **different.**

Two words that are especially confusing are *good* and *well*. *Good* is always used as an adjective. *Well* is usually used as an adverb, but it can also be used as an adjective that means "healthy" or "satisfactory."

The preliminary *findings* look **good.** (*adjective*)

Janet *dances* **well.** (*adverb*)

The town crier shouted, "*All* is **well!**" (*adjective*)

Notice the difference between the following two sentences:

He feels good.
He feels well.

The adjective *good* describes the person's mood. The adjective *well* describes his health.

Some verbs can be used as both action verbs and linking verbs. (See pages 128–132.) These verbs include the following:

die	grow	feel	turn
go	look	smell	taste

Action: The customs officer *looked* **carefully** through our luggage. (*adverb*)

Linking: This *book* looks **interesting.** (*adjective*)

Action: The cute little puppy *grew* **quickly** into a 150-pound dog. (*adverb*)

Linking: After drinking the potion, the old *man* grew **young** before our very eyes. (*adjective*)

Action: He *died* **peacefully** in his sleep. (*adverb*)

Linking: The *poet* died **young.** (*adjective*)

18c Comparative and Superlative Forms of Adjectives and Adverbs

Form the comparative of most one-syllable adjectives and adverbs by adding the suffix *-er* (or *-r*) to the base, or positive, form of the word. Form the superlative of most one-syllable adjectives and adverbs by adding the suffix *-est* (or *-st*) to the base form.

Positive	*Comparative*	*Superlative*
slow	slower	slowest
late	later	latest
deep	deeper	deepest

Form the comparative of most longer adjectives and adverbs by placing the word *more* before the base word. Form the superlative of most longer adjectives and adverbs by placing the word *most* before the base word.

Positive	*Comparative*	*Superlative*
graceful	more graceful	most graceful
gracefully	more gracefully	most gracefully
sensible	more sensible	most sensible
sensibly	more sensibly	most sensibly

Some adjectives and adverbs have irregular comparative and superlative forms.

Positive	*Comparative*	*Superlative*
good well	better	best
bad ill badly	worse	worst
many much	more	most
little (quantity)	less	least

A dictionary usually lists the *-er* and *-est* comparative and superlative forms for adjectives and adverbs that have these forms.

Use the comparative form to compare two things. Use the superlative form to compare three or more things.

This dish is **spicier** than that one.
This dish is the **spiciest** one on the menu.

Harry is a **more skillful** carpenter than his partner.
Harry is the **most skillful** carpenter in town.

Lois works **harder** than Carol.
Lois works the **hardest** of the three students.

Sharon speaks **more distinctly** than her sister.
Sharon speaks the **most distinctly** of anyone in her family.

Do not use the superlative form when only two things are
being compared.

Not: Of the two sexes, women live **the longest.**
But: Of the two sexes, women live **longer.**

Not: Both of the proposals were reasonable, but Johnson's was
the most complex.
But: Both of the proposals were reasonable, but Johnson's was
more complex.

Not: Henry James and Edith Wharton both wrote of a certain
type of society—the society of the very rich and the very
secure—and of the effects of this society on the idealistic
woman. It is hard to say whose vision was the **clearest.**
But: Henry James and Edith Wharton both wrote of a certain
type of society—the society of the very rich and the very
secure—and of the effects of this society on the idealistic
woman. It is hard to say whose vision was the **clearer.**

Do not make double comparisons (comparisons using both -er
or -est and more or most).

Not: He was **more wealthier** than John D. Rockefeller.
But: He was **wealthier** than John D. Rockefeller.

Not: It is the **most sleekest** craft on the lake.
But: It is the **sleekest** craft on the lake.

Do not compare words like *complete, dead, perfect, round,
square,* and *unique.*

These words, called *absolutes,* name conditions that cannot be
compared. For example, people are either dead or not dead;
one person cannot be *more dead* than another person. If

something is perfect, something else cannot be *more perfect.*
Except for *dead,* however, you can compare the steps in
reaching these conditions. For example, something may be
more nearly perfect than something else, or one thing may be
the most nearly complete of three.

> *Not:* His solution was **more perfect** than John's.
> *But:* His solution was **more nearly perfect** than John's.

18d Double Negatives

Use only one negative word to express a negative meaning.

A **double negative** occurs when two negative words are used
to make a negative statement. Although this device was often
used in earlier centuries to emphasize the idea of negation, it
is not acceptable in standard modern English.

> *Not:* Felicity **didn't** bring **nothing** to the party.
> *But:* Felicity **didn't** bring **anything** to the party.
> *Or:* Felicity brought **nothing** to the party.

> *Not:* I **don't** know **no one** by that name.
> *But:* I **don't** know **anyone** by that name.
> *Or:* I know **no one** by that name.

> *Not:* She **can't hardly** see in this light.
> *But:* She **can hardly** see in this light.

Exercise

Identify the incorrect adjective and adverb forms in the following
sentences. One sentence is correct as written.

1. In the late eighteenth and early nineteenth centuries, some social critics looked close at the plight of the child laborer.

2. Among these critics were two of the most famousest writers of their time, William Blake and Charles Dickens.

3. One job usually held by children was that of the chimney sweep. since most adults couldn't hardly fit through the real tortuous passageways connecting chimneys and fireplaces.

4. Blake and Dickens could not help considering a chimney sweep's job dangerously, since many sweeps died young from consumption and black lung disease.

5. In his poem "The Chimney-Sweeper," William Blake tells of a pitiful sweep who mournfully cries the words "Weep! Weep!"

6. In *Oliver Twist,* Charles Dickens writes very moving of the real dreadful conditions of a sweep's daily life.

7. A sweep who felt badly was not given the day off to rest.

8. In spite of their health, sweeps had to get up early to be ready to work prompt at 5:00 A.M.

9. They had to crawl through passageways that were often unbearable hot and uncomfortable narrow, while scraping the soot meticulously.

10. Often, when the young sweeps seemed wearily, they had to endure harsh treatment by their masters, who tried to keep their youngsters moving rapid and working hard.

19 Comparisons

In addition to using the appropriate comparative or superlative form of an adjective or adverb, a writer who is making a comparison has to keep a number of other points in mind. Be sure that your comparisons are sensible, complete, and unambiguous; do not leave out anything necessary to make your meaning clear.

19a False Comparisons

Be careful that your comparative statements compare what you intended to compare. Do not compare things that are essentially unlike.

> *False:* Mark's smile was broader than Dora.

In the preceding sentence, the writer is trying to compare Mark's smile with Dora's smile. But the sentence as written compares Mark's smile with Dora herself.

> *Valid:* Mark's smile was broader than Dora's.

> *False:* Her style of dressing is like the 1960's.

The preceding sentence compares a style of dressing with a period of time. Obviously, it should compare this style of dressing with the style of dressing popular in that period.

> *Valid:* Her style of dressing is like **that of** the 1960's.

> *False:* Tuition at private colleges has become much more expensive than state colleges.

> *Valid:* Tuition has become much more expensive at private colleges than **at** state colleges.

19b Incomplete Comparisons

Do not introduce the idea of a comparison without specifying one of the things being compared.

Incomplete: This cake tastes better.

Tastes better than what?

Complete: This cake tastes better than any of the others.

Incomplete: Growing up in a small town is different.

Different from what?

Complete: Growing up in a small town is different from growing up in a large city or a suburb.

19c Ambiguous Comparisons

Do not make a comparative statement that has two possible meanings.

Ambiguous: I know Eliot better than Pound.

The preceding sentence is unclear. You can interpret it in two ways.

Clear: I know Eliot better than I know Pound.
Clear: I know Eliot better than Pound knows him.

Ambiguous: I can recall the family vacation we took when I was five better than my sister.

Clear: I can recall the family vacation we took when I was five better than my sister can recall it.

Clear: I can recall the family vacation we took when I was five better than I can recall my sister.

19d Omitted Comparative Words

Do not omit the words *as* or *than* when they are necessary in a comparative construction.

> *Not:* The candidate was better prepared although not as well spoken as her opponent.
>
> *But:* The candidate was better prepared **than,** although not as well spoken as, her opponent.

> *Not:* His grades were as good, if not better than, his brother's.
>
> *But:* His grades were as good **as,** if not better than, his brother's.

> *Not:* All of their friends were as poor or even poorer than they.
>
> *But:* All of their friends were as poor **as** they or even poorer. (*than they* is understood)

Use the word *other* or *else* when you compare one thing with other members of the group to which it belongs.

> *Not:* The flutist plays more beautifully than any member of the orchestra.
>
> *But:* The flutist plays more beautifully than any **other** member of the orchestra.

> *Not:* Hal can throw farther than anyone on his team.
>
> *But:* Hal can throw farther than anyone **else** on his team.

> *Not:* The clipper cut through the water more gracefully than any of the ships.
>
> *But:* The clipper cut through the water more gracefully than any of the **other** ships.

Exercise

Rephrase the following sentences to eliminate any false, ambiguous, or incomplete comparisons. Where necessary, supply any comparative words that have been omitted.

1. Mark wanted to date Christine as much as Lee.

2. James Michener's novels are longer than most other writers.

3. That jockey has ridden more winners than any rider in his race.

4. The child speaks as clearly if not more clearly than other children her age.

5. Arabic is harder to learn than almost any language.

6. Jean paid more for her car than her husband.

7. Harry likes football better than his girlfriend.

8. Drinking water in Cairo is as pure as many other big cities.

9. The train's schedule is the same as the bus.

10. This peanut butter tastes better.

20 Shifts

While variety is desirable in writing, some kinds of variety are not desirable. Shifting for no good reason from the active to the passive voice or from the past to the present tense is confusing and irritating to the reader. Be consistent in your use of number, person, tense, voice, and mood.

20a In Number

Do not shift awkwardly and inconsistently between the singular and the plural.

Many shifts of this kind are actually problems with pronoun-antecedent agreement (see pages 206–210).

Inconsistent:	Just before **a person** speaks in public, **they** should do several relaxation exercises.
Consistent:	Just before **a person** speaks in public, **he or she** should do several relaxation exercises.
Or:	Just before speaking in public, a person should do several relaxation exercises.

Inconsistent:	**A warthog** may appear ungainly, but **these animals** can run at a speed of 30 miles an hour.
Consistent:	**A warthog** may appear ungainly, but **this animal** can run at a speed of 30 miles an hour.
Or:	**Warthogs** may appear ungainly, but **these animals** can run at a speed of 30 miles an hour.

Inconsistent:	**Anyone** who travels to Greece will see many sites about which **they** have read.
Consistent:	**People** who travel to Greece will see many sites about which **they** have read.
Or:	**Travelers** to Greece will see many sites about which **they** have read.

20b In Person

Do not shift awkwardly between the second person and the third person.

All nouns and all indefinite pronouns are in the third person. However, personal pronouns may be in the first person, the second person, or the third person.

	Singular	*Plural*
First person:	I, me, my, mine	we, us, our, ours
Second person:	you, your, yours	you, your, yours
Third person:	he, him, his she, her, hers it, its	they, them, their, theirs

Inconsistent:	It has been said that unless **you** have a knowledge of history, **a person** is condemned to repeat the mistakes of history.
Consistent:	It has been said that unless **you** have a knowledge of history, **you** are condemned to repeat the mistakes of history.
Or:	It has been said that without a knowledge of history, a person is condemned to repeat the mistakes of history.
Inconsistent:	When **a person** reads Jefferson's *Notes on Virginia,* **you** are amazed by his wide range of interests.
Consistent:	When **people** read Jefferson's *Notes on Virginia,* **they** are amazed by his wide range of interests.
Or:	People who read Jefferson's *Notes on Virginia* are amazed by his wide range of interests.
Inconsistent:	As **you** read about the slaughtering of the rhinoceros for its horn and the elephant for its tusks, **one** becomes appalled by the selfishness of humankind.
Consistent:	As **you** read about the slaughtering of the rhinoceros for its horn and the elephant for its tusks, **you** become appalled by the selfishness of humankind.
Or:	Reading about the slaughtering of the rhinoceros for its horn and the elephant for its tusks, one becomes appalled by the selfishness of humankind.

20c In Tense

Do not shift awkwardly between the present tense and the past tense.

When writing about literature or history, you can often use either the present tense or the past tense. However, if you start writing in the present tense, continue writing in this tense. If you start writing in the past tense, continue writing in this tense.

> *Inconsistent:* At the end of the war, Ezra Pound **is accused** of treason. He **was confined** at St. Elizabeth's Hospital, where he **spends** the next twelve years.
>
> *Consistent:* At the end of the war, Ezra Pound **is accused** of treason. He **is confined** at St. Elizabeth's Hospital, where he **spends** the next twelve years.

> *Inconsistent:* *The Day of the Scorpion* **is** the second book in Paul Scott's *The Raj Quartet.* It **tells** the story of an English family living in India in the last years of British rule. The book **opened** on August 9, 1942. On this day Gandhi and other prominent Indians who had voted for independence from Britain **were sent** to prison.
>
> *Consistent:* *The Day of the Scorpion* **is** the second book in Paul Scott's *The Raj Quartet.* It **tells** the story of an English family living in India in the last years of British rule. The book **opens** on August 9, 1942. On this day Gandhi and other prominent Indians who had voted for independence from Britain **are sent** to prison.

> *Inconsistent:* Lincoln **came** to national attention as a result of a series of debates with Stephen A. Douglas. Although he **loses** the senatorial election to Douglas, two years later he **gains** the Republican nomination for president.
>
> *Consistent:* Lincoln **came** to national attention as a result of a series of debates with Stephen A. Douglas. Although he **lost** the senatorial election to Douglas, two years later he **gained** the Republican nomination for president.

20d In Voice

Do not shift awkwardly between the active voice and the passive voice.

Inconsistent:	John F. Kennedy **won** the presidency with only 49.7 percent of the popular vote because a majority of the electoral vote **was captured** by him.
Consistent:	John F. Kennedy **won** the presidency with only 49.7 percent of the popular vote because he **captured** a majority of the electoral vote.
Inconsistent:	André-Jacques Garnerin **made** the first parachute jump, and the first aerial photographs **were taken** by Samuel Archer King and William Black.
Consistent:	André-Jacques Garnerin **made** the first parachute jump, and Samuel Archer King and William Black **took** the first aerial photographs.
Inconsistent:	A group of ants **is called** a colony, but you **refer** to a group of bees as a swarm.
Consistent:	A group of ants **is called** a colony, but a group of bees **is referred** to as a swarm.

20e In Mood

Do not shift awkwardly between the indicative, imperative, and subjunctive moods.

Inconsistent:	First **brown** the onions in butter. Then you **should add** them to the beef stock.
Consistent:	First **brown** the onions in butter. Then **add** them to the beef stock.
Inconsistent:	If I **were** president of this club and he **was** my second in command, things would be very different.
Consistent:	If I **were** president of this club and he **were** my second in command, things would be very different.
Inconsistent:	First **proofread** your paper and **make** any necessary changes. Next you **ought to retype** it.

> *Consistent:*   First **proofread** your paper and **make** any nec-
> essary changes. Next **retype** it.

Exercise

Rephrase each of the following items to eliminate awkward shifts in number, person, tense, voice, and mood.

1. Boil the pasta for ten minutes. The sauce will already have been made.

2. Pretoria's homelands have profited from gambling casinos and nightclubs, but residents have been victimized by such playgrounds.

3. At the start of his adventures, Huckleberry Finn meets Jim; then the two started down the Mississippi on a raft.

4. It is necessary that a welder take certain precautions, one of which is that he wears his goggles.

5. When you apply for a passport, a person should bring a copy of his or her birth certificate.

6. A student should take their education seriously; certainly they should never cut class excessively.

7. Before one condemns somebody for some insult or injury, you should check the facts carefully.

8. To parallel park, first pull the car alongside the car in front. Then the wheel should be turned sharply, and you are ready to back in slowly.

9. Salespeople cannot afford to let personal feelings show. One must be friendly and polite even to rude customers.

10. Jogging is dangerous on city streets at night, because you have to watch for cars, potholes, and muggers.

21   Sequence of Tenses

Maintain a logical sequence of tenses to indicate when events happen in relation to one another.

The English tense system may seem complicated, but most of the time, native speakers of the language have few problems using it correctly. One problem that some people do have is shifting unnecessarily from one tense to another (see pages 239–240). Some writers, on the other hand, have the opposite problem: they do not change tenses when they need to in order to show that one event happened before or after another. The following rules cover some of the most common problems with sequence of tenses.

21a   With Clauses

If you begin a sentence in the present tense, shift to the past tense or the present perfect tense when you begin to write about past action.

Not: To a large extent, we **remember** Alice B. Toklas because she **is** Gertrude Stein's friend.

But: To a large extent, we **remember** Alice B. Toklas because she **was** Gertrude Stein's friend.

> *Not:* Today he **supports** moving the embassy, while just three weeks ago he **opposes** this action.
>
> *But:* Today he **supports** moving the embassy, while just three weeks ago he **opposed** this action.

> *Not:* She always **goes** to the mountains on vacation because she **loved** them since childhood.
>
> *But:* She always **goes** to the mountains on vacation because she **has loved** them since childhood.

Use the past perfect tense to indicate that one past action occurred before another past action.

> *Not:* Hitler **purged** the Nazi Party before he **gained** complete control of the state.
>
> *But:* Hitler **had purged** the Nazi Party before he **gained** complete control of the state.

> *Not:* They **double-checked** the results of their experiment because they **made** an error.
>
> *But:* They **double-checked** the results of their experiment because they **had made** an error.

> *Not:* Since spring **came** early, they **were hoping** for a long growing season.
>
> *But:* Since spring **had come** early, they **were hoping** for a long growing season.

Use the future perfect tense to indicate that an action in the future will occur before another future action or point in time.

> *Not:* By next Tuesday we **will cover** half the course.
>
> *But:* By next Tuesday we **will have covered** half the course.

> *Not:* When they **pay** off the loan, they **paid** twice the cost of the car.
>
> *But:* When they **pay** off the loan, they **will have paid** twice the cost of the car.

21b With Infinitives

Use the present infinitive to express action that occurs at the same time as or later than the action of the main verb. Use the present perfect infinitive to express action that occurs before the action of the main verb.

Not: They **need to purchase** their tickets by now.

But: They **need to have purchased** their tickets by now. (*The need is in the present; the purchase, if it happened, was in the past.*)

Not: The artist **wanted to have captured** the variations in the light.

But: The artist **wanted to capture** the variations in the light. (*The wanting occurred before the capturing.*)

Not: The designer **had hoped to have gotten** the job.

But: The designer **had hoped to get** the job.

Compare the following three sentences.

He **would like to review** the book favorably. (would like *in the present* to review *in the present*)

He **would have liked to review** the book favorably. (would have liked *in the past* to review *in the past*)

He **would like to have reviewed** the book favorably. (would like *in the present* to have reviewed *in the past*)

21c With Participles

Use the present participle to express action that occurs at the same time as the action of the main verb. Use the present perfect participle or the past participle to express action that occurs before the action of the main verb.

The present perfect participle of a verb consists of the word *having* followed by the past participle of the verb: *having done, having been, having seen,* and so forth.

Not: **Winning** the battle, the general planned the next day's campaign.

But: **Having won** the battle, the general *planned* the next day's campaign. (*action of participle occurred before action of main verb*)

Not: **Having hoped** for good news, he rushed for the telephone.

But: **Hoping** for good news, he *rushed* for the telephone. (*action of participle occurred at the same time as action of main verb*)

Not: **Being encouraged** by her friends, she eagerly filled out the form for entrance in the marathon.

But: **Having been encouraged by her friends,** she *filled out* the form eagerly for entrance in the marathon. (*action of participle occurred before action of main verb*)

Or: **Encouraged** by her friends, she eagerly *filled out* the form for entrance in the marathon.

Exercise

Correct any error in sequence of tenses in the following sentences. Identify any correct sentences.

1. The seven-year-old knows since he was five the truth about Santa Claus.

2. The committee had drawn up its plans by the time the conference convened.

3. As we left, we told our hosts we had a wonderful time.

4. By tomorrow we will cover half the trail.

5. Having waited for the letter for a week, she had been happy to get it.

6. I was sorry to have missed your visit.

7. Although very little rain fell so far this season, farmers still hope to save their crops.

8. Parking his car close to the building's entrance, he arrived on time for his appointment.

9. Selling two paintings, the young artist felt confident enough to have given up his job as a plumber.

10. After shopping in the bazaar for an hour, she discovered she spent almost all the money she brought.

22 Sentence Structure

The parts of a sentence, like those of a building or a jigsaw puzzle, must be put together in a certain way in order to fit with one another. For example, verbs must agree with their subjects, and pronouns with their antecedents. In constructing sentences, you must also be sure to maintain a consistent structure throughout a sentence, to make subjects and predicates fit together logically, to express parallel grammatical elements in parallel form, and to place modifiers correctly.

22a Mixed Structure

Maintain a consistent sentence structure. Do not start a sentence with one type of structure and end it with another type.

> *Inconsistent:*   First rub olive oil over the outside of the
>   chicken; then salt the chicken lightly, but no
>   pepper.

The writer of the sentence above begins with an independent clause, continues with another independent clause, and then begins the third part of the sentence with the conjunction *but,* indicating that another independent clause will follow. However, the writer then ends the sentence with a phrase rather than a clause. The problem can be eliminated by turning the phrase into a clause.

> *Consistent:*   First rub olive oil over the outside of the
>   chicken; then salt the chicken lightly, but do not
>   pepper it.

Another kind of mixed sentence structure is created by clauses that are not clearly related to one another.

> *Inconsistent:*   When your parents were poorly educated and
>   you yourself have attended substandard schools,
>   what kind of odds for success are those?

In this sentence, the writer begins with an adverb clause that should modify a word in an independent clause. However, the independent clause that follows does not contain any word for the adverb clause to modify. To correct the problem, simply provide such a word.

> *Consistent:*   What kind of odds for success do you have when
>   your parents were poorly educated and you
>   yourself have attended substandard schools?

> *Inconsistent:*   Those black pilots who fought so valiantly dur-
>   ing World War II, many people do not even
>   know of their existence.

Here the writer begins with a noun modified by an adjective clause but does not provide a predicate for the noun. Instead, ss

the sentence ends with an independent clause that is not grammatically related to what precedes it.

> *Consistent:* Many people do not even know of the existence of those black pilots who fought so valiantly during World War II.

The following sentence is from a television program about training business executives to answer (or evade) reporters' questions.

> *Inconsistent:* How you could be a newsperson and work with people you might one day have to interview, I could not do it.
>
> *Consistent:* As a newsperson, I could not work with people I might one day have to interview.
>
> *Or:* I do not understand how you could be a newsperson and work with people you might one day have to interview.

22b Faulty Predication

Make the subject and predicate of a sentence fit together both grammatically and logically.

A sentence with a poorly matched subject and predicate is said to have **faulty predication.**

> *Not:* More versatile and more manageable account for the popularity of the latest breed of home computers.

In the preceding sentence, the writer used two adjectives as the subject of the predicate *account for . . . computers.* A subject, however, must always be a noun or a noun equivalent.

> *But:* Their greater **versatility** and increased **manageability** account for the popularity of the latest breed of home computers.

Other sentences with faulty predication are grammatically acceptable but make no sense or do not say what the writer intended.

> *Not:* Flattery and snobbery are people who will not be effective as political advisers.

The nouns *flattery* and *snobbery* do not sensibly fit the predicate *are people.*

> *But:* The flatterer and the snob will not be effective as political advisers.
>
> *Not:* My opinion of his latest movie is poorly directed and ineptly filmed.

According to the preceding sentence, it is the writer's opinion that is poorly directed and ineptly filmed. Obviously, the writer meant to say this of the movie, not of the opinion.

> *But:* In my opinion, his latest movie is poorly directed and ineptly filmed.
>
> *Or:* My opinion of his latest movie is that it is poorly directed and ineptly filmed.
>
> *Not:* Our criminal-justice system, which allows the victims of crime to suffer more than the perpetrators of crime, should be punished more severely.

The subject *our criminal-justice system* does not fit the predicate *should be punished more severely.*

> *But:* Our criminal-justice system, which allows the victims of crime to suffer more than the perpetrators of crime, should be changed.
>
> *Or:* Our criminal-justice system should be changed so that perpetrators of crime suffer more than their victims.

Do not use an adverb clause as a subject or as a predicate nominative.

> *Not:* Because the British were occupying Philadelphia is the reason the Liberty Bell was moved to Allentown during the Revolutionary War.

The word *because* introduces what must be an adverb clause.

> *But:* Because the British were occupying Philadelphia, the Liberty Bell was moved to Allentown during the Revolutionary War.

> *Not:* The reason the Liberty Bell was moved to Allentown during the Revolutionary War is because the British were occupying Philadelphia.

Change this *because* adverb clause to a noun clause, or omit it.

> *But:* The reason the Liberty Bell was moved to Allentown during the Revolutionary War is **that** the British were occupying Philadelphia.

> *Not:* The year 1778 is when the Liberty Bell was returned to Independence Hall.
> *But:* The Liberty Bell was returned to Independence Hall in 1778.

> *Not:* Ironically, England is where the Liberty Bell was cast.
> *But:* Ironically, the Liberty Bell was cast in England.

22c Faulty Parallelism

Use the same grammatical form for elements that are part of a series or a compound construction.

> The speech was **concise, witty,** and **effective.**
> Today's "supermom" is both **a mother** and **an executive.**
> He tried to be honest **with himself** as well as **with others.**

Sentence elements that have the same grammatical structure are said to be *parallel*. When elements that are part of a series or a compound construction do not have the same form, a sentence is said to have **faulty parallelism.**

Repeat articles, prepositions, and the word *to* before the infinitive to make the meaning of a sentence clear.

The audience applauded the composer and lyricist.

The preceding sentence is clear if the composer and the lyricist are the same person. It is misleading if they are not the same person. Repeat the article *the* to indicate two people.

The audience applauded **the** composer and **the** lyricist.

Unclear:	She was a prominent critic and patron of young poets.
Clear:	She was **a** prominent critic and **a** patron of young poets.
Unclear:	She quickly learned to supervise the maid and cook.
Clear:	She quickly learned to supervise **the** maid and **the** cook.
Clear:	She quickly learned **to** supervise the maid and **to** cook.
Unclear:	His father had taught him to shoot and ride a horse.
Clear:	His father had taught him **to** shoot and **to** ride a horse.

Place elements joined by a coordinating conjunction in the same grammatical form. Balance a noun with a noun, an adjective with an adjective, a prepositional phrase with a prepositional phrase, and so on.

Not parallel: The scientific community in general regarded

> adjective   adjective   noun
> ↓   ↓   ↓
> him as **outspoken, eccentric,** and a **rebel.**

Parallel: The scientific community in general regarded

> adjective   adjective   adjective
> ↓   ↓   ↓
> him as **outspoken, eccentric,** and **rebellious.**

Not parallel: In *Searching for Caleb,* the protagonist is a

> noun   noun   clause
> ↓   ↓   ↓
> **wife,** a **mother,** and **she tells fortunes.**

Parallel: In *Searching for Caleb,* the protagonist is a

> noun   noun   noun
> ↓   ↓   ↓
> **wife,** a **mother,** and a **fortune-teller.**

> adjective
> ↓

Not parallel: Reviewers praised the play for its **realistic**

> noun
> ↓
> **portrayal** of a sensitive young woman and

> adverb clause
> ↓
> **because it gave a penetrating depiction of a family.**

Parallel:

adjective
↓
Reviewers praised the play for its **realistic**

noun
↓
portrayal of a sensitive young woman and its

adjective   noun
↓   ↓
penetrating depiction of family life.

Not parallel:

Prepositional phrase
↓
A hobbit is a creature **with a hearty appetite**

adjective clause
↓
and **who loves home.**

Parallel:

verb
↓
A hobbit is a creature who **has** a hearty appetite

verb
↓
and **loves** home.

Place elements joined by correlative conjunctions in parallel form.

Not parallel:	He was not only **her husband** but also **she considered him her friend.**
Parallel:	He was not only **her husband** but also **her friend.**
Not parallel:	Knute Rockne would be either **a science teacher** or **someone who coached football.**
Parallel:	Knute Rockne would be either **a science teacher** or **a football coach.**

| *Not parallel:* | After his vision, Scrooge becomes not only **a generous man** but also **happy**. |
| *Parallel:* | After his vision, Scrooge becomes not only **a generous man** but also **a happy one**. |

Take care with the placement of correlative conjunctions.

| *Not parallel:* | Solar energy is **both** used to heat houses **and** to run small appliances. |

In the preceding sentence, the first part of the correlative conjunction (*both*) is followed by a verb, but the second part (*and*) is followed by an infinitive. The problem can be corrected by moving the *both* to a later position in the sentence so that it, too, is followed by an infinitive.

Parallel:	Solar energy is used **both** to heat houses **and** to run small appliances.
Not parallel:	She would **either** run as the presidential candidate **or** the vice presidential candidate.
Parallel:	She would run as **either** the presidential candidate **or** the vice presidential candidate.
Not parallel:	He **not only** wanted money **but also** fame.
Parallel:	He wanted **not only** money **but also** fame.

22d Dangling Modifiers

An introductory phrase must clearly and sensibly modify the noun or pronoun that follows it.

A phrase that does not do this is called a **dangling modifier,** because it is not clearly attached to the rest of the sentence.

| *Unclear:* | **Frightened by the huge, gnarled tree outside his window,** his head dived under the covers. |

In the sentence above, the introductory participial phrase seems to modify his head, but it was obviously not the boy's head, but the boy himself, who was frightened. A simple way to revise this sentence is to rewrite the independent clause so that it begins with the noun that the introductory phrase actually refers to.

> *Clear:*   **Frightened by the huge, gnarled tree outside his window,** the boy hid his head under the covers.

> *Unclear:*   **Unable to make a living in Detroit,** relocating to Houston seemed a good idea.

The introductory phrase does not sensibly modify *relocating,* the gerund that follows it. This sentence can also be revised by rewriting the independent clause so that it begins with the noun or pronoun that the introductory phrase actually refers to.

> *Clear:*   **Unable to make a living in Detroit,** she thought relocating to Houston was a good idea.
> *Or:*   **Unable to make a living in Detroit,** she thought she might move to Houston.

Another way to revise the sentence is to turn the phrase into a clause.

> *Clear:*   **Since she was unable to make a living in Detroit,** relocating to Houston seemed a good idea.

Here are some more examples of dangling modifiers.

> *Unclear:*   **While trying to control my temper,** the sergeant forced me to do a hundred push-ups.
> *Clear:*   **While trying to control my temper,** I was forced to do a hundred push-ups by the sergeant.
> *Or:*   **As I tried to control my temper,** the sergeant forced me to do a hundred push-ups.

| Unclear: | **As a young girl,** my grandfather told me stories of his life in Sweden. |
| Clear: | **When I was a young girl,** my grandfather told me stories of his life in Sweden. |

A few introductory phrases are idiomatic. They modify the entire sentence, not a particular word.

To tell the truth, no one knows where he is.
Relatively speaking, my grades are not that bad.
As a matter of fact, the sea is not wine-red but blue.

22e Misplaced Modifiers

Place a modifying word or phrase as close as possible to the word it modifies. Be careful not to place it so that it seems to refer to a word other than the one you intended.

The placement of a modifier in a sentence is very important. Notice the difference in meaning between the following two sentences.

He **almost** spent two hundred dollars.
He spent **almost** two hundred dollars.

In the first sentence, *almost* modifies the verb *spent*. It tells us that he did not complete his action. In the second sentence, *almost* modifies *two hundred*. It tells us that the amount he spent came close to, but did not total, two hundred dollars.

Misplaced modifiers make a sentence confusing or even ridiculous, as shown in the following examples.

| Unclear: | He almost spoke for two hours. |
| Clear: | He spoke for **almost** two hours. |

| Unclear: | She only quoted from three sources. |
| Clear: | She quoted from **only** three sources. |

Unclear:	He sang a ditty about filling a bottomless hole with his sister.
Clear:	**With his sister,** he sang a ditty about filling a bottomless hole.
Or:	He sang a ditty **with his sister** about filling a bottomless hole.
Unclear:	He described his years spent alone on the island after the rescue.
Clear:	**After the rescue** he described his years spent alone on the island.

22f Squinting Modifiers

Do not place a modifier in such a way that it could refer to either the preceding or the following element in the sentence.

Such a modifier is called a **squinting modifier.**

Unclear:	The mayor announced **in March** he would run for reelection.

Was it the announcement or the election that was in March?

Clear:	The mayor announced he would run for reelection in March.
Clear:	In March, the mayor announced he would run for reelection.
Unclear:	Carlson said **today** he is leaving for California.
Clear:	Carlson said he is leaving for California today.
Clear:	Today Carlson said he is leaving for California.
Unclear:	Professor Quinn asked us **before we left** to turn in our papers.
Clear:	Before we left, Professor Quinn asked us to turn in our papers.
Clear:	Professor Quinn asked us to turn in our papers before we left.

Exercise

Revise each of the following sentences to eliminate the problem in sentence structure.

1. In his spare time he likes to cook and knit mittens.

2. For emergencies she kept a flashlight and umbrella in her car.

3. The men rowed all night, but no progress.

4. The reason I did not write is because I lost your address.

5. Hunting shells on the seaward side of the island, the ferry left without him.

6. How people could live under such conditions, I could not understand it.

7. Not only did we have to boil the water but also disinfect the vegetables.

8. Popped fresh for every show, the movie-goers couldn't resist buying the popcorn.

9. The nurse succeeded in getting the patient to nearly eat all of his meal.

10. The sunflowers grew slowly turning their faces to the sun.

Part IV

Punctuation
and
Mechanics

Punctuation marks are signals designed to help people understand what they are reading. They tell readers when to pause, when to stop, and when to read something with emphasis.

Mechanics deals with the technical aspects of writing. These aspects include when to underline, when to use numerals, and how to form contractions.

23 End Punctuation

End punctuation separates sentences and marks the end of other elements, such as abbreviations. The three end punctuation marks are the *period,* the *question mark,* and the *exclamation mark.*

23a The Period

Use a period to end a sentence that makes a statement.

> In 1979, the United States ceded control of the Panama Canal Zone to the Panamanian government.
> The Japanese painter Hokusai changed his style many times.
> Adlai E. Stevenson ran for the presidency against Dwight D. Eisenhower.

Use a period to end a sentence that makes a request, expresses a mild command, or gives directions.

> Please help the needy.
> Open your books to page 178.
> Turn left at the next corner.

If you wish the command or request to be given a great deal of emphasis or force, use an exclamation point instead of a period.

> Help!
> Sign up now!
> Quit smoking!

Use a period at the end of a sentence that asks an indirect question.

> The editorial questions whether NATO is effective.
> The reporter asked how the fire had started.
> The doctor wondered why the patient's temperature had risen.

Use a period at the end of a request politely expressed as a question.

> Will you please type this letter for me.
> Will you kindly keep your voices down.

(See pages 296–297 for the use of the period with parentheses. See page 305 for the use of the period with quotation marks.)

Use a period after most abbreviations and initials.

If a sentence ends with an abbreviation requiring a period, use only one period.

> The first admiral in the U.S. Navy was David G. Farragut.
> The Marine Corps traces its beginnings to Nov. 10, 1775.
> Thomas Jefferson's home, Monticello, is near Charlottesville, Va.

The current trend in abbreviations is away from the use of periods. The following two rules are now considered standard.

However, if you are in doubt about whether to use a period after an abbreviation, consult your dictionary.

Do not use a period with abbreviations of units of measure.

> 86 **m**   275 **kg**   2.4 **cm**   20 **cc**   20 **ft**
>   10.5 **yd**   20 **lb**

> *Exceptions:*   For *mile* use *m.* or *mi.* to prevent confusion with
>   *m* for *meter;* for *inch* use *in* only when there is no
>   possibility of confusion with the word *in;* the ab-
>   breviation *in.* avoids all confusion.

Do not use a period with acronyms or other abbreviations of businesses, organizations, and government and international agencies.

> The **NAACP** has not endorsed a presidential candidate.
> My mother served in the **WACs** for eight years.
> The impartiality of **UNESCO** is being questioned.

23b The Question Mark

Use a question mark at the end of a sentence that asks a direct question.

> Who invented the safety pin**?**
> Have you registered to vote**?**
> Why did Nixon go to China**?**

Use a question mark at the end of an interrogative element that is part of another sentence.

> How can I keep my job**?** was the question on every worker's
> mind.

Will he actively support women's rights? she wondered.
The telegram said that Malcolm is alive—can it be true?—and
will be returned to the United States on Friday.

In general, when a question follows an introductory element, use a capital letter to begin the question and a question mark to end it.

The question to be decided is, How can we improve our public
transportation system?
Before buying on credit, ask yourself, Do I really need this?
A good detective inquires, What was the motive for the crime?

Usage varies somewhat on capitalization of questions following introductory elements. The more formal the question, the greater the tendency to use a capital letter. The less formal, the greater the tendency to use a lowercase letter.

Formal: The book raises the question, What role should the
United States play in the Middle East?
Informal: I wondered, should I bring my umbrella?

Use a question mark, usually in parentheses, to express doubt or uncertainty about a date, a name, or a word.

The *Vedas* (written around 1000 B.C.?) are the sacred books of
Hinduism.
A dialect of Germanic, called Angleish (?), is the basis of modern-day English.
Sir Thomas Malory (?–1471) wrote *Morte d'Arthur,* an account of
the exploits of King Arthur and his knights.

23c The Exclamation Point

Use an exclamation point at the end of a sentence, word, or phrase that you wish to be read with emphasis, with surprise, or with strong emotion.

Don't give up!
We shall resist this onslaught!
Impossible!
What a terrible time!

However, do not overuse the exclamation point. Too many exclamation points are distracting and ineffective. The more you use, the less effective each one will be.

Exercise

Identify the end punctuation missing from the following sentences. Some of the sentences need more than one punctuation mark.

1. Have you ever wondered why people go trick-or-treating on Halloween

2. The Christian church created Christian holidays to take the place of pagan holidays

3. All Saints' Day—did you know this—was established to replace the Celtic holiday Samhain, the festival of the dead

4. St Patrick (AD 389–461) helped convert the Celts to Christianity

5. Will you please check these dates

6. How can we use the customs of the Celts to convert these people was the question the Church considered

7. You might wonder, Is *hallow* another word for *saint*

8. An excellent question

9. All Saints' Day, or All Hallows' Day, is celebrated on Nov 1;

therefore, All Saints' Eve, or All Hallows' Eve, or Halloween, is Oct 31

10. The custom of dressing like ghouls and goblins and trick-or-treating mimics the Celtic belief that the dead walk the earth during Samhain, doesn't it

24 The Comma

The **comma** groups elements within the sentence in four ways: a comma *separates coordinate elements;* it *sets off introductory elements;* it *sets off certain terminal elements;* a pair of commas *set off interrupting elements.*

24a Between Coordinate Elements

Independent clauses

Use a comma between two independent clauses (sentences) joined by a coordinating conjunction—*and, but, for, nor, or, so, yet.*

Many Caribbean people emigrate to other countries, and 700,000 of these emigrants settled in the United States between 1971 and 1979.

Halloween has its origins in the Celtic religious festival of the dead, but today Halloween is largely a children's holiday of tricks and treats.

Travel to the countryside to buy fresh apples, for there at roadside stands you can find many varieties not available in supermarkets.

The comma may be omitted between two short independent clauses.

> She handed him the note and he read it immediately.
> Take notes in class and study them.

If in doubt, use the comma.

Items in a series

Use commas to separate three or more items—words, phrases, or clauses—in a series.

Words in a series

> A zoo veterinarian is called upon to treat such diverse animals as elephants, gorillas, and antelopes.
> Murillo, Velázquez, and El Greco were three major seventeenth-century Spanish painters.
> The sporting goods store carries equipment for skiing, track, hockey, and weight lifting.

Phrases in a series

> The subway carried children going to school, adults going to work, and derelicts going to nowhere at all.
> The children playing hide-and-seek hid behind boulders, under bushes, or in trees.
> Running in the halls, smoking in the bathrooms, and shouting in the classrooms are not allowed.

Clauses in a series

> Edward Steichen photographed the Brooklyn Bridge, Georgia O'Keefe painted it, and Hart Crane wrote about it.
> Foster stole the ball, he passed it to Kennedy, and Kennedy made a basket.
> The yellow press proclaimed boldly that the man's character was hateful, that he was guilty as sin, and that he should be punished severely.

Note: The comma before the conjunction with items in a series is often omitted in newspapers and magazines. Follow your instructor's preference. Most handbooks recommend its use because it prevents misreading, as in the following cases.

> Harry, Anita, and Jayne have left already.

Without a comma before the conjunction, it is possible to read such sentences as directly addressing the first person named.

> Harry, Anita and Jayne have left already. (*Someone is addressing Harry and giving him information about Anita and Jayne.*)
> The menu listed the following sandwiches: bologna, chicken salad, pastrami, ham and cheese. (*four sandwiches*)
> The menu listed the following sandwiches: bologna, chicken salad, pastrami, ham, and cheese. (*five sandwiches*)

Coordinate adjectives

Use commas between coordinate adjectives that are not joined by *and*.

Coordinate adjectives each modify the noun independently.

> The comic was censored for his *audacious, vulgar* routine.
> The traveler paused before walking into the *deep, dark, mysterious* woods.
> The advertisement requested a *cheerful, sensitive, intelligent* woman to serve as governess.

Do not use a comma between cumulative adjectives.

Cumulative adjectives each modify the whole group of words that follow them.

> He gave her a *crystal perfume* bottle.
> On top of the stove was a set of *large shiny copper* pots.
> She carried an *expensive black leather* briefcase.

How can you distinguish coordinate adjectives from cumulative adjectives? In general, coordinate adjectives would sound natural with the word *and* between them, since each modifies the noun independently.

> The comic was censored for his audacious and vulgar routine.
> The traveler paused before walking into the deep and dark and mysterious woods.
> The advertisement requested a cheerful and sensitive and intelligent woman to serve as governess.

In addition, coordinate adjectives would sound natural with their order changed or reversed.

> The comic was censored for his vulgar, audacious routine.
> The traveler paused before walking into the mysterious, dark, deep woods.
> The advertisement requested an intelligent, sensitive, cheerful woman to serve as governess.

The order of cumulative adjectives cannot be changed. For example, no native English speaker would write sentences like the following:

> He gave her a perfume crystal bottle.
> On top of the stove was a set of copper shiny large pots.
> She carried an expensive leather black briefcase.

24b After Introductory Words, Phrases, and Clauses

Use a comma after an introductory word or expression that does not modify the subject of the sentence.

Why, we didn't realize the telegram was merely a hoax.
Yes, Washington did sleep here.
Well, that restaurant is certainly expensive.
On the other hand, its prices are justified.
By the way, what were you doing last night?

Use a comma after an introductory verbal or verbal phrase.

Smiling, she greeted us at the door.
While sleeping, Coleridge conceived the idea for "Kubla Khan."
To sketch a tree accurately, you must first study it closely.
Hoping to find happiness at last, Poe married his cousin.

Use a comma after an introductory series of prepositional phrases.

Under cover of night, the secret agent slipped across the border.
In this album of music from the 1960s, you will find several traditional folk songs.
In Jack London's famous story of a fight for survival in the Arctic, the man fails to light a fire.

Use a comma after any introductory phrase if there is a possibility that the sentence will be misread without it.

The day before, he had written her a letter.
After the tournament, winners received trophies and certificates.
Without hunting, the deer would soon become too numerous for the available food supply.

Use a comma after an introductory adverb clause.

Because John F. Kennedy was assassinated on the same day Aldous Huxley died, Huxley's death was given little attention by the press.
Although the alligator once faced extinction, its numbers are now increasing dramatically.
If the earth were to undergo another ice age, certain animals would flourish.

The comma after a very short introductory adverb clause is considered optional, unless its placement prevents misreading.

24c Before Certain Terminal Elements

Contrasted elements

Use a comma to set off an element that is being contrasted with what precedes it.

> Robert Graves claims he writes novels for profit, not for pleasure.
> Birds are warm-blooded, unlike reptiles.

Interrogative elements

Use a comma before a short interrogative element at the end of a sentence.

> I don't know anyone who hasn't seen at least one of Hitchcock's films, do you?
> Tom Stoppard's new play is wonderful, isn't it?
> The Vietnam War was never officially a war, or was it?

Terminal adverb clauses

In general, do not use a comma before an adverb clause that follows the main clause.

> Many people wept *when they saw the monument honoring the veterans of the war in Vietnam.*
> A national holiday has been established *so that Americans can honor Martin Luther King, Jr.*
> Who ruled England *before the Normans invaded it?*

However, there are several exceptions to the preceding rule.

Use a comma before a terminal adverb clause that begins with *although* or *even though*.

> Columbus found a rich world for the Spanish, although it was not the world he set out to reach.

Use a comma before a terminal adverb clause that begins with *since* or *while* when these words express cause or condition. Do not use a comma when these words express time.

> *Cause:*   He advocated prison reform, *since he knew first-hand the dehumanizing effects of prison life.*
>
> *Time:*   Mighty empires have come and gone *since the world began.*
>
> *Condition:*   Many critics praised her new play, *while others felt it was the worst she had ever written.*
>
> *Time:*   She wrote her first play *while she was vacationing in Venice.*

Use a comma before a terminal adverb clause beginning with *because* if the clause does not modify the verb nearest it.

Notice the difference in meaning between the two sentences below.

> I knew he *was absent* from work *because his supervisor was looking for him.*
>
> I *knew* he was absent from work, *because his supervisor was looking for him.*

In the first sentence above, the adverb clause modifies *was* (*absent*). It tells why he was absent—because his supervisor was looking for him. In the second sentence, the comma tells us that the adverb clause does not modify the verb closest to it.

Instead, it modifies the verb *knew*. It tells how I knew he was absent—because his supervisor was looking for him.

Use a comma before a terminal adverb clause that begins with *so that* when *so that* indicates result. Do not use a comma when *so that* indicates purpose.

> **Result:**   *Huckleberry Finn* combines strong plot and characterization with a profound insight into the human condition, *so that it can be read by children and adults alike.*
>
> **Purpose:**   Oliver Twist set out for London *so that he could escape punishment by the beadle.*

24d   Around Interrupting Elements

With nonessential appositives and adjective clauses

Use commas to set off a nonessential appositive. Do not use commas to set off an essential appositive.

A nonessential, or nonrestrictive, appositive gives additional information about the noun it refers to but is not essential for the identification of the noun it renames. In the following sentences, the nonessential appositives appear in *italics.*

> Neil Armstrong, *winner of the 1970 Silver Buffalo award for distinguished service to youth,* was the first man to walk on the moon.
> Duke Ellington, *a famous composer and bandleader,* helped gain acceptance for jazz as a serious musical form.
> St. Augustine, *the oldest city in the United States,* was founded by the Spanish.

An essential, or restrictive, appositive identifies the noun it refers to. As its name suggests, it is essential to the meaning of the sentence. In the following sentences, the essential apposi-tives appear in *italics*.

> My friend *George* works in a bookstore.
> The word *nice* has undergone many changes in meaning.
> Truman Capote's book *In Cold Blood* established a new literary form.

Use commas to set off a nonessential adjective clause. Do not use commas to set off an essential adjective clause.

A nonessential, or nonrestrictive, adjective clause provides extra information about the noun it modifies but is not essen-tial to identify the noun it modifies. In the following sen-tences, the nonessential adjective clauses appear in *italics*.

> Dinah Washington, *whom many consider the queen of the blues,* sang with Lionel Hampton's band.
> Elvis Presley, *whose records still sell well,* is regarded as the king of rock 'n' roll.
> Modern dance, *which was originated by Martha Graham,* has had a profound influence on the dance world.

An essential, or restrictive, adjective clause limits or identifies the noun it refers to. It is essential to the meaning of the sentence. In the following sentences, the essential adjective clauses appear in *italics*.

> The person *who buys the first ticket* will win a trip to Mexico.
> The scientist *whose research is judged the most important* will be given a grant.
> The performance *that they gave last night* was not up to their usual standard.

Note: The pronoun *that* is used only with essential clauses. The pronoun *which* may be used with either essential or non-essential clauses.

Whether or not an adjective clause is set off with commas can make a major difference to the meaning of a sentence. For example, compare the following two sentences:

Essential: The first president who was born in Virginia was George Washington.

Nonessential: The first president, who was born in Virginia, was George Washington.

The first sentence tells you that George Washington was the first Virginia-born president. The second sentence tells you that George Washington was the first president. As additional information, it mentions that he was born in Virginia.

Now compare the next two sentences.

Essential: The first president who was born in New York was Martin Van Buren.

Nonessential: The first president, who was born in New York, was Martin Van Buren.

The first sentence tells you that Martin Van Buren was the first New York-born president. This statement is true. However, the second sentence says that Martin Van Buren was the first president. This statement is obviously not true.

Finally, compare these two sentences.

Essential: The tenants who did not pay their rent were evicted.

Nonessential: The tenants, who did not pay their rent, were evicted.

The first sentence tells you that only the tenants who did not pay their rent were evicted. The second sentence tells you that all the tenants were evicted. As additional information, it tells the reason they were evicted: they did not pay their rent.

With adverb clauses and interrupting or parenthetical adverbs

In general, use commas to set off an internal adverb clause that is parenthetical or that separates the subject of the main clause from its predicate.

> Harry Truman, although a newspaper headline prematurely declared otherwise, won the 1948 election over Thomas E. Dewey.
>
> Columbus, as we have seen, died without his true accomplishments recognized or honored.

Use commas to set off adverbs (*however, accordingly, moreover, nevertheless,* and so on) and transitional phrases (*in addition, to sum up, on the other hand, for example*) used parenthetically.

> Many acclaimed writers, however, have written mysteries.
>
> A popular mystery set in a fourteenth-century monastery, moreover, was written by a professor of semiotics.
>
> Edmund Wilson, on the other hand, considered mysteries simply a waste of time.

With parenthetical expressions

Use commas to set off a parenthetical expression within a sentence.

Expressions that comment on or give additional information about the main part of the sentence are considered parenthetical.

> Jazz, many critics feel, is America's greatest contribution to the arts.
>
> You, like most people, probably do not know that the person responsible for the completion of the Brooklyn Bridge was a woman.

George Washington, according to the old-style calendar used by the colonists, was born on February 11.

Use commas to set off words that identify the source of a quotation within a sentence.

"The advance for the book," said Calvin Trillin, "should be at least as much as the cost of the lunch at which it was discussed."

"You can be a little ungrammatical," Robert Frost claimed, "if you come from the right part of the country."

"Just get it down on paper," advised Maxwell Perkins, "and we'll see what to do with it."

Use commas after or around words in direct address.

Here, my fellow citizens, is an issue we can agree on.
Ladies and gentlemen, may I present our speaker.
Sam, you've won the prize!

With dates and addresses

With dates, use commas to separate the day of the week from the month, the day of the month from the year, and the year from the rest of the sentence.

Please reply by Tuesday, January 7.
The *Titanic* hit an iceberg and sank on April 15, 1912.
The Allies landed at Normandy on Tuesday, June 6, 1944, and began the offensive that would lead to the downfall of the Third Reich.

Note: Do not use a comma when only the month and the day (e.g., April 15) or only the month and the year (e.g., April 1912) are given or when the following form is used: 15 April 1912.

With addresses, use a comma to separate the name from the street address, the street address from the city, and the city from the state. Use a comma after the zip code (or after the state if no zip code is given) to separate the entire address from the rest of the sentence. Do not use a comma between the state and the zip code.

> The book is available from the Macmillan Publishing Company, 866 Third Avenue, New York, New York 10022.
>
> He lived at 579 Montenegro Avenue, Frisco, Colorado, until 1982.

24e Misused commas

Do not use a comma to separate a subject from its predicate.

> *Not:* The album that he cut last year, sold over a million copies.
>
> *But:* The album that he cut last year sold over a million copies.
>
> *Not:* The painting hanging on the wall, was of the last duchess.
>
> *But:* The painting hanging on the wall was of the last duchess.
>
> *Not:* How a bill becomes a law, was the subject discussed in class today.
>
> *But:* How a bill becomes a law was the subject discussed in class today.

Do not use a comma to separate a verb from its complement.

> *Not:* Did you know, that chimpanzees can communicate through sign language?
>
> *But:* Did you know that chimpanzees can communicate through sign language?
>
> *Not:* After discussing the issue for several hours, we realized that our decision must be, to place safety concerns before cost considerations.

But: After discussing the issue for several hours, we realized that our decision must be to place safety concerns before cost considerations.

Not: The speaker declared that the government must let us know, why we are involved in this conflict.
But: The speaker declared that the government must let us know why we are involved in this conflict.

Do not use a comma between cumulative adjectives.

Not: She declared him to be a handsome, young man.
But: She declared him to be a handsome young man.

Not: He was sentenced to a nine-year, prison term.
But: He was sentenced to a nine-year prison term.

Not: She wore a knee-length, red, suede skirt.
But: She wore a knee-length red suede skirt.

Do not use a comma to separate the two parts of a compound subject, a compound verb, or a compound complement.

Not: High ceilings, and cathedral windows are two features I look for in a house.
But: High ceilings and cathedral windows are two features I look for in a house.

Not: The skier cleaned his boots, and then sprayed them with a water repellent.
But: The skier cleaned his boots and then sprayed them with a water repellent.

Not: For breakfast she ordered a ham omelet, and a side dish of home fries.
But: For breakfast she ordered a ham omelet and a side dish of home fries.

Do not use a comma to separate two dependent clauses joined by *and*.

Not: They promised that they would obey the laws of their new country, and that they would uphold its principles.

But: They promised that they would obey the laws of their new country and that they would uphold its principles.

Not: Anyone who attends this school, and who lives off-campus must sign this list.

But: Anyone who attends this school and who lives off-campus must sign this list.

Not: He wrote that he would stop loving her when dogs could fly, and when fish could sing.

But: He wrote that he would stop loving her when dogs could fly and when fish could sing.

Do not use a comma to separate the parts of a comparison.

Not: During the five months she spent alone in the woods, she was more productive, than she had ever been before.

But: During the five months she spent alone in the woods, she was more productive than she had ever been before.

Not: The situation is not as bad, as we had expected.

But: The situation is not as bad as we had expected.

Not: It is difficult to imagine another museum containing such a magnificent collection of medieval art, as the Cloisters in New York City.

But: It is difficult to imagine another museum containing such a magnificent collection of medieval art as the Cloisters in New York City.

Do not use a comma before an opening parenthesis. However, a comma may follow a closing parenthesis.

Not: David McCullough, who wrote *The Path Between the Seas*, (winner of a National Book Award) visited the Panama Canal.

But: David McCullough, who-wrote *The Path Between the Seas* (winner of a National Book Award), visited the Panama Canal.

Exercise 1

Place commas where they are needed in the following sentences. Some of the sentences are correct as written.

1. Angola is rich in minerals diamonds and iron ore.

2. Scald the milk with the rice and then set it aside.

3. Read Jane Austen's *Persuasion* to understand the nineteenth-century woman and Dickens' *Hard Times* to understand the century's economic conditions.

4. I don't think I can afford the trip nor am I sure I want to go.

5. The fine structure and genetic organization of the chromosomes of humans and chimpanzees may be very similar say some researchers.

6. In the back of this book you will find a glossary, a brief atlas, and an index.

7. We will choose three new officers: president vice-president and secretary and treasurer.

8. Public figures caught in scandals can often make their fortunes by writing books and giving lectures and interviews.

9. A few of her poems seem to refer to a happy marriage but divorce is the topic of many.

10. Bees swarm because the hive is overcrowded or the queen bee is old.

Exercise 2

Place commas where they are needed in the following sentences. Some of the sentences are correct as written.

1. The chairperson opened the meeting with a long boring recital of her goals.
2. Did you read their list of the twenty best modern novels?
3. The senator was praised for her long distinguished career.
4. In the sun on the porch steps lay my plump Persian cat sleeping peacefully.
5. To tell the truth I have no intention of going to the exhibition.
6. Dag Hammarskjold secretary general of the United Nations, was killed in a plane crash.
7. I am hungry aren't you?
8. Dean Payne may I meet with you sometime in the next few days?
9. The conference will be held in Abilene not in Amarillo.
10. The poet Edna St. Vincent Millay is now receiving attention by literary critics.

Exercise 3

Place commas where they are needed in the following sentences. Some of the sentences are correct as written.

1. Hammurabi, you probably know was a Babylonian king.

2. The Carthaginian general Hannibal led his army across the Alps.

3. Benito Juárez, a Mexican hero took part in the overthrow of Santa Anna.

4. His defeat, however, was a long and bloody process.

5. Robotics and fiber optics are technological fields in which the United States hopes to keep ahead of others.

6. Little is known about the life of Confucius whose teachings are the basis of Confucianism.

7. Children used to collect stamps and coins and also baseball cards which came in packs of bubble gum.

8. Swarming bees will not sting since they have no defensive sense of place about their temporary location.

9. "Few people can be happy" claimed Bertrand Russell "unless they hate some other person, nation, or creed."

10. "Anybody who hates children and dogs," said W. C. Fields "can't be all bad."

Exercise 4

Place commas where they are needed in the following sentences. Some of the sentences are correct as written.

1. As a result of *Brand* and *Peer Gynt* Ibsen became known around the world.

2. The author of what is considered one of the great novels of modern times Marcel Proust had to subsidize the publishing of *Swann's Way* himself.

3. Because most of us have read *The Scarlet Letter* we are familiar with Hawthorne's views on the nature of sin.

4. Hawthorne gained notice after the publication of *The Scarlet Letter.*

5. The story is long enough to be a novel only because of the preliminary material about the Customs House.

6. Samuel Johnson who wrote *Lives of the Poets* which consists of fifty-two brief biographies is perhaps best remembered for his dictionary.

7. James Boswell on the other hand is best remembered for his biography of his friend Dr. Johnson.

8. Some readers prefer biography and history while others prefer all their reading to be fiction.

9. Celebrities may choose biographers and select the material for the books so that their lives will be reported as they would like them to have been lived.

10. That the Russians particularly like William Faulkner's novels is surprising since Faulkner is not easy for native Americans to read.

25 The Semicolon

The **semicolon** links independent clauses or separates items in a series. The semicolon indicates a pause longer than that taken for a comma but not so long as that taken for a period.

25a Between Independent Clauses

Use a semicolon between two closely related independent clauses not joined by a coordinating conjunction.

> Years ago caviar was an inexpensive food often given away free at taverns; today it is one of the most expensive foods in the world.
> Truffles are the food of the rich; turnips are the food of the poor.
> Truffles are the food of the rich; turnips, the poor.

The comma in the third sentence indicates that a part of the second clause has been left out.

Use a semicolon between two independent clauses joined by a conjunctive adverb or by a transitional phrase.

> Columbus sent cacao beans back to Spain; however, the Spanish were not particularly impressed.
> Cortez brought back more cacao beans; moreover, he brought back the knowledge of how to prepare them.
> In some cultures insects are considered delicacies; for example, the ancient Romans thought the cicada a delightful morsel.

Use a semicolon between two independent clauses joined with a coordinating conjunction if one or both of these clauses contain internal commas or if the clauses are particularly complex.

With fairly short clauses, either a comma or a semicolon is acceptable.

Persephone was the daughter of Demeter, the goddess of agriculture, and she was represented by the pomegranate, the symbol of fertility.

Persephone was the daughter of Demeter, the goddess of agriculture; and she was represented by the pomegranate, the symbol of fertility.

With longer and more complex clauses, the semicolon is preferred.

In Greek mythology Persephone was the daughter of Demeter, the goddess of agriculture; and she was represented by the pomegranate, the symbol of fertility, of which she ate the seeds after Hades carried her down into the underworld.

In Italy during the Renaissance, the inside of the opened pomegranate, which is divided into compartments containing colorful seeds, was used as the basis for a popular fabric design; and in the Middle East during ancient times, this beautiful fruit figured prominently in the decorative arts.

Because of its abundance of seeds, some Westerners find the pomegranate, which originated in the Middle East, unpalatable as a food, although pleasing as a decoration; but supporters of the pomegranate, of whom there are many, find the seeds no drawback, since they like to chew these crunchy tidbits.

25b   Between Items in a Series

Use semicolons to separate items in a series if the individual items are long or contain commas.

In the language of flowers, each flower represents a particular attribute: belladonna, which is a deadly poison, silence; citron, which produces a sour, inedible fruit, ill-natured beauty; blue periwinkle, which is small and delicate, early friendship.

The guide grouped wildflowers into many families, four of which were the cattail family, Typhaceae; the arrowhead family, Alismataceae; the yellow-eyed grass family, Xyridaceae; and the lizard-tail family, Saururaceae.

25c Misused Semicolons

Do not use a semicolon between noncoordinate elements.

Not: In Shakespeare's *Hamlet,* after Ophelia is rebuffed; she communicates her despair through the language of flowers.

But: In Shakespeare's *Hamlet,* after Ophelia is rebuffed, she communicates her despair through the language of flowers.

Not: She became famous for her photographs of wildflowers; especially for those of mountain laurel.

But: She became famous for her photographs of wildflowers, especially for those of mountain laurel.

Exercise

Circle where the punctuation mark should be replaced by a semicolon in each of the following sentences. Two of the sentences are correct as written.

1. Some people collect rocks and minerals, others, seashells.

2. The color of turquoise ranges from sky blue to apple green, however, gem-quality turquoise is blue.

3. Turquoise can be found in the American Southwest; however, the finest turquoise comes from Iran.

4. Quartz is abundant in North America, for example, it can be found in Ontario, New Jersey, Arkansas, Colorado, and California.

5. Amethyst, which is a violet to red-purple quartz, is particularly beautiful, as a result, it is often used for jewelry.

6. Tigereye, a quartz with a changeable luster, is often used for cameos, which are stones cut in such a way that the raised design is of one hue and the background of another, and, like adventurine and rose quartz, it is fashioned into cabochons, which are highly polished, unfaceted gems.

7. Like rocks and minerals, seashells can be used for decoration, in fact, they can be found on Greek and Roman vases as well as in modern jewelry.

8. Some members of the cowry family are particularly interesting: the measled cowry, *Cypraea zebra,* which has circular white spots on its back, the chestnut cowry, *Cypraea spadicea,* which has an irregular spot of light chestnut or grayish brown on the middle of its back, and the Atlantic gray cowry, *Cypraea cinerea,* which has small blackish spots or streaks on its sides.

9. One living mollusk that is particularly beautiful is the ringed top shell, another is the four-toothed nerite.

10. Many of the shells called jewel boxes are also brightly colored, but most jingle shells are translucent.

26 The Colon

The **colon** introduces elements that explain, illustrate, or expand the preceding part of the sentence. It calls attention to the word, phrase, clause, or quotation that follows it.

26a Before Elements Introduced Formally

Use a colon when formally introducing a statement or a quotation.

Capitalize the first word of a formal statement or a quotation following a colon.

> One of the guiding principles of our government may be stated as follows: All people are created equal.
> Though Murphy's identity is not known, Murphy's Law seems to be a truth: "If anything can go wrong, it will."

Use a colon when formally introducing a series of items.

> The picture gallery at the Vatican contains magnificent treasures: Raphael's *Madonna of Foligno,* Titian's *Madonna of San Niccolô dei Frari,* Leonardo's *St. Jerome,* Caravaggio's *Deposition,* Rouault's *Autumn,* and Utrillo's *The Church of St. Auxonne.*
> From 1933 through 1981, unsuccessful assassination attempts were made on the lives of the following presidents: Franklin Roosevelt, Harry Truman, Gerald Ford, and Ronald Reagan.
> Nine planets circle the sun: Mercury, Venus, Earth, Mars, Jupiter, Saturn, Uranus, Neptune, and Pluto.

26b Before Formal Appositives

Use a colon before a formal appositive, including one beginning with a phrase such as *namely, that is, specifically,* or *in other words.*

In many cases a dash would also be appropriate in this situation.

> The scholar wrote mysteries for one reason and one reason only: to make money.

> Domenikos Theotocopoulos, whom many consider one of the
> greatest painters of all times, is better known by his pseu-
> donym: El Greco.
> In 1961, Kennedy made one of the toughest decisions of his
> presidency: namely, to back the invasion at the Bay of Pigs.

Notice that the colon in the third example appears *before* the
word *namely*.

26c Between Two Independent Clauses

**Use a colon between two independent clauses when the sec-
ond clause explains or expands the first.**

> Cubism was more than a new movement: it was a revolution.
> After reading the letter, he did something that surprised me: he
> laughed.

The clause following the colon may begin with a capital or a
lowercase letter. However, a lowercase letter is preferred.

26d In Salutations and Bibliographical Entries

Use a colon after a salutation in a formal letter or speech.

> Dear Dr. Jacoby:
> Ladies and Gentlemen:
> Members of the Board:

**Use a colon between the city and the publisher in a biblio-
graphical entry.**

> New York: Macmillan
> London: John Murray
> Chicago: The University of Chicago Press

Use a colon between a title and its subtitle.

> *Tutankhamen:* The Untold Story
> *Nooks and Crannies:* An Unusual Walking Tour Guide to New
>   York City
> *The Seeing Hand:* A Treasury of Great Master Drawings

26e   Misused Colons

Do **not** use a colon after a form of the verb *be,* after a preposition, or between a verb and its object.

Not: Three devices the ancient Romans used to tell time were: sundials, water clocks, and sand-filled glasses.

But: Three devices the ancient Romans used to tell time were sundials, water clocks, and sand-filled glasses.

Or: The Romans used three devices to tell time: sundials, water clocks, and sand-filled glasses.

Not: In 1966, France effectively withdrew from NATO, which thereafter consisted of: Belgium, Canada, Denmark, Great Britain, Greece, Iceland, Italy, Luxembourg, the Netherlands, Norway, Portugal, Turkey, the United States, and West Germany.

But: In 1966, France effectively withdrew from NATO, which thereafter consisted of Belgium, Canada, Denmark, Great Britain, Greece, Iceland, Italy, Luxembourg, the Netherlands, Norway, Portugal, Turkey, the United States, and West Germany.

Not: The store manager ordered: six microwave ovens, four dishwashers, seven coffee makers, and eleven toasters.

But: The store manager ordered six microwave ovens, four dishwashers, seven coffee makers, and eleven toasters.

Exercise

Place a colon where it is necessary in each of the following sentences. Some of the sentences are correct as written.

1. Poets would do well to listen to Ezra Pound "Music rots when it gets *too far* from the dance. Poetry atrophies when it gets *too far* from music."

2. The United Kingdom includes England, Scotland, Wales, and Northern Ireland.

3. Although titled *Trout Fishing in America,* Brautigan's book is not about trout fishing it is about life.

4. She subscribes to the following magazines *Smithsonian, Newsweek, Time,* and *The Atlantic.*

5. The reference books he has at home are an atlas, an almanac, two dictionaries, and an encyclopedia.

27 The Dash

The **dash** is less formal than the colon. It is used to give emphasis or clarity to extra information in a sentence. When typing, produce a dash by two hyphens without a space before, after, or between them (– –).

27a With an Introductory Series

Use a dash to separate an introductory series from its summarizing clause.

His own party, the opposition, and the public——all were astounded by his resignation.
Chaucer, Shakespeare, Malory——these were her favorite writers.

27b With Parenthetical Elements

Use dashes to set off a parenthetical element you wish to emphasize.

> The castle was surrounded by a moat and contained——I found this astounding——an actual dungeon.
> On his first day as a volunteer, he fought a fire in——of all places——the firehouse.

Use dashes to clarify a parenthetical element that contains commas.

> Of our first five presidents, four——George Washington, Thomas Jefferson, James Madison, and James Monroe——came from Virginia.
> The first recorded Olympic Games——which, you will be surprised to know, this reporter did not see——were held in 776 B.C.

27c With Terminal Elements

Use a dash to introduce informally a terminal element that explains or illustrates the information in the main part of the sentence.

> They pledged to prevent what seemed inevitable——war.
> He battled his worst enemy——himself.
> He little appreciated her greatest attribute——her sense of humor.

Use a dash to introduce informally a terminal element that is a break in thought or a shift in tone.

> He confessed that he was desperately in love——with me.
> No one loves a gossip——except another gossip.
> "But she said she had——I can't believe it," Patrick exclaimed.

Exercise

Circle where dashes belong in each of the following sentences.

1. Wordsworth, Keats, Shelley, Byron these are the most popular of the Romantic poets.

2. People who live in glass houses shouldn't throw stones and neither should you!

3. Three of the most beautiful bridges in the world the Brooklyn Bridge, the George Washington Bridge, and the Verrazano-Narrows Bridge are in New York City.

4. We found Dr. Jekyll in his library no one will believe this changing into Mr. Hyde.

5. The speaker hesitated, then sputtered, "I just want to let me start again."

28 Parentheses

Parentheses enclose information or comments that break the continuity of the sentence or paragraph. Unlike the dash, which tends to emphasize, parentheses minimize the importance of the material they enclose. The information within parentheses should be of such a nature that it may be omitted without changing the essential meaning of the sentence.

28a With Parenthetical Comments and Additional Information

Use parentheses to enclose comments or additional information that you do not wish to emphasize.

> On August 11, 1960, Chad (see map) became independent.
> Charles Darwin (1809–1882) was a contemporary of Abraham Lincoln.
> Ibsen's *A Doll's House* (which was quite revolutionary for its time) ends with Nora walking out on her husband.

Do not use a capital letter or a period for a parenthetical sentence within another sentence. Use a capital letter and a period for a parenthetical sentence that stands by itself.

Sentence within another sentence

> After the Civil War, carpetbaggers (their name came from their habit of carrying their belongings in a bag made of carpet material) took advantage of Southern blacks who had just been given the vote.
> Demosthenes warned the Athenians against King Philip of Macedon (he felt King Philip was a threat to their liberty).
> The Democratic Party (this is the party founded by that lover of liberty, Thomas Jefferson) was divided on the question of slavery.

Notice that in the second example the period ending the main sentence goes *outside* the closing parenthesis.

Sentence standing by itself

> In the fifteenth century, Christian I founded the Oldenburg dynasty. (In modern Denmark, the ruling family traces its roots to him.) Christian II, however, was removed from the throne in 1523.
> Elizabeth Barrett Browning is remembered in part for her beautiful love poems. (She was married to Robert Browning.)

In the original *King Kong,* the huge creature climbed what was then the tallest building in the world, the Empire State Building. (In the second version of the movie, he climbed the World Trade Center.) There he was attacked by airplanes.

Notice that the period ending the parenthetical sentence goes *inside* the closing parenthesis.

28b With Items in a Series

Use parentheses to enclose numerals and letters designating items in a series.

When accepting a credit card from a customer, you should (a) check the customer's signature against the card, (b) call the credit-card company for approval, and (c) write the approval code on the credit slip.

In the nineteenth century, the United States was involved in four wars: (1) the War of 1812, (2) the Mexican War, (3) the Civil War, and (4) the Spanish-American War.

28c With Other Punctuation Marks

Place a comma, semicolon, or colon *outside* a closing parenthesis.

Although most Americans have heard of the Battle of Lexington and Concord (which occurred on April 19, 1775), many do not know that it is commemorated as Patriots' Day in Massachusetts.

Maine has successfully preserved its northern moose population (the moose is Maine's official state animal); however, the state's deer population is now endangered by the growing moose herd.

Carter carried only six states (plus the District of Columbia**):**
Georgia, Hawaii, Maryland, Minnesota, Rhode Island, and
West Virginia.

Place a question mark or exclamation point *inside* a closing
parenthesis if the parenthetical expression itself is a question
or an exclamation.

Sean was astonished when he opened the door to his room and
found a letter (who could have put it there**?)** lying on the
floor.

The Founding Fathers considered many different animals (Benjamin Franklin suggested the turkey**!)** before they decided
to make the bald eagle the national symbol of the United
States.

Place a question mark or exclamation point *outside* a closing
parenthesis if the sentence is a question or exclamation but the
parenthetical expression is not.

Did you know that Lewis Carroll wrote *Alice in Wonderland* for
a real girl named Alice (Alice Liddell**)?**

Never was I more surprised than when I found wild berries
growing in a New York City park (there were both raspber-
ries and blackberries**)!**

29 Brackets

Brackets enclose information inserted into quotations, and
they take the place of parentheses within parentheses.
Brackets are used mainly in formal writing.

29a With Inserted Information

Use brackets to enclose information inserted into direct quotations for clarification.

"The fellow [Rubens] mixes blood with his colors," claimed Guido Reni.

Groucho Marx quipped, "From the moment I picked your [S. J. Perelman's] book up until I laid it down, I was convulsed with laughter. Someday I intend reading it."

"Government [in a democracy] cannot be stronger or more tough-minded than its people," said Adlai Stevenson.

Use brackets to enclose editorial comments inserted into quoted material.

According to Clarence Darrow, "The first half of our lives is ruined by our parents [how many people under twenty agree with this!] and the second half by our children."

Notice that the exclamation point is placed inside the closing bracket because it is part of the editorial comment.

The word *sic* or *thus* enclosed in brackets is used to indicate that an incorrect or seemingly incorrect or inappropriate word is not a mistake on the part of the present writer but appears in the original quotation.

Jane Austen parodied the popular melodramatic fiction of her day in "Love and Freindship [*sic*]," which she completed at the age of fourteen.

Notice that the comma is placed *outside* the closing bracket.

29b With Parentheses

Use brackets to replace parentheses within parentheses.

Some humpback whales reach a length of over fifty feet. (See p. 89 [chart] for a comparison of the size of whales.)

Several books are available on the life and times of "Boss" Tweed. (For a revisionist picture of Tweed, we suggest Leo Hershkowitz's *Tweed's New York* [Garden City, N.Y.: Anchor Press/Doubleday, 1977].)

Notice that the period is placed *inside* the closing parenthesis because the entire sentence is enclosed by parentheses.

> The reading list contains several books dealing with the issue of freedom of the press (for example, Fred W. Friendly's *Minnesota Rag: The Dramatic Story of the Landmark Supreme Court Case that Gave New Meaning to Freedom of the Press* [New York: Random House, 1981]).

Notice that the period is placed *outside* the closing parenthesis because only part of the sentence is enclosed by parentheses.

Exercise

Add parentheses and/or brackets where necessary to enclose information in each of the following sentences.

1. According to George Bernard Shaw, ''The road to ignorance is paved with good editions *sic*.''

2. Until recently, Picasso's *Guernica* see p. 458 could be seen at the Museum of Modern Art.

3. A month after the assassination of Archduke Franz Ferdinand on June 28, 1914, Emperor Franz Josef Austria declared war on Serbia.

4. Unlike many paintings of the time, the portraits of Modigliani show a world of tranquility how far away this world is from the reality of Modigliani's life!.

5. Dance plays an important role in the art of the early part of the

twentieth century. (In 1909, Matisse completed his mural *The Dance* [see plate 7.

---

30 Quotation Marks

Quotation marks enclose quoted material and certain kinds of titles. They are always used in pairs.

30a For Direct Quotations

Use quotation marks to enclose a direct quotation—the exact words of a speaker or writer.

> When one character says to Mae West, "My goodness, those diamonds are beautiful," West replies, "Goodness had nothing whatever to do with it."
>
> In *The Code of the Woosters,* Bertie vividly describes the aunt he fears: "Aunt Agatha, who eats broken bottles and wears barbed wire next to the skin."
>
> The opening lines set the tone of the poem: "I will be the gladdest thing/Under the sun!" (*The slash indicates the end of a line in a poem.*)

When writing dialogue, begin a new paragraph each time the speaker changes.

> "This coat costs $25.00," said the seller at the flea market.
> "That's too much," said the customer.
> "Did I say $25.00?" responded the seller. "I meant $15.00."

30b Block Quotations

When quoting a **prose** passage of considerable length, you omit quotation marks as you use the block quotation form. The Modern Language Association's (MLA) guidelines advise **block quotation** form for four or more lines of prose; The American Psychological Association (APA) specifies its use for passages of forty or more words. Type the material double-spaced. If you are using MLA form, indent ten spaces from the left-hand margin. Further indent three spaces for a paragraph, but only where a paragraph appears in the original. APA guidelines suggest that you indent only five spaces from the left-hand margin, indenting five additional spaces for a paragraph. Bear in mind that these instructions apply principally to material that is being prepared for publication. Common sense and your instructor may adjust these rules when you are preparing a paper for a class assignment and may suggest single-spacing in block form.

Here are two examples following MLA rules:

In "The American Scholar" Ralph Waldo Emerson warns:

> Meek young men grow up in libraries, believing it their duty to accept the views which Cicero, which Locke, which Bacon have given; forgetful that Cicero, Locke, and Bacon were only young men in libraries when they wrote these books.
>
> Hence, instead instead of Man Thinking, we have the bookworm. Hence the book-learned class. . . . Hence the restorers of readings, the emendators, the bibliomaniacs of all degrees.

In a speech he made in New York in 1911, Woodrow Wilson underscored the importance of business:

> Business underlies everything in our national life, including our spiritual life. Witness the fact that in the

Lord's Prayer the first petition is for daily bread. No one can
worship God or love his neighbor on an empty stomach.

Here is an example following APA rules:

In <u>Psychological Types</u>, Jung stated:

> The dynamic principle of fantasy is play, which belongs also
> to the child, and as such it appears to be inconsistent with the
> principle of serious work. But without this playing with fantasy no
> creative work has ever yet come to birth. The debt we owe to the
> play of imagination is incalculable.

When quoting four or more lines of *poetry,* double-space
lines and indent, according to MLA guidelines, ten spaces or
fewer if the poetic lines are long (APA style holds to five
spaces as with prose quotations). Type the poem line for line,
following the spatial arrangement of the original. Do not use
quotation marks.

Thoreau, as he explains in <u>Walden, or Life in the Woods</u>, lived less
than two miles from the village of Concord and yet felt that he was living
on a distant star, like the shepherd in the anonymous poem he quotes:

> There was a shepherd that did live,
> And held his thoughts as high
> As were the mounts whereon his flocks
> Did hourly feed him by.

In the first four lines of "Oysters," Anne Sexton makes the oysters seem
human:

> Oysters we ate,
> sweet blue babies,

twelve eyes looked up at me,

running with lemon and Tabasco.

30c　For Quotations Within Quotations

Use single quotation marks to enclose quoted material contained within a quotation.

In "Silence," Marianne Moore wrote: "My father used to say, 'Superior people never make long visits.' "

The British humorist Robert Morley once joked, "Beware of the conversationalist who adds 'in other words.' He is merely starting afresh."

Jensen looked up from his research and declared, "I've found the answer. It was Henry Clay who said, 'I would rather be right than President.'"

30d　For Titles of Short Works

Use quotation marks to enclose the quoted titles of short stories, short poems, one-act plays, essays, articles, subdivisions of books, episodes of a television series, songs, short musical compositions, and dissertations.

In his poem "Son of Frankenstein," Edward Field reveals the loneliness of the Frankenstein monster.

In the second half of *Brideshead Revisited*, which is entitled "A Twitch upon the Thread," Charles returns from South America, and Lord Marchmain returns to Brideshead to die.

Joan Didion details the pattern of shopping malls in "On the Mall."

Use underlining for the titles of longer works (see pages 309–310.

30e With Other Punctuation Marks

Place a period or a comma *inside* a closing quotation mark.

> In "Perseid," John Barth writes, "Stories last longer than men, stones than stories, stars than stones."
>
> "I don't want to talk grammar," Eliza Doolittle says in *Pygmalion.* "I want to talk like a lady."
>
> "After all," says Scarlett, "tomorrow is another day."

Place a semicolon or a colon *outside* a closing quotation mark.

> The critic wrote that the play demonstrated the playwright's "dissatisfaction with satisfaction"; this comment, I felt, was more preposterous than the play itself.
>
> In the American detective story, few women are private eyes. One of the best known of these women appears in Stuart Palmer's "The Riddle of the Twelve Amethysts": Hildegarde Withers.

Place a question mark or an exclamation point *inside* a closing quotation mark if the quotation itself is a question or exclamation.

> The song I was trying to recall is "Will You Love Me in December?"
>
> Upon reaching the summit of Mount Everest, Sherpa Tensing declared, "We've done the bugger!"

Place a question mark or an exclamation point *outside* the closing quotation mark if the sentence is a question or exclamation but the quotation itself is not.

> Who first said, "Big Brother is watching you"?
>
> What a scene she caused by saying, "I don't want to"!

If both the sentence and the quotation are questions or exclamations, use only one question mark or exclamation point, and place it *inside* the closing quotation mark.

Why did she cause a scene by asking, "Who is that woman**?**"

Of course, the rules for using other punctuation marks with quotation marks apply to single quotation marks as well.

Harold asked, "Do you know who coined the term 'the brain trust'**?**" (*Question mark ends Harold's quotation.*)

Gordon said, "I can hear the crowd shouting, 'Long live the king**!**' " (*Exclamation point ends quotation within quotation.*)

30f Misused Quotation Marks

Do not use quotation marks to enclose indirect quotations.

Not: The seer declared that **"**they would win the war against the Macedonians.**"**

But: The seer declared that they would win the war against the Macedonians.

Not: The editorial proclaimed that **"**the President would win the next election.**"**

But: The editorial proclaimed that the President would win the next election.

Note: The word *that* is used to introduce an indirect quotation, *not* a direct quotation.

Do not use quotation marks to enclose a title used as the heading of a paper, theme, or essay.

Suicide and the Modern Poet
Science Fiction in the 1930s
Communication Among Chimpanzees

Exercise

Identify where quotation marks are needed in the following sentences. Some of the sentences do not need quotation marks.

1. Aristotle said, There is no great genius without a mixture of madness.

2. Aristotle claimed that genius needs a mixture of madness.

3. Drew asked, Do you know who called a best-seller a gilded tomb of mediocre talent?

4. Have you read Joyce Carol Oates' short story Where Are You Going, Where Have You Been?

5. Charlotte advised, Try to remember Cicero's statement on grief: There is no grief which time does not lessen and soften.

6. Balzac said, If we could but paint with the hand as we see with the eye!

7. The best, said Ben Franklin, is the cheapest.

8. Disraeli declared that Nature, like man, sometimes weeps for gladness.

9. Robert Frost concludes his poem Birches with the line, One could do worse than be a swinger of birches.

10. John Kennedy told the German people that he felt himself to be a Berliner.

31 Ellipsis Points

Ellipsis points are equally spaced dots, or periods. They indicate that part of a quotation has been omitted.

Use three ellipsis points within a quotation to indicate that part of the quotation has been left out, or omitted.

Partial quotations do not need ellipsis points at beginning and end.

> *Not:*   Stewart Udall declares that Indians have "● ● ● a reverence for the life-giving earth● ● ●"
>
> *But:*   Stewart Udall declares that Indians have "a reverence for the life-giving earth."

When typing, leave a space before the first ellipsis point, a space between each of the points, and a space after the last point.

> In *The Other America: Poverty in the United States,* Michael Harrington writes: "They [the poor] are not simply neglected ● ● ● they are not seen."
>
> In *The Quiet Crisis,* Stewart Udall writes: "The most common trait ● ● ● is a reverence for the life-giving earth, and the native American shared this elemental ethic: the land was alive to his touch, and he, its son, was brother to all creatures."
>
> The Atlantic Charter states: "Eighth, they believe that all of the nations of the world ● ● ● must come to the abandonment of the use of force."

Use a period and three ellipsis points to indicate that the end of a sentence has been left out of a quotation.

> Huck said, "It most froze me to hear such talk● ● ● Thinks I, this is what comes of my not thinking."

The review said, "The book promises a cornucopia of unusual characters● ● ● That promise is fully realized."

In Susan Fromberg Schaeffer's *The Madness of a Seduced Woman*, Margaret says, "I don't read books much anymore because I don't much care about how things turn out● ● ● What interests me, I suppose, is how people get to where they find themselves in the end."

32 Underlining

Underlining in a typed or handwritten paper serves the same purpose as *italics* in a printed work. It highlights, or sets apart, certain titles, words, or phrases.

Underline the titles of books, full-length musical compositions, plays, and long poems and the names of newspapers, magazines, ships, boats, and aircraft.

The Light in the Forest (*book*)
Madame Butterfly (*opera*)
The Rape of the Lock (*long poem*)
the Mayflower (*ship*)

Be careful to underline only the exact title or name. Do not underline words added to complete the meaning of the title.

The Atlantic magazine (*The word* magazine *is not part of the name.*)
the London Times or The Times of London (London *is not part of the name.*)

Be careful to underline all the words that make up the title.

The Decline and Fall of the Roman Empire (The *is part of the title.*)

<u>A Childhood</u> (A *is part of the title.*)
<u>Standard & Poor's New Issue Investor</u> (Standard & Poor's *is part of the title.*)

(Do not underline the heading of your own paper.)

Underline foreign words or phrases that are not commonly used in English.

In general, a word or phrase need not be underlined if it is listed in a standard English dictionary. For example, the Spanish word *siesta,* the French phrase *coup de grace,* and the Latin phrase *ad infinitum* are now considered part of English and are not underlined.

German women were traditionally expected to confine themselves to <u>Kinder</u>, <u>Kirche</u>, <u>Küche</u>.
<u>Chacun à son goût</u> proved a difficult principle to apply in this case.
The great English public schools attempted to follow the ideal of <u>mens sana in corpore sano</u>.

Underline letters, words, or phrases being named.

How many <u>i</u>'s are in <u>Mississippi</u>?
His life demonstrates the meaning of the word <u>waste</u>.
What is the derivation of the phrase <u>on the ball</u>?

In most cases, it is also appropriate to use quotation marks instead of underlining for this purpose.

Underline words and phrases for emphasis.

I did <u>not</u> say I would do that.
You <u>must</u> stop overeating!
You plan to do <u>what</u>?

Do not overuse this device. Too much underlining weakens the effect. Emphasize only what deserves emphasis.

Exercise

Identify which items should be underlined in each of the following sentences.

1. Satirical portraits were a regular feature in the Tatler and the Spectator, two periodicals of the eighteenth century.

2. The meaning of the word satire is not explained by the meaning of its Latin root, satira.

3. Satirist Jonathan Swift is best remembered for Gulliver's Travels, which brought the words yahoo and Lilliputian into our language.

4. Hogarth, eighteenth-century painter, satirized manners and morals of his time in his sequence called Rake's Progress.

5. A satirist can find traits of human nature to ridicule even in tragic situations—the fictional events in Voltaire's novel Candide, for example, or the real-life tragedy in the sinking of the Titanic.

33 Abbreviations

In general, avoid abbreviations in formal writing. However, abbreviations are acceptable in certain situations.

Use an abbreviation for the following designations preceding names.

Mr.	Messrs.	St. or Ste. (Saint)
Mrs.	Mmes.	Mt. (Mount)
Ms.	Dr.	Rev. (unless preceded by *the*)

Is **Mrs.** Dalloway a fully realized character?
For what musicals are **Messrs.** Rogers and Hart responsible?
Rev. James Spenser read the service.

Note: Spell out *Reverend* when it is preceded by *the*.

The **Reverend** James Spenser read the service.

Do not use an abbreviation for any other designation preceding a name.

Not: No one was surprised when **Pres.** Reagan said that he would run again.

But: No one was surprised when **President** Reagan said that he would run again.

Not: Are you campaigning for **Sen.** Jones?
But: Are you campaigning for **Senator** Jones?

Not: In his new book, **Prof.** Rosenthal discusses the use of imagery in the poetry of Ted Hughes.
But: In his new book, **Professor** Rosenthal discusses the use of imagery in the poetry of Ted Hughes.

Use an abbreviation preceded by a comma for a designation or an academic degree following a name.

Jr.
Sr.
Esq.
B.A. or BA (Bachelor of Arts)
B.S. or BS (Bachelor of Science)
M.A. or MA (Master of Arts)
M.S. or MS (Master of Science)

M.D. or MD (Doctor of Medicine)
Ph.D. or PhD (Doctor of Philosophy)
Ed.D. or EdD (Doctor of Education)

D.D.S. or DDS (Doctor of Dental Science)
D.D. or DD (Doctor of Divinity)

J.D. or JD (Doctor of Jurisprudence)
D.V.M. or DVM (Doctor of Veterinary Medicine)

> The speaker will be Thomas Dean, **Jr.**
> The academy announced the appointment of Marion Unger, **Ph.D.,** as chairman. (or **PhD** without periods)

Do not use the abbreviation *Dr.* before a name that is followed by an abbreviation denoting a doctoral degree.

Use abbreviations without periods for many well-known agencies, organizations, and businesses, and also for other familiar abbreviations using capital letters.

> The newspaper accused the **CIA** of covert activities in that country.
> The **YMHA** is presenting a revival of Arthur Miller's *All My Sons.*
> The candidate sought the support of the **AFL–CIO.**

An **acronym** is a pronounceable word made from initials or parts of words. Consult your dictionary about its capitalization, and be sure to explain, in parentheses, an acronym that might be unfamiliar to your readers.

> The next meeting of **OPEC** will be an important one.
> Bring your **scuba** equipment with you.
> America's **ZIP** code (**Z**one **I**mprovement **S**ystem) has improved the postal service.
> The lecture explained **quasars** (quasi-stellar objects).

With numerals, use the abbreviations *B.C.* or *BC* (before Christ) and *A.D.* or *AD* (*anno Domini,* "in the year of the Lord") for dates. Use the abbreviations *A.M.* or *AM* or *a.m.* (before noon) and *P.M.* or *PM* or *p.m.* (after noon) for time.

> Confucius, China's most important teacher and philosopher, was born in 551 **BC**.
> In **AD** 37, Caligula was made emperor of Rome.
> The child was born at 6:37 **a.m.**

The abbreviation *B.C.* or *BC* should be put after the date, and the abbreviation *A.D.* or *AD* is usually put before the date. However, the practice of putting *AD* after the date is now also considered acceptable. *BC* and *AD* are sometimes replaced with the abbreviations *B.C.E.* (Before the Common Era) and *C.E.* (Common Era), respectively.

A.M. or *AM* and *P.M.* or *PM* may be written with either capital or lowercase letters, but be consistent within a single piece of writing. Lowercase letters require periods—*a.m.* or *p.m.*

Use the following abbreviations for common Latin words and expressions.

c. or *ca.* (about)	*etc.* (and others)
cf. (compare)	*i.e.* (that is)
e.g. (for example)	*viz.* (namely)

> Moses (*c.* 1350–1250 B.C.) led his people out of slavery.
> Taoism is based on the teachings of Lao-zu (*cf.* Confucianism).
> Monotheistic religions (*e.g.,* Christianity and Islam) worship only one god.

Do not overuse these Latin abbreviations. Where possible, try substituting the English equivalent.

Spell out the names of days and months.

> *Not:* The first game of the World Series will be played on **Oct.** 11.
> *But:* The first game of the World Series will be played on **October** 11.

Not: The committee met on **Wed.,** not **Thurs.**
But: The committee met on **Wednesday,** not **Thursday.**

Not: It snowed heavily on the first **Sat.** in **Dec.**
But: It snowed heavily on the first **Saturday** in **December.**

Spell out the names of cities, states, and countries, except in addresses.

Not: He came to **N.Y.C.** to study music.
But: He came to **New York City** to study music.

Not: Emily Dickinson was born in Amherst, **Mass.**
But: Emily Dickinson was born in Amherst, **Massachusetts.**

Not: The Mediterranean fruit fly was accidentally introduced into the **U.S.**
But: The Mediterranean fruit fly was accidentally introduced into the **United States.**

Spell out first names.

Not: The editor of this collection is **Thom.** Webster.
But: The editor of this collection is **Thomas** Webster.

Not: **Benj.** Disraeli worked for passage of the Reform Bill of 1867.
But: **Benjamin** Disraeli worked for passage of the Reform Bill of 1867.

Not: **Chas.** Lindbergh was the first person to fly nonstop across the Atlantic Ocean.
But: **Charles** Lindbergh was the first person to fly nonstop across the Atlantic Ocean.

In names of businesses, spell out the words *Brothers, Corporation,* and *Company,* except in addresses or in bibliographic information.

Not: She was employed by the firm of Magnum **Bros.**
But: She was employed by the firm of Magnum **Brothers.**

Not: The employees at Thomas Smythe and **Co.** are on strike.
But: The employees at Thomas Smythe and **Company** are on strike.

In formal, nontechnical writing, spell out units of measure.

Not: The pamphlet claims that anyone who is more than ten **lbs.** overweight is a candidate for a heart attack.
But: The pamphlet claims that anyone who is more than ten **pounds** overweight is a candidate for a heart attack.

Not: The father rebuked his lazy children with tales of how he had had to walk fifteen **mi.** to school each day.
But: The father rebuked his lazy children with tales of how he had had to walk fifteen **miles** to school each day.

Not: How many **qts.** of milk did you sell?
But: How many **quarts** of milk did you sell?

In technical writing, abbreviations are acceptable and often preferred.

34 Contractions

A **contraction** is a shortened form of a word or words. In a contraction, an apostrophe takes the place of the missing letter or letters. Contractions are widely used in speech and in informal writing.

In general, avoid contractions in formal writing.

Informal: During his lifetime, Mark Twain **didn't** receive the serious critical attention he deserved.
Formal: During his lifetime, Mark Twain **did not** receive the serious critical attention he deserved.

Informal: He asserted that it **isn't** necessary to separate Sam-uel Clemens from Mark Twain.

Formal: He asserted that it **is not** necessary to separate Sam-uel Clemens from Mark Twain.

Informal: She, on the other hand, claimed that **it's** important to know where the autobiography stops and the fic-tion begins.

Formal: She, on the other hand, claimed that **it is** important to know where the autobiography stops and the fic-tion begins.

35 Numerals

A **numeral** is a symbol that denotes a number. In formal, nontechnical writing, use numerals only in specific instances.

Use numerals for numbers that cannot be written as one or two words.

During its first year, the book sold only **678** copies.
There are **365** days in the normal year, and **366** days in the leap
year.
Last Saturday this shop sold **1,059** doughnuts.

However, never begin a sentence with a numeral.

Nine hundred seventy-six people bought tickets for the con-cert, but only 341 attended.
Two hundred twenty-six poems are anthologized in this volume.
Three hundred sixteen photographs of San Francisco are on exhibit.

Spell out all numbers that can be written as one or two words and that modify a noun.

She sang a medley of **sixteen** Sondheim songs.
The gestation period for a rabbit is about **thirty-one** days.
We need **one hundred** squares to make this quilt.

Use numerals for decimals or fractions.

We had **2½** inches of rainfall last month.
What do they mean when they claim that the average family has **2.3** children?

Use numerals for addresses.

702 West **74**th Street   **1616** South Street

However, it is acceptable to spell out the name of a numbered street in an address.

417 **Eleventh** Avenue   201 East **Seventh** Street

Use numerals for page numbers, percentages, degrees, and amounts of money with the symbol *$* or *¢*.

Turn to **page 82** for an analysis of the works of Van Gogh.
The survey found that **70.2%** of registered voters favor Brosnan.
The account yields **9.5 percent** interest annually.
An acute angle is an angle under **90°.**
The computer costs **$1,667.99.**

Use numerals for dates and for hours expressed with *A.M.* (*AM*) or *P.M.* (*PM*).

At **6:07 AM** the snow began to fall.
The First International Peace Conference, held at The Hague, began on May **18, 1899.**

Use numerals with units of measurement.

The course is **127** kilometers.
The room is **11'7″** × **13'4″.**
The tree is **6'5″** from the garage door.

However, simple numbers may be spelled out: *six feet*.

Use numerals with numbers in a series.

A grizzly bear can run at a speed of **30** miles per hour; an elephant, **25**; a chicken, **9**; but a tortoise, only **0.17**.

The commercial traveler logged his sales for his first five days on the job: **7, 18, 23, 4, 19**.

Use numerals for identification numbers.

His social security number is **142–45–1983**.

For service call the following number: **(800) 415–3333**.

Flight **465** has been canceled.

When one number immediately follows another, spell out the first number and use a numeral for the second number.

He ran in **two 50**-meter races.

We have **three 6**-foot ladders in the garage.

There are **five 7**-foot players in the conference.

Exercise

Identify the errors in the use of abbreviations and numbers in the following sentences. Two of the sentences contain no error.

1. The kindly Dr. Jekyll turned into the terrible Mr. Hyde.

2. Has the Rev. Joseph Parker been assigned to this church?

3. Relations between Egypt and the U.S. were improved by Pres. Carter's Camp David meeting between Sadat and Begin.

4. The speaker at yesterday's meeting was James Colby, Junior.

5. J. Edgar Hoover headed the F.B.I.

6. The comet fell at 6:57 A.M.

7. The program cannot be shown until Wed., Dec. nineteenth.

8. 32 African nations formed the O.A.U. in May 1963.

9. An excellent source for information about N.A.T.O. is Jas. Huntley's *The NATO Story,* which was published in nineteen sixty-nine.

10. Honduras has a Caribbean coastline of six hundred forty-four kilometers.

36 Manuscript Form

The following are general guidelines for preparing handwritten and typewritten papers. If your college or your instructors specify different or additional guidelines, however, follow their directions.

36a For Handwritten Papers

1. Use blue or black ink. Do not use pencil.
2. Use 8½″ × 11″ ruled white paper. If you tear the paper from a notebook, cut off the ragged edge. Do not use paper with narrowly spaced lines.
3. Skip every other line, unless your instructor tells you otherwise. (Do not skip lines between the lines of a quotation.)
4. Write on only one side of the paper.
5. Center your title. Leave an extra line of space between the title and the first line of text. Do not underline or put

quotation marks around the title. (Of course, if a part of your title is a quotation or the title of another work, use the appropriate punctuation for this part.)

6. Capitalize all words in the title except articles, short (under five letters) conjunctions, and short prepositions. Do not put a period at the end of the title.

7. Leave about an inch and a half of space at the top of each page. (The first rule on ruled paper is usually about an inch and a half from the top.) Leave about an inch of space at the bottom of each page.

8. Leave about an inch-and-a-half margin at the left-hand side of each page. (Ruled paper usually has a vertical line on the left-hand side to indicate this margin.) Leave about a one-inch margin at the right-hand side.

9. Indent the first line of each new paragraph about one inch from the left margin.

10. Use hyphens to divide words at the end of lines. (See pages 357–358 for information on word division at the end of a line.)

11. Do not end a line with an opening bracket, parenthesis, or quotation mark. Do not begin a line with a comma, a colon, a semicolon, or an end punctuation mark. Do not separate ellipsis points over two lines.

12. When underlining, underline the complete item, including the space between words.

13. Correct an error by drawing a line through it and writing the correction above it. (Rewrite any page that contains more than one error.)

14. Number each page with arabic numerals. On the first page, center the number at the bottom of the page. (You may omit the number from the first page.) On all other pages, write the number in the upper right-hand corner of the page.

15. Follow carefully your instructor's directions for writing your name and any other necessary identifying information on your paper.

16. Fold your paper only if your instructor says you may do so.
17. Write legibly.
18. Proofread your paper carefully before turning it in.

36b For Typewritten Papers

1. Use a black typewriter ribbon.
2. Use 8½″ × 11″ unruled white bond paper. Do not use onionskin.
3. Double-space each line.
4. Type on only one side of the paper.
5. Center your title. Leave an extra line of space between the title and the first line of text. Do not underline or put quotation marks around the title. (Of course, if a part of your title is a quotation or the title of another work, use the appropriate punctuation for this part.)
6. Capitalize all words in the title except articles, short (under five letters) conjunctions, and short prepositions. Do not put a period at the end of the title.
7. Leave about an inch and a half of space at the top of each page. Leave about an inch of space at the bottom of each page.
8. Leave about an inch-and-a-half margin at the left-hand side of each page. Leave about a one-inch margin at the right-hand side.
9. Indent the first line of each new paragraph five spaces from the left margin.
10. Use hyphens to divide words at the end of lines. (See pages 357–358 for information on word division at the end of a line.)
11. Do not end a line with an opening bracket, parenthesis, or quotation mark. Do not begin a line with a comma, a colon, a semicolon, or an end punctuation mark. Do not separate ellipsis points over two lines.
12. Leave two spaces after end punctuation marks and colons. Leave one space after all other punctuation marks.

13. Indicate a dash with two hyphens (--). Do not leave space before or after the hyphens.
14. When underlining, underline the complete item, including the space between words.
15. If your typewriter does not have the numeral 1 on its keyboard, use a lowercase "el" for this numeral.
16. Number each page with arabic numerals. Do not number the first page. On all other pages, type the number in the upper right-hand corner of the page.
17. Follow carefully your instructor's directions for typing your name and any other necessary identifying information on your paper.
18. Fold your paper only if your instructor says you may do so.
19. Make corrections neatly. Use correction fluid where possible. Retype any page that appears messy.
20. Proofread your paper carefully before turning it in.

Note: These guidelines also apply to a paper produced on a word-processor.

Part V

Spelling

Mastery of English spelling is a difficult task, though perhaps not as difficult as poor spellers believe. Simply remember to follow a few simple guidelines and—most important—to use your dictionary when you are not sure of a spelling.

37 Spelling Rules

Although spelling rules are not infallible, mastery of the few described here will help you. They cover some of the most common spelling problems: adding suffixes to words, forming noun plurals, and choosing between *ei* and *ie*.

37a Doubling the Final Consonant

In a word ending with a consonant-vowel-consonant (c-v-c) combination, the vowel usually has a short vowel sound.

bat	dot	shun
pen	begin	occur

When a suffix is added to such a word, sometimes the final consonant is doubled to maintain the short vowel sound.

With suffixes beginning with a consonant

Do not double the final consonant of a c-v-c word when adding a suffix beginning with a consonant.

ship + ment = shi**p**ment   mob + ster = mo**b**ster
wet + ness = we**t**ness   pen + man + ship = pe**n**ma**n**ship

With suffixes beginning with a vowel

Double the final consonant of a one-syllable c-v-c word when adding a suffix beginning with a vowel.

pen + ed = pe**nn**ed   brag + art = bra**gg**art
skip + er = ski**pp**er   grip + ing = gri**pp**ing

Exception: bus + ing = busing

When adding a suffix beginning with a vowel to a c-v-c word of more than one syllable, double the final consonant if the word is accented on the last syllable. Do not double the consonant, however, if the accent shifts to the first syllable when the suffix is added.

begín + er = begi**nn**er   regrét + ed = regre**tt**ed
recúr + ence = recu**rr**ence defér + ence = défe**r**ence
emít + ing = emi**tt**ing   prefér + ence = préfe**r**ence

When adding a suffix beginning with a vowel to a c-v-c word of more than one syllable, do not double the final consonant if the word is not accented on the last syllable.

pénal + ize = pena**l**ize   bánter + ing = bante**r**ing
lábor + er = labo**r**er   abándon + ed = abando**n**ed

Do not double the final consonant when adding any suffix to any word that does not end in a consonant-vowel-consonant.

cheap + er = cheaper   ordain + ed = ordained
chant + ing = chanting   pretend + er = pretender

37b   Dropping the Silent *e*

Many English words end with a silent *e*. At times this *e* indicates that the vowel before the consonant should have a long sound. For example, notice the difference in the vowel sound in each of the following word pairs.

hat—hate	rot—rote	pan—pane
din—dine	run—rune	spit—spite

At times the silent *e* indicates that the *c* or *g* preceding it should have a soft, rather than a hard, sound.

notice	trace	courage
peace	engage	outrage

Drop a final silent *e* when adding most suffixes beginning with a vowel.

fade + ing = fading	grimace + ed = grimaced
pleasure + able = pleasurable	cohere + ence = coherence
use + age = usage	escape + ist = escapist

Exceptions

acre + age = acreage	line + age = lineage
dye + ing = dyeing	mile + age = mileage
hoe + ing = hoeing	singe + ing = singeing

Retain a final silent *e* when adding the suffix *-able* or *-ous* to a word in which the silent *e* is preceded by a *c* or a *g*.

notice + able = noticeable	advantage + ous = advantageous
peace + able = peaceable	change + able = changeable
outrage + ous = outrageous	courage + ous = courageous

Retain a final silent *e* when adding a suffix beginning with a consonant.

delicate + ness = delicateness	move + ment = movement
loose + ly = loosely	decisive + ness = decisiveness

Exceptions

acknowledge + ment = acknowledgment
argue + ment = argument
judge + ment = judgment
nine + th = ninth
true + ly = truly
whole + ly = wholly

37c Changing *y* to *i*

When a final *y* is preceded by a consonant, change the *y* to *i*
when you add most suffixes.

lovely + er = lovelier   happy + ly = happily
likely + hood = likelihood   lazy + ness = laziness
risky + est = riskiest   tally + ed = tallied

Exceptions

dry + er = dryer (machine)   sly + ly = slyly
dry + ly = dryly   sly + ness = slyness
dry + ness = dryness   wry + ly = wryly
shy + ly = shyly   wry + ness = wryness
shy + ness = shyness

However, do not change a final *y* to *i* when you add the suffix
-ing or *-ist*.

spy + ing = spying   hurry + ing = hurrying
copy + ist = copyist   pacify + ing = pacifying

If a final *y* is preceded by a vowel, do not change the *y* to *i*
when you add a suffix.

employ + ee = employee   destroy + er = destroyer
essay + ist = essayist   convey + ance = conveyance
survey + ing = surveying   overstay + ed = overstayed

Exceptions

day + ly = daily   pay + ed = paid
gay + ly = gaily   say + ed = said
lay + ed = laid

37d Choosing Between *ei* and *ie*

In most cases, place *i* before *e* except after *c*. Place *e* before *i*
when these letters are pronounced as *ā*.

i before e

pierce   niece   mien
believe   interview   shield

After c

receive   deceit   deceive
conceive   perceive   ceiling

Pronounced as ā

neighbor   weight   feign
freight   vein   reign

Exceptions

either   height   neither
feisty   heir   seize
heifer   leisure   weird

Note: The rule does not apply to words in which the *i* and the *e*
or the *e* and the *i* are pronounced as parts of separate syllables:
piety, deity, hierarchy, science.

37e Forming Noun Plurals

For most nouns, form the plural by adding *s* to the singular.

pot—pots	table—tables	magazine—magazines
lamp—lamps	picture—pictures	recorder—recorders

For nouns ending in *y* preceded by a vowel, form the plural by adding *s* to the singular.

monkey—monkeys	holiday—holidays
display—displays	jersey—jerseys
journey—journeys	odyssey—odysseys

For nouns (except proper nouns) ending in *y* preceded by a consonant, form the plural by changing the *y* to *i* and adding *es*.

jelly—jellies	theory—theories
quality—qualities	frequency—frequencies
heresy—heresies	fraternity—fraternities

For nouns ending in *s, ch, sh, x,* or *z,* form the plural by adding *es* to the singular.

genius—geniuses	miss—misses
ditch—ditches	brush—brushes
hoax—hoaxes	waltz—waltzes

For nouns ending in *o* preceded by a vowel, form the plural by adding *s* to the singular.

cameo—cameos	trio—trios
duo—duos	folio—folios
radio—radios	scenario—scenarios

For nouns ending in *o* preceded by a consonant, form the plural by adding either *s* or *es* to the singular.

Add s

piano—pianos	memo—memos
burro—burros	dynamo—dynamos
alto—altos	magneto—magnetos

Add es

hero—heroes	echo—echoes
mosquito—mosquitoes	tomato—tomatoes
potato—potatoes	mulatto—mulattoes

Add s or es

flamingo—flamingos *or* flamingoes
salvo—salvos *or* salvoes
banjo—banjos *or* banjoes
lasso—lassos *or* lassoes
domino—dominos *or* dominoes
cargo—cargos *or* cargoes

For most nouns ending in *f* or *fe* and for all nouns ending in *ff*, form the plural by adding *s* to the singular.

belief—beliefs	muff—muffs
waif—waifs	staff—staffs
safe—safes	rebuff—rebuffs

For some nouns ending in *f* or *fe*, form the plural by changing the *f* or *fe* to *ve* and adding *s*.

calf—calves	knife—knives
leaf—leaves	wife—wives
self—selves	life—lives

The following nouns ending in *arf* have alternative plural forms.

dwarf—dwarfs *or* dwarves
scarf—scarfs *or* scarves
wharf—wharfs *or* wharves

For compound nouns written as one word, form the plural by applying the preceding rules to the last part of the compound.

cupful—cupfuls	tablespoon—tablespoons
handful—handfuls	hemstitch—hemstitches
housewife—housewives	toolbox—toolboxes
takeoff—takeoffs	horsefly—horseflies

Exception: passerby—passersby

For compound nouns in which the words are joined by a hyphen or written separately, make the chief word plural.

mother-in-law	mothers-in-law
sergeant at arms	sergeants at arms
runner-up	runners-up
attorney general	attorneys general
father-to-be	fathers-to-be

but

tape recorder	tape recorders
sound track	sound tracks
high school	high schools
hope chest	hope chests

Exceptions

drive-in	drive-ins
five-year-old	five-year-olds
jack-in-the-box	jack-in-the-boxes
frame-up	frame-ups
sit-in	sit-ins
stand-in	stand-ins

For numbers, letters, symbols, and words being named, form the plural by adding 's to the singular.

9's　　　*'s　　　a's
and's　　abc's　　+'s

Learn the irregular plural forms.

Some nouns have an irregular plural or form the plural according to the rules of their language of origin.

woman—women	louse—lice	foot—feet
man—men	mouse—mice	tooth—teeth
ox—oxen	alumnus—alumni	analysis—analyses
child—children	radius—radii	crisis—crises

Learn the nouns that have the same form for both singular and plural.

deer	trout	species	moose
salmon	sheep	series	

Form the plural of proper nouns by adding s or es.

Tuesdays　　the Joneses　　the Kennedys

In the example on the right, note that no apostrophe is used and that the final *y* is not changed to *i*.

Exercise

Circle any misspelled word in each of the following groups.

1. shipped, remitted, driped, excelled, distilled

2. quitting, outwitting, outfitting, benefitting, permitting

3. committee, committment, committed, committing, committable

4. recurence, deference, inference, reference, preference

5. describing, singeing, placing, juiceing, liking

6. acknowledgement, ninety, noticeable, outrageous, peaceably

7. rectifing, slyly, wryly, satisfying, hurriedly

8. travesties, journeys, salaries, delays, frequencys

9. hitches, quizzes, folioes, mosquitoes, heroes

10. deign, deceive, hienous, relieve, frontier

38 Troublesome Words

A large number of spelling errors are caused by omitting one or two letters from a word or by adding letters where they do not belong. The most common errors of this kind are caused by not doubling a consonant or by doubling one incorrectly. The following is a list of words that are often misspelled by adding or omitting letters. The part or parts of the word that commonly cause spelling problems are in **boldface**.

abando**n**ed
a**c**ademic
academic**all**y
a**cc**elerator
acce**p**table
a**cc**essible
a**cc**ident**all**y
a**cc**o**mm**odate
a**cc**ompanied
a**cc**ompanying
a**cc**omplish
a**cc**umulate
a**cc**uracy

a**cc**ustomed
achie**v**ement
acknowle**dg**e
acknowledgment (no *e* after *g*)
a**c**quaintance
a**c**quire
a**c**quit
acr**e**age
a**c**ross
actua**ll**y
a**dd**ress
admi**ss**ion
admi**tt**ance

adolescent
advantageous
advertisement
aerial
aggravate
aggressive
aisle
allotting
almost
already
altogether
always
amateur
among (no *u* after *o*)
amount
analysis
analyze
ancestry (no *a* after *t*)
annihilate
announcement
annual
another
apartment
apologetically
apology
apparatus
apparent
appearance
applies
appoint
appreciate
appropriate
appropriately
approximate
approximately
arctic
arguing (no *e* after *u*)
argument (no *e* after *u*)
aspirin

assassination
association
atheist
athlete (no *e* after *h*)
athletic (no *e* after *h*)
attitude
awful (no *e* after *w*)
bankruptcy
bargain
basically
battalion
beautiful
becoming
before
beginning
benefited
biggest
biscuit
biting
boundary
bracelet
bulletin
business
calendar
camouflage
candidate
career
carrying
challenge
changeable
channel
characteristics
chocolate
chosen (no *o* after *o*)
clothes
column
coming
commercial
commission

commitment
committee
communism
communists
compel
compelled
competition
completely
conceivable (no *e* after *v*)
condemn
conferred
confused
connoisseur
conscience
conscientious
consists
continuous
controlled
controlling
controversial
convenient
coolly
criticism
crowded
cruelty (no *i* after *l*)
curriculum
dealt
decision
decorate
deferred
define
definitely
definition
descend
desirable (no *e* after *r*)
desperate
develop (no *e* after *p*)
diarrhea
different

dilemma
dilettante
dining
disagree
disappear
disappoint
disapprove
disaster
disastrous (no *e* after *t*)
discipline
discussion
dispel
dissatisfied
disservice
dissipate
distinct
drunkenness
during
ecstasy
efficiency
efficient
eliminate
embarrass
eminent
empty
endeavor
enemy
enthusiastically
entirely
entrance (no *e* after *t*)
environment
equipment (no *t* after *p*)
equipped
especially
essential
everything
exaggerate
excellent
excess

exercise (no *c* after *x*)
exhaustion
exhibition
exhilarate
existence (no *h* after *x*)
experience
explanation (no *i* after *l*)
extremely
fallacy
familiar
family
fascinate
fascism
favorite
February
fiery
final (no *i* after *n*)
financially
fission
fluorine
foreign
foresee
forfeit (no *e* after *r*)
forty (no *e* after *r*)
forward (no *e* after *r*)
fourth
frantically
fulfill
gaiety
generally
genius (no *o* after *i*)
government
grammatically
grievous (no *i* after *v*)
gruesome
guarantee
guerrilla
handicapped
handkerchief

harass
height (no *h* after *t*)
hemorrhage
heroes
hindrance (no *e* after *d*)
holiday
hopeless
hurriedly
hygiene
hypocrite
ideally
illogical
imagine
imitate
immediately
immense
impossible
incidentally
indispensable (no *e* after *s*)
individually
ingenious
initially
initiative
innocent
innocuous
inoculate
intellectual
intelligence
intelligent
interest
interfered
interference
interrupt
iridescent
irrelevant
irresistible
irritable
jewelry (no *e* after *l*)
judgment (no *e* after *g*)

knowledge
laboratory
larynx
later
laundry (no *e* after *d*)
lenient
liable
liaison
library
lightning (no *e* after *t*)
likely
listening
literature
loneliness
lonely
magazine
maintenance
manageable
maneuver
manner
manual
marriage
marriageable
mathematics
meanness
meant
medicine
medieval
mileage
millennium
miniature
miscellaneous
mischievous (no *i* after *v*)
missile
misspelled
mortgage
muscle
narrative
naturally

necessary
necessity
nineteen
ninety
ninth (no *e* after *in*)
noticeable
nowadays
nuisance
numerous
occasion
occasionally
occurred
occurrence
official
omission
omit
omitted
operate
opinion
opponent
opportunity
opposite
oppression
outrageous
pageant
pamphlet (no *e* after *h*)
panicked
paraffin
parallel
parliament
particular
pastime
peaceable
peculiar
permissible
picnicked
planned
playwright
pneumonia

pollute
Portuguese
possess
possession
possible
practically
preference
preferred
prejudiced
primitive
privilege (no *d* after *le*)
probably (no *a* after *ab*)
procedure (no *e* after *ce*)
profession
professor
pronunciation (no *o* after *on*)
psalm
psychology
ptomaine
publicly (no *al* after *c*)
pumpkin
quantity
quarrel
questionnaire
realize
rebellion
recession
recommend
reference
referring
relative
remember
remembrance (no *e* after *b*)
reminisce
remittance
restaurant
rhythm
roommate
saccharine

safety
satellite
scientists
scintillate
sergeant
shepherd
sheriff
shining
shrubbery
similar (no *i* after *l*)
sincerely
skiing
sophomore
souvenir
specifically
statistics (no *s* after *a*)
strenuous
stretch
stubbornness
studying
subtle
succeed
success
succession
sufficient
summary
summation
summed
supposed
suppress
surely
surrounding
swimming
syllable
symmetric
tariff
temperament
temperature
therefore

thorough
tobacco
tomorrow
transferred
trespass
truly (no *e* after *u*)
tyranny
unconscious
uncontrollable
undoubtedly
unmistakably (no *e* after *k*)
unnatural
unnecessary
until
used
useful
usually

vacuum
valuable
various
vaudeville
vegetable
vehicle
vengeance
villain
violence
warring
where
whether
whistle
wholly
whose
writing
written

The following is a list of other words that are often misspelled.

abundant
acre
against
a lot
anonymous
arithmetic
article
attendance
ballet
beggar
behavior
believe
beneficial
bibliography
blasphemy
boulevard
buffet
bureaucrat
burial

buried
carburetor
caricature
catalogue
catastrophe
category
cellar
cemetery
children
circumstantial
colossal
comparative
complexion
counselor
courtesy
criticize
debacle
despicable
detrimental

dictionary
diphtheria
doesn't
eighth
eligible
emphasize
espionage
exuberant
financier
galaxy
guidance
hers
hospital
hundred
hypocrisy
idiomatic
imagery
incredible
independent

inevitable
insurance
interpretation
involve
January
leisurely
license
liquor
luxurious
magnificent
malicious
martyrdom
mediocre
melancholy
minuscule
minute
naive
neurotic
nickel
nuclear
nucleus
ogre
optimism
ours
paid
paralysis
penicillin

performance
permanent
perseverance
perspiration
phenomenon
physician
pigeon
poison
predominate
prescription
prestige
prevalent
proceed
propaganda
propagate
pursue
pursuit
repetition
ridiculous
sacrifice
salary
schedule
secretary
seize
seizure
separate
siege

significance
source
specimen
speech
supersede
surprise
susceptible
technical
technique
tendency
theirs
themselves
tolerance
tortoise
tragedy
tried
Tuesday
unscrupulous
versatile
vigilance
vinegar
Wednesday
woman
yacht
yours
zinc

Exercise

Circle the misspelled word in each of the following groups.

1. assassination, acquit, salery, permanent, galaxy

2. intepretation, ogre, paralysis, communism, appearance

3. challenge, artic, ancestry, forfeit, vigilance

4. technique, colossal, lightning, curriculum, nineth

5. pronounciation, interrupt, diarrhea, compel, inoculate

6. iridescent, necessary, harrass, acquire, aerial

7. embarass, disaster, nuisance, parallel, annihilate

8. condemn, biscuit, souvenir, rememberance, bureaucrat

9. carburetor, mischievous, irritable, sacharine, occasion

10. millennium, hemorrhage, questionaire, benefited, ecstasy

39 Capitalization Rules

Capitalize the first word of a sentence, the pronoun *I*, and the interjection *O*.

> **M**any writers have created imaginary universes.
> **Do I** think that life exists on other planets?
> **T**hese creatures, **O** mighty Gork, come from the other side of the universe.

Capitalize the first word of a direct quotation that is a complete sentence.

> At the climax of the movie, Rhett says, "**F**rankly, my dear, I don't give a damn."
> The book begins with the present Mrs. de Winter recounting a dream: "**L**ast night I dreamt I went to Manderley again."
> When Cuyloga prepares to leave his son, he tells him, "**G**ive me no more shame."

Capitalize the first word of every line of verse unless the poet has written the line with a lowercase letter.

The first two lines of Reed Whittemore's poem "Still Life" immediately capture your interest: "**I** must explain why it is that at night, in my own house,/**E**ven when no one's asleep, I feel I must whisper."

Keats's poem ends with the lines, "**T**hough the sedge is withered from the lake/**A**nd no birds sing."

The Eliot poem that I am trying to remember begins with the following two lines: "**M**acavity's a Mystery Cat: He's called the hidden paw—/**F**or he's the master criminal who can defy the Law."

Note: In quotations, always capitalize whichever words the writer has capitalized.

Capitalize proper nouns.

Sharon	**K**eats
Andrew **J**ackson	**L**ake **M**ichigan
Portuguese	**H**awaii
Greta **G**arbo	the **E**mpire **S**tate **B**uilding
the **M**iddle **A**ges	the **R**evolutionary **W**ar

Do not capitalize compass points unless they are part of a proper noun: *northwest of Chicago* but *the Pacific Northwest.*

Capitalize an official title when it precedes a name.

The guest speaker will be **C**ongresswoman Katherine Murphy.
The nation mourned the death of **P**resident Lincoln.
The changes were supported by **G**overnor Celeste.

Capitalize the title of a high official when it is used in place of the person's name.

The guest speaker will be the **C**ongresswoman.
The nation mourned the death of the **P**resident.
The changes were supported by the **G**overnor.

Note: Do not capitalize a title that does not name a specific individual.

Capitalize abbreviations and designations that follow a name. Do not capitalize titles used as appositives.

Eugene Anderson, **J**r.
Anne Poletti, **P**h.**D**. (PhD)
Louise Tate, **A**ttorney at **L**aw
Seymour Rosen, a **c**hemistry **p**rofessor, submitted an article to the magazine.
Lois Kean, a first-year **l**aw student, won the award.
Malcolm Kennedy, an **i**ntern at the hospital, was interviewed on television.

Capitalize the title of a relative when it precedes a name or is used in place of a name. Do not capitalize the title if it is used with a possessive pronoun.

Aunt Joan   **C**ousin Mary
Uncle Carlos   **G**randfather Tseng

Is **G**randmother coming to visit?
You look well, **G**randpa.
My **u**ncle Bill could not come to the performance.

Capitalize proper adjectives.

Shakespearean sonnet   **M**achiavellian goals
Parisian style   **G**recian urn
Islamic teacher   **C**hristian faith

Do not capitalize most proper adjectives that are part of a compound noun.

french fries   **d**anish pastry
roman numeral   **v**enetian blind

Note: Usage in this area varies. Consult your dictionary for capitalization of compound nouns formed from proper adjectives.

Capitalize the names of specific academic courses. Do not capitalize general subject areas unless the subject area is a proper noun, such as a language.

History 121   *but* a world history course
The Modern American Novel   *but* an American literature course
Advanced Biology   *but* a biology course

Capitalize words naming the Deity, sacred books, and other religious documents and names of religions, religious denominations, and their adherents.

Jehovah   Allah   the Lord
the Bible   the Koran   the Upanishads
Catholicism   Moslem   Lutheran

Note: Pronouns referring to the Deity are usually capitalized.

Capitalize names of months, days of the week, and holidays.

April   December   January
Tuesday   Saturday   Wednesday
Halloween   New Year's Eve the Fourth of July

Note: Do not capitalize the names of the seasons.

Capitalize the abbreviations *A.D. (AD)* and *B.C. (BC)*.

A.D. 172   500 B.C.
AD 356   275 BC

For titles of literary works, capitalize the first and the last word and all other important words, including prepositions of five or more letters.

Do not capitalize articles, short prepositions, or coordinating conjunctions that do not begin or end a title.

> ***The Decline and Fall of the Roman Empire***
> "**The Case of the Irate Witness**"
> ***Much Ado About Nothing***
> "**On the Morning After the Sixties**"

Capitalize both parts of a hyphenated word in a title.

> "**Home-Thoughts from Abroad**"
> "**Good-Bye, My Fancy!**"
> ***The Sot-Weed Factor***
> *Giles Goat-Boy*

Exercise

In each of the following items, change a lowercase letter to a capital letter wherever necessary. Some of the sentences are correct as written.

1. E. B. White once said, "writing is an act of faith, nothing else."

2. In "Morning song," Sylvia Plath describes the birth of her child: "Love set you going like a fat gold watch./the midwife slapped your footsoles and your bald cry/took its place among the elements."

3. A leading character in Faulkner's story of the south and his fictional Yoknatapawpha county is a strong black woman named aunt Molly.

4. In "When Lilacs last in the Dooryard bloom'd," Walt Whitman mourns the death of president Abraham Lincoln: "O powerful western fallen star!/O shades of night—o moody, tearful night!"

5. The word *sideburns* comes from general Ambrose Burnside, a union commander during the civil war who sported this style of whiskers.

6. The traveler to new york city will be impressed by the twin towers on the lower tip of the island and trump tower in upper manhattan.

7. Syngman Rhee, who was the first president of South Korea, sought Korean independence from Japan.

8. At the Yalta conference held near the end of world war II in the crimean peninsula, the allies planned the postwar reorganization of Europe.

9. I plan to take a course called women's literature, examining works written from the time of the renaissance through colonial america.

10. The eighteenth-century followers of methodism, which is based on the teachings of John Wesley, were barred from the church of England.

40 The Apostrophe

40a In Possessive Forms

The possessive case forms of all nouns and of many pronouns are spelled with an apostrophe. The following rules explain when to use an apostrophe for possessive forms and where to place the apostrophe.

Note: Do not be misled by the term *possessive*. Rather than trying to see "ownership," consider the possessive case form as an indication that one noun modifies another in some of the ways adjectives do. (See pages 147–150.) Consider these examples:

a **week's** vacation	the **flower's** fragrance
Egypt's history	a **car's** mileage
the **river's** source	your **money's** worth

Singular nouns

To form the possessive of a singular noun, add an apostrophe and *s*.

Kirsoff's review emphasized the **dramatist's** outstanding contribution to the arts.

A **woman's** effort to free herself from the past is the concern of Alice **Walker's** novel *Meridian*.

The Greeks tried to appease **Zeus's** anger, just as the Romans tried to avoid **Jupiter's** wrath.

Exception: Use only an apostrophe when a singular noun ending in *s* is followed by a word beginning with *s*.

The **boss'** salary is three times that of her assistant.

We discussed **Keats'** sonnets in class today.

In Langston **Hughes'** story "Thank You, M'am," a young boy finds kindness where he expected punishment.

Plural nouns

To form the possessive of a plural noun not ending in *s*, add an apostrophe and *s*.

The **women's** proposal called for a day-care center to be set up at their place of employment.

Dr. Seuss is a well-known name in the field of **children's** literature.

The store has introduced a new line of **men's** fragrances.

To form the possessive of a plural noun ending in s, add an apostrophe alone.

The **doctors'** commitment to their patients was questioned at the forum.

This course highlights two **composers'** works—Haydn and Mozart.

The **soldiers'** tales of atrocities enraged the public.

Compound nouns

To form the possessive of a compound noun, make the last word possessive.

Does anyone welcome a **mother-in-law's** advice?

As a result of the **Vice President's** remarks, the party asked for his removal from the ticket.

The editorial defended the **police officers'** conduct in the case.

Noun pairs or nouns in a series

To show joint possession, add an apostrophe and s to the last noun in a pair or a series.

Sociologists were concerned that **Charles and Diana's** announcement would set off a new baby boom in Britain.

Carter and Pollard's book examines certain nineteenth-century forgeries.

Lennon and McCartney's music had a dramatic effect on their contemporaries.

To show individual possession, add an apostrophe and s to each noun in a pair or series.

Anne Tyler's and **Sam Shepard's** styles have many similarities.

In *48 Hrs.*, **Nolte's** and **Murphy's** characters come from opposite sides of the law.

The **President's** and the **Vice President's** duties are clearly defined.

Nouns naming periods of time and sums of money

To form the possessive of a noun naming a period of time or a sum of money, add an apostrophe and *s* or an apostrophe if the noun is plural.

The value of **today's** dollar is less than the value of last **year's** dollar.

A good rule of thumb is that a **week's** salary should cover a **month's** rent.

Taxes can easily swallow several **days'** pay.

Indefinite pronouns

To form the possessive of some indefinite pronouns, add an apostrophe and *s*. (Note that *each, both, all* and some others can have no possessive form.)

We can learn from **each other's** mistakes.

How we can improve our care of the elderly is a subject on almost **everyone's** mind.

It can be argued that **no one's** life has been so poignant as that of David, the boy who lived almost his entire short life in an isolation bubble.

Personal pronouns

Do not use an apostrophe with the possessive forms of personal pronouns.

Her analysis of the problem was more complete than **yours.**

The druids' methods of telling time were quite different from **ours.**

Our troops are better prepared than **theirs.**

40b In Plural Forms

Add an apostrophe and *s* to form the plural of words being named, letters of the alphabet, abbreviations, numerals, and symbols. Apostrophe may be omitted with capitals without periods: TVs, UFOs, PhDs.

> One drawback of this typeface is that the capital *i*'s and the lowercase *l*'s look exactly alike.
> Avoid weakening your argument by including too many *but*'s and *however*'s.

40c In Contractions

Use an apostrophe to indicate a missing letter or letters in a contraction.

In general, use contractions only in informal writing.

> The Sherlock Holmes stories **weren't** Arthur Conan Doyle's only success.
> She claimed that enough attention **isn't** being paid to the threat of nuclear war.

Note: It's is a contraction that means "it is" or "it has." *Its* is a possessive pronoun that means "belonging to it." Do not confuse the two.

40d For Omissions

Use an apostrophe to indicate that part of a word or number has been omitted.

> In **'64** the Beatles invaded the United States with a new style of rock **'n'** roll.
> The manager told the singer to "go out and knock **'em** dead."

Exercise

In each of the following groups, circle the items that show the correct use of the apostrophe.

1. Shakespeare's sonnets, Dumas's stories, Brontë's novels

2. childrens' clothes, women's rights, mens' clothing

3. three employee's complaints, two student's papers, five athletes' visas

4. a year's salary, a season's growth, a day's labor

5. it's buzzer, his' youth, one of ours

6. anyone's knowledge, everybody's home, no ones' speech

7. the swinging '60's, the roaring '20's, the fabulous '50s

8. ca'nt, o'er, you're

9. Hal and Marie's apartment, Annette and Tom's house, Sid's and Fran's car (*joint ownership*)

10. Nancy's and Jack's papers, Chris' and Paul's checks, Sal's and Harry's remarks (*individual ownership*)

41 The Hyphen

41a In Compound Nouns

Use a dictionary to determine whether to spell a compound noun with a hyphen.

Relatively few compound nouns are hyphenated; most are written either solid (as one word) or open (as two or more separate words). The only kinds of compound nouns that are usually hyphenated are those made up of two equally important nouns and those made up of three or more words.

philosopher-king	city-state	man-hour
mother-in-law	free-for-all	jack-of-all-trades

41b In Compound Adjectives

Hyphenate two or more words that serve as a single adjective preceding a noun.

well-known painter   **law-school** degree
soft-spoken man   **sure-to-win** candidate
too-good-to-be-true behavior

Do you know the difference between **mass-market** paperbacks and trade paperbacks?
Cheever's stories provide insight into **middle-class** suburban life.
The company is investigating both the **short-term** and the **long-term** benefits of scattered work hours.

In general, do not hyphenate such words when they follow a noun.

painter who is **well known**
degree from a **law school**
man who is **soft spoken**
candidate who is **sure to win**
behavior that is **too good to be true**

Do you know the difference between novels that are considered **mass market** and novels that are considered trade?

> Cheever's stories provide insight into the lives of suburban people who are **middle class.**
>
> The benefits of scattered work hours are both **short term** and **long term.**

Do not hyphenate two or more words that precede a noun when the first of these words is an adverb ending in *-ly.*

> Critics attacked the President's **rapidly expanding** budget.
>
> When Menudo first came to this city, the police were called in to restrain the crowd of **wildly screaming** teenagers.
>
> The government's **widely criticized** policies are the subject of the debate on television today.

Use a "hanging" hyphen after the first part of a hyphenated compound adjective used in a series, where the second part of the compound adjective is implied but omitted.

> both **paid-** and complimentary-ticket holders
>
> both **short-** and long-term disability
>
> all **first-, second-,** and third-year students

41c In Compound Numbers and Fractions

Hyphenate spelled-out numbers from *twenty-one* through *ninety-nine* and spelled-out fractions used as adjectives.

In spelled-out numbers larger than *ninety-nine,* do not use a hyphen before or after *hundred, thousand,* and so forth.

> The Protestant Bible has **thirty-nine** books in the Old Testament and **twenty-seven** in the New Testament.
>
> **Two hundred fifty-seven** people were killed in the fire.
>
> The installation of computers has effected a **one-third** increase in productivity and an expected **three-quarter** growth in profits.

Do not hyphenate spelled-out fractions used as nouns.

> About **one half** of Yugoslavia is covered with mountains.
> Only **three eighths** of the adults in this community voted in the
> last election.

41d With Prefixes and Suffixes

In general, do not use a hyphen between a prefix and its root
or a suffix and its root. However, there are several exceptions.

Use a hyphen between a prefix and its root to avoid am-
biguity.

the **re-creation** of the world	*but*	tennis as **recreation**
to **re-count** money	*but*	to **recount** an event
a **co-op** apartment	*but*	a chicken **coop**

Use a hyphen between a prefix and its root when the last
letter of the prefix and the first letter of the root are the same
vowel or when the first letter of the root is capitalized.

sem**i-i**ndustrial	ant**i-i**ntellectual
supr**a-a**uditory	r**e-e**cho
un-**A**merican	pro-**W**estern

Exceptions:
Frequent usage may allow the elimination of the hyphen.
(Consult the dictionary.)

> *Example:*   *Cooperation, preempt, reexamine,* and so on.

Use a hyphen between the prefixes *all-, ex-* ("former"), and
self- and their roots and between the suffix *-elect* and its root.

all-star	all-time
ex-senator	ex-husband

self-control   self-sufficient
mayor-elect   president-elect

41e For Word Division
at the End of a Line

A hyphen is used to indicate that a word has been divided at the end of a line. However, some words may not be divided, and no word should be divided except between syllables. The following are some general rules for word division; consult a dictionary for words not covered by these rules.

Do not divide a one-syllable word.

truth   strayed   twelve
fifth   strength   gauche

Do not divide a word so that a one-letter syllable appears on a separate line.

Not: a-mount   e-rase   sand-y
But: amount   erase   sandy

Do not divide proper names.

Not: Eliza-beth   Mal-ory   Pas-cal
But: Elizabeth   Malory   Pascal

In general, divide words between double consonants.

sad-dle   com-mit-ted   cor-ruption   refer-ral
daz-zle   as-sistant   im-mortal   dif-ferent

In general, divide words between the prefix and the root or between the suffix and the root.

non-violent	in-sincere	re-dedicate
appease-ment	fellow-ship	mother-hood

Note: Do not carry over a two-letter suffix—*loaded* not *load-ed.*

Try to divide a hyphenated word at the hyphen.

Not:	self-de-nial	quick-tem-pered	cold-blood-edness
But:	self-denial	quick-tempered	cold-bloodedness

Exercise 1

Circle the correct form of each word in parentheses in the following sentences.

1. According to (*well informed/well-informed*) sources, Smith believes that (*three eighths/three-eighths*) of the voters now favor her, while (*one quarter/one-quarter*) are still undecided.

2. The (*beatup/beat-up*) car in the (*parking-lot/parking lot*) had a (*for-sale/for sale*) sign in its window.

3. His (*winner-take-all/winner take all*) attitude prevented him from turning his (*newly-defeated/newly defeated*) opponents into allies.

4. The (*in house/in-house*) (*newsletter/news letter*) contained an article that was (*well-researched/well researched*).

5. This (*thought-provoking/thought provoking*) article contained comments by (*twenty one/twenty-one*) lawyers on the emotional entanglements that can arise from a (*lawyer client/lawyer-client*) relation.

Exercise 2

Circle any correctly hyphenated words in each of the following groups.

1. self-control, in-discreet, dis-interested

2. anti-intellectual, semi-formal, de-escalate

3. bi-annual, mid-September, pro-West

4. all-time, all-star, all-American

5. senator-elect, non-aligned, un-democratic

Exercise 3

Imagine the following words appear at the end of lines. Circle any correctly divided words in each group.

1. non-committal, gam-y, brid-ge

2. self-con-fident, distrust-ful, impossibil-ity

3. impres-sion, pos-sess, specula-tion

4. avoid-ed, special-ty, adapt-able

5. Bo-wen, Eu-ler, Py-thagoras

Part VI

Diction

Diction is the choice and arrangement of words in writing. Good diction helps you reach your audience, achieve your purpose, maintain an appropriate tone, and write with style.

42   Appropriate Word Choice ▬▬▬

Whenever you write, the most basic decision you have to make about diction is whether to use formal or informal English. Formal English, as its name suggests, adheres strictly to the conventions of standard English. Most of the writing you do in college or in a profession—term papers, formal essays, theses, reports—should be in formal English. Informal English takes a more relaxed attitude to the conventions of standard English and may include contractions, colloquialisms, jargon, and sometimes even slang. It is appropriate for informal writing situations—journal and diary entries, informal essays, and creative writing in which you try to capture the sound of everyday speech.

Informal: The delegates **were savvy of the fact** that the document they were signing **wasn't** perfect.

Formal: The delegates **understood** that the document they were signing **was not** perfect.

Informal: The candidate **knocked** her opponent for often **changing his tune** on the issues.

Formal: The candidate **criticized** her opponent for often **changing his views** on the issues.

Informal: Stickley furniture may not be **real cushy,** but **it's pricey** and **in.**

Formal: Stickley furniture may not be **very comfortable,** but **it is expensive** and **fashionable.**

A good dictionary will not only help you determine whether a word or expression is formal or informal but also provide other useful information. Here is a list of three good desk dictionaries and a sample listing from the first one.

1. *The American Heritage Dictionary*. 2nd coll. ed. Boston: Houghton Mifflin, 1982.
2. *Webster's New World Dictionary of the American Language*. 2nd coll. ed. New York: Simon & Schuster, 1982.
3. *The Random House College Dictionary*. New York: Random House, 1987.

Pronunciation **doubt** (dout) *v.* doubt-ed, doubt-ing, doubts. —*tr.* **1.** To be undecided or skeptical about. **2.** To tend to disbelieve; distrust: *doubts the promises of all politicians.* **3.** *Archaic.* To suspect; fear. —*intr.* To be undecided. —*n.* **1.** A lack of conviction or certainty. **2.** A lack of trust. **3.** A point about which one is uncertain or skeptical. **4.** An uncertain state of affairs: *an outcome still in doubt.* —*idioms.* beyond (or without) doubt. Without question; certainly; definitely. no doubt. **1.** Certainly. **2.** Probably. [ME *douten* < OFr. *douter* < Lat. *dubitare*, to waver.] —doubt'er *n.*

Forms and usage as a verb

Definitions as a noun

Etymology

Explanation of usage

Usage: *Doubt* and *doubtful* are often followed by clauses introduced by *that, whether,* or *if.* A choice among the three is guided by the intended meaning of the sentence, but considerable leeway exists. Generally, *that* is used when the intention is to express more or less complete rejection of a statement: *I doubt that he will even try* (meaning, "I don't think he will even try"); or, in the negative, to express more or less complete acceptance: *I don't doubt that you are right.* On the other hand, when the intention is to express real uncertainty, the choice is usually *whether: We doubt whether they can succeed. It is doubtful whether he will come.* According to a majority of the Usage Panel, *whether* is the only acceptable choice in such examples; a minority would also accept *if* (which is more informal in tone) or *that.* In sum, *that* is especially appropriate to the denial of uncertainty or to implied disbelief but is sometimes used also when the intention is to express real uncertainty. *Doubt* is frequently used in informal speech, both as verb and as noun, together with *but: I don't doubt but* (or *but what*) *he will come. There is no doubt but it will be difficult.* These usages should be avoided in writing; substitute *that* or *whether* as the case requires.

Syllabication

doubt · ful (dout'fəl) *adj.* **1.** Subject to or tending to cause doubt; uncertain: *It's doubtful if we'll ever know what hap-*

Beginning of a listing of related words

42a Slang

Slang is extremely informal language. It consists of colorful words, phrases, and expressions added to the language, usually by youthful or high-spirited people, to give it an exciting or ebullient flavor. Carl Sandburg described slang as "language that rolls up its sleeves, spits on its hands, and goes to work."

Slang is usually figurative and highly exaggerated. Each generation has its own slang; for example, in the 1960s someone who was approved of was *cool,* in the 1970s such a person was *with it,* and in the early 1980s, *awesome.* Although slang often begins as street language, some of it becomes so popular that with time it is accepted as part of formal language. Until a slang term becomes accepted, however, it is usually inappropriate in college writing.

> *Slang:*   Some parents **came unglued** when they were **clued in to** how some children's programs on the **boob tube** were really just extended commercials.
>
> *Formal:*   Some parents **became upset** when they were **made aware of** how some children's **television** programs were really just extended commercials.

> *Slang:*   **It's a real downer to rap about** the number of employees who **got the boot** during the late 1970s and early 1980s.
>
> *Formal:*   **It is sad to discuss** the number of employees who **were laid off** during the late 1970s and early 1980s.

> *Slang:*   Elizabeth Blackwell was **bummed out** by the nineteenth century's view of the ideal woman, but she managed to find a doctor who was **in groove with** her goal of studying medicine.
>
> *Formal:*   Elizabeth Blackwell was **disheartened** by the nineteenth century's view of the ideal woman, but she managed to find a doctor who was **sympathetic to** her goal of studying medicine.

Slang can be used judiciously for effect in formal writing. When you use slang this way, do not enclose it in quotation marks or underline it.

> The educated were turning in their diplomas for guitars, the rich were trading in their furs for jeans and love beads, and the middle-aged were pretending they were fifteen, not fifty; in fact, during this topsy-turvy time, everyone seemed to be **going bananas.**
>
> She was thoughtful, politically aware, well spoken, and well educated, but the movie directors of the 1950s preferred **bubblebrains.**
>
> As he grew older, he realized that his **old man** had been smarter than he thought.

42b Colloquialisms

Colloquial language is the conversational and everyday language of educated people. **Colloquialisms** are the words and expressions that characterize this language. While not as informal as slang, colloquial language is generally still too casual to be considered appropriate for formal writing.

Colloquial: The meeting will begin at 7:00 P.M. **on the dot.**
Formal: The meeting will begin **promptly** at 7:00 P.M.

Colloquial: In *Bodily Harm,* Rennie realizes she is **in a jam** when she opens the box and finds illegal guns.
Formal: In **Bodily Harm,** Rennie realizes she is **in trouble** when she opens the box and finds illegal guns.

Colloquial: When Colonel Pickering expresses doubt as to Higgins's ability to make a lady of Eliza, Higgins **tells him to put up or shut up.**
Formal: When Colonel Pickering expresses doubt as to Higgins's ability to make a lady of Eliza, Higgins **invites him to make a bet.**

Notice how the following sentences are improved when the colloquial qualifiers are replaced by more formal adverbs.

Colloquial: Harriet Tubman was a **terribly** brave woman, for she made several trips back into slave territory to lead fugitives into freedom.
Formal: Harriet Tubman was a **truly** brave woman, for she made several trips back into slave territory to lead fugitives into freedom.

Colloquial: General Harrison considered Tecumseh's plan to force the United States to relinquish its claims to Indian lands **awfully** clever, but not workable.
Formal: General Harrison considered Tecumseh's plan to force the United States to relinquish its claims to Indian lands **extremely** clever, but not workable.

Colloquial:	Television viewers were **pretty** moved by the program about nuclear war.
Formal:	Television viewers were **greatly** moved by the program about nuclear war.

42c Jargon

Jargon is the special language used by people in a particular field or group to communicate with others in the same field or group. The problem with jargon, or "shop talk," is that people outside the group have trouble understanding it. Language aimed at people with a specific technical or professional knowledge may be appropriate for some classes, but it is not appropriate for most general college writing. If you must use a technical term in general college writing, make sure you define it.

Consider the following paragraph aimed at people with a specialized knowledge of word processing.

> All your files will be stored on diskettes, including text files and any data files you may require. For that matter, WordStar's program files are also stored on a diskette. A disk file can hold either text, data, or a computer program. You can have Word-Star's files on one diskette and your typing files on another. Make sure you ask someone how the files are stored for your system. One typical set-up would be for you to have one Word-Star disk, one working disk, and several backup disks kept on a shelf for emergencies. (The more you work with computers, the more you will learn to value backup disks.)

Someone who is familiar with word-processing programs will easily understand this paragraph. However, the general audience at which you aim most of your college writing will not understand the jargon; they will not know the meaning of the terms *diskette, text file, data file, program file, disk file, typing file, stored, system, working disk,* and *backup disk.*

Now consider the following paragraphs in which William Zinsser tells how he began to overcome his frustration with learning word processing.

> A diskette, for example, was just a disk. But which kind of diskette was which? What exactly was the difference between the "program diskette" and the "work diskette"? Surely some kind of "work" got done on the program diskette. And where was the "work station" that the menu kept inviting me to use? I didn't remember unpacking it.
>
> As it turned out, the work station is the printer and the table that it sits on. As for the work diskette, it's the diskette that I'm supposed to put into the "diskette unit" (the toaster) to store my own work on. It's a blank disk that I can buy at the store, like a blank tape for a tape recorder. The program diskette is the disk that IBM does *its* work on; it's patented, and I can't buy it at any store. In short, the work diskette is my disk and the program diskette is their disk.
>
> William Zinsser
> *Writing with a Word Processor*

These paragraphs also contain jargon. Notice, though, that they are directed at a general audience of people who want to learn about word processing but right now do not have knowledge of it. Therefore, the author uses technical terms, but he defines these terms for his readers. In fact, to make his audience feel comfortable with so many technical terms, Zinsser creates a persona for himself—that of someone who is technically inept and quite confused by all the jargon. If I can learn word processing, he implies, so can you.

42d Gobbledygook

Gobbledygook is stuffy, pretentious, inflated language that often contains an abundance of jargon. It is found in much government, legal, and academic writing, as well as in many other places, and it is sometimes called *governmentese* or *legalese*. Avoid gobbledygook, since it obscures meaning and lends both a timid and a pompous quality to your writing.

A major advocate of eliminating gobbledygook, especially from government writing, is Rudolf Flesch. In his book *How to Write Plain English,* he shows how Oregon's 1976 income tax instructions were rewritten in 1977 to eliminate gobbledygook.

1976

Deceased persons. A return must be made by the executor or administrator of the decedent's estate or by the surviving spouse or other person charged with the care of the property of the deceased. If the surviving spouse or next of kin desires to claim the refund, an affidavit should be submitted with the return. This affidavit (Form 243) is available at all Oregon Department of Revenue district offices, or it can be obtained by writing the Oregon Department of Revenue, State Office Building, Salem, Oregon 97310.

1977

My husband died last year. Can I file for him? Yes. The husband or wife of someone who dies, or the legal representative, must file the return. Use the form the person would have used if living. If you claim a refund, attach Form 243 to show you have the right to the deceased person's refund. Write for Form 243 to: Oregon Department of Revenue, Salem, Oregon 97310, or pick it up at any of our district offices.

Exercise

Rephrase each of the following sentences in formal English.

1. When we turn our gray matter ~~minds~~ to the fate of the Cherokees, we

    can see that it was a real down ~~sad~~ day in our history when these

    folks ~~Indians removed from~~ were kicked out of their lands by Uncle Sam. ~~the govt.~~

2. Hamlet knows that his old man ~~father~~ didn't kick the bucket ~~die a~~ natural

    like ~~death~~ but was knocked off ~~killed~~ by his brother, Hamlet's unk. ~~uncle.~~

3. The Model T was the super-duper ~~fantastic~~ idea of Henry Ford, the whiz ~~founder~~

    of the auto biz. ~~marvel~~ ~~bus~~

4. The nurse recorded the deceased's expiration date ~~date of death~~ on his chart.

5. Kennedy didn't punk out ~~cower~~ when he came up against the Reds

    during the Cuban missile crisis; instead he stood pat ~~remained firm~~ and kept

    cool until Khrushchev chickened out ~~backed down~~ and agreed to pull ~~remove~~ the

    missiles out ~~from~~ of Cuba.

6. After he was caught with the goods, ~~arrested with the stolen property~~ even his legal beagle ~~atty~~

    couldn't keep him out of the monkey cage. ~~jail~~

7. During the 1950s, idiot boxes ~~TVs~~ sold like hotcakes, ~~so quickly~~ and whole ~~entire~~

    families spent their evenings glued to the tube. ~~watching TV.~~

8. We hung out and chewed the fat ~~talked and visited~~ about the latest glad rags ~~fashions~~ from

    Paris.

9. For eight years the actress was an also-ran, ~~a has been~~ but now she's nu-

    mero uno. ~~#1~~

10. The colonists merely kicked ~~thought about~~ about the Sugar Act, but the Stamp

    Act got them real ticked off. ~~very angry.~~

43 Exact Word Choice

Choose words that express your thoughts precisely. Do not settle for a near-synonym or an almost-right word, but pay attention to shades of meaning and nuances.

43a Specific and General Words

Specific words are precise, focused, and restricted in scope. General words are not focused; they refer to a large group or a wide range of things. For example, compare the following general and specific words.

General:	painter	make	hungry	some
Specific:	Mary Cassatt	coerce	voracious	thirty-five

The word *painter* refers to a whole group of people. *Mary Cassatt* refers to just one. The word *make* refers to a wide range of actions; *coerce* limits this range, meaning "to make someone do something or to make something happen through the use of force or pressure." The word *hungry* indicates a desire for food or for something else, but *voracious* indicates that this desire is overwhelming and insatiable. The word *some* indicates a number larger than a few, but *thirty-five* indicates a specific number.

Consider how the following sentences are improved through the use of a specific word.

General:	The **official** was accused of **working** for a **foreign government.**
Specific:	**Alger Hiss** was accused of **spying** for the **Soviet Union.**
General:	This **woman,** who is best known for **longer things,** also wrote **several good** ghost stories, which are collected in a **book.**

Specific:	**Edith Wharton,** who is best known for her **novels,** also wrote **eleven riveting** ghost stories, which are collected in ***The Ghost Stories of Edith Wharton.***
General:	**Some writers** are **liked** for their **sense of humor.**
Specific:	**Dorothy Parker and Robert Benchley** are **appreciated** for their **wry, and sometimes biting, wit.**

Of course, general words do have a place in your writing. They introduce topics that you can later elaborate on or narrow. When you use a general word, however, consider narrowing the scope of this word later in your writing, if not immediately. Always search for an alternative before using adjectives and adverbs such as *good, nice, bad, very, great, fine, awfully, well done,* or *interesting.* Words like these are so general, that is, have so many meanings, that paradoxically they convey almost no meaning at all.

43b Concrete and Abstract Words

Concrete words create vivid impressions. They name things that can be seen, touched, heard, smelled, or tasted—in other words, things that can be perceived by the senses. The words *skyscraper, microfilm, buzzer, gourmet, pizza,* and *porcupine* are concrete words. *Abstract words* name concepts, ideas, beliefs, and qualities—in other words, things that cannot be perceived by the senses. For example, the words *democracy, honesty, childhood,* and *infinity* are abstract words. Use abstract words with care, since, in general, they create less intense impressions and so are often ineffective.

Abstract:	He argued that this nation could no longer accept poverty.
Concrete:	Hungry children crying themselves to sleep, families evicted from their homes and sleeping in the streets, old people in cold-water flats surviving by

eating cat food—these are conditions, he argued, that we as Americans can no longer tolerate.

Abstract: Immigrants came to America in search of a better life.

Concrete: Immigrants came to America to farm their own land, to earn a living wage, to put a roof over their heads and food in their stomachs, and to speak and believe as they wished without fear of being thrown in jail.

Abstract: One reason supermarkets began to replace ma-and-pa grocery stores is that they offered more variety.

Concrete: One reason supermarkets began to replace ma-and-pa grocery stores is that they offered not one brand of peas, but seven brands; not one kind of coffee, but six kinds; not one type of paper towel, but ten in five different colors—all under one roof.

Of course, abstract words do have a place in your writing. However, too many of them can create an impression of vagueness. When you do use abstract words, try to provide concrete examples to make their meaning vivid. Compare the following pairs of sentences. The second sentence in each pair contains a concrete example that clarifies the meaning of the abstract word or words in the first sentence.

Hating people is self-destructive.
Hating people is like burning down your own house to get rid of a rat.

Harry Emerson Fosdick

Circumstance makes heroes of people.
A light supper, a good night's sleep, and a fine morning often made a hero of the same man who by indigestion, a restless night, and a rainy morning would have proved a coward.

Earl of Chesterfield

Americans are absorbed in the present but are unaware of the past.

We Americans are the best informed people on earth as to the events of the last twenty-four hours; we are not the best informed as to the events of the last sixty centuries.

Will and Ariel Durant

Exercise

Each of the following sentences is vague or unclear. Rewrite each sentence, replacing general and abstract words with specific or concrete ones.

1. A bad storm can do a great deal of damage.

2. Houseplants may substitute for pets.

3. Hope is a basic requirement of human life.

4. Modern sculptors sometimes use unusual materials.

5. Many people will not take a stand on an issue.

6. The couple felt that their landlord had been unfair.

7. The landlords felt they had grounds for eviction.

8. Most fairy tales end in the same way.

9. The movie was interesting, exciting, and full of action.

10. The media have become very important.

43c Denotation and Connotation

Besides their **denotation,** or basic dictionary definition, many words also have **connotations**—associations that the word brings to mind and emotions that it arouses. Words that have the same dictionary meaning may have quite different connotations. For example, consider the following two sentences.

The clothes at this boutique are quite **cheap.**
The clothes at this boutique are quite **reasonable.**

Both *cheap* and *reasonable* have the dictionary meaning of "not expensive." However, *cheap* carries a negative connotation of low value, while *reasonable* carries a positive connotation of fair value.

When you write, you must choose words with the appropriate connotations.

Inappropriate:	The quality of **childish** innocence shines through her poetry.
Appropriate:	The quality of **childlike** innocence shines through her poetry.
Inappropriate:	The editorial praised the candidate for being a rugged **egocentric.**
Appropriate:	The editorial praised the candidate for being a rugged **individualist.**
Inappropriate:	In 1873, the Supreme Court prevented Myra Bradwell from becoming a lawyer, since it did not consider the law an **effeminate** profession.
Appropriate:	In 1873, the Supreme Court prevented Myra Bradwell from becoming a lawyer, since it did not consider the law a **ladylike** profession.

Some words have such strong connotations that they are said to be *loaded.* When used, they go off with a deafening emotional bang. For example, the words *slumlord, witch-hunt,* and *imperialism* are all loaded. Their connotative effect drowns out their denotative meaning. Be careful of loaded words, since they can make your writing appear biased. (See pages 18–20; 108.)

Exercise

In each of the following pairs, the words have the same or almost the same denotative meaning but different connotations. Write a sentence for each word that shows you understand its connotative value. You may use your dictionary to help you.

1. harm/hurt

2. skinny/slim

3. idealistic/unrealistic

4. sweet/sugary

5. circumspect/sly

6. learned/pedantic

7. conflict/war

8. dress/gown

9. murmur/mutter

10. taste/savor

43d Wordiness and Repetition

Write as concisely as possible. Do not use five words where one will do. Avoid using empty words and unnecessary repetitions. Conciseness gives vigor to your style.

One way to achieve conciseness is to eliminate wordy expressions. Notice how each of the following phrases can be changed to a single-word equivalent.

Wordy	*Concise*
at all times when	whenever
at this point in time	now

Wordy	Concise
at that point in time	then
because of the fact that	because
bring to a conclusion	conclude
by means of	by
due to the fact that	because
during the time that	while
in the event that	if
in spite of the fact that	although
make reference	refer
be of the opinion that	think
on a great many occasions	often
prior to this time	before
until such time as	until
have a conference	confer

You can also make your writing more concise by deleting superfluous words, using exact words, and reducing larger elements to smaller elements. Notice how the following sentence is improved when the author uses these revision strategies:

Wordy: In the month of April in the year 1984, men who were flying in space on board the spaceship that was named *Challenger* made an attempt to catch hold of and perform a repair job on a satellite that had been disabled.

Concise: In April 1984, astronauts on board the spaceship *Challenger* attempted to grab and repair a disabled satellite.

The words *the month of* and *in the year* add nothing to the meaning of the sentence; they simply fill up space and can be deleted. The noun phrase *men who were flying in space* can be replaced by one exact noun—*astronauts*. The words *that was named* are also deadwood. The phrase *made an attempt* can be reduced to the more direct *attempted, catch hold of* to *grab,* and *perform a repair job on* to *repair.* The clause *that had been disabled* can be reduced to the single word *disabled.*

Wordy:	A man named Allan Dwan, who was a pioneer in the field of filmmaking, began his career as a director in the year 1910.
Concise:	Allan Dwan, a pioneer filmmaker, began directing in 1910.
Wordy:	The film that is called *The Birth of a Nation* and that was made by D. W. Griffith has caused a lot of controversy among people.
Concise:	D. W. Griffith's film *The Birth of a Nation* is highly controversial.

Avoid the wordiness that comes from overuse of prepositional phrases, the weak verb *be,* and relative pronouns.

Wordy:	The book examines the twentieth century **in terms of** its wars, depressions, and social changes.
Concise:	The book examines the twentieth century, its wars, depressions, and social changes.
Wordy:	1941 **was** the year **when, on** December 7, the Japanese bombed Pearl Harbor.
Concise:	On December 7, 1941, the Japanese bombed Pearl Harbor.
Wordy:	The car **that** was parked on the street, **close to** the curb is the **kind of** car **that** I have always wanted to own.
Concise:	I have always wanted a car like the one parked at the curb.

Using the active voice instead of the passive voice will usually make a sentence more concise. Sometimes, however, the passive voice is the simplest and most concise way to express an idea. For example, the sentences *Her husband was killed in Vietnam* or *The President is inaugurated on January 20* would be much wordier and more awkward if they were rewritten to make the verbs active. In general, however, the passive voice is wordier than the active voice. Notice how the following sentences are improved by changing the passive voice to the active voice and eliminating other kinds of wordiness.

Wordy: Studies **are being undertaken** by doctors who specialize in psychology to find out what effects the divorce of two parents has on the children of the two parents.

Concise: Psychologists **are studying** the effects of divorce on children.

Wordy: According to the author, whose name is Freeman Dyson, *Weapons and Hope* **was chosen** by him as the title for his book because a desire **was felt** by him "to discuss the gravest problem facing mankind, the problem of nuclear weapons."

Concise: Freeman Dyson **titled** his book *Weapons and Hope* because he **wanted** "to discuss the gravest problem facing mankind, the problem of nuclear weapons."

Wordy: Advice about gardening **is given** every day by Blair Michels, and this advice **is printed** on page 13 of this newspaper.

Concise: Blair Michels **gives** daily gardening advice on page 13 of this newspaper.

Try to avoid the constructions *it is, it was, there is,* and *there was.* Like the passive voice, these constructions are sometimes useful and appropriate, but often they are an unnecessarily wordy way of introducing an idea. Notice how the following sentences are improved by eliminating them.

Wordy: It is known that there is a need for security in children.

Concise: Children need security.

Wordy:	It is a fact that the painting is a forgery.
Consise:	The painting is a forgery.
Wordy:	There is a need among modern people to gain an understanding of the risks of modern technology.
Concise:	We need to understand the risks of modern technology.

Another cause of wordiness is redundant elements, words or phrases that unnecessarily repeat the idea expressed by the word to which they are attached. For example, the phrase *to the ear* is redundant in the expression *audible to the ear* because *audible* itself means "able to be perceived by the ear." Here is a list of some other common expressions that contain redundant elements.

Redundant	*Concise*
and etc.	etc.
bibliography of books	bibliography
mandatory requirements	requirements
refer back	refer
tall in height	tall
collaborate together	collaborate
visible to the eye	visible
repeat again	repeat
advance forward	advance
negative complaints	complaints
humorous comedy	comedy
close proximity	proximity
expensive in price	expensive
past history	history
continue to remain	remain
component parts	components

Not:	The plot of Le Carré's **fictional novel** *The Little Drummer Girl* involves the **emotionally passionate** claims of the Israelis and the Palestinians.

But: The plot of Le Carré's novel *The Little Drummer Girl* involves the **passionate** claims of the Israelis and the Palestinians.

Not: The **consensus of opinion** is that the **true facts** of the **fatal assassination** may never be known.

But: The **consensus** is that the facts of the **assassination** may never be known.

Not: Copies of the **biography of his life** quickly **disappeared from sight** on the shelves, although the book was **large in size** and **heavy in weight.**

But: Copies of the **biography** quickly **disappeared** from the shelves, although the book was **large** and **heavy.**

Repetition has an important place in writing. It can be used effectively to emphasize a point or to complete a parallel structure. However, needless or excessive repetition weakens your writing. You can eliminate it by deleting the repeated words or by substituting synonyms or pronouns for them.

Not: Lady **Macbeth** urges **Macbeth** to murder the **king** so that **Macbeth** can become **king.**

But: Lady **Macbeth** urges **her husband** to murder the **king** so that **he** can gain **the crown.**

Not: One admirer of the rock group Devo has found similarities between **the works of Devo** and the **works** of the Dadaists.

But: One admirer of the rock group Devo has found similarities between **their works** and **those** of the Dadaists.

Not: After they decided to shoot the movie in a **shopping mall,** they examined thirty-five **shopping malls** until they found the right **shopping mall.**

But: After they decided to shoot the movie in a **shopping mall,** they examined thirty-five **malls** until they found the right **one.**

43e Flowery Language

Wherever possible, use simple and direct words and phrases instead of showy and pretentious ones.

Flowery: Travelers on the road of life cannot help looking back and considering the possibility of whether any companion on this lonely journey will remember them after they have passed from this vale of tears.

Direct: People cannot help wondering whether anyone will remember them after they die.

Flowery: Even a person who passes his daily hours by contemplating the strange little tricks played on unsuspecting victims by cruel and relentless fate receives a jolt that shakes him to the depths of his being when, at the Huntington Library, he sets his eyes upon the pass that Lincoln inscribed in his own hand to allow his trusted bodyguard to be absent from his side on that fateful night of April 14, 1865.

Direct: Even people who appreciate the ironies of life receive a jolt when, at the Huntington Library, they see the pass that Lincoln wrote for his bodyguard to have the night off on April 14, 1865.

Flowery: The streets of this fair city were graced on this day of May 19, 1984, by the arrival of Hank Morris, an artist of more than well-deserved distinction.

Direct: The distinguished artist Hank Morris arrived in town on May 19, 1984.

Exercise

Revise each of the following sentences to eliminate wordiness, needless repetition, or flowery language.

1. Operators of motor vehicles must conduct themselves defensively behind the wheel at all times while driving on congested

metropolitan thoroughfares and when wending their way along country lanes as well.

2. A story about ghosts that many critics feel has not been surpassed by any other story about ghosts was written by a writer who was an American and who was named Henry James, and it was called *The Turn of the Screw.*

3. All of the students who participated in the two trips in the field are reminded that their reports of those excursions will be overdue unless they are submitted promptly in accordance with the prearranged time schedule.

4. In this day and age in which we find ourselves today, no living human being can look ahead to forecast coming events.

5. The trials and tribulations of daily life, in the midst of which the breadwinner must keep body and soul together, the wolf from the door, and food on the table for his or her loved ones, are enough to drive many individuals, both male and female, to a state in which they might forcibly remove the hairs from their heads.

6. It is interesting and enlightening to compare and to show the similarity between the writer Edgar Allan Poe's story ''The Oval Portrait'' and the writer Oscar Wilde's novel *The Picture of Dorian Gray.*

7. The stranger in the Western community, who was unknown and who spoke an Eastern dialect with which those townspeople were unfamiliar, was living dangerously and asking for trouble when he risked joining them to participate in a card game of chance.

8. A flaw is shown by Billy Budd that mars his otherwise perfect beauty; his flaw is that at each time that he is confronted by a situation that makes him feel upset and ill at ease, he experiences an interruption in his speech, a spasmodic hesitation or prolongation of sounds.

9. The vitamin supplement that was to be added to the diet of the dog to improve the luster of the coat of the dog was recommended by the doctor who specializes in the treatment of animals.

10. In Gina Berriault's *The Infinite Passion of Expectation,* it is shown that the happiness and contentment of a person must come from the inside of the person; this "passion of expectation" gives to the person the ability to continue to go on.

43f Figurative Language

Franklin P. Jones once quipped, "You're an old-timer if you can remember when setting the world on fire was a figure of speech." In a **figure of speech,** or **figurative language,** words are used in an imaginative and often unusual way to create a vivid impression. For example, as a figure of speech, *setting the world on fire* means "doing something astounding that gains recognition." Literally, of course, setting the world on fire means burning it. Most figures of speech make a direct or indirect comparison between two things that are essentially unlike each other. Three common types of figures of speech are *simile, metaphor,* and *personification.*

Simile

A **simile** uses the word *like* or *as* to make a direct comparison between two essentially unlike things: for example, "He was like a lion in the fight." Here are some other examples of simile.

> The land was perfectly flat and level but it shimmered like the wing of a lighted butterfly.
>
> Eudora Welty

> He wore faded denims through which his clumsy muscles bulged like animals in a sack.
>
> Ross MacDonald

> Art is like a border of flowers along the course of civilization.
>
> Lincoln Steffens

> The man's tie was as orange as a sunset.
>
> Dashiell Hammett

> He [Monet] paints as a bird sings.
>
> Paul Signac

exact

Metaphor

A **metaphor** is an indirect comparison between two essentially unlike things that does not use the word *like* or *as*. In a metaphor the writer says or implies that one thing *is* another: for example, "He was a lion in the fight." Here are some other examples of metaphor.

> Advertising is the rattling of a stick inside a swill bucket.
>
> George Orwell

> His elegance was the thorn. And he was well aware that his aversion to coarseness, his delight in refinement, were futile; he was a plant without roots.
>
> Mishima Yukio

> Roads became black velvet ribbons with winking frost sequins. Pines became whispering flocks of huge, dark birds and the hilltop and pasture cedars were black candle flames.
>
> Hal Borland

> He gave her a look you could have poured on a waffle.
>
> Ring Lardner

> A California oak is a tough, comforting thing—half tree, half elephant—its gray, baggy elbows bending solicitously close to the ground, following the contours of the hill.
>
> Phyllis Theroux

Personification

Personification is the attributing of human qualities to inanimate objects or abstract ideas. You may have noticed the word *solicitously* in the preceding example of metaphor. This is an example of personification, since an oak cannot be solicitous; solicitousness is a human quality. Here are some other examples of personification.

> His clothes were dark and a white handkerchief peeped coyly from his pocket and he looked cool as well as under a tension of some sort.
>
> Raymond Chandler

> A painting in a museum hears more ridiculous opinions than anything else in the world.
>
> Edmond De Goncourt

> In all its career the Rio Grande knows several typical kinds of landscape, some of which are repeated along its great length.
>
> Paul Horgan

> I am for an art that is political—erotical—mystical, that does something other than sit on its ass in a museum.
>
> Claes Oldenburg

Mixed Metaphor

A **mixed metaphor** is one that is not logically consistent. Complete your figurative comparisons appropriately.

- *Not:* The river was a giant **snake** that **galloped** through the valley. (*Snakes cannot gallop.*)
- *But:* The river was a giant **snake** that **slithered** through the valley.
- *Not:* The bill **rolled** through the House with little opposition, but it **ran aground** in the Senate. (*Something that is rolling cannot run aground, since one action occurs on a solid surface and the other on water.*)

But:	The bill **rolled** through the House with little opposition, but it **hit a stone wall** in the Senate.
Or:	The bill **sailed** through the House with little opposition, but it **ran aground** in the Senate.
Not:	Her **shallow** arguments were easily refuted by the more **solid** reasoning of her opponent. (*You cannot contrast something shallow with something solid;* shallow *refers to depth, whereas* solid *refers to firmness.*)
But:	Her **shallow** arguments were easily refuted by the more **profound** reasoning of her opponent.
Or:	Her **flimsy** arguments were easily refuted by the more **solid** reasoning of her opponent.

Exercise

Use figurative language to complete each of the following items in a vivid and consistent manner.

1. The flock of birds (*the call of the loon/the donkey's bray*) sounded like . . .

2. From the airplane the river (*the town/the fields*) looked like . .

3. When he opened the test, he felt . . .

4. At the good news she felt . . .

5. The silence was like . . .

6. The bed of flowers was . . .

7. The little boat . . .

8. Dogs and cats are as different as . . .

9. Her words were as . . . as . . .

10. The loss of . . . was like . . .

43g Clichés

A **cliché** is an overused phrase or figure of speech that has lost its freshness and its ability to express thoughts exactly. Chlichés bore the reader and give the impression that the writer is lazy or unimaginative. Avoid staleness in your writing; strive for freshness and originality. Eliminate all clichés.

The following is a list of clichés. Avoid them and others like them.

shadow of a doubt	all walks of life
busy as a beaver	as luck would have it
bee in your bonnet	the crack of dawn
babbling brook	green with envy
depths of despair	take the bull by the horns
face the music	the acid test
bite the bullet	as happy as a lark
to the bitter end	in the nick of time
a thinking person	as sly as a fox
never a dull moment	as proud as a peacock
in the final analysis	callow youth
a crying shame	fly in the ointment
a bundle of joy	out of the woods
as quick as a wink	count on one hand
by the skin of our teeth	by hook or by crook
interesting to note	in the blink of an eye
slowly but surely	by the seat of my pants
in his heart of hearts	the depths of her soul

Clever writers or speakers often use clichés in an original way.

> Marriage is a great institution, but I'm not ready for an institution, yet.
>
> Mae West

> There nearly always is a method in madness. That's what drives men mad, being methodical.
>
> G. K. Chesterton

Life is just a bowl of pits.

Rodney Dangerfield

Ecologists believe that a bird in the bush is worth two in the hand.

Stanley C. Pearson

43h   Euphemisms

Euphemisms are words that disguise seemingly harsh or offensive realities. Euphemisms are quite rightly used in many situations to be polite or to avoid giving offense. There is nothing really wrong with referring to old people as *senior citizens* or to dead people as having *passed on.* However, many euphemisms have become clichés; they also tend to be wordy and to give writing a timid quality. In addition, euphemism can be improperly used to cover up the truth. Euphemism is commonly used in this way in gobbledygook.

Not: The employees who had been notified of an interruption in their employment were referred to their outplacement manager.

But: The laid-off employees were told to speak to the person who would try to help them find new jobs.

Not: The official acknowledged that he had misspoken when he said the troops had not engaged in any protective-reaction missions.

But: The official admitted that he had lied when he claimed the troops had not engaged in any offensive missions.

Or: The official admitted he had been lying when he claimed the troops had not attacked any enemy positions.

Not: The prisoner's life will be terminated at dawn.

But: The prisoner will be shot at dawn.

Exercise

Rewrite each of the following sentences to eliminate clichés and euphemisms.

1. The machine is not operational at this point in time.

2. He passed the test by the skin of his teeth.

3. The funds came through in the nick of time.

4. Although the interment of his bosom buddy upset him, he knew that into each life some rain must fall.

5. The company announced that it was relocating to another state and releasing its employees.

6. A good time was had by all at the party to mark the entrance into this world of a little bundle of joy.

7. He experienced a temporary setback to his earning potential.

8. Although she felt as fit as a fiddle, she was disturbed by the appearance of a large beauty mark on her left cheek.

9. Residents in this correctional facility dine on Salisbury steak every Monday.

10. It was raining cats and dogs when the government tested its new antipersonnel device.

44 Correct Word Choice

A **malapropism** is a word or expression that sounds unintentionally humorous when it is used in place of the similar-sounding one that the writer intended. The term is derived from Mrs. Malaprop, a pretentious character in Richard Sheridan's eighteenth-century play *The Rivals,* who uses near-miss words with a hilarious effect. For example, she refers to an "allegory [*rather than* alligator] on the banks of the Nile" and to another character's "historical [*rather than* hysterical] fit."

Do not be a Mrs. Malaprop. If you are not sure of the meaning of a word, look it up.

Not: Women charged with witchcraft were often accused of using spells and **incarnations** to cause their neighbors misfortune.

But: Women charged with witchcraft were often accused of using spells and **incantations** to cause their neighbors misfortune.

Not: At the end of the book are several helpful **appendages.**
But: At the end of the book are several helpful **appendixes.**

Not: The author argues that environmental damage is not necessarily a **coronary** of industrial development.
But: The author argues that environmental damage is not necessarily a **corollary** of industrial development.

Exercise

Choose the word in parentheses that sensibly completes each of the following sentences. Use your dictionary where necessary.

1. As soon as the sun came up, we (*ascended/descended*) from the top of the mountain.

2. Often on the desert what appears to be an oasis is only an (*allusion/illusion*).

3. The room was so hot that the flowers quickly dropped their (*pedals/petals*).

4. Most people know what their (*conscience/conscious*) advises them to do.

5. Not every business closes its (*fiscal/physical*) year on December 31.

6. My sister studied in France to become a (*gourmand/gourmet*) cook.

7. The burglar found a most (*ingenious/ingenuous*) way to get into the locked house.

8. Those who (*gesticulate/matriculate*) this September must take four courses in physical education.

9. She applied for a job in the (*Personal/Personnel*) Department.

10. A vigorously barking dog is an effective (*detergent/deterrent*) to crime.

44a Homonyms

A writer can get into difficulty with careless choice among **homonyms,** words that sound alike but have different meanings and spellings. Here are some examples of many that can give trouble.

altar/alter	presence/presents
cite/sight/site	there/their/they're
dual/duel	to/too
hole/whole	weather/whether
pair/pare	who's/whose
past/passed	your/you're

Part VII

Writing the Research Paper

The word *research* comes from an Old French word meaning "to seek out" or "to search again." A research paper is one in which you seek out information about a topic from a variety of sources. However, a research paper should not be merely a recapitulation of the findings of others. It should also reflect your own ideas and understandings.

A research paper is both informative and objective. It seeks to provide information about a topic by examining a variety of sources objectively and by reaching a conclusion about the findings.

A research paper is formal. It contains little, if any, colloquial language or slang and few, if any, contractions.

45 Choosing and Limiting a Topic

What interests you? Since you will be spending several weeks researching your topic, make sure you choose one that appeals to you. Are you interested in finding information about any particular person? Andrew Johnson? Diane Arbus? Woody Allen? Gwendolyn Brooks? Are you interested in studying any particular place? Spain? Jupiter? The Great Plains? Grenada? Are you interested in exploring any particular time period? The turn of the century? The sixteenth century? The fifth century BC? The 1920s? Are you interested in examining any particular event? The Civil War? The birth of Christianity? The first space flight to the moon? The building of the first transcontinental railroad? Are you interested in studying any particular object or activity? Clocks? Vitamins? Jazz? Cooking? Are you interested in exploring any particular idea or doctrine? Rationalism? Buddhism? Transcendentalism? Dada? Are you interested in investigating a controversial issue? Abortion? Nuclear power? School desegregation? The military draft?

When faced with the task of writing a research paper, many students go blank; they can think of nothing that interests them. Some solve this problem by thumbing through magazines, newspapers, and encyclopedias. A letter in the *New York Times* Book Review interested one student, Gail Young, in Mercy Otis Warren, a minor writer of Colonial New England. But what could Gail write about her?

A typical research paper is between 2,000 and 3,000 words long. Therefore, after you decide on a topic you must limit it so that you can cover it effectively within these boundaries. What aspect of your topic do you wish to cover? Notice how the following topics are narrowed.

Woody Allen → his life → his life as an artist → his artistic output → his movies → *Annie Hall* → the making of *Annie Hall*

Grenada → the history of Grenada → the military history of Grenada → Grenada's strategic importance to the United States

the fifth century B.C. → the fifth century B.C. in China → religion in China in the fifth century B.C. → the teachings of Confucius → modern Chinese reaction to the teachings of Confucius

the Civil War → important generals of the Civil War → important Union generals of the Civil War → General Sherman's role in the Civil War → General Sherman's Atlanta campaign

vitamins → types of vitamins → the use of vitamin supplements → vitamin therapy → the controversy over megadose vitamin therapy

transcendentalism → New England transcendentalists → the influence of transcendentalism on the works of Henry David Thoreau → the influence of transcendentalism on *Walden*

Of course, limiting your topic is not always such a simple, straightforward process. It is more a trial-and-error procedure that is open to revision, wisely delayed until you have investigated options.

Gail Young first consulted the encyclopedias in the reference area of the library. It seemed obvious from those brief entries that Warren's life would not be as interesting as Woody Allen's. But the encyclopedias included with each of their entries a brief bibliography, a start for Gail's research. The encyclopedias also gave Gail several clues to possible areas for investigation. For example, Gail noted with surprise that the *Britannica* declares Warren's poems and plays to be of "no permanent value." What the *Americana* calls Warren's "chief work"—*History of the Rise, Progress, and Termination of the American Revolution*—was "bitterly resented" by John Adams, notes the *Britannica*. So Gail was on her way to choosing a topic: What did Warren's contemporaries think of her poems and plays? Why is her work apparently of so little worth today? What caused Adams' resentment? Was Warren an early feminist?

When choosing a topic to write about, you must first be sure that the topic lends itself to research. If the topic you have chosen is a narrow one or very new, you probably will not be able to find sufficient written information about it. For example, the topic *the increase in popcorn consumption in the United States during the last six months* will most likely not lend itself to adequate research. It is too recent. Further, the topic *why I like popcorn* calls for personal opinion, not research. It might be appropriate for an essay, but not for a research paper.

46 Doing Research

After you have chosen your topic, the next step is to gather information. The best place to start is your library.

46a Finding Information

The library card catalog

Begin your research in the library's **card catalog,** which lists alphabetically on index cards all the books, magazines, and journals in the library. Usually the card catalog contains at least three cards for each book: a *subject card,* a *title card,* and an *author card.* (Often it contains more than one subject card.) If you have no particular title or author in mind, the best place to start is the subject cards, which are often grouped separately from the author and title cards.

Gail started her research by looking in the author/title card catalog, where she found cards listing Warren's works and some biographies, giving the location of the materials in the library, and providing other information as well (e.g., publisher and date of publication, length, number of illustrations, presence of bibliography, and so on). Gail also discovered that although few of Warren's plays are available in book form, all are contained on microfilm in a collection of Colonial drama located in a special section of the library. Also, Gail found that Warren's history of the Revolution is in a special area for rare books since it is a facsimile of the original volume that Warren autographed and sent to Thomas Jefferson. When Gail followed the call numbers to the books, she found, shelved with the Warren material, books by and about other authors of the period—suggestions for new topics if this research proved unproductive.

Gail also consulted the subject card catalog, where she found some duplicate listings. Other books listed here and not in the author/title catalog she could have found by looking on the shelves near the call numbers she had already gathered. Gail needed catalog call numbers, however, for others—history books, for example, in which Warren is not the central topic.

Today, in a large library, you may find that the drawers of catalog cards are missing. Instead, the catalog is kept in books, on microfilm, or on microfiche. If you cannot find the catalog or do not know how to use a microfilm or microfiche catalog, ask the librarian for help. The subject catalog that Gail used was on computer. In using a subject catalog in any form, you may find it helpful to consult, in the reference section of your library, a volume called *Library of Congress Subject Headings.* Gail checked several headings and found these for Warren: Colonial American Literature, American Historians, Dramatists, and Women, among others.

Periodical indexes

After using the card catalog, you may want to use **periodical indexes** to locate magazine and journal articles. The more current your topic, the more likely you will be to use magazine, journal, and newspaper articles for information. Probably, the index you will find most useful for locating articles is the *Readers' Guide to Periodical Literature,* which provides a monthly, quarterly, and annual index to almost 200 periodicals. For literary topics, the *Humanities Index* is useful, as is the *Essay and General Literature Index.* Another useful index is *The New York Times Index.* The following is a list of these and other indexes to periodicals.

General

> *Cumulative Index to Periodical Literature,* 1959–
> *New York Times Index,* 1851–
> *Nineteenth Century Readers' Guide to Periodical Literature,* 1890–1899
> *Poole's Index to Periodical Literature,* 1802–1906
> *Popular Periodicals Index,* 1973–
> *Readers' Guide to Periodical Literature,* 1900–

Special

> *Abstracts of Popular Culture,* 1976–
> *Agricultural Index,* 1916–1964

The American Humanities Index, 1975–
Applied Science and Technology Index, 1958–
Art Index, 1929–
Bibliography and Index of Geology, 1961–
Biography Index, 1946–
Biological Abstracts, 1926–
Biological and Agricultural Index, 1964–
Book Review Digest, 1905–
Business Periodicals Index, 1958–
Cumulative Index to Nursing and Allied Health Literature, 1977–
Cumulative Index to Nursing Literature, 1961–1976
Current Index to Journals in Education, 1969–
Economics Abstracts, 1969–
Education Index, 1929–
Engineering Index, 1906–
General Science Index, 1978–
Humanities Index, 1974–
Index to Jewish Periodicals, 1963–
Index to Legal Periodicals, 1908–
Industrial Arts Index, 1913–1957
International Index to Periodicals, 1907–1965
International Political Science Abstracts, 1951–
MLA International Bibliography of Books and Articles on the Modern Languages and Literatures, 1921–
Music Index, 1949–
Public Affairs Information Service (bulletin), 1915–
Social Sciences and Humanities Index, 1965–1974
Social Sciences Index, 1974–
U.S. Government Publications (monthly catalog), 1895–

Another student, Tim Gomez, chose as his topic for a research paper sleep disorders. After consulting the card catalog, Tim felt his topic might be too vague, so he decided to restrict it somewhat by narrowing it to current information on sleep disorders. Consulting periodical indexes seemed the logical next step. The *Readers' Guide* entry for 1987 under "Sleep" follows. A bit later in his research, Tim will recall the "*See also*" list of terms in this entry, and he will find there help in narrowing his topic productively.

Sleep

See also
Dreams
Insomnia
Nightmares
Snoring
Wakening from sleep

The A to ZZZ of better sleep. L. J. Brown and P. Gadsby. il *Good Housekeep* 204:146–7 Ja '87

All through the night? Not quite [getting children to sleep] E. Klavan. il *Parents* 62:80–4 F '87

Asleep in the cosmos [astronauts] S. J. Nadis. il *Omni* 9:26+ Je '87

Bedtime battles [toddlers] J. T. Gibson. il *Parents* 62:201 My '87

"But I don't want to go to bed!" [children's problems] A. E. Nourse. il *Good Housekeep* 205:134+ S '87

Can toddlers have nap schedules? J. T. Gibson. il *Parents* 62:110 Ja '87

Feeling sleepy? Shhh! Bacteria at work. il *Discover* 8:12 Ap '87

For too many, life is just a snore. S. N. Wellborn. il *U.S. News World Rep* 102:56–7 Je 15 '87

From yawn to dawn: the science of sweet sleep. il *Prevention* 39:34–6+ Jl '87

Getting bedtime right. J. A. Reimer. il *Parents* 62:95–8 O '87

How to get the kids to go to bed and stay there. J. K. Rosemond. il *Better Homes Gard* 65:109–10 N '87

Nap-time strategies that work. V. Lansky. il *Parents* 62:343–4 N '87

REM sleep: pilot light of the mind? L. Miller. il *Psychol Today* 21:8+ S '87

Sleeping better. *Vogue* 177:474 O '87

The sleepless sportsman. J. Poppy. il *Esquire* 108:712 O '87

Sweet dreams are made of this (how to get a good night's sleep). E. Royte. il *Mademoiselle* 93:82 Ja '87

What is this thing called sleep? M. E. Long, il *Natl Geogr* 172:786–821 D '87

Whose bed is it anyway? [children sleeping in parents' bed] L. G. Katz. il *Parents* 62:188 Mr '87

Instead of continuing to search the volumes of periodical indexes, Tim took another step available in many libraries. He consulted a computer database.

A computer database

A **database** is a computerized index of articles, books, and other materials on a specific subject. Information is indexed like the card catalog by author and title and like the subject catalog by key words (called *descriptors*). A strong advantage of the computer database index is that subjects, topics, and concepts can be combined, so focusing and narrowing can be quickly accomplished.

A library may permit you to use the computer yourself, but there are hundreds of databases available, and the process may be complicated, particularly for a subject search. You may need to use the services of a librarian, and usually there will be a charge for the service.

After choosing an appropriate database from those available in your library, the first step in your search is to plan a search strategy. Break down the topic into its major concepts, then list terms to cover each concept. Some databases have lists of standardized subject terms that are used in the database. Such a list is called a *thesaurus* and is similar in function to the *Library of Congress Subject Headings*. Then determine how the subject terms relevant to your topic may be crossed or combined. Next, you or the librarian enter on the computer the terms you have chosen. The computer then searches for all citations included in the database indexed under your terms, and provides you with a printout of the references you are interested in. Some cases the databases also provide you with a brief summary of each text.

The database chosen for Tim's research was *PsycINFO,* a database produced by the American Psychological Association and available on the Bibliographic Retrieval Services (BRS) system. The first term entered was Tim's original broad topic, sleep disorders, and the query was the number of items on that topic. The computer's answer—413 documents—confirmed Tim's earlier suspicion that his topic was too broad. He entered next a narrowed topic, nightmares. The number of documents now, though smaller, was still discouragingly high for Tim, so he continued the search by combining the terms (descriptors). He asked the computer to look for material concerning first the sleep disorders of young adults, then of students, then of young adult students, and finally college students' nightmares. Within only a few minutes the computer narrowed the field to a workable list of twenty-four items. After the computer had located the citations appropriate for Tim's topic, Tim requested that the computer give him the titles of several articles and their subject headings to determine whether he was on target in his search. Then, after viewing this sample, Tim could obtain bibliographic information and an abstract of any or all of the citations.

Gail also searched her topic in a database. She used the database *America: History and Life,* produced by ABC Clio and available on the DIALOG system. Before using the database Gail had spent hours searching only a few years of printed indexes and had found listings for only four articles. With the *America: History and Life* database, however, she searched 200,000 references dating back to 1964 and retrieved eleven articles in just a few minutes. Gail asked for abstracts of all eleven of the articles on her topic, one of which is shown here.

380462 14A-00632

John Adams' Opinion of Benjamin Franklin

Evans, William B.

Pennsylvania Mag. of Hist. and Biog. 1968 92(2): 220–238.

Document Type: ARTICLE

Traces John Adams' animosity toward Benjamin Franklin in 10 1807
letters to Mercy Otis Warren questioning her favorable treatment
of Franklin in History of the Rise, Progress, and Termination of
the American Revolution. Differences between the two
revolutionary giants began in 1776 when Franklin supported a
unicameral legislature in Pennsylvania, and continued in Paris
(1776–79) until their joint presence on the Peace commission in
1780 brought an open breach when Adams opposed Franklin's
supposedly pro-French policy. Not only differences on policy but
Adams' envy and pride may have colored his view of Franklin.
Based primarily on the papers of John Adams; 67 notes. (R. B.
Mitchell)

Descriptors: Adams, John (letters, opinion); Politics, 1774–1810;
Franklin, Benjamin; Warren, Mercy Otis

Notice that since Warren's name is not in the title, Gail might
have had difficulty in finding this article as she searched her
printed indexes. The computer, however, could also search
the abstract and find the reference.

Most often you will use the computer database just as you
use the card catalog and periodical indexes, to identify books
and articles that you will then locate and read in the process of
your research. Occasionally, you may use a database to provide
the complete article for you. The database systems used by
Gail and Tim—DIALOG and BRS—are among those that provide, in addition to references and abstracts, full texts of articles from a selected list of magazines. Other systems have
complete texts of newspapers and reference books. Computer
database material does, of course, require documentation like
any printed source. Sample bibliographic entries for computerized sources appear in sections 47b and 48b (pp. 415
and 420).

46b Primary and Secondary Sources of Information

The sources of information for a research paper can be divided into primary and secondary sources. A **primary source** gives you firsthand information about a topic. For example, for a paper on the causes of and treatment for sleep disorders of college students, a primary source would be an article by a researcher or an interview with a person who had experienced nightmares. A book describing the experiments of others is a **secondary source.** For a paper on a literary subject, primary sources would include the literature itself and the writer's letters and diaries. For Gail's literary topic on writer Mercy Otis Warren or a historical study of Warren's quarrel with John Adams or the politics of the times, primary sources would include Warren's poems and plays, Adams' letters, and records of the proceedings of the Continental Congress. Secondary sources would include critical studies of the literature, histories of the period, and biographies of Warren and Adams.

In your research, try to use as many primary sources as possible. However, for many topics, you will have to use secondary sources. Remember, though, that in many cases the closer you are to the original source, the more accurate your information is likely to be.

Keep in mind the reliability of your sources. If the source is primary, ask yourself the following questions:

1. Is the source objective?
2. Is the source an expert in the field?
3. If the source reports the results of an experiment, did the experiment follow established procedures?
4. How recent is the information? (Obviously, this question is not important for all situations.)

If the source is secondary, ask yourself these questions:

1. What is the author's reputation in the field?
2. What sources did the author use?
3. How sound are the author's conclusions?
4. How recent is the book or article? (Once again, in some situations, this will not apply.)
5. Was the book published by a reputable publisher or was the article in a reputable magazine? (An article in a scholarly journal is more likely to contain reliable information than an article in a magazine that seeks to entertain its readers.)

Of course, your choice of sources depends on your purpose.

Sources of information can also be divided into the three categories of yourself, others, and written and broadcast materials. Your first source of information is yourself. What do you know about the subject? What experiences have you had that relate to the subject?

Your second source of information is other people. Interview people who have firsthand information about the topic. Attend discussions and lectures about the subject. Take an opinion poll. Conduct a survey. When Tim Gomez started working on his research paper, he took an informal survey of students at his school to find out about their experiences with nightmares.

Your third source of information is books, magazine and journal articles, newspaper articles, films, and radio and television news programs and documentaries. Read as much about your topic as you can. View films and documentaries.

When you are beginning your research, you may find reference books helpful in getting an overview of your topic. Your library contains many general reference aids. Learn what they are and use them appropriately, but do not depend on encyclopedias or other general reference works for all your research. After getting an overview of your topic, you will need to consult more specialized books and articles for more detailed information.

The following is a sampling of general reference aids.

General encyclopedias

Collier's Encyclopedia, 24 vols.
Encyclopedia Americana, 30 vols.
The New Encyclopaedia Britannica, 32 vols.

Almanacs and yearbooks

Americana Annual, 1923–
Britannica Book of the Year, 1938–
Collier's Year Book (titled *National Year Book* before 1942), 1939–
Facts on File Yearbook, 1940–
Statesman's Year-Book, 1864–
United Nations Yearbook, 1947–
World Almanac and Book of Facts, 1868–

Art and architecture

Art Books 1876–1949: Including an International Index of Current Serial Publications, 1981
Art Books 1950–1979: Including an International Directory of Museum Permanent Collection Catalogs, 1979
Art Books 1980–1985, 1985
Cyclopedia of Painters and Paintings, 4 vols., 1978
Encyclopedia of World Architecture, 2 vols., 1979, repr. 1983
Encyclopedia of World Art, 15 vols., 1959–1968; and supplement, 1983
A History of Architecture, 19th ed., 1987

Atlases and gazetteers

Columbia-Lippincott Gazetteer of the World, 1952; and supplement, 1961
Commercial Atlas and Marketing Guide, 1988
Hammond Gold Medallion World Atlas, 1988
National Geographic Atlas of the World, 5th ed., 1981
Oxford Economic Atlas of the World, 4th ed., 1972

Biography

Contemporary Authors: A Bio-Bibliographical Guide to Current Writers in Fiction, General Nonfiction, Poetry, Journalism, Drama, Motion Pictures, Television, and Other Fields, rev. ed., 106 vols., 1967–1982
Current Biography, 1940–
Dictionary of American Biography, 20 vols., 1928–1936; and supplements, 1944–1981
Dictionary of National Biography (British), 22 vols., 1885–1901; and supplements, 1912–1981
McGraw-Hill Encyclopedia of World Biography, 12 vols., 1973; and supplement, 1987
Webster's New Biographical Dictionary, 1983
Who's Who (British), 1849–
Who's Who in America, 1899–

Business and economics

American Business Dictionary, 1957–
Encyclopedia of Banking and Finance, 8th ed., 1983
Encyclopedia of Computer Science and Engineering, 2nd ed., 1982
Encyclopedia of Computer Science and Technology, 15 vols., 1975–1980
Encyclopedia of Computers and Data Processing, 1978–
Encyclopedia of Management, 3rd ed., 1982

Education

> *Cyclopedia of Education,* 5 vols., 1968, reprint of 1911 ed.
> *Encyclopedia of Educational Research,* 4 vols., 5th ed., 1982
> *International Encyclopedia of Higher Education,* 10 vols., 1977

History and political science

> *Cambridge Ancient History Series,* 12 vols., 3rd ed., 1984
> *Cambridge Medieval History,* 9 vols., 2nd ed., 1966
> *Concise Dictionary of World History,* 1983
> *Cyclopedia of American Government,* 3 vols., 1963 reprint of 1914 ed.
> *Dictionary of American History,* 8 vols., rev. ed., 1978
> *Dictionary of Political Economy,* 3 vols., 1976, reprint of 1910 ed.
> *Encyclopedia of the Third World,* 3 vols., rev. ed., 1981
> *Encyclopedia of World History,* 5th ed., 1972
> *New Cambridge Modern History,* 14 vols., 1957–1979

Literature, theater, film, and television

> *Bartlett's Familiar Quotations,* 15th ed., 1980
> *Cambridge History of American Literature,* 3 vols., 1943
> *Cambridge History of English Literature,* 15 vols., 1907–1933
> *Cassell's Encyclopaedia of World Literature,* 3 vols., 1973
> *Granger's Index to Poetry,* 8th ed., 1986
> *International Encyclopedia of Film,* 1972
> *International Television Almanac,* 1956–
> *Larousse World Mythology,* 1965
> *McGraw-Hill Encyclopedia of World Drama,* 5 vols., 2nd ed., 1983
> *Mythology of All Races,* 13 vols., 1964; reprint of 1932 ed.
> *Oxford Companion to American Literature,* 5th ed., 1983
> *Oxford Companion to Classical Literature,* 2nd ed., 1937

Oxford Companion to English Literature, 5th ed., 1985
Play Index, 1949–
Short Story Index, 1900–

Medicine/nursing

Encyclopedia and Dictionary of Medicine, Nursing, and Allied Health, 4th ed., 1987

Music

Encyclopedia of Pop, Rock, & Soul, 1977
Harvard Dictionary of Music, 2nd ed., 1969
International Cyclopedia of Music and Musicians, 11th ed., 1985
Musician's Guide, 6th ed., 1980
New Grove Dictionary of Music and Musicians, 20 vols., 1980

Philosophy and religion

Encyclopedia of Philosophy, 4 vols., 1973
Encyclopedia of Religion, 1976, reprint of 1945 ed.
The Interpreter's Dictionary of the Bible, 5 vols. and supplement, 1976

Science

Cambridge Encyclopedia of Astronomy, 1977
Cambridge Encyclopedia of Earth Sciences, 1982
Grzimek's Animal Life Encyclopedia, 13 vols., 1972–1975
McGraw-Hill Encyclopedia of Science and Technology, 15 vols., 6th ed., 1987

Social science

A Dictionary of Psychology and Related Fields, 1974
Encyclopedia of Psychology, 2nd ed., 1979
Encyclopedia of Social Work, 2 vols., 18th ed., 1987; and supplement, 1987
Encyclopedia of the Social Sciences, 15 vols., 1974

International Encyclopedia of the Social Sciences, 8 vols., 1977; biographical supplement, 1979

Special dictionaries

Dictionary of American Slang, 2nd ed., 1975
Dictionary of Modern English Usage, 2nd ed., 1965
Dictionary of Slang and Unconventional English, 8th ed., 1985
Harper Dictionary of Contemporary Usage, 2nd ed., 1985
Modern American Usage, 1966
New Roget's Thesaurus in Dictionary Form, 1986

Unabridged dictionaries

The Oxford English Dictionary, 13 vols., 1933
The Random House Dictionary of the English Language, 1987
Webster's Third New International Dictionary of the English Language, 1986

46c Compiling a Working Bibliography

A **working bibliography** is a record of sources you plan to consult for information about your topic. Since a working bibliography is open to change, most instructors suggest you keep it on index cards, thus making it easy to add or delete books and articles.

Keep the following points in mind when developing your working bibliography.

1. List each source on a separate 3 × 5-inch index card.
2. Arrange these cards alphabetically by author. (You may also find alternate arrangements convenient. For example, you may find it useful to organize the cards by subcategory.)

3. Include the name of the author, with the last name first. (If the book has an editor or a compiler rather than an author, indicate this.)
4. Include the complete title of the source.
5. Include the place and date of publication.
6. Include the name of the publisher.
7. Include the library call number.
8. Include any other pertinent information, such as volume number or edition.

When Gail Young was preparing a working bibliography, she first consulted the encyclopedias—the *Encyclopedia Americana,* the *Encyclopedia Britannica, Collier's Encyclopedia*—checking the bibliography at the end of each article she read about Mercy Warren or John Adams. Then she consulted the card catalog, the periodical indexes, and a computerized database. As she worked, Gail kept adding titles to her working bibliography and eliminating titles that were not relevant to her topic. One of Gail's bibliography cards follows. Notice that the book she listed has two editors rather than an author.

Berky, Andrew S. and James P. Shenton, eds.
The Historians' History of the United States
New York: Putnam's, 1966.

47 Bibliographic Form— MLA Style

Eventually, you will turn your working bibliography into a formal bibliography or list of works cited or consulted, which will appear on a separate page at the end of your paper. Before compiling your working bibliography, check with your instructor to determine which guidelines for bibliographic form to follow. The guidelines of the Modern Language Association in the *MLA Handbook for Writers of Research Papers,* 3rd ed. (1988) are used in the following examples. Consult the *Handbook* for situations not covered by these examples.

47a General MLA Guidelines

1. Always include the author's name (as listed on the title page), the complete title, and the complete publication information.
2. Separate these three parts (and any additional items of information) with periods followed by two spaces.
3. Give the author's last name first. A second or third author, or the name of an editor after the author, is listed in normal order. For more than three authors, list only the first, followed by "et al."
4. Indicate an editor or compiler by the abbreviation *ed.* or *comp.* or *eds./comps.* if there is more than one.
5. In the publication information for books, you may use the shortened form of publishers' names as listed in the *MLA Handbook* or other standard sources. Give the name of the city. Add the state or country only if the city alone would not be familiar to the reader. Use the standard postal abbreviations for states.
6. In publication dates for periodicals, abbreviate the names

of all months except May, June, and July. Put the dates in parentheses for periodicals with continuous pagination.

7. Include page numbers for a periodical article; a work that is part of an anthology or collection; or an introduction, preface, foreword, or afterword. Do *not* use *p.* or *pp.*

47b Sample Bibliographic Entries

Books

Book by one author

Fritz, Jean. Cast for a Revolution: Some American Friends and Enemies, 1728–1814. Boston: Houghton, 1972.

Book by two authors

Commager, Henry Steele, and Elmo Giordanetti. Was America a Mistake? An Eighteenth-Century Commentary. New York: Harper, 1967.

Book by three authors/Edition after the first

Millett, Fred B., Arthur W. Hoffman, and David R. Clark. Reading Poetry. 2nd. ed. New York: Harper, 1968.

Book by more than three authors

Adams, Russell, et al. Great Negroes Past and Present. Chicago: Afro-American Pub., 1964.

More than one book by the same author

Morrison, Samuel Eliot. Harrison Gray Otis 1765–1848: The Urban Federalist. Boston: Houghton, 1969.

---. Three Centuries of Harvard. Cambridge: Harvard UP, 1936.

Book by a corporate author

Group for the Advancement of Psychiatry. Symposium No. 8: Medical

Uses of Hypnosis. New York: Mental Health Material Center, 1962.

Book in more than one volume/Work by one, prepared for printing by an editor

Adams, John. The Works of John Adams. Ed. Charles Francis Adams.

10 vols. Boston: Little, 1850–56.

Selection from an anthology, collection, or critical edition

Bowen, Francis. "Life of James Otis." Library of American Biography.

Ed. Jared Sparks. Boston: Little, 1847.

(Note that you may omit the name of a publisher before 1900. The previous two references might have read: . . . vols. Boston, 1850–56; . . . Sparks. Boston, 1847.)

Book with two publishers/Book previously published/Book without publication date (n.d. = not dated)

Boswell, James. Boswell in Search of a Wife, 1776–1779. Ed. Frank

Brady and Frederick A. Pottle. 1956. New Haven: Yale UP; New

York: McGraw, n.d.

Book or pamphlet previously published/Book without publication data (N.p. = no place; n.p. = no publisher)

Warren, Mercy Otis. The Adulateur, a Tragedy. The Massachusetts Spy.

N.p.: n.p., 1722. Rpt. in The Magazine of History. 63. Tarreytown,

NY, 1918.

An introduction, preface, foreword, or afterword

Bryan, William J., Jr. Foreword. Helping Yourself with Self-Hypnosis. By

Frank S. Caprio and Joseph R. Berger. Englewood Cliffs, NJ:

Prentice, 1963. 7–8.

Periodicals

Article in a monthly periodical

Morrison, Samuel Eliot. "Three Great Ladies Helped Establish the
United States." Smithsonian Aug. 1975: 96–103.

Article in a weekly or biweekly periodical

Seliger, S. "In the Dead of the Night." Interview with E. Hartmann.
People Weekly 11 Mar. 1985: 128–30.

Article in a journal with continuous pagination

Weales, Gerald. "The Duality of Mercy, or Mrs. Warren's Profession."
Georgia Review 33 (1977): 881–894.

Article in a daily newspaper

Brown, Patricia Leigh. "Home Sweet Scary Home." Herald Tribune
[Rome] 31 Oct. 1987, internatl. ed.: 18.

Unsigned article

"Notes and Comments." New Yorker 11 June 1984: 29.

Encyclopedias and other sources

Article in an encyclopedia

"Warren, Mercy." Encyclopedia Americana. 1985 ed.

Government document

United States. Dept. of Commerce. Bureau of the Census. "Population
Profile of the United States, 1977." Current Population Reports.
Series P-20, No. 303. Washington: GPO, 1979.

Other published material

Weitzenhoffer, A. M., and E. R. Hilgard. <u>Stanford Hypnotic</u>
<u>Susceptibility Scale, Form C.</u> Palo Alto, CA: Consulting
Psychologists Press, 1962.

Personal or telephone interview

Wilfong, James. Personal interview. 23 Sept. 1987.

Bethke, Teresa. Telephone interview. 1 Oct. 1987.

Material from a computer service

Evans, William B. "John Adams' Opinion of Benjamin Franklin."
<u>Pennsylvania Magazine of History and Biography:</u> 92 (1968): 220–
238. Dialog file 38, item 380462.

48 Bibliographical Form— APA Style

Whereas MLA style is usually followed in the humanities, the guidelines of the American Psychological Association (APA) usually are required in the social sciences. (There are other styles as well, and you should follow your instructor's suggestions.)

If you choose to use APA bibliographical style, use the following examples to guide you in preparing your working bibliography. For situations that are not covered by these examples, refer to the *Publication Manual of the American Psychological Association,* 3rd edition (1983). Unlike the writer following MLA style, you may not list in your final bibliography everything you consulted as sources. Instead you may list only those sources you use directly in your paper. There are some other differences between the two styles, as well as some general suggestions about using APA style of which you should be aware.

48a General Distinctions Between APA and MLA Styles

1. The alphabetized bibliography at the end of your paper is to be titled "References." (In MLA style, that list may be titled "Works Cited," "Works Consulted," or "Bibliography.")

2. APA style inverts all authors' names, except a name that is part of a title. (MLA style inverts the first author's name only.)

3. Use capitals for proper nouns and the first word only of titles and subtitles of books and articles. For titles of periodicals use normal capitalization. (MLA does not omit capitals.)

4. For more than one work by an author, repeat the author's name for each entry and arrange works by publication date, the earliest first. (MLA style does not repeat the author's name; instead, it uses three hyphens, a period, and two spaces, and the works are listed alphabetically.)

5. List all names of multiple authors (et al. is not used in the list of References). See p. 466 for how to cite multiple authors in the text. (MLA allows a listing of up to three authors (names in normal order except for the first); for works with more than three authors, only the first author's name is given followed by et al.)

6. APA puts *all* publication dates in parentheses. (MLA uses parentheses only for dates of periodicals with continuous pagination.) Follow parentheses with a period. In dates for periodical articles, give the year first, followed by the month/day. Do not abbreviate months. (MLA gives the

day/month before the year of publication and abbreviates the month.)

7. Omit the quotation marks from titles of articles in periodicals. (MLA does not omit these quotation marks.)

8. Precede page numbers by *p.* or *pp.* in referring to articles or chapters in an edited book and to articles in popular magazines and newspapers, but *not* in reference to journal articles. (MLA does not use *p.* or *pp.*)

48b Sample Bibliographic Entries

Books

Book by one author

Jolly, A. (1985). The evolution of primate behavior (3rd ed.). New York: Macmillan.

Book by more than one author

Kagan, D., Ozment, S., & Turner, F. (1987). The western heritage (3rd ed.). New York: Macmillan.

Book translated

De La Varende, J. (1956). Cherish the sea: A history of sail (M. Savill, Trans.). New York: Viking.

Book in a series

Henle, M. (1986). 1879 and all that: Essays in the theory and history of psychology (Critical Assessments of Contemporary Psychology. D Robinson, Gen. Ed.). New York: Columbia University Press.

Book of a multivolume work

Sandburg, C. (1939). <u>Abraham Lincoln: The war years</u> (Vol. 2). Orlando,
FL: Harcourt.

Periodicals

Article in a newspaper

DePalma, A. (1986, May 18). The scramble for elusive "affordables."
<u>New York Times</u> sec. 8, p. 1.

Article in a popular magazine, weekly

Donahue, D., & Reed, S. (1986, May 12). A hyannis hitching. <u>People</u>, pp.
53–56, 59.

Article in a popular magazine, monthly

Moine, D. J. (1982, August). To trust, perchance to buy. <u>Psychology
Today</u>, pp. 51–52.

Article with no author, in popular magazine

SALT shaker; Reagan might breach a treaty. (1986, May 19). <u>Time</u>, p. 18.

Article in a journal with continuous pagination

Vesilind, P. J. (1986). Rising, shining Tennessee. <u>National Geographic</u>,
<u>169</u>, 602–636.

Article in a journal, pagination by issue

Lottmann, H. R. (1936). A bustling bologna. <u>Publisher's Weekly</u>,
<u>229</u>(20), 26–30.

Article published in a book

Fader, D. (1983). Literacy and family. In R. Baily & R. M. Fosheim (Eds.), Literacy for life: The demand for reading and writing (pp. 236–247). New York: The Modern Language Association of America.

Government document

U.S. Department of Commerce, Bureau of the Census. (1979). Population profile of the United States, 1977. Current population reports. Series P-20, 303. Washington, DC: U.S. Government Printing Office.

Material from a computer service

Bower, Bruce. (1987, Jan. 17) The fragile, creative side of nightmares. Science News, p. 37. (DIALOG file 647: MAGAZINE ASAP, item 04645291).

49 Writing the Paper

49a Writing a Thesis Statement and Making a Working Outline

Once you have completed your preliminary research, you should formulate a plan for writing. Your first two steps in formulating a plan are to write a thesis statement and to prepare a working outline.

As in an essay, your **thesis statement** should express the idea you wish to develop in your paper. The formulation of this statement will help you focus your research. Word your thesis statement carefully, but at this point, do not worry about the style with which you express your main idea. Most likely, you will reword your thesis statement many times before you are satisfied with it. Gail Young's initial thesis statement was the following: *Colonial New England author Mercy Otis Warren is best known for insulting in print her friend John Adams.* Tim Gomez's was this: *Minor anxieties and the fear of death cause college students' nightmares, which may be relieved sometimes by simple means, or, in serious cases, only with professional help.*

Your **working outline** should include all the main points you wish to include in your paper. Of course, as you do more research, you may find you have overlooked some points and add them to your outline. At this time your outline need not be in perfect form, for it is certainly subject to change, but it should be complete enough to serve as a guide for your research and your note taking. Gail Young developed the following working outline based on the research she had done so far. As she gathered more information about her topic, she added to her outline.

A NEW ENGLAND WOMAN'S WAR

Thesis Statement: Mercy Otis Warren would probably be forgotten as author and/or feminist but for her quarrel with John Adams.

I. Attitudes toward women
   A. Gov. Winthrop
   B. Lord Chesterfield

II. Women who succeeded as writers
   A. Anne Bradstreet
   B. Mercy Warren
   C. Phillis Wheatley

III. Contemporary reception of Warren's work

   A. Poems

   B. Plays

   C. History

IV. John Adams' reaction

   A. To poems and plays

   B. To history

      1. Political climate

      2. Adams' personal situation

      3. Politics of Warren's family

49b Taking Notes

Note taking is a way of keeping track of information that you think is important and that you may use later in your paper. Some people take notes on legal pads. A more efficient way is to use 4 × 6-inch index cards. The size prevents you from mixing up your note cards with your bibliography cards. The cards themselves allow you to arrange and rearrange your information as the need arises.

What information should you put on your note cards? First, each card should have at the top of it a heading indicating the category under which the information falls. Second, it should have a summary or paraphrase of the information or a quotation. Third, it should give the source of the information. Usually this need be only the author and the page number, since you will have the complete information on your bibliography card. If you are using more than one source by the same author, include the title or a shortened form of it.

Be sure to use a separate card for each piece of information. This will make it easier to arrange your notes when it comes time to write.

Summarize

One method of taking notes is to write a **summary** of the information you wish to record. A summary presents the substance of the information in a condensed form. It does not use the words of the author but conveys the thoughts of the author in your own words. Following is a summary card Gail Young wrote.

Adams – Quarrel
    Fritz 303
Adams' ten letters were an expression
of his own frustration at being
retired, out of favor, and "misunderstood,"
particularly by this friend, Mercy Warren.

Compare the summary with the original.

> Actually, these letters—ten in six weeks, some running to twenty pages—were his long pent-up cry of outrage at the world in general, at his age which had reduced him to the role of a spectator, at his enemies who had defeated him, at his friends who had misunderstood him, at himself for not being sufficiently dignified (like Washington) or sufficiently genial (like Franklin) to be forgiven his foibles, and at all historians, present and fu-

ture, who would not write history as he would have it written, who would not let him play his part as he knew he had played it.

Jean Fritz
*Cast for a Revolution: Some
American Friends and Enemies*

Paraphrase

A second method of taking notes is to paraphrase the information. A **paraphrase** is a restatement of someone else's statement in your own words. A good paraphrase reflects your own style of writing and extracts important information but does not lose the original meaning of the statement. Following is a paraphrase card Gail Young wrote.

Governor Winthrop on Women
Brown / 56
If the wife of the Governor of Hartford had not strained her weak wits by behaving like a man and neglecting her role and duties as a female, she would not have lost her mind.

Compare the paraphrase with the original.

". . . For if she had attended her household affairs, and such things as belong to women, and not gone out of her way and calling to meddle in such things as are proper for men, whose minds are stronger, &c., she had kept her wits, and might have improved them usefully and honourably in the place God had set her.''

Alice Brown
Mercy Warren

Note that a paraphrase reproduces another's words without editorial comment.

Record quotations

A third method of recording information is to write down exact quotations. You may find that the information you wish to record has been so well expressed or contains such precise facts and details that you wish to use the exact words of the source rather than summarize or paraphrase the information. Following is a quotation card Gail Young wrote.

Women and reading
Warren, The Group stage directions
n.p.
"In one corner of the room is discovered
a small cabinet of books....Hobb's [sic]
Leviathan, Winthrop's sermons,
Hutchinson's History, Fable of the Bees...
Hoyle on Whist, Lives of the Stewarts...
and Acts of Parliament for 1774."

With quotation cards, you must be extremely careful to record the exact words of the original and to transfer these words exactly if you use the quotation in your paper. (Review pages 305–306 for the use of punctuation marks with quotations.) Be careful not to overuse quotations in your paper, since too many quotations leave the reader with the impression that you did not truly master the material. Remember that a research paper expresses your understanding of a subject based on information gleaned from research. Even if you have written a quotation card, you can always summarize or paraphrase the information when you write your paper.

A fourth method of recording your information is to combine quotation and paraphrase. This method allows you to record the information in your own words while retaining a few particularly well-chosen words from the original. Following is a combination quotation and paraphrase card Gail Young wrote.

Political Situation, 1795
        Fritz 276
Neither side was pleased with John
Jay's treaty. If the Federalists were
"disappointed," the Republicans were
"outraged." Mercy believed america
"humiliated."

Be judicious in taking notes. Do not record everything you read, but only what you think will be relevant. Even when you write your paper, you will not use all your notes but will cull them, using only the notes that develop your thesis.

49c Making a Formal Outline

After you have taken notes, the next step is to turn your working outline into a formal outline. Your **formal outline** must include a formal statement of your thesis and all of the main points you will develop in your paper arranged in a logical sequence. Ask your instructor whether you should develop a topic outline or a sentence outline. (Review the procedures for outlining on pages 23–26.) Remember that your working outline is for yourself; your formal outline will be read and evaluated by your instructor.

49d Begin Writing the Paper

The process of actually writing the research paper is much like that of writing an essay, except that you are relying to a large extent on source material outside your own mind. Using your formal outline, write a first draft, let it sit for a while, and then go back to it and begin the process of criticism and revision. In particular, consider your paper as a piece of research. Are you relying too heavily on one or two sources? Perhaps you need to do some more research. Do you seem to be using a great many quotations? Perhaps it would be more effective to summarize or paraphrase some of them. Does any section of the paper seem to need strengthening? Perhaps you could use some of the note cards you didn't use in the previous draft.

When Gail wrote her first draft, she gave a good bit of attention to Warren's plays and poems. As she worked, Gail realized her interest was in Warren's *History,* Adams' reaction, and Warren's response, as part of the political controversy of the times. Her working outline (see pages 423–424) reflects that change in emphasis in the subdivisions beginning with that part of the topic.

Write or type your final draft according to the guidelines for manuscript form on pages 320–323, and do not forget to proofread it for spelling and punctuation. In addition, be sure to acknowledge all of your outside sources according to the guidelines described in Chapters 50–51.

50 Acknowledging Sources

An absolute requirement in writing a research paper is that you must acknowledge all of your sources according to accepted guidelines. Plagiarism, or using the words or thoughts of others as though they were your own, is a serious offense, and you must be scrupulous about avoiding it in your writing. Acknowledge all quotations and all summaries and paraphrases of information that is not generally known and readily available from other sources. For example, since the information that Sally Ride was the first American woman to travel in space is commonly known and readily available, you need not acknowledge a source for it. Since information about how Sally Ride's performance during her first flight was evaluated by NASA is not commonly known or readily available, you do need to acknowledge your source for it. If in doubt about whether to acknowledge a source, always do so.

50a MLA Style

The traditional method of acknowledging sources uses superscript numbers in the text to refer the reader to notes identifying the sources. The notes are placed either at the bottom of the text pages on which the superscripts appear (footnotes) or together at the end of the paper (end notes). However, the most recent edition of the *MLA Handbook for Writers of Research Papers* (1988) recommends a newer method in which sources are briefly identified in parentheses within the text itself. These parenthetical acknowledgments refer the reader to the full source information contained in the bibliography, or list of works cited, at the end of the paper. The following guidelines are based on the *MLA Handbook.* Consult the *Handbook* for situations not covered by these guidelines.

At times, you may wish to refer to the entire work. In this case, give the author's name and the title of the work in the text itself.

In Cast for a Revolution: Some American Friends and Enemies, Jean

Fritz tracks the political dissension surrounding the war.

Or your text may give both author and location of your reference.

Alice Brown, on page 156 of her biography, Mary Warren, quotes

Governor Winthrop's comments.

Usually, however, you will credit your source as concisely as possible, citing the author's last name only. You must identify also the location of borrowed information, giving the page number and/or the stanza, line, act, scene, and chapter, as appropriate. As you work through your paper, you will find yourself using parentheses for much of this information, as shown in the following examples.

Directly quoted material, author's name in text

Brown says that John Adams' language was "warmer than that of the

courtier to Aspasia" (157).

Author's name in parentheses

"Governor Winthrop . . . consigned them to the limbo they had earned"

(Brown 156).

Note the absence of punctuation between the author's name and the page number, as well as the position of the punctuation closing the sentence—outside the parentheses.

Reference to material, author's name in text

Fritz (259) lists the recipients of Warren's autographed copies.

Author's name in parentheses

Warren mailed complimentary copies to a list of distinguished friends (Fritz 259).

Work listed by title, not author

The Encyclopedia Britannica finds Warren's poems "of no value."

Judgment in our time contradicts the high praise Warren's friends gave to her poems (Encyclopedia Britannica).

Note that you need not give page numbers for material arranged alphabetically as in an encyclopedia or a dictionary.

Place the citation as close as possible to the material it acknowledges, in midsentence if it is brief.

Brown quotes Governor Winthrop (156) in his harsh condemnation of the sick wife of a fellow governor.

50b APA Style

APA style for crediting sources within the paper is much the same as MLA's. However, note the following differences:

1. A title does not appear in the text reference, unless the author is unknown.
2. APA style always gives the year of publication, in addition to the author's last name and page or line numbers for quotations.
3. Items in parentheses—the author's name, publication date, and page numbers—are separated by commas. Page numbers are signaled by *p.* or *pp.* and are required for direct quotations.
4. For works with more than one and fewer than six authors, the first text reference lists the last names of all authors. For subsequent references, if the work has two authors,

cite both names; if the work has more than two authors, give only the surname of the first author followed by et al.

Author's name in text

According to Jolly (1985), social behavior. . . .

Author's name in parentheses

Social behavior may be defined as the interaction of individual organisms (Jolly, 1985).

Specific part of a source

Humans do not use these higher-thought processes while speaking (Wittgenstein, 1965, p. 9).

Source with two authors

There are inconsistencies in theories (Morris & Fox, 1978, pp. 16–17).

Reference to several sources in the same parenthetical citation

Some cruel experiments produce no knowledge (Ogilvie, 1954, p. 1195; Ryder, 1976, p. 3).

Note that multiple citations within the same parentheses are grouped alphabetically and separated by semicolons.

51 Preparing the List of Sources

After you have written the final draft of your paper, you must prepare the list of the sources you used, giving the full author, title, and publication information for each work.

1. Start the list on a new page following the text of the paper. Number each page of the list in the upper right-hand corner, continuing the page numbers of the text. (For example, if the text ended on page 8, the first page of the list would be page 9.)

2. In MLA style, type the title *Works Cited* centered one inch from the top of the page. In APA style, use the title *References.*

3. Double-space between the title and the first entry, and then double-space the entire list, within entries and between entries.

4. In MLA style, list the works alphabetically by author, or by title for works by anonymous authors. (Disregard *A, An,* and *The* in alphabetizing titles.) In APA style do the same, but works by the *same author* are listed chronologically, from earliest to most recent publication.

5. If you have followed the guidelines for the working bibliography on pages 412–413, your sources are already listed in the proper form; simply copy the information for each source that you actually used in your paper.

6. Begin each entry at the left-hand margin; if an entry is longer than one line, indent the subsequent lines five spaces for MLA style and three spaces for APA style.

Even if you use the parenthetical method of acknowledging sources, you can still use footnotes or end notes to give additional information or commentary about points in the text. If you use end notes of this kind, they should be typed on a separate numbered page at the end of the paper (before the list of works cited) under the title *Notes.* Like the list of works cited, the end notes are double-spaced, but the indentation system is reversed: the first line of each note is indented five spaces, and any subsequent lines begin at the left margin.

52 Two Sample Term Papers

Two model research papers, one utilizing The Modern Language Association's (MLA) style of documentation, the other using The American Psychological Association's (APA) style of documentation, are presented for reference. The first sample research paper is a literary essay using MLA style of documentation, which is usually required in the humanities. It is an analysis of Addie Bundren, a character in William Faulkner's *As I Lay Dying,* and her relation to the overall theme of the novel. The second and abbreviated sample essay illustrates the APA style of documentation, which is usually required in the social sciences. This essay argues that the use of animals in research is in some ways immoral and unethical. For a detailed explanation of the distinctions between MLA and APA documentation styles, see pages 430–433.

52a MLA-Style Research Paper

The sample research paper that follows is a literary analysis or expository essay that utilizes the style of documentation recommended in the *MLA Handbook for Writers of Research Papers,* 3rd ed. In his analysis, the author, Peter Conlin, explains his assessment of Addie Bundren's character. As in any kind of writing, Conlin must "prove" his assertions by developing his paragraphs with specific details and examples. However, this analysis differs from an argumentative essay (see the sample APA research paper on pages 461–475 for an example of an argumentative essay) in that there is no need to persuade the reader of anything other than the honesty of the writer's considered opinion and the soundness of his evidence. Throughout, Conlin's tone remains reasoning.

1 **Title page format.** A title page is not required by MLA guidelines and there is no fixed form for it. You should follow your instructor's specific requirements. Conlin has decided to use a separate title page. He centers the title, placing it about one-third of the way down from the top of the page, and includes the date, his name, his instructor's name, and the section number, one inch below the title, centered and double-spaced.

If instead you omit the title page, the MLA guidelines recommend placing your name and course information in a block beginning at the left margin of the first page of the paper. Starting about one inch from the top of the page at the margin, type, double-spaced, with each item on a separate line, your name, your instructor's name, the course number, and date. Double space once again and then center the title. If the title uses more than a line, double space a second line; then double space before beginning the text. Do not underline your title, put it in quotation marks, or type it in capital letters. There is no need to follow your title with a period.

1

Addie: A Woman of Works

5 November 1988

Peter A. Conlin

Professor David Payne

ENG 233G

2 **Outline.** If your instructor requires an outline with your paper, it should follow the title page and appear on a separate, unnumbered page. Included with the sample paper are Conlin's two outlines. The first (above) is an informal, preliminary sentence outline that Conlin used to organize his ideas prior to and while writing the paper. The second (opposite) is a formal topic outline that was submitted, as required, with the paper. As you will note, the formal outline uses only short phrases, does not include the introduction found in the sentence outline, and is presented in standard outline form with roman numerals for major categories, indented capital letters for the next series of ideas, and indented arabic numerals for the third level.

2 Working Outline: Addie: A Woman of Works

Thesis: Addie Bundren epitomizes Faulkner's ideal of one who lives by deeds.

1. Introduction: Reviewers praised the book but were puzzled over Addie's character.

2. Those who live on words are foils to Addie: Anse, Whitfield, and Cora.

3. Those who live on words deceive themselves, not others; Anse, for example, deceives neither Darl nor Addie.

4. The Reverend Whitfield also deludes himself with words.

5. Addie interprets religion as works, in contrast to Cora who, first, judges Addie and, second, lets her life be shaped by fate.

6. Addie understands the difference between words and works and her own stance, rooted in the morality of nature but split from traditional religion.

7. Addie's final deed: she extracts from her family the promise to bury her in Jefferson.

2   Outline: Addie: A Woman of Works

Thesis: Addie Bundren epitomizes Faulkner's ideal of one who lives by deeds.

    I.   Foils to Addie
       A.   Anse
       B.   Whitfield
       C.   Cora
   II.   The self-deceivers
       A.   Anse
          1.   seen by Darl
          2.   seen by Addie
       B.   Whitfield
 III.   Traditional religion
       A.   For Addie
          1.   works
          2.   rejection of the Word
       B.   For Cora
  IV.   The deed

3   **Paper format.**   All pages of the paper itself are numbered with arabic numerals in the upper right-hand corner, typed one half-inch from the top of the page. MLA guidelines recommend typing your last name before the page number for easy reorganization if a page is misplaced. Do not use the abbreviation "p." before a page number or add any punctuation or symbols.

The text of your paper is double-spaced throughout with a margin of one inch at the top, bottom, and on both sides of the page. Indent the first word of a paragraph five spaces from the left margin.

4   **In-text documentation.**   Peter Conlin follows MLA style. Unless the author's name is given in the text discussion, a parenthetical citation should include the author's name and the page number with no punctuation. A single-page article needs no page number. The parentheses are included within the sentence; a period follows them.

5   **Introduction.**   One way to capture a reader's interest is to open the paper with a brief anecdote, as Conlin does. Faulkner's friend, Anthony West, told the story in a magazine article about Faulkner as a dinner guest. Conlin abbreviated West's account and paraphrased it in his paper, documenting it to credit West.

6   **No documentation.**   The publication date of the novel is the kind of information readily available in such a source as a dictionary or an encyclopedia and so does not require documentation.

7   **The article preceding the title of a newspaper or periodical.**   The is not treated as part of the title; therefore it is not italicized.

8   **Citing an indirect source.**   Boskin was quoted in a periodical article, a fact Conlin indicates by the phrase "qtd. in" in the citation.

(See p. 442 for items 9 and 10.)

3   The day that William Faulkner finished the manuscript of As
4   I Lay Dying, the novel received its first critical judgment. Faulkner
5   told the story himself (West 23). A "female relative" was
"outraged" by some of the details of the story, and so she seized
the opportunity to throw the whole thing out the window of
Faulkner's automobile. After a mighty paper chase, the author
managed to retrieve most of the four hundred-plus pages, and the
6   novel was published on October 6, 1930. Professional reviewers
7   were kinder than the female relative. The Herald Tribune's critic
called it a "meaty tale" and "the terrifying, mysterious, and
intimate picture of a soul" (Dawson). The New Yorker described it
as a "novel to wonder over," "keenly told" (Coates). Critical
acclaim continued. William Boskin of the New York Evening Post
called it one of the "best books" published that season. He found in
it, he said, "eloquent evidence of William Faulkner's power in
conveying tragical and satirical messages through his study of
8, 9   abnormal psychologies" (qtd. in "Twenty Four Novels . . .").
Faulkner himself declared it his "best" and "real easy" to write
10   (Lion in 8, 13, 222).

When the novel was published in England in 1935, the
anonymous reviewer for the Times Literary Supplement called it an
"odyssey of human misery, courage, and cowardice." The Bundren
family, outraging the whole countryside, takes the coffin holding
the unembalmed corpse of Addie, the mother, on a four-day
"tortuous and illogical" journey (Hewes). Though illogical, there is
a reason for the journey: Addie had exacted a promise from her
husband, Anse, that she would be buried in a grave next to her

9   **Citing an anonymous work listed by title only.**   An anonymous book or article is listed in Works Cited by its title, so the
parenthetical reference lists it the same way. ("Works Cited" is
the MLA-recommended title for the list of references given at
the end of the paper.)

10   **Citing one of two or more works by the same author.**   The
author is named in the text (Faulkner). The title of the work
(here in shortened form) appears in parentheses, followed by
the page reference (here more than one page).

11   **Raised arabic numeral.**   Any kind of note is signalled by an
arabic number, without a period, placed slightly above the
line. This number signals a content note (see page 443). If
Conlin had chosen to use end notes or footnotes instead of
in-text citations, such numbers would signal those documentation notes.

12   **Thesis.**   The thesis of the essay usually appears somewhere
near the beginning of the essay, as here after the introduction
and in the first paragraph of the essay's body. Conlin also, in
this brief thesis paragraph, forecasts the principal method of
development of his essay—the differences between Addie, his
topic, and the other characters in the story. Such an organizing
sentence is a help to reader and writer, but not a necessity.
(See page 443).

13   **A work available in several editions.**   The parenthetical reference here includes first the page number, then a semicolon,
then the additional information the reader will need to find
the reference in any copy of the work. Here the chapter title is
necessary—"Addie."

14   **Use of quotations.**   Conlin fits quoted material smoothly into
his own sentences, using a minimum of such signal phrases as
"Somebody says. . . ." and avoiding the fault of letting quoted

(See p. 444 for item 15.)

father's. Was Addie insane to so make that trip necessary? Only a
psychiatrist could tell, and there have been some psychiatrists
among the critics.[1] Common sense can see Addie as just a
"wronged" wife aiming for revenge. The London reviewer was of
the opinion that she was "worn out by life." Faulkner in interviews
is silent. Although her character and motivation defy complete
understanding, what does seem clear, however, is that Addie is
quite different from those who surround her.

In As I Lay Dying, William Faulkner paints a bright contrast
between those people who live by deeds and those who live on
words. Addie Bundren epitomizes Faulkner's ideal of one who lives
by deeds. She sees words as "just a shape to fill a lack" (158;
"Addie").

Faulkner sets several foils to Addie's character, chiefly to
illustrate how those who live on words vastly outnumber those who
live by deeds. Anse, Whitfield, and Cora offer mere words to offset
Addie's deeds. Addie sees Anse as one who is dead but "[does] not
know that he [is] dead" (159; "Addie"). Whitfield exhibits the
ultimate self-deception by substituting words of his mind for a deed
in reality. Faulkner presents Cora as the traditional religious
hypocrite who uses "high dead words . . . [which] seemed to lose
even the significance of their dead sound" (161; "Addie"). Addie's
whole life can be seen as a struggle with those who would have her
abandon her natural adherence to living through her works. Her
struggle begins when she marries Anse.

Those who live on words deceive themselves, not others. Anse
gives proof to this assertion. When he says to Tull, "I give my

sentences stand alone. Where he needs to add something to the quotation, he puts his addition in square brackets. To signal the omission of one or more words or even sentences within a quotation, Conlin uses ellipsis points—three spaced periods. A fourth point signals the fact that a sentence ends within the quotation. No other punctuation accompanies the ellipsis points, and ellipsis points are ordinarily not needed at the beginning and end of quoted material.

15 **Primary sources versus secondary sources.**   Textbooks, this one included, advise the writer of the research paper to use primary sources as much as possible. This is easy for the writer of a literary analysis since the topic—the book or story or poem—is a primary source. Most of Peter Conlin's references are to the work itself. He does use secondary sources—materials about the novel, professional critics' analyses—and documents his use of their ideas. But most of the support for his assertions is in the form of primary source material, quoted from the novel itself, as shown on this page by the number of such citations.

16 **Ellipsis marks at the end of a quotation.**   Most often, when a quoted sentence's meaning is complete, even though more words may follow in the original, no ellipsis marks are needed. Here, however, Conlin uses ellipsis marks at the end of the sentence (". . . twenty-two years old . . ."). The ellipsis points signal that Conlin has omitted from the original the end of this sentence and also another sentence that follows it: "He was sick once from working in the sun when he was twenty-two years old, and he tells people that if he ever sweats he will die. I suppose he believes it." Conlin has incorporated that omitted material, condensing it and using it to comment on Anse's character as he paraphrases: "Anse has convinced himself he will die if he ever sweats. . . ."

17 **Ellipsis marks at the end of a quotation.**   Conlin's sentence is complete, and it is obvious that he is using only a partial quo-

(See p. 446 for item 18.)

promise, . . . [Addie] is counting on it" (126; "Tull"), he tries to
appear as a selfless, honorable man. However, quite the contrary is
true. Anse can make such a promise because he knows "he can
depend on his children" to make his promise good (Brooks 148).
Anse has spent his life leaning on others. Darl, his second son,
makes note of this. Darl admits he "never seen a sweat stain on
6   . . . [Anse's] shirt" (15; "Darl"). Anse has convinced himself he
will die if he ever sweats because "he was sick once from working
in the sun when he was twenty-two years old . . ." (15). Another
example of Anse's empty talk manifests itself when the team of
mules drowns in the river. He boasts that "[he] wouldn't be
beholding [to no man], God knows" (191; "Darl"). However, when
it comes time to replace the mules, he coerces Jewel to make up
part of the replacement cost by contributing his horse to a barter
deal (176; "Armstid"). Anse never quite takes credit for his own
actions, and he blames his misfortunes on "the Hand of God."
Anse lives on lies.

These lies alienate him from Addie. She realizes the difference
7   between "the trickery of words and the implacability of deeds . . ."
(Brooks 152). Her first taste of the discrepancy between words and
deeds comes when she bears Cash, and she thinks thus:

    And when I . . . had Cash, I knew that living was
8   terrible and that this was the answer to it. That was
        when I learned that words are no good; that words don't
        ever fit even what they are trying to say at. When he
        was born I knew that motherhood was invented by
        someone who had to have a word for it because the ones

tation, a few words from Brooks. In such a situation, usually no ellipsis points are required. Brooks' sentence reads: "Addie sees as the difference between them the trickery of words and the implacability of deeds, but she soon comes to put the difference in terms of life and death." Because the end of Brooks' sentence contains a new idea not relevant to Conlin's discussion, Conlin omits it. But in fairness to Brooks, he indicates by the ellipsis points that he has omitted material important to Brooks' discussion.

18 **Using block quotation.**   A quotation of more than four lines should be typed in block form, indented ten spaces from the left margin, and double-spaced (or single-spaced if your instructor permits). No quotation marks are needed to enclose indented quotations. The reference, since it ends the passage, stands after the sentence-ending punctuation.

19 *Changing capitalization in a quotation.*   As Conlin incorporates a quotation into his sentence, to make the sentence grammatically correct, he must change the capital letter *L* in the original to a lowercase letter *l*. He does this with square brackets. In the block quotation following, Conlin handles the same problem in reverse. He must change the lowercase letter *a* in the original to a capitalized and bracketed [*A*].

20 *Introducing block quotations.*   Although it stands apart from the text, a block quotation must have a logical connection with the sentence that precedes it. Conlin often uses a colon, the appropriate punctuation mark to introduce most block quotations. He is careful, too, to complete the sentence before the colon.

However, the colon is not the only punctuation possible. Other marks may be used or none, as required by the grammar of the introductory sentence preceding the quotation. For example, a comma would be used in the following instance:

Cora describes Addie as she lay dying,

propped on the pillow, with her head raised so

that had the children didn't care whether there was a
word for it or not. (157; "Addie")

She also owes the second phase of her education to Anse. Addie
found that he "had a word. . . . Love, he called it" (158; "Addie").
This revelation does not deceive her because she "had been used to
words for a long time [and she] knew that that word was like the
others: just a shape to fill a lack" (158). She vows to "[l]et Anse
use it, if he wants . . . [but] Cash did not need say it to me, nor I to
him" (158). Addie's soul craves a "direct expression . . . [like] the
welt raised by the switch on the limbs of schoolchildren, or the pain
of childbed," or the suckling of a child at her breast (Brooks 153).

Addie's lover, the Reverend Mister Whitfield, further
emphasizes the difference between words and deeds. When Addie
falls ill, Whitfield, being her pastor, has been summoned to her
bedside. He plans to confess his sin to Anse before Addie dies, and
on the ride to her home, he rehearses just what he will say. He
words it thus:

> [A]nd, as I rode across the firm earth again and the scene
> of my Gethsemane drew closer and closer, I framed the
> words which I should use. I would enter the house; I
> would stop her before she had spoken; I would say to her
> husband: "Anse, I have sinned. Do with me as you will."
> (165; "Whitfield")

In his mind, he thinks of the deed "as though it were done" (165).
However, the scenario he envisions never comes to pass for he
arrives at the home to find Addie has died: "He continues to dread

> she can see out the window. . . . Her face is
> wasted away so that the bones draw. . . .

For an example of a situation where no punctuation is needed
to introduce the block quotation, see page 472–473.

21 **Word choice.**   The word <u>quote</u> is a verb, a colloquialism
when it is used as a noun. Choice of the noun <u>quotation</u> would
be no better here. A character's speech is not a "quotation"
when he or she makes it! Conlin's instructor suggested these
substitutions: "train of thought," "way of thinking," or "inner
dialogue."

22 **Repetition of words.**   The word <u>assert</u> repeated and then emphasized by the quotation marks provides a transition between
paragraphs.

the confession that he must make" until the youngest Tull
daughter gives him the grim word (Brooks 151). At this point,
Whitfield's "confession" shows itself as hypocritical self-delusion.
He fashions a scenario in his mind that ultimately ends in his
vindication--with mere words. The delusion becomes apparent when
his thoughts run the following course:

> I have sinned, O Lord. Thou knowest the extent of my
> remorse and the will of my spirit. But He is merciful; He
> will accept the will for the deed, Who knew when I
> framed the words . . . it was to Anse that I spoke them,
> even though he was not there. (165; "Whitfield")

21   This quote plumbs the depths of Whitfield's delusion. He builds his
entire world on the words he creates and he becomes "the shape
and echo of his words" (160; "Addie").

Addie Bundren transposes "the spiritual (and, [most]
specifically, the Christian spiritual) into secular terms" and places
herself in opposition to the "conventional religious tradition"
(Brooks 153).[2] She feels improper not living a life full of works. She
believes "man must not simply vegetate . . . [but] he must assert
himself through some unique gesture to indicate that he has lived"
(Brooks 153).

22   When Addie "asserts" herself by committing adultery, critic
Charles Palliser sees that act as not just an expression of contempt
for the unreality of the word <u>sin</u> but as a rejection of the Word
(with the capital letter). That is, she is escaping "from the
pressures which mold human beings, reducing them to the
predictable . . . [making them] puppets . . . [subject to]

23   The repeated use of <u>thus</u> to introduce block quotations has
become, by this point in the paper, obtrusive and awkward.
Conlin's sentence is complete without <u>thus</u> before the colon:
    ". . . She scornfully judges Addie:"

24   **Transitions.**   Phrases that refer to what has been discussed
provide logical transitions within and between paragraphs:
"Such a critique. . . ." and, in the following paragraph, "All
these struggles. . . ."

25   **The essay's conclusion.**   Beginning with "All these struggles
and deeds. . . ." Conlin expands his original thesis and now
connects Addie's character with the religious and moral values
that are part of the theme of the novel as a whole.

predestination" (563). Faulkner, further to show Addie's disdain
for conventional religion, sets Cora Tull as a character foil to
Addie's "fierce energy" (153; "Cora") against which Cora is a pale
shadow. Faulkner makes <u>this</u> character seem typical of a
traditional Christian woman. Cora delights in exalting her superior
spiritual morality over those she perceives as less than herself.
When she describes how Addie looks on her deathbed, she
23 scornfully judges Addie thus:

> Her face is wasted away so that the bones draw just under
> the skin in white lines. Her eyes are like two candles
> when you watch them gutter down into the sockets of iron
> candle-sticks. But the eternal and everlasting salvation
> and grace is not upon her. (7; "Cora")

24 Such a critique comes from a "charitable Christian woman."
Faulkner's irony stings harshly. Cora also stands opposite to Addie
in another respect. Addie takes an active hand in shaping her life
while Cora lets her life be shaped by the fate she calls the "will of
God." Such "vegetating" would make Addie furious.

25   All these struggles and deeds have made up Addie's life. She
constantly finds herself at odds with people who shape their worlds
with words. She understands the enormous difference between
words and works, which she explains when she says the following:

> And so when Cora Tull would tell me I was not a true
> mother, I would think how words go straight up in a
> line, quick and harmless, and how terribly doing goes
> along the earth, clinging to it, so that after a while the
> two lines are too far apart for the same person to

26 **Transition.**   A referring word—the demonstrative adjective <u>that</u>—together with the repetition of the word <u>deed</u> connects the last paragraph with the one preceding it.

27 *Closing by returning to the beginning.*   Here Conlin echoes Addie's words, those he quoted in support of his thesis in the first body paragraph of the essay on page 3 of the essay. However, he gives them a different slant, applying them, following O'Donnell's suggestion, to Addie's coffin. That coffin is first introduced in the essay in the beginning of paragraph two. Such a circle, tying the beginning and end of an essay together without repetition, is a satisfying conclusion.

straddle from one to the other; and that sin and love and
fear are just sounds that people who never sinned nor
loved nor feared have for what they never had and
cannot have until they forget the words. Like Cora, who
could never even cook. (160; "Addie")

This passage lays Cora's hypocrisy bare for all the world to see.
Faulkner did not intend for such gross hypocrisy to be able to hide.
It also splits Addie from traditional religion. Traditional religion
takes its form in the dogma of words, and hence shoots straight off
from earth. Addie, in her "doing," follows the course of the earth,
and stays firmly rooted in the morality of nature. This passage
condemns all who rely on words, including Anse, Whitfield, and
Cora. In this profession, Addie forever frees herself from any
sharing in their hypocrisy. Addie's salvation must be in Jefferson
in the earth of her kin, because to hypocrites like Cora and the
others, "to whom sin is just a matter of words, to them salvation is
just words, too" (163; "Addie"). Her salvation comes through a
deed, her burial, which she forces from her family.

That deed, Addie's burial, introduces a coffin, put together by
Cash in the yard outside the room where Addie is dying. The coffin
becomes, like Addie's view of words, "just a shape to fill a lack," a
"shell surrounding nothingness" (O'Donnell 73). Addie, who has
lain unmoving in bed for ten days, raises herself up and looks out,
her face framed by the window. Soon she herself is nothing more
than a shape without life, "framed" by the coffin. The final irony
for Addie would be that the story through which Faulkner shapes
and frames her life can be constructed only of words.

28 **Content notes.** Information, comment, or explanation that could be interesting or valuable to the reader but that would be inappropriate or distracting in the text itself may appear in note form on a separate sheet at the end of the paper before the Works Cited.

Endnotes/footnotes. Notes of all kinds follow the form of these content notes: raised arabic numerals in the text signal notes; the numbering is consecutive throughout the paper. The first line of each note is indented five spaces and all subsequent lines begin at the left margin. <u>Endnotes</u> are listed, double-spaced and numbered, on a separate page following the paper. <u>Footnotes</u> are typed on the pages where they appear, two double-spaces below the text. The footnote itself is single-spaced with double spacing between footnotes.

29 **Bibliographical information.** This content note contains bibliographical information because the book is only peripherally related to Conlin's topic and therefore is not listed in the Works Cited. This bibliographical content note illustrates the form of the first reference note wherever it appears—as endnote or as footnote. Note several differences in form between this listing and those in the Works Cited list on the following page:

1. The author's name appears in normal order; it is not reversed.
2. The author's name is followed by a comma, not by a period.
3. The publishing information appears within parentheses.

Subsequent notes referring to the same work follow the same form as in-text citations, except that they do not require parentheses because they do not interrupt the text. (The terms <u>op.</u> <u>cit.</u> and <u>ibid.</u> are no longer used.)

30 **Reference to a published thesis.** A dissertation would be indicated by "Diss."

31 **Book title within a book title.** Italics are omitted.

Notes

28   [1] Cleanth Brooks mentions Rollo May, Viktor Frankl, and
Existential philosophers Kierkegaard and Nietzsche, noting some of
their theories as relevant to Addie's condition (399–400). For an
interpretation of Addie's character in connection with the theories of
29   Jung and Freud, see Dixie M. Turner, A Jungian Psychoanalytic
30   Interpretation of William Faulkner's As I Lay Dying (Thesis, Olivet
31   Nazarene College, 1981. Washington: UP of America, 1981), 5–11.

[2] Philip C. Rule, S. J., however, finds an Old Testament parallel
for Addie's attitude toward words. Rule notes that Jeremiah warned
against "deceptive words" and advised that only actions could lead
Israel to salvation (112).

32   **Works Cited.**   "Works Cited" is the heading suggested by MLA guidelines for a bibliography that lists only works to which the writer refers directly in the text. If you use endnote or footnote form of documentation instead of the MLA-preferred in-text citation form, you may, if your instructor permits, omit a separate list of works cited because the bibliographic information would already have appeared in the reference notes.

33   **Format of the list.**   Begin the list of works cited on a separate page, center the heading "Works Cited," and type it one inch from the top of the page. Double space all lines unless instructed otherwise. All entries must be alphabetized.

The first line of each work is typed flush with the left margin. Second and subsequent lines are indented five spaces from the left margin. Each entry begins with the author's name, surname first. In instances where there are multiple authors, only the name of the first author is inverted. For more than three authors, list only the name of the first, followed by "et al."

34   **Entry without an author.**   Alphabetize the entry by the first word of its title; if it is a review, signal that fact by "Rev. of."

35   **Weekly or monthly magazine or a newspaper.**   Give the date and page number; no volume number is needed.

36   **Two or more works by the same author.**   A second work by the same author is introduced by three hyphens, a period, and two spaces.

37   **Periodicals using continuous pagination.**   Identify the date by a volume number; give the year in parentheses.

38   **Article in an edited book.**   Information about the article is given first. The editor's name is signaled by "Ed." (See also note 22.)

39   **Page information.**   None is needed if the book as a whole is the reference. The sign after the page number in the West reference indicates that the article continues on later pages.

Works Cited

Rev. of <u>As I Lay Dying</u>. <u>Times Literary Supplement</u> 26 Sept. 1935: 594.

Brooks, Cleanth. <u>William Faulkner: The Yoknapatawpha Country</u>. New Haven and London: Yale UP, 1963.

Coates, Robert M. "Recent Books." <u>New Yorker</u> 25 Oct. 1930: 104.

Dawson, Margaret Cheny. "Beside Addie's Coffin." <u>New York Herald Tribune</u> 5 Oct. 1930, sec. XI: 6.

Faulkner, William. <u>As I Lay Dying</u>. New York: Vintage Books, 1985.

---. <u>Lion in the Garden: Interviews with William Faulkner: 1926–1962</u>. Ed. James B. Meriwether and Michael Millgate. New York: Random, 1968.

Hewes, Henry. "Broadway Postscript." <u>Saturday Review</u>. 4 June 1960: 30.

O'Donnell, Patrick. "The Spectral Road: Metaphors of Transference in Faulkner's <u>As I Lay Dying</u>." <u>Papers on Language and Literature</u> 20 (1984): 60–79.

Palliser, Charles. "Predestination and Freedom in <u>As I Lay Dying</u>." <u>American Literature</u> 58 (1986): 557–573.

Rule, Philip C., S. J. "The Old Testament Vision in <u>As I Lay Dying</u>." <u>Religious Perspectives in Faulkner's Fiction: Yoknapatawpha and Beyond</u>. Ed. J. Robert Barth, S. J. Notre Dame: UP Notre Dame, 1972. 107–118.

"Twenty-Four Novels of the Season." <u>Literary Digest</u> 24 Jan. 1931: 18.

West, Anthony. "Remembering William Faulkner." <u>Gourmet</u> Jan. 1969: 22+.

40 **Works Consulted.** This title heads a list of works that Conlin read for background information but did not quote from or refer to in his essay. If this list had been more extensive, he might have chosen to include only what he would have titled a "Selective Bibliography."

41 **Name of state.** If the city of publication may be unfamiliar to readers—Madison, NJ or Madison, WI?—the state name is given in postal-code form.

42 **Reference to an edited book.** If you refer primarily to the work of an editor, then he or she becomes the "author" and his or her name begins the citation, followed by a comma and "ed." (See also note 38.)

43 **Periodical with continuous pagination.** The parentheses may include the season or the month in addition to the year of publication. (See also note 37.)

44 **Pages that are not consecutive.** Format is indicated in this Volke entry.

40   Works Consulted

41   Beck, Warren. <u>Man in Motion: Faulkner's Trilogy</u>. Madison, WI: U of
           Wisconsin P, 1961.

42   Blotner, Joseph, ed. <u>Selected Letters of William Faulkner</u>. New York:
           Random, 1977.

      Brooks, Cleanth and Robert Penn Warren. <u>The Scope of Fiction</u>. New
           York: Appleton, 1960.

43   Rossky, William. "<u>As I Lay Dying</u>: The Insane World," <u>Texas Studies in
           Literature and Language</u> 4 (Spring 1962): 87–97.

44   Volke, Edmond L. <u>A Reader's Guide to William Faulkner</u>. New York:
           Farrar, 1964. 126–140, 377–382, 413–422.

52b APA-Style Research Paper

The sample research paper that follows uses the method of documentation recommended in the <u>Publication Manual of the APA</u>, Third Edition. In this abbreviated version of a longer paper, Sheila Woody argues that the use of animals in research is often immoral and unethical. In the last half of the paper, which has been omitted, Woody proposes that changes in the spirit and methods of using animals in research would be profitable and productive for that research. Since this is an argumentative essay, Woody's tone is persuasive. She points to weaknesses in her opponents' case while presenting strong evidence to support her position. In her concluding section, she acknowledges the good intention of researchers, but also asserts the benefits that would accompany new attitudes and techniques in research. Note that the outline on page 2 of the paper encompasses the whole essay.

1 **Title page format.** Although APA guidelines do not prescribe a form for the title page, a sample paper in the <u>APA Publication Manual</u> (the source for those guidelines) provides Woody with a model to follow: her title, her name, and the name of the university she attends are centered on the page and double-spaced. Since Woody's paper is a class assignment, she adds course title, instructor's name, and the date about two inches below her university affiliation. A running title (a brief encapsulation of the essay title) appears in the top right-hand corner above each page number. This serves the purpose of identification and reordering of pages in the instance of page misplacement and eliminates the need to include one's name alongside each page number (as is done in MLA style). Note that running titles most often appear on papers submitted for publication.

1

Ethics of Nonhuman Animal Experimentation

Sheila Roxanne Woody

University of Georgia

Psychology

Dr. Stuart Katz

October 20, 1987

2   Outline: Ethics of Nonhuman Animal Experimentation

Thesis: An evaluation that takes into account that the concerns
of both sides of the issue of animal rights in laboratory
experiments can lead to guidelines for preserving those
rights and still promoting worthwhile research.

     I.   Number of animals used
    II.   Flaws in experiments
        A.   Unnecessary
        B.   Repetitious
        C.   Cruel
   III.   Justification for experiments
        A.   Double standard
            1.   Animals
            2.   Humans

2   **Outline.**   The sample APA paper in the <u>APA Publication Manual</u> includes no outline but instead presents an abstract of the paper on page 2. Woody's essay includes a formal outline as required by her instructor. Like the formal outline that accompanies the MLA research paper, the outline here appears on a separate unnumbered page and only short phrases are used. Roman numerals indicate major categories; indented capitals and then arabic numerals, indented further, indicate subsidiary categories.

2

  B. Language test

  C. Consciousness

  D. Ability to feel pain

    1. Neurological evidence

    2. Behavioral evidence

    3. Evolutionary evidence

 IV. Guidelines for reform of research

  A. Reexamination of question

  B. Alternate procedures

    1. Computer simulation

    2. Use of human organs and tissues

  C. Value of research vs. cost in suffering

 V. Benefits for research

  A. Creativity

  B. Holistic view of life

3   **Introduction.**   Woody uses two paragraphs to introduce the essay, delaying the thesis sentence until the last sentence of paragraph two. She opens with some startling statistics to arouse the reader's interest in the topic and emphasize its importance.

4   **In-text documentation.**   Woody follows APA documentation style. When the author's name is not given within the text itself, a parenthetical reference includes the name and page number as in MLA style, but there are differences. Commas separate the elements in the reference. The publication date is always cited and "p." or "pp." accompanies the number(s) of the page. Also, a title does not appear in the text reference unless the author is unknown.

5   **Thesis.**   The basis for the thesis is an arguable point: the assertion that to inflict pain on animals is immoral. Woody begins to develop the argument in the body of her essay, beginning in paragraph three.

6   **Page numbering.**   APA style requires that pages be numbered with arabic numerals starting with the number 2 on the second page. Page numbers are placed in the upper right-hand corner, one-half inch from the top of the page.

7   **Paragraph development.**   Woody uses several examples to support the first point in her argument: research using animal subjects is flawed in three ways.

3   Accurate statistics are not available concerning the actual number of animals used in American laboratories each year for research and experimentation because researchers are not compelled to report these figures. However, based on the number of published studies each year, as well as comparison with official reports from the United Kingdom, estimates of the number of living animals used yearly in American laboratories range between twenty

4   million and 125 million (Ryder, 1975, p. 35).

       The ethical issue of animal rights in laboratory experiments has become an increasingly controversial topic in the last ten years. Experimenters resent what they see as intrusion into their decisions about research, and animal welfare activists often deny the value of any experimentation. An evaluation that takes into

5   account the legitimate concerns of both sides could form a base for establishing guidelines concerning nonhuman animal welfare while still promoting the pursuit of worthwhile research.

6   Questioning the morality of using nonhuman animals in laboratories is not merely an academic exercise. Numerous examples can be cited of experiments that are unnecessary, cruel, or repetitious.

       Some studies may appear on the surface to be worthwhile, but they may accomplish very little in real terms. This is frequently true when a researcher attempts to extrapolate from animal

7   research to humans, particularly with hereditary diseases. For example, methods can be devised to create ulcers or epilepsy in animals. While the symptoms and behaviors of these induced

8   **Block quotation.**   APA guidelines indent a block quotation five spaces from the left margin, not ten spaces as in MLA style. Also, the period is placed at the end of the last sentence but before the citation, as in MLA style.

9   **Citing a work by two or more authors.**   When citing a source with two or more authors <u>within parentheses</u>, use an ampersand (&) in place of the word <u>and</u>. However, when the citation is not parenthetical but part of the text itself, the word <u>and</u> is used.

10   **Summarizing or paraphrasing.**   Woody paraphrases relevant research to present information economically. She documents her sources just as she would if she had quoted them directly.

disorders closely resemble those of the natural disorders in
humans, the origins are different in crucial respects:

> They [gastric and duodenal ulcers] never occur naturally in
> animals, and they are hard to reproduce experimentally. They
> have been so produced, but usually by methods of gross
> damage that have no relation to any possible causative factor
> in man; moreover, these experimental ulcers are superficial
> and heal rapidly and bear little resemblance to the indurated
> chronic ulcers we see in our patients. ("Reactions to," 1954,
> p. 1195)

There are many examples of nonessential research. Some of
the studies are undertaken to reach conclusions that common
sense could have reached. For example, Professor P. L. Broadhurst
reports that psychologists have blinded rats, then deafened them,
and finally eliminated olfaction to find out how rats learn in a
maze. It is no wonder that "it was found that rats deprived in this
way showed very little ability to learn" (Regan & Singer, 1976, p. 3).

Other studies are costly repetitions. The National Institute of
Health underwrote a thirty-year study of sleep deprivation costing
$51,000. In this study, animals were forced to run for 23 hours,
rest an hour, then run for 23 more hours. During the hour of rest, a
gun was shot off to disturb the weary animals. The experiment was
a repetition of others performed in 1927, 1929, and 1946 (Morse,
1968, p. 29).

11 **Transitional paragraph.** This paragraph serves a dual purpose. First, it briefly explains scientists' justifications for the experiments discussed in earlier paragraphs as examples of cruelty to animals; it concludes and summarizes this section of the essay. Second, it serves as a transition to the essay's following section, in which Woody asserts the connection between human and nonhuman animals.

12 **Rhetorical question.** In the slow, logical building of evidence in an argumentative essay, a rhetorical question is useful to frame a paragraph or a part of an essay. The answer to Woody's question becomes the three divisions of the first half of the chief argument of the essay: animals are not unlike humans, although researchers declare their differences.

10   Many studies seem unnecessarily cruel. The University of Michigan conducted an experiment in which cats were repeatedly struck on the head by a pneumatic hammer. Although the cats were given a relaxant to reduce their motor activity and facilitate their handling, they were still conscious when struck, and none of them received anesthesia. All of the cats suffered severe brain concussions, as anticipated (Morse, 1968, p. 29). Similar experiments have been conducted at other major universities with other species.

11   Various reasons were given for these studies. Broadhurst's could shed light on learning theory. The repeated sleep deprivation experiments could improve statistical controls and physiological measurements of the earlier studies. Information about the course of severe concussions was gained in the last study. However, the issue at hand is not only the practical value of the studies but also the cost in animal suffering.

       One justification for such abuses is many scientists' opinion that animals do not fall within the bounds of moral concern. Laws protect human subjects, but even without laws, researchers would consider trauma studies, drug addiction studies, and so on to be 12 unethical if human subjects were required. What is the basis for the double standard? The major distinction seems to be the level of intellect. We assume that human beings are capable of abstract thought and rationalization and that other animals are not.

13   **Line of spaced periods.**   The line of spaced periods indicates
the omission of a section of Woody's essay as we have
abridged it here. This device is not necessary for omissions in
prose material; three ellipsis points and a period are enough to
signal the omission of even a paragraph or two. Such a full line
of spaced periods is necessary when you are block quoting a
poem and omitting a line or more.

14   **Audience.**   Woody seems to consider her audience to be both
her psychology instructor and classmates and also what could
be called a "general" audience. Along with her discussion of
scientific experiments, she refers to theories of philosophy
and language.

13

Many writers and researchers maintain that because language users (humans) are assumed to be able to form concepts, any being unable to use human language must lack that ability. Theories of language that are based on the heritability of linguistic rules, such as Noam Chomsky's theory of universal grammar, would rule that any communication among animals could not be considered "language" unless it followed these presumed genetic grammatical rules found in human languages of all cultures (Chomsky, 1959, pp. 26–58). If human language is viewed as the central trait proving that a being has intelligence, then no other animal could possibly have it.

On such a basis was vivisection justified when it was first practiced. For example, in the thirteenth century Saint Thomas Aquinas wrote:

> Dumb animals and plants are devoid of the life of reason whereby to set themselves in motion; they are moved, as it were, by another, by a kind of natural impulse, a sign of which is that they are naturally enslaved and accommodated to the uses of others. (Regan & Singer, 1976, p. 57)

The irony of using language as a test is that while nonhuman animals are considered to be similar to humans for the convenience of research, they are considered to be completely separate for moral purposes. In addition, use of the language test as a basis for a moral decision does not exempt all humans from painful

15 **Audience, tone, and diction.** Woody maintains a balance between technical language, appropriate for part of her audience, and nontechnical diction for others. Language also becomes part of Woody's argument in a subtle way. The homely picture of Spot "wagging his tail" at the sight of his leash is contrasted by the following sentence, which contains the kind of jargon that can cloud meaning rather than clarifying it: "Spot has not demonstrated a sophisticated refinement of thought complete with an extemporaneous discourse on his expectations." This juxtaposition is a good-natured (because veiled) attack on her opponents, those researchers who would defend their actions with high-sounding words.

16 **Block quotation.** The quotation is a long noun subordinate clause, used as the object of the sentence verb <u>noted</u>; therefore, no punctuation follows <u>noted</u>, and the first word of the quotation does not begin with a capital letter.

experiences. Infants, comatose persons, autistic persons, and the severely mentally retarded could ethically be used if language alone were a valid criterion, since they cannot speak to demonstrate their intelligence.

Furthermore, an animal's inability to say what it is aware of does not determine the range of its awareness. When Spot sees his owner take out his leash and responds by running in a circle, wagging his tail, and looking what can only be described as excited, is it not reasonable that Spot has an expectation of being taken for a run in the fresh air? Spot has not demonstrated a sophisticated refinement of thought complete with an extemporaneous discourse on his expectations, yet his actions would lead a reasonable person to believe he did know what was about to happen. Of course, granting that animals have a modicum of intelligence does not imply that they are capable of a full range of abstract thoughts. On the other hand, Charles Darwin noted

> how little can the hard-worked wife of an Australian savage,
> who uses very few abstract words and cannot count above
> four, exert her self-consciousness or reflect on the nature of
> her own existence. (Regan & Singer, 1976, p. 77)

Since language is simply a tool for expressing meaning, rather than the meaning itself, the best way to judge the intelligence of a being is to evaluate its behavior in the whole context of its natural environment. Human language would indicate the cognitive

17 **Concrete detail.** Woody uses details and examples effectively throughout the essay. In these last two paragraphs, for example, a generalization about humans is illustrated by the borrowed example of "the hard-worked wife of an Australian savage," and in her discussion of animal qualities Woody pictures the typical family pet, "Spot," and also mentions chimpanzees.

17   abilities of humans, but other animals, such as chimpanzees, also
      indicate intelligence with communication complex enough and
      spontaneous enough to be called language. Though chimpanzees do
      not have the abstract conceptualization behind their
      communication, often humans, as Wittgenstein notes, do not use
      these "higher" thought processes while speaking (1965, p. 9).

18   **Format of references.**   The alphabetized bibliography at the end of a paper following APA style is titled "References," whereas in MLA style that list may be titled "Works Cited," "Works Consulted," or "Bibliography." The title "References" indicates that all works are cited in the essay. Although APA style does not call for it, if Woody's instructor had suggested that she list her background reading, she would have titled that list "Bibliography."

Notice the particular features of APA bibliographic style in this list:

—Initials substitute for authors' first names, and an ampersand is used in place of the word <u>and</u>.

—All authors' names are inverted. Recall that MLA style inverts the first author's name only (see pages 414, 419).

—Titles of books and articles are not capitalized except for the first letter of the initial word and any proper nouns. MLA style does not omit capitals.

—Titles of periodicals are capitalized.

—Italics designate book and periodical titles.

—The first line of the reference is flush with the left margin, and all subsequent lines are indented three spaces.

—Chapter titles and titles of magazine and journal articles are not enclosed in quotation marks in the reference list.

19   **Review of a book.**   Since the review is untitled, the information that describes the review takes the place of the title and is put in brackets to show that it is not the title. If the review had a title, this material would follow it, in brackets as shown here. Note too, that APA style places all publication dates in parentheses followed by a period. MLA uses parentheses only for dates of periodicals with continuous pagination.

(See p. 478 for items 20–22.)

18   References

19   Chomsky, N. (1959). [Review of Verbal behavior by B. F. Skinner].
          Language, 35, 26–58.

20   Dewsbury, D. (1978). Comparative animal behavior. New York: McGraw-
          Hill.

20   Fox, M. (1980). Returning to Eden. New York: Viking.

21   Griffin, D. (1976). The question of animal awareness. New York:
          Rockefeller University Press.

21   Kummer, H. (1971). Primate societies. Arlington Heights, MA: AHM
          Publishing.

21   Midgley, M. (1984). Animals and why they matter. Athens, GA:
          University of Georgia Press.

     Morse, M. (1968). Ordeal of the animals. Englewood Cliffs, NJ: Prentice-
          Hall.

     Reactions to stress. (1954, May 22). British Medical Journal, p. 1195.

     Regan, T. (1983). The case for animal rights. Berkeley: University of
          California Press.

22   Regan, T., & Singer, P. (Eds.). (1976). Animal rights and human
          obligations. Englewood Cliffs, NJ: Prentice-Hall.

     Ryder, R. (1975). Victims of science. London: Davis-Poynter.

     Wittgenstein, L. (1965). The blue and brown books. New York: Harper &
          Row.

Journal article. The volume number, underlined, follows the name of the journal and a comma. A comma then follows the volume number, and pages are given without the signal "p." or "pp." (Page numbers are preceded by "p." or "pp." in referring to articles or chapters in an edited book and to articles in popular magazines and newspapers.) MLA does not use "p." or "pp."

20 **Publisher's name in brief.** Nonessential words such as <u>Publishing Co., Inc.</u>, are omitted. Viking Press becomes Viking; McGraw-Hill stands without "Book Company."

21 **Publisher's name in full.** The name of a university press is spelled out in full; the word <u>Publishing</u> is needed to identify this publisher.

22 **Edited book.** The abbreviation <u>Eds</u>. (or <u>Ed</u>.) within parentheses is used when referring to an edited book, as shown in Woody's reference list. However, if the reference is to a chapter or article within an edited book, the author of the chapter or article is given first, and the reference is formatted like this:

> Author, A., Author, B., & Author, C. (1976). Can the chimpanzee think? In T. Regan & P. Singer (Eds.), <u>Animal rights and human obligations</u> (pp.   –   ). Englewood Cliffs, NJ: Prentice-Hall.

Part VIII

Business
Writing

memo

53

The Memo

Like all good writing, business writing should be clear, concise, and correct. In addition, writers in a business setting must meet certain conventions of form, record information accurately for later referral (sometimes with legal implications), and pay special attention to the needs of their readers.

53 The Memo

The most common form of communication in business is the memo. A **memo** addresses one or many readers within an organization or company. It is generally short in length (no more than a page or two), focuses on a single topic, is clearly directed to its audience, and, to a noticeable degree, follows conventions or formulas in form and content. A memo can be sent on paper or electronically through mail systems that link company offices.

53a The Parts of a Memo

The memo has two parts: heading and message.
The memo **heading** is often printed on company memo sheets and looks something like this:

Date:

To:

From:

Subject:

The writer fills in these elements to *record* vital information for the file and to inform the reader directly about the message to come.

Message

In writing the **message,** the memo writer focuses on a single topic. Short paragraphs and company abbreviations that are clear to readers are used. For example, the abbreviations for Emergency Services (ES) and Intensive Care Unit (ICU) are used in the sample memo in section 54b. Important information is highlighted in headings and lists and these items are kept parallel. Further, drawings and diagrams often accompany the memo to support its purpose and message and to avoid lengthy discussion. The sample in the following section is a good example of a typical business memo.

53b Sample Memo

Date: 23 March 1989

To: All Employees, Emergency Services
From: Peter Parker
          Director, Patient Services
Subject: New Procedure for Patient Admission to ICU

Effective April 15, new procedures will be implemented in the Patient Records Office to ensure that patient admissions from ES to ICU will be handled quickly.

After that date, ES personnel must complete the new Form ES-27 for any patient transferred to ICU. A copy of this form should be sent to ICU and to Patient Records.

All ES employees are asked to cooperate with this new procedure. Address any questions to me at ext. 8887.

cc: Patient Records Office

54 The Business Letter

A **business letter** is appropriate when you write to an organization or when you write on behalf of an organization to customers or clients. The letter is more formal than the memo and thus also may be used for recording important matters of policy or confidential personnel decisions within an organization.

54a Business Letter Formats

Business letters generally follow one of the three following formats:

1. Block format.
2. Modified block format (sometimes with indented paragraphs).
3. Simplified format.

Each format is shown in a model business letter in section 54d. Of course, you should check with your organization to see which format is preferred.

The business letter is typed on 8½ × 11-inch white or off-white bond paper (erasable paper is not used because it tends to smudge). The text is centered vertically on the paper and wide margins are used. Further, the text of the letter must be neatly typed; messy erasures, cross-outs, and ink corrections are unacceptable. Each part of the business letter is single-spaced with double space separating the parts.

54b The Parts of a Business Letter

A typical business letter has these parts: heading, inside address, salutation, subject line, body, closing, notations, and an addressed envelope in which the letter is sent.

Heading

The **heading** includes the sender's address and the date of the letter. If you use letterhead stationery, you need only note the date. Otherwise, write your address (*without* your name).

Inside address

The **inside address** is simply the name and address of the reader to whom the letter will be sent. Readers are often pleased to be identified by their names, so when you write your job application letters, try to use the *names* of the persons responsible for new employee hirings. If you are unable to obtain the reader's name, then address the appropriate office or person by job title. For example:

Personnel Department

Director of Personnel

Customer Service

Write out the full name of the company—do not abbreviate. Spell all names correctly; if you are unsure of a spelling, check it—do not guess.

Salutation

The conventional **salutation,** or greeting, is "Dear [Mr./Ms.] Lastname:" (the formal greeting ends in a colon). If you are unsure of the gender of the reader (e.g., if you are responding to a letter signed "S. H. Phillips"), then write "Dear S. H. Phillips." The simplified letter format shown on pages 489–490 omits the salutation and thus avoids such cumbersome and archaic greetings as "Dear Sir or Madam" or "To Whom it may Concern."

Subject line

Although **subject lines** are common in memos, they are less often used in business letters. Subject lines may be seen in sequential letters about a project, in routine correspondence concerning orders and responses to orders, and in sales letters. Simplified format letters may include a subject line that is typed in capital letters; for example:

YOU MAY ALREADY HAVE WON!

Body

The **body** of the letter should be brief and arranged in relatively short paragraphs for ease of reading. The text is single-spaced with double-spacing between paragraphs. Begin the first sentence of each paragraph at the left-hand margin if you are using the block format (see the sample memo on pp. 486–488). If instead you are using the modified block format, use indented paragraphs with the first sentence of each paragraph indented five spaces (see p. 488).

Closing

The **closing** consists of the complimentary close and the writer's signature. The most common closing phrases are "Sincerely," "Sincerely yours," and "Yours truly." The phrase "Respectfully yours" shows a bit more deference and respect, whereas "Cordially" and "Best regards" are more informal.

Only the first letter of the closing is capitalized and the entire phrase is followed by a comma. Your name is typed several spaces (usually four spaces, leaving enough space for your signature) below the complimentary close, as in the following example:

Truly yours,

Janet P. Smith

Janet P. Smith

The company name and/or your job title may also appear below your typed name. Although you type your full name, you may sign the letter with a nickname if your relationship with the reader warrants it.

In the simplified format, the closing is omitted if you have also omitted the salutation (see the sample memo on p. 481). In the modified block format, the closing is indented (see p. 488), whereas in the block format it is positioned at the left-hand margin (see p. 488).

Notations

Beneath the closing and flush with the left-hand margin you may include **notations,** such as *Enclosure*(*s*) (sometimes abbreviated *enc.* or *encl.*) to direct the reader to items enclosed with the letter, *DCA:dtd* to indicate the initials of the writer and typist or secretary, and *cc:* to note circulation of copies (*pc:* for photocopy) followed by the names of the recipients of the copies.

Envelope

Your name and address are typed in the upper left-hand corner of the envelope, unless of course the return address is already printed there. The recipient's name and address are typed exactly as they appear in the letter, in block form, as shown in the model on page 487.

54c Writing the Business Letter

As you write a business letter, imagine that you are the letter's reader. What would you as the reader need to know? How would you react to the letter? Writing from the reader's point of view can show, for example, your knowledge of a particular company and of its needs in terms of employment. When writing a job application letter, first develop a profile of the company and assess the demands of the position you seek. If you are responding to an advertisement, let the description of the job shape your response in the letter. Describe how your skills match the employer's needs, as in the model on page 487.

When you write a letter to claim an adjustment for some error in service or faulty product, or to complain, think about the remedy you seek and about the information the reader will need to meet your claim. Present yourself as someone credible, rational, deserving of the requested adjustment. Do not attack the reader. Announce your claim, and then provide a narrative of the error. For a product, include such information as the product's name, model, serial number, and warranty information. Describe the requested action (e.g., specify whether you are requesting a refund, repair, or replacement). The model letter on pages 489–490 claims an adjustment, whereas the model on page 488 requests information. Note how the latter sample letter encourages a response through its specific questions and pleasant tone. A response letter in any situation should be written with the request in hand.

54d Sample Business Letters

Block format

96 Forest Ave.
Portland, ME 04103
25 March 1989 ⎤ — *heading*

R. H. Dawson
Director of Personnel
The Big Company
800 N. French St.
Wilmington, DE 19801

inside address

Dear Mr. Dawson:

salutation

paragraphs are not indented

From both Professor Richard H. McKinley at the University of Southern
Maine and your advertisement in the 15 March issue of the Wilmington
News Journal, I have learned of your opening for an entry-level
accountant. I am writing to apply for that position.

As my resume shows, I will receive a degree in accounting in June. My
course work has concentrated on the financial management of large
multinationals like The Big Company. Each course required extensive
case analyses and practical problem solving. My high grade-point
average indicates my strengths in those skills necessary to do well in
your position.

body

single-spaced text

In addition, through my work with POM Recoveries and the Publisher's
Clearing House, I have gained experience in the day-to-day operation of a
small and a large operation. For much of my work I was given an
assignment that I completed largely on my own. I also learned and
demonstrated skills with computerized accounting systems. Thus, I am
confident that I can be the "knowledgeable self-starter" your
advertisement seeks. A position with The Big Company especially
interests me because of your recent acquisition of Steitman AG and the
potential for learning about German accounting practices as I apply my
knowledge of the German language and culture.

double space between → paragraphs

I will be visiting Delaware during my spring break, 17-22 April, and will
gladly meet with you any time during that period for an interview. If
these dates are not suitable, please let me know and I'll make other
arrangements for a time convenient to The Big Company.

I look forward to talking with you.

bz/ltr

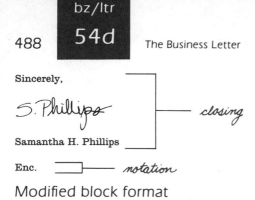

Sincerely,

S. Phillips

Samantha H. Phillips

— *closing*

Enc. — *notation*

Modified block format

September 14, 1989
1111 Carriage House Drive
Tallahassee, FL 32312

— *indented heading*

John C. Jones
Department of Entomology
Florida State University
Tallahassee, FL 32306

Dear Professor Jones:

   I saw a strange-looking insect in my garden yesterday. It was
slender but large for an insect--about an inch long. It was a rather
violent green, had greenish gossamer wings, and a tiny head with
prominent black eyes. It appeared to be able to turn its head in a
complete circle. As I watched the creature, it rose on its hind legs
and folded its front legs. Could you identify it from this description?

— *paragraphs indented 5 spaces*

   1. What is the name of the insect?
   2. Is it destructive to plants?
   3. If so, which plants?
   4. What kind of spray should I use to destroy it, if necessary?

   I would appreciate any information you can send me.

indented closing —

Sincerely,

Mark H. Hocking

Mark H. Hocking

Sample business letter envelope

Samantha H. Phillips
96 Forest Ave.
Portland, ME 04103

R. H. Dawson
Director of Personnel
The Big Company
800 N. French St.
Wilmington, DE 19801

Simplified format

Box 983
Ketchum, ID 83340
May 18, 1989

Customer Service
Get Mugged, Inc.
12 Adams Lane
Newton Highlands, MA 02161

← *salutation omitted*

I am writing about a problem with a recent order.

On May 1, I ordered 6 "Bunnies in Heaven" mugs from your spring catalog. The stock number is 45-66-77; the mugs appeared on page 10 of the catalog. On May 15, I received a package from you marked "1/2 dozen bunnies in heaven." It contained, however, a combination of bunny mugs and "Moose in Maine" mugs. Moreover, the count was wrong. The case contained a total of 8 mugs: 4 bunnies and 4 moose.

In accordance with your guarantee, I am returning the improperly
packaged case to you. Please reimburse me for the postage costs and
send me 6 "Bunnies in Heaven" mugs. Thank you.

Martha Simpson   ← *closing phrase omitted*

Martha Simpson

55 The Résumé

Your résumé represents *you* as a potential employee. It must
be concise, accurate, easy to read, and well designed. And it
must be *correct.*

Start by making an inventory of your skills, education, and
relevant experience. Note all of the jobs you have held, including their dates and responsibilities, as well as all paid
positions, internships, and volunteer work. Also list major
courses, and academic achievements, and activities, especially
offices held and leadership roles. Then select and arrange this
information to provide a profile of yourself. Although the form
of the résumé may vary to suit individual tastes, most résumés
conform to conventions in content and design.

55a The Parts of a Résumé

The typical résumé of a college graduate contains these parts:
a stated objective, personal data, educational background,
work experience, references, and other miscellaneous information.

Objective

Although not all résumés include a statement of **objective,**
some employers look for this indication of your career goal.

The objective can serve as a thesis that is supported by the evidence presented later in the résumé.

Personal data

The **personal data** should include your name, address, (home and school, if different), and phone number.

Educational background

The **education** section should list the schools you have attended since high school, starting with the most recent (reverse chronological order) and including dates of attendance and degrees received or expected. Major and minor fields of study and your grade-point average should also be identified.

Work experience

In the **work experience** section you should list the jobs you have held, starting with the most recent. For each job, note the dates of employment, title of your position, and the name and address of the company. Briefly describe your responsibilities. Avoid full sentences in the description; instead, use fragments beginning with action verbs, as in the model on page 493. Quantify your work wherever possible. Show independent work or a progression of responsibilities if that occurred.

References

Most prospective employers will expect you to provide **references,** the names of people who can vouch for you. You may keep a file of letters of reference at your college placement office; if so, note that on the résumé. Because you may wish to select different references for different positions while keeping one résumé for several possibilities, and because of a need to save space, you may elect not to name the references directly on the résumé. Instead you would write, "References available on request."

Other information

Include mention of scholarships, awards, athletic activities, or other extracurricular participation in drama groups or clubs if you feel such information provides a more overall view of yourself as a potential employee. Such information also gives an interviewer a good opener for an interview. It is *your* résumé. Just be brief and honest.

55b The Design of a Résumé

The design of the résumé is probably almost as important as its content. The résumé is printed or typed on a sheet of 8½ × 11-inch paper. Be careful in your typing, or take advantage of a typing service to ensure excellence in the final result. If you have access to a word-processing system and high-quality printer, and your skills are equal to the task, then prepare your résumé on the system. You can select an appropriate typeface, deploy boldface and underlining for emphasis, and insert, for example, different objective statements to match different jobs you seek. However, do not get carried away with too many options in type. Finally, *proofread* the final résumé many times. One error in spelling may very well send your résumé to the reader's wastebasket. The model on page 493 shows one good résumé form.

55c Sample Résumé

SAMANTHA H. PHILLIPS

College address (until June 1, 1989): 96 Forest Ave., Portland, ME 04103.

Permanent address: 210 Waverly St., Jericho, NY 11753 (516) 432-9655.

Objective
A position in internal auditing with a large multinational organization in which I can combine my accounting skills with my knowledge of different languages and cultures

Education
BS in accounting, University of Southern Maine, expected 1990. Courses in managerial accounting, cost accounting, business law, finance, operations management, marketing. GPA 3.5 out of 4.0. Earned 75% of college expenses.

Experience

Summer 1988
POM Recoveries. Syosset, NY.
Posted financial statements by hand and on computer.

Spring 1988
Publisher's Clearing House. Port Washington, NY.
Sorted checks, processed magazine orders, validated contest entry forms.

Summers 1985, 1986
Camp Thistle. Rabbit Lake, NY.
Organized games, taught swimming, supervised campers.

Activities
German Club; intramural soccer and baseball.

Personal
Born September 17, 1969. Have traveled widely in the United States and Europe. Willing to relocate.

References
Available upon request.

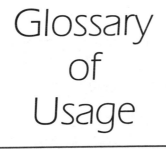

Glossary of Usage

The items in this glossary reflect current usage among experienced writers. Use the glossary to check the appropriateness of your word choices.

A, An Use the article *a* before a consonant sound; use *an* before a vowel sound.

a receipt	a history	a one-liner	a unit	a B
an idea	an hour	an officer	an umbrella	an F

Aggravate *Aggravate* means "to make worse." In formal writing, do not use *aggravate* with its informal meaning of "to annoy, irritate, or vex."

Agree To, Agree With Use *agree* with *to* when you mean "to grant or give approval." Use *agree* with *with* when you mean "to be in harmony," "to conform," or "to hold similar views."

The senator could not **agree to** the amendment.
The senator could not **agree with** his colleague on the need for the amendment.

495

Ain't Nonstandard contraction. In general, avoid it in your writing.

All Right Always write *all right* as two words, not as *alright*.

Allusion, Illusion An *allusion* is an indirect or casual reference to something. An *illusion* is a false or misleading perception or concept.

> The poem is filled with many **allusions** to the Bible.
> Five years in the theater stripped him of his **illusions** about the glamour of an actor's life.

A Lot Always write *a lot* as two words, not as *alot*. In general, avoid using *a lot* in formal writing.

A.M., P.M. *or* AM, PM *or* a.m., p.m. Use these abbreviations only with figures.

> *Not:* The lecture ends at eleven in the **A.M.**
> *But:* The lecture ends at **11:00 A.M.**

Among, Between Use *among* with three or more people or objects. Use *between* with only two.

> According to the will, the funds were to be divided equally **between** the two children.
> He decided to leave his entire estate to his eldest son, rather than divide it **among** his six children.

Amount, Number *Amount* refers to mass or quantity. It is followed by the preposition *of* and a singular noun. *Number* refers to things that can be counted. It is followed by *of* and a plural noun.

> The **amount** of time he spent completing the job was far greater than the reward he derived from it.
> The **number** of domestic animals that have contracted rabies is alarming.

An   *See* **a**

And Etc.   The abbreviation *etc.* means "and other things" or "and so forth." Therefore, *and etc.* is redundant.

Anxious, Eager   *Anxious* means "worried, uneasy, uncertain." In formal writing, do not use *anxious* for *eager,* which means "expectant" or "desirous" but carries no implication of apprehension.

> The doctor was **anxious** about her patient's condition.
> Since we have heard so many good things about them, we are **eager** to meet our new neighbors.

Anyone, Any One   *Anyone* means "any person at all." It refers indefinitely to any person whatsoever. *Any one* refers to a specific, though unidentified, person or thing within a group. Similar cases are *everyone, every one* and *someone, some one.*

> **Anyone** willing to work hard can get good grades.
> **Any one** of these plans is acceptable.

Anyplace   *Anywhere* is preferred.

Anyways   *Anyway* is preferred.

Anywheres   *Anywhere* is preferred.

As   In general, use the stronger and clearer conjunctions *because, since,* and *while.*

> *Not:*   We could no longer see the river from our terrace, **as** the new building blocked our view.
> *But:*   We could no longer see the river from our terrace **because** the new building blocked our view.

As, Like   *See* **like.**

Awful   In general, use a more specific adjective such as *shocking, ugly, appalling,* or *great.* In formal writing, do not use *awfully* or *awful* as an intensifier meaning "very."

Awhile, A While *Awhile* is an adverb meaning "for a short time." It is not preceded by the preposition *for*. *A while* is an article plus a noun. It is usually preceded by *for*.

We asked our guests to stay **awhile.**
They could stay for **a while** longer.

Bad, Badly Use the adjective *bad* before nouns and after linking verbs. Use the adverb *badly* to modify verbs or adjectives.

Several **bad** strawberries were hidden under the good ones.
The students felt **bad** about the loss.
The dancer performed **badly.**
The book was **badly** written.

Being As, Being That Use the more formal *because*.

Not: **Being as** the sketch was signed, it was valuable.
But: **Because** the sketch was signed, it was valuable.

Not: **Being that** they needed money badly, they took a second mortgage on their home.
But: **Because** they needed money badly, they took a second mortgage on their home.

Beside, Besides *Beside* is a preposition that means "next to." When used as a preposition, *besides* means "in addition to" or "except for." When used as an adverb, *besides* means "in addition" or "furthermore."

She was buried **beside** her husband.
Besides mathematics, there are no required courses.
To keep warm, she wore a coat, a hat, and gloves—and a muffler **besides.**

Between *See* **among.**

Between You And I   A common grammatical mistake. Write *between you and me.* (*You* and *me* are objects of the preposition *between.*)

Bring, Take   Use *bring* when you mean movement from a farther person or place toward a nearer one. Use *take* when you mean movement away from a nearer person or place toward a farther one.

> **Bring** me the book I left in the bedroom.
> **Take** this package to the post office.

Bunch   Do not use *bunch* to refer to a group of people.

Burst, Bursted, Bust, Busted   *Burst* is a verb that means "to come apart suddenly." Its past and past participle forms are both *burst,* not *bursted.* Bust, a verb meaning "to come apart suddenly" or "to break," is considered slang. Do not use it or its past form, *busted,* in formal writing.

Can, May   In formal writing, use *can* to indicate ability and *may* to indicate permission. In informal writing, you may use them interchangeably.

> **Can** the defendant answer the question? (Is he or she able to?)
> **May** the defendant answer the question? (Does he or she have permission to do so?)

Can't Hardly, Can't Scarcely   Avoid these double negatives. Use *can hardly* and *can scarcely* instead.

Center Around   Use *center on* instead.

Climactic, Climatic   *Climactic* refers to the climax, or highest point of intensity. *Climatic* refers to the climate, or characteristic weather conditions.

Compare To, Compare With   Use *compare to* when referring to the similarities between essentially unlike things. Use *compare with* when referring to the similarities and differences between things of the same type.

Hart Crane **compares** the sound of rain **to** "gently pitying laughter."

The professor **compared** a poem by Hart Crane **with** one by Edna St. Vincent Millay.

Contemptible, Contemptuous   *Contemptible* means "deserving contempt." *Contemptuous* means "feeling contempt."

She claimed that efforts to cut back funds for food programs for the poor were **contemptible.**

She was **contemptuous** of people who ignored the suffering of others.

Continual, Continuous   *Continual* means "recurring regularly." *Continuous* means "occurring without interruption."

He was kept awake by the **continual** dripping of the faucet.

The nation was experiencing a period of **continuous** growth.

Convince, Persuade   *Convince,* which is often used with *of,* means "to cause to believe." *Persuade,* which is often used with an infinitive, means "to cause to do."

The physicist **convinced** his colleague **of** the correctness of his methods.

The doctor **persuaded** her patient **to undergo** therapy.

Could Of   Nonstandard. Use *could have.*

Criteria, Data, Phenomena   These words are plural and in formal writing take plural verbs. The singular forms are *criterion, datum,* and *phenomenon.*

Deal   As a word meaning "agreement," "bargain," or "business transaction," this word is informal and overused.

Disinterested, Uninterested   *Disinterested* means "impartial." *Uninterested* means "indifferent" or "not interested."

The jury paid special attention to the testimony of one **disinterested** witness.

She did not finish the book, because she was **uninterested** in the subject.

Done   *Done* is the past participle of *do*. Do not use *done* as the past tense.

Not: He always read the last page of a mystery first to find out who **done** it.

But: He always read the last page of a mystery first to find out who **did** it.

Don't   Avoid using *don't*, which is a contraction of *do not*, in formal writing. Never use *don't* as a contraction of *does not*.

Due To   In formal writing, do not use *due to* to mean *because of.*

Not: The shipment was delayed **due to** the bad weather.

But: The shipment was delayed **because of** the bad weather.

Or: The delay in the shipment **was due to** the bad weather.

Eager   *See* **anxious.**

Enthused   In formal writing, use *enthusiastic.*

Etc.   *See* **and etc.**

Everyday, Every Day   Use *every day* as an adverb. Use *everyday* as an adjective.

During training, he took vitamins **every day.**
He needed an **everyday** suit.

Everyone, Every One   *See* **anyone.**

Everywheres   Nonstandard. Use *everywhere.*

Exam   In formal writing, use *examination.*

Expect   In formal writing, do not use *expect* to mean "to presume or suppose."

Not: I **expect** the performance went well.
But: I **suppose** the performance went well.

Explicit, Implicit *Explicit* means "stated forthrightly." *Implicit* means "implied" or "suggested."

The warning was **explicit:** Beware of the dog.
Although he never said a word, his threat was **implicit** in his action.

Farther, Further In formal writing, use *farther* to refer to geographical distance. Use *further* to refer to time, quantity, or degree.

We were **farther** from home than we had imagined.
The court demanded **further** documentation of his expenses.

Fewer, Less Use *fewer* to refer to things that can be counted. Use *less* to refer to a collective quantity that cannot be counted.

This year **fewer** commuters are driving their cars to work.
In general, smaller cars use **less** fuel than larger cars.

Finalize *Finalize* is an example of bureaucratic language. Do not use it in place of *complete, conclude,* or *make final.*

Fine *Fine* is informal and weak when used for the words *very well.* In formal writing, use a more exact word.

Firstly, Secondly, Etc. Use *first, second,* etc., instead.

Fix In formal writing, avoid using *fix* to mean "predicament."

Flunk *Flunk* is informal. In formal writing, use *fail.*

Folks In formal writing, avoid using the informal word *folks* for *parents, relatives,* or *family.*

Former, Latter *Former* means "the first mentioned of two." When three or more are mentioned, refer to the first mentioned as *first. Latter* means "the second mentioned of two." When three or more are mentioned, refer to the last mentioned as *last.*

Anita and Jayne are athletes: the **former** is a gymnast, the **latter** a tennis player.
The judges sampled four pies—apple, plum, rhubarb, and apricot—and gave the prize to the **last.**

Funny   In formal writing, avoid using *funny* for *odd* or *peculiar.*

Further   *See* **farther.**

Get   In formal writing, avoid using slang expressions beginning with *get: get even, get going, get on with it,* etc.

Good, Well   *Good* is an adjective. *Well* is usually an adverb, but it can also be used as an adjective meaning "healthy."

She looks **good** in that color.
The baby looks **well** today.
They work **well** together.

Great   In formal writing, do not use *great* to mean "wonderful."

Had Ought, Hadn't Ought   Use *ought* and *ought not* instead.

Hanged, Hung   Use *hanged* as the past and past participle form when referring to a method of execution. Otherwise, use *hung.*

In the Old West, horse thieves were **hanged.**
The clothing was **hung** out to dry.

Has Got, Have Got   In formal writing, use simply *has* or *have.*

Herself, Himself   *See* **myself.**

Hisself   Nonstandard. Use *himself.*

Hopefully   *Hopefully* means "in a hopeful manner." Avoid using *hopefully* to mean "it is hoped" or "let us hope."

Not: **Hopefully** it will not rain again this weekend.
But: **Let us hope** it will not rain again this weekend.

Illusion *See* **allusion.**

Implicit *See* **explicit.**

Imply, Infer *Imply* means "to suggest or hint." *Infer* means "to draw a conclusion." A writer or speaker implies something; a reader or listener infers it.

> He **implied** that he knew someone had cheated.
> From his remark I **inferred** that he is worried about her.

In, Into *In* indicates position. *Into* indicates direction of movement.

> When the sergeant came **into** the barracks, she found several of the new recruits still **in** bed.

Infer *See* **imply.**

In Regards To Use *in regard to* or *regarding* or *as regards.*

Into *See* **in.**

Irregardless Nonstandard. Use *regardless.*

Is When, Is Where Do not use these constructions in giving definitions.

> *Not:* Improvisation *is when* actors perform without preparation.
>
> *But:* Improvisation **occurs when** actors perform without preparation.
>
> *Or:* Improvisation **is** a performance by actors without preparation.

> *Not:* An aviary **is where** a large number of birds are housed.
>
> *But:* An aviary **is a place where** a large number of birds are housed.
>
> *Or:* An aviary **is** a house for a large number of birds.

Its, It's *Its* is the possessive case of the pronoun *it. It's* is a contraction of *it is* or *it has.*

> The cat was cleaning **its** paws.
> **It's** too late to submit an application.

Kind Of, Sort Of In formal writing, avoid using *kind of* and *sort of* as adverbs. Use instead the more formal words *rather* and *somewhat*.

> *Not:* His description was **kind of** sketchy.
> *But:* His description was **rather** sketchy.
>
> *Not:* She left **sort of** abruptly.
> *But:* She left **somewhat** abruptly.

Kind Of A, Sort Of A When using these expressions to mean "type of," delete the *a*.

> What **kind of** fabric is this?
> What **sort of** person was he?

Lay *See* **lie.**

Lead, Led *Lead* is the present infinitive form of the verb. *Led* is the past tense and past participle form.

Learn, Teach *Learn* means "to receive knowledge." *Teach* means "to give knowledge."

> We can **learn** from the mistakes of history.
> History can **teach** us many lessons.

Leave, Let In formal writing, use the verb *leave* to mean "to depart (from)." Use the verb *let* to mean "to allow to."

> Paul Simon wrote about the many ways to **leave** a lover.
> The natives would not **let** themselves be photographed.

Less *See* **fewer.**

Let *See* **leave.**

Liable *See* **likely.**

Lie, Lay *Lie* is an intransitive verb that means "to recline." Its past and past participle forms are *lay* and *lain*. *Lay* is a transitive verb that means "to place." Its past and past participle forms are both *laid*. (See also pp. 192–193.)

Although he **lay** in bed for hours, he could not sleep.
Please **lay** the book on the table.
Then let it **lie** there.

Like   In formal writing, do not use *like* as a conjunction. Instead use *as, as if,* or *as though.*

> *Not:*   The headlines claim that it looks **like** peace is at hand.
> *But:*   The headlines claim that it looks **as if** peace is at hand.

Likely, Liable   *Likely* indicates probability. *Liable* indicates responsibility or obligation.

> The Kremlin asserted that changes in the makeup of the government were not **likely** to lead to changes in U.S.-Soviet relations.
> The court determined that the driver of the truck was **liable** for all damages.

Lose, Loose   *Lose* is a verb. *Loose* is an adjective.

> In what year did Nixon **lose** the election to Kennedy?
> **Loose** talk can cause much trouble.

Lot   *See* **a lot.**
Lot Of, Lots Of   In formal writing, use *a great deal of, much, plenty of,* or *many* instead.
May   *See* **can.**
May Be, Maybe   *May be* is a verb phrase. *Maybe* is an adverb meaning "perhaps."

> His findings **may be** accurate.
> **Maybe** they will find a solution.

May Of, Might Of, Must Of   Use *may have, might have,* or *must have* instead.
More Importantly, Most Importantly   Use *more important* and *most important* instead.

Most   In formal writing, do not use *most* to mean "almost."

> *Not:* The survey predicted that **most** everyone would vote.
> *But:* The survey predicted that **almost** everyone would vote.

Myself, Yourself, Himself, Herself, Etc.   Pronouns ending in
-self or *-selves* are reflexive or intensive. In formal writing,
do not use them in place of *I, me, you, he, her*, and so on.

> *Not:* My friend and **myself** are campaigning actively.
> *But:* My friend and **I** are campaigning actively.

Nice   In formal writing, replace this weak word with a more
exact one—*attractive, appealing, kind*, and so forth.

Not Hardly   Avoid this double negative. Use *hardly* instead.

Nowhere Near Enough   Colloquial. In formal writing, use *not
nearly enough* instead.

> *Not:* The concessions the company made its employees were
> **nowhere near enough** to avoid a strike.
> *But:* The concessions the company made its employees were
> **not nearly enough** to avoid a strike.

Nowheres   Nonstandard. Use *nowhere*.

Number   *See* **amount.**

Off Of   Use *off* without *of.*

> *Not:* During the tremor the paintings fell **off of** the wall.
> *But:* During the tremor the paintings fell **off** the wall.

OK, O.K., okay   Avoid these expressions in formal writing.

People, Persons   Use *people* to refer to a large group collectively. Use *persons* to emphasize the individuals within
the group.

> The committee is investigating ways in which **people** avoid pay-
> ing their full taxes.

The group thought it was near agreement when several **persons** raised objections.

Percent, Percentage   Use *percent* after a specific number. Use *percentage* after a general adjective indicating size.

The poll showed that 75 **percent** of Americans supported the President's foreign policy.

The poll showed that a large **percentage** of Americans supported the President's foreign policy.

Persuade   *See* **convince.**
Phenomena   *See* **criteria.**
P.M.   *See* **A.M.**
Quote, Quotation   *Quote* is a verb. *Quotation* is a noun.

During her speech she **quoted** from one of Blake's poems.
She began her speech with a **quotation** from one of Blake's poems.

Raise, Rise   *Raise* is a transitive verb meaning "to lift." Its past and past participle forms are both *raised. Rise* is an intransitive verb meaning "to go up." Its past and past participle are *rose* and *risen.* (See also pp. 194–195.)

Inflation is **raising** the cost of living.
The cost of living is **rising.**

Real, Really   *Real* is an adjective. *Really* is an adverb.

What is the **real** value of the dollar?
Mortgage rates are **really** high this year.

Reason Is Because   Use *that* instead of *because* or rewrite the sentence.

Not: The **reason** for the patient's lethargy **is because** his diet is inadequate.

But: The **reason** for the patient's lethargy **is that** his diet is inadequate.

Or: The reason for the patient's lethargy is an inadequate diet.

Or: The patient is lethargic because of an inadequate diet.

Respectably, Respectfully, Respectively *Respectably* means "in a manner deserving respect." *Respectfully* means "in a manner showing respect." *Respectively* means "in the order given."

The tenor performed his aria **respectably,** but his voice cracked during the duet.

The defendant **respectfully** asked permission to address the court.

Baghdad and Damascus are the capitals of Iraq and Syria, **respectively.**

Rise *See* **raise.**

Sensual, Sensuous Both of these adjectives mean "appealing to the senses," but *sensual* describes something that arouses physical appetites, while *sensuous* describes something that leads to aesthetic enjoyment.

The censors claimed that the dancing was too **sensual.**

The painter was praised for the **sensuous** quality of his still lifes.

Set, Sit *Set* is a transitive verb that means "to put or place." Its past and past participle forms are both *set. Sit* is an intransitive verb that means "to be seated." Its past and past participle forms are both *sat.* (See also pp. 193–194.)

The stagehands **set** the chairs on a raised platform.

The actors will **sit** in the chairs during the rehearsal.

Shall, Will The distinction between *shall* and *will* is fading. However, for strictly formal writing, use *shall* with first-person pronouns and *will* with second- and third-person pronouns to indicate simple futurity. Reverse the order to indicate determination, duty, or need.

Simple futurity

> I **shall** see you at the theater.
> He **will** meet us at the theater.

Determination

> We **will** find a solution to this problem.
> They **shall** not defeat us.

Should Of   Nonstandard. Use *should have.*

Sit   *See* **set.**

Someone, Some One   *See* **anyone.**

Sometime, Some Time   Use *sometime* as an adverb to mean "at an indefinite or unnamed time." Use *some time* after a preposition.

> The announcement will be made **sometime** next month.
> He has been retired for **some time** now.

Sort Of   *See* **kind of.**

Sort Of A   *See* **kind of a.**

Suppose To   *See* **use to.**

Sure, Surely   *Sure* is an adjective that means "certain." *Surely* is an adverb that means "undoubtedly" or "certainly."

> The expedition was **sure** to succeed.
> The expedition was **surely** a success.

Sure And, Try And   In formal writing, use *sure to* and *try to* instead.

> *Not:*   Be **sure and** pay attention to the speaker's body language.
> *But:*   Be **sure to** pay attention to the speaker's body language.

Teach   *See* **learn.**

That, Which   Use *that* to introduce a restrictive clause. Use *which* to introduce either a restrictive or a nonrestrictive clause. (In order to maintain a clearer distinction between *which* and *that,* some writers use *which* to introduce only a nonrestrictive clause.)

Is this the manuscript **that** he submitted yesterday?
This contract, **which** is no longer valid, called for a 30 percent royalty.

Theirself, Theirselves   Nonstandard. Use *themselves.*

These Kind, Those Kind; These Sort, Those Sort   Since *kind* and *sort* are singular, use singular adjectives: *this kind, that kind, this sort, that sort.* For the plural use *these kinds, those kinds, these sorts, those sorts.*

Thusly   Use *thus.*

Try And   *See* **sure and.**

Uninterested   *See* **disinterested.**

Unique   The word *unique* means "unequaled" or "unparalleled," a quality that is not capable of comparison.

Not: He has the **most unique** sense of humor I have encountered.
But: His sense of humor is **unique.**

Use To, Suppose To   The correct forms are *use**d** to* and *suppose**d** to.*

Not: In *My Dinner with André,* Wally **use to** be a Latin teacher.
But: In *My Dinner with André,* Wally **used to** be a Latin teacher.

Wait For, Wait On   Use *wait for* to mean "await" or "attend to." Use *wait on* to mean "serve."

Many young actors **wait on** tables while they **wait for** the right role.

Ways   Use *way* to mean "distance."

> *Not:* He lives only a short **ways** from London.
> *But:* He lives only a short **way** from London.

Well *See* **good.**
When, Where *See* **is when, is where.**
Where Do not use *where* for *that.*

> *Not:* I read in the magazine **where** flood victims were now receiving federal aid.
> *But:* I read in the magazine **that** flood victims were now receiving federal aid.

Which, Who Use *which* to refer to objects. Use *who* to refer to people. (*That* usually refers to objects but at times may be used to refer to people.)

> The book, **which** was written by Nat Hentoff, is called *Jazz Is.*
> Nat Hentoff, **who** wrote *Jazz Is,* contributes articles to many magazines.

Will *See* **shall.**
-wise Avoid using *-wise* as a noun suffix—*budgetwise, careerwise, marketwise.*
Without Do not use *without* for *unless.*

> *Not:* The director could not act **without** the committee approved.
> *But:* The director could not act **unless** the committee approved.
> *Or:* The director could not act **without** the committee's **approval.**

Yourself *See* **myself.**

Glossary
of
Grammatical Terms

Absolute Phrase A group of words containing a noun and a nonfinite, or incomplete, verb. It modifies the entire clause to which it is attached, instead of an individual word within the clause. (See also section 5a; 9b.)

His energy depleted, the fighter conceded the bout.

Abstract Noun *See* **noun.**

Acronym A kind of abbreviation that creates a word from parts of words or initials without periods: *radar; CARE; ROM.*

Active Voice *See* **voice.**

Adjective A word that modifies, or describes, a noun or pronoun. An adjective tells what kind, how many, or which one. (See also section 8d; 18.)

In **his latest** novel, **this prodigious** writer uses **several historical** studies to create **a realistic** portrait of **the** man often considered **our greatest** president—Abraham Lincoln.

Adjective Clause   A dependent clause that acts as an adjective and modifies a noun or pronoun. Usually, an adjective clause begins with a relative pronoun (*who, whose, whom, that,* or *which*). (See also 10b.)

> The king of England **who broke with the Catholic Church** was Henry VIII.

Adverb   A word that modifies, or limits the meaning of, a verb, an adjective, or another adverb. An adverb tells when, where, to what extent, or how. (See also 8e; 18.)

> This **extremely** absorbing book deals **quite successfully** with the way computers function **today** and the way they will affect our lives **tomorrow.**

Adverb Clause   A dependent clause that begins with a subordinating conjunction (*although, because, while,* etc.) and acts as an adverb in the sentence. (See also 10b.)

> The museum was closed **because it was being renovated.**

Agreement   The correspondence in form between a verb and its subject or a pronoun and its antecedent to indicate person, number, and gender. (See also 15 and 16a.)

> **Each** of these women **makes her** position understood.

Antecedent   The word or words to which a pronoun refers. A pronoun must agree with its antecedent in number and gender. (See also 8c and 16a.)

> **Jack** pledged **his** support for the project.

Appositive   A noun or group of words acting as a noun that renames, identifies, or gives additional information about the preceding noun or pronoun. (See also 24d and 5a.)

> Typhoid Mary, **the notorious carrier of typhoid fever,** died in 1938.

Article   The indefinite articles are *a* and *an;* the definite article is *the.* Articles are classified as adjectives. (See also 8d.)

Auxiliary Verb   A form of *be* or *have* used to form perfect tenses, progressive forms of tenses, and the passive voice. (See also 8b.)

> I **am** leaving.
> They **have** left.
> The money **had been** left in the safe.

Case   The structural function of a noun or a pronoun in a sentence. English has three cases—subjective, objective, and possessive. The subjective case indicates the subject of a verb or a subject complement:

> The **umpire** called a strike. The **umpire** was he.

The objective case indicates the object of a verb or of a preposition:

> Connors returned the **serve** to **McEnroe.** He returned it to **him.**

The possessive case indicates possession, description, or origin:

> The **team's** overall performance was disappointing. **Their** overall performance was disappointing.

Nouns and some pronouns have the same form in the subjective and the objective cases; an apostrophe and *s* or an apostrophe alone is added to form the possessive case: *investor's, investors', anybody's.* The pronouns *it* and *you* have special possessive forms: *its, your,* or *yours.* The following pronouns have different forms in all three cases.

Subjective: I, he, she, we, they, who
Objective: me, him, her, us, them, whom
Possessive: my, mine; his; her, hers; our, ours; their, theirs; whose

(See also 8a, 8c, 17, and 40a.)

Clause   A group of words with a subject and a predicate. A clause may be independent or dependent. An independent (main) clause is structurally independent and can stand by itself as a simple sentence:

The President honored the Unknown Soldier.

A dependent (subordinate) clause is not structurally independent and cannot stand by itself as a simple sentence. Therefore, it must be joined to or be part of an independent clause:

Although newspapers strive for accuracy, they sometimes make mistakes.
What you see *is* **what you get.**

Dependent clauses, which can function as adjectives, adverbs, or nouns, usually begin with a subordinating conjunction or a relative pronoun. (See also 10.)

Collective Noun   *See* **noun.**
Comma Splice   An error that occurs when a comma is used to separate two independent clauses not joined by a conjunction. (See also 13a.)
Common Noun   *See* **noun.**
Comparative, Superlative   Forms of adjectives and adverbs

used to make comparisons. The comparative form is used to compare two things; the superlative form is used to compare more than two. The comparative and superlative of most one-syllable adjectives and adverbs are formed by adding *-er* and *-est* to the base, or positive, form: *long, longer, longest.* The comparative and superlative of most longer adjectives and adverbs are formed by placing the words *more* and *most* before the positive form: *beautiful, more beautiful, most beautiful.* (See also 8d, 8e, and 18c.)

Complement   A word or group of words that completes the meaning of a verb. The five types of complements are direct objects, indirect objects, objective complements, predicate nominatives, and predicate adjectives. (See also 7b and 7c.)

Complete Predicate   *See* **predicate.**

Complete Sentence   *See* **sentence.**

Complete Subject   *See* **subject.**

Complex Sentence   *See* **sentence.**

Compound   A word or group of words that is made up of two or more parts but functions as a unit. Compound words consist of two or more words that may be written as one word, as a hyphenated word, or as separate words but that function as a single part of speech: *hairbrush, well-to-do, toaster oven.* A compound subject consists of two or more nouns or noun substitutes that take the same predicate:

Chemistry and **physics** were required courses.

A compound verb consists of two or more verbs that have the same subject:

The doctor **analyzed** the results of the tests and **made** a diagnosis.

(See also 8a, 15a, 24e, and 41.)

Compound-Complex Sentence   *See* **sentence.**

Compound Sentence   *See* **sentence.**

Concrete Noun   *See* **noun.**

Conjunction   A word or set of words that joins or relates other words, phrases, clauses, or sentences. There are three types of conjunctions: coordinating conjunctions, correlative conjunctions, and subordinating conjunctions. Coordinating conjunctions (*and, but, for, nor, or, so,* and *yet*) join elements that have equal grammatical rank. Correlative conjunctions (*both . . . and, either . . . or, neither . . . nor, not only . . . but also, whether . . . or, just as . . . so*) function as coordinating conjunctions but are always used in pairs. Subordinating conjunctions (*after, as long as, because, if, since, so that, unless, until, while,* etc.) join subordinate, or dependent, clauses to main, or independent, clauses. (See also 8g.)

Conjunctive Adverb   An adverb that provides transition between independent clauses. (See also 8g.)

> The movie received many excellent reviews; **consequently,** people across the country lined up to see it.

Coordinating Conjunction   *See* **conjunction.**

Correlative Conjunction   *See* **conjunction.**

Dangling Modifier   An introductory phrase that does not clearly and sensibly modify the noun or pronoun that follows it. (See also 22d.)

Degrees Of Modifiers   *See* **comparative, superlative.**

Demonstrative Pronoun   *See* **pronoun.**

Dependent Clause   *See* **clause.**

Direct Object   *See* **object.**

Double Negative   A construction, considered unacceptable in standard modern English, that uses two negative words to make a negative statement. (See also 18d.)

Elliptical Clause   A clause in which a word is omitted but understood. (See also 10b and 17.)

> He works harder than his partner [does].

Expletive   The word *there, here,* or *it* used to fill the position before a verb of being but not to add meaning to the sentence. (See also 7a and 43d.)

There are several excellent reasons for taking this course. **Here** is one of them. **It** is wise to register early.

Fragment   *See* **sentence fragment.**

Fused Sentence   Two independent clauses written without a coordinating conjunction or a punctuation mark between them. (See also 13b.)

Gender   The classification of nouns and pronouns as masculine (*man, he*), feminine (*woman, she*), or neuter (*skillet, it*). (See also 8a, 8c, and 16a.)

Gerund   *See* **verbal.**

Gerund Phrase   *See* **phrase.**

Imperative   *See* **mood.**

Indefinite Pronoun   *See* **pronoun.**

Independent Clause   *See* **clause.**

Indicative   *See* **mood.**

Indirect Object   *See* **object.**

Infinitive   *See* **verbal.**

Infinitive Phrase   *See* **phrase.**

Intensive Pronoun   *See* **pronoun.**

Interjection   A word that expresses emotion and has no grammatical connection to the sentence in which it appears. (See also 8h).

Oh, how happy he was! **Wow,** that was painful!

Interrogative Pronoun   *See* **pronoun.**

Intransitive Verb   *See* **verb.**

Inverted Word Order   A change in the normal English word order of subject-verb-complement. (See also 7a and 15h.)

In the doorway stood **Tom**.

Irregular Verb   A verb that does not form its past tense and past participle according to the regular pattern of adding *-ed* or *-d* to the present infinitive: *begin, began, begun; draw, drew, drawn; put, put, put.* (See also 14.)

Linking Verb   *See* **verb.**

Main Clause   *See* **clause.**

Misplaced Modifier   A modifier placed so that it seems to refer to a word other than the one intended. (See also 22e.)

Modal   A verb form used with a main verb to ask a question, to help express negation, to show future time, to emphasize, or to express such conditions as possibility, certainty, or obligation. The following words are modals: *do, does, did; can, could; may, might, must; will, shall; would, should,* and *ought to.* (See also 8b.)

Modifier   A word or group of words that limits the meaning of or makes more specific another word or group of words. The two kinds of modifiers are adjectives and adverbs. (See also 8d and 8e.)

Mood   The aspect of a verb that indicates the writer's attitude toward the action or condition expressed by the verb. In English there are three moods: the indicative, the imperative, and the subjunctive. The indicative expresses a factual statement or a question:

The weather **is** fine today. **Will** it **rain** tomorrow?

The imperative indicates a command or a request:

Buy your tickets today.
Will you please **be** quiet.

The subjunctive indicates a wish, an assumption, a recommendation, or something contrary to fact:

She wished she **were** home.
If she **were** mayor, she would eliminate waste from the city budget.

(See also 8b and 20e.)

Nominative Case   *See* **case.**

Nonessential Element   A modifying phrase or clause that does not limit, qualify, or identify the noun it modifies. Since a nonessential element is not necessary to the meaning of the clause in which it appears, it is set off with commas. (See also 24d.)

> *Hurlyburly,* **which was written by David Rabe,** conveys the confusion and aimlessness of modern American life.

Noun   A word that names a person, place, object, or idea. Proper nouns name particular people, places, objects, or ideas: *Gertrude Stein, Spain, Corvettes, Puritanism.* Common nouns name people, places, objects, and ideas in general, not in particular: *poet, country, cars, religion.* Concrete nouns name things that can be seen, touched, heard, smelled, or tasted: *portrait, mansion, chorus, garlic.* Abstract nouns name concepts, ideas, beliefs, and qualities: *honesty, consideration, fascism, monotheism.* Collective nouns refer to groups of people or things as though the group were a single unit: *committee, choir, navy, team.* (See also 8a, 15c, and 43b.)

Noun Clause   A dependent clause that acts as a noun in a sentence. It functions as a subject, an object, or a predicate nominative. (See also 10b.)

> **That an agreement would be reached before the strike deadline** seemed unlikely.

Noun Substitute   A pronoun, gerund, clause, or other group of words that functions as a noun in a sentence. (See also 8c, 8i, and 10b.)

Number   The quality of being singular or plural. (See also 8a, 8b, 8c, and especially 15 and 16.)

Object   A noun or noun substitute that completes the meaning of or is affected by a transitive verb or a preposition. A direct object specifies the person, place, object, or idea that directly receives the action of a transitive verb:

The three heads of state *signed* the **treaty.**

An indirect object tells to whom or what or for whom or what the action of a transitive verb is performed:

They *gave* the **refugees** food and clothing.

An object of a preposition is the noun or noun substitute that the preposition relates to another part of the sentence:

The cat is sleeping *under* the **table.**

(See also 7, 8f, 9a, and 17.)

Objective Case   *See* **case.**
Objective Complement   A noun or adjective that completes the action of a transitive verb by modifying or renaming that verb's object. (See also 7c)

Delilah cut his *hair* **short.**

History calls *Thomas More* a **martyr.**

Parenthetical Expression   An expression that comments on or gives additional information about the main part of a sentence. Since a parenthetical expression interrupts the thought of the sentence, it is set off by commas. (See also 24d.)

Music, **I believe,** is good for the soul.

Participial Phrase   *See* **phrase.**
Participle   *See* **verbal.**

Parts of Speech   The eight groups into which words are traditionally classified based on their function in a sentence:
noun, verb, adjective, adverb, pronoun, preposition, conjunction, and interjection. (See also 8.)

Passive Voice   *See* **voice.**

Past Participle   *See* **verbal.**

Personal Pronoun   *See* **pronoun.**

Phrase   A group of words lacking a subject and a predicate
that often functions as a single part of speech. (See also
9.)

Positive Degree   *See* **comparative, superlative.**

Possessive Case   *See* **case.**

Predicate   The part of a sentence that tells what the subject
does or is. The simple predicate is the main verb, including any auxiliaries or modals:

The rice **was** lightly **flavored** with vinegar.

The complete predicate consists of the simple predicate
and all the words that modify and complement it:

The rice **was lightly flavored with vinegar.**

(See also 7b.)

Predicate Adjective   An adjective that follows a linking verb
and describes the subject of the verb. (See also 7c.)

Lestrade's solution was too **simplistic.**

Predicate Nominative   A noun or noun substitute that follows
a linking verb and renames the subject of the verb. (See
also 7c.)

The model for Nora Charles was **Lillian Hellman**

Preposition   A function word used to show the relationship of a noun or pronoun to another part of the sentence. (See also 8f.)

Prepositional Phrase   A phrase consisting of a preposition, the object of the preposition, and all the words modifying this object. (See also 9a.)

The narrator **of the story** is a young man who lived **with the writer** and assisted him **in his work.**

Pronoun   A word that stands for or takes the place of one or more nouns. A personal pronoun takes the place of a noun that names a person or a thing: *I, me, my, mine; you, your, yours; he, him, his; she, her, hers; it, its; we, us, our, ours; they, them, their, theirs.* A demonstrative pronoun points to someone or something: *this, that, these, those.* An indefinite pronoun does not take the place of a particular noun. It carries the idea of "all," "some," "any," or "none": *everyone, everything, somebody, many, anyone, anything, no one, nobody.* An interrogative pronoun is used to ask a question: *who, whom, whose, what, which.* A relative pronoun is used to form an adjective clause or a noun clause: *who, whose, whom, which, that, what, whoever, whomever, whichever, whatever.* An intensive pronoun is used for emphasis. It is formed by adding *-self* or *-selves* to the end of a personal pronoun. A reflexive pronoun, which has the same form as an intensive pronoun, is used to show that the subject is acting upon itself. (See also 8c, 16, and 17.)

Proper Adjective   An adjective formed from a proper noun. (See also 39.)

Machiavellian scheme, **Byronic** disposition, **Parisian** dress.

Proper Noun   *See* **noun.**
Reflexive Pronoun   *See* **pronoun.**
Regular Verb   A verb whose past tense and past participle are

formed by adding *-d* or *-ed* to the present infinitive: *analyze, analyzed, analyzed; detain, detained, detained.*
(See also 8b; 14.)

Relative Pronoun *See* **pronoun.**

Restrictive Element A modifying phrase or clause that limits,
identifies, or qualifies the idea expressed by the noun it
modifies. Since a restrictive element is necessary for the
basic meaning of the clause in which it appears, it is not
set off with commas. (See also 24d.)

The woman **wearing the blue suit** just received a promotion.

Run-on Sentence Two or more complete sentences incorrectly written as though they were one sentence. (See
also 13.)

Sentence A group of words with a subject and a predicate that
expresses a complete thought. Sentences can be classified into four basic groups according to the number and
kinds of clauses they contain. A simple sentence contains
only one independent clause and no dependent clause:

The relationship between the United States and the Soviet Union
needs to be improved.

A compound sentence contains two or more independent
clauses but no dependent clause:

The senator worked hard for passage of the bill, but his efforts
proved futile.

A complex sentence contains one independent clause
and one or more dependent clauses:

Although the two nations were technically at peace, their secret
services were fighting a covert war.

A compound-complex sentence contains two or more independent clauses and one or more dependent clause:

Voter confidence in the administration grew as interest rates went down; however, it quickly faded when interest rates started to rise.

(See also 7 and 11.)

Sentence Fragment   An incomplete sentence written as a complete sentence. (See also 12.)

Simple Predicate   *See* **predicate.**

Simple Sentence   *See* **sentence.**

Simple Subject   *See* **subject.**

Squinting Modifier   A modifier that, because of its placement, could refer to either the preceding or the following element in a sentence. (See also 22f.)

Subject   The part of a sentence that answers the question "who?" or "what?" in regard to the predicate, or verb. The simple subject is the main noun or noun substitute in the subject:

Women's **fashions** from the 1950s are becoming popular again.

The complete subject is the simple subject together with all the words that modify it:

Women's fashions from the 1950s are becoming popular again.

(See also 7a.)

Subject Complement   *See* **complement.**

Subjective Case   *See* **case.**

Subjunctive   *See* **mood.**

Subordinate Clause   *See* **clause.**

Subordinating Conjunction   *See* **conjunction.**

Superlative Degree   *See* **comparative, superlative.**

Tense   The time expressed by the form of the verb. There are six tenses: (simple) present, present perfect, (simple) past, past perfect, (simple) future, future perfect. Each of the tenses has a progressive form that indicates continuing action. The present tense is used to write about events or conditions that are happening or existing now:

She **writes** a column for the local newspaper.

The present tense is also used to write about natural or scientific laws, timeless truths, events in literature, habitual action, and (with an adverbial word or phrase) future time. The present perfect tense is used to write about events that occurred at some unspecified time in the past and about events and conditions that began in the past and may still be continuing in the present:

She **has written** a series of articles about child abuse.

The past tense is used to write about events that occurred and conditions that existed at a definite time in the past and do not extend into the present:

The researcher **studied** voting trends in this district.

The past perfect tense is used to write about a past event or condition that ended before another past event or condition began:

They **had studied** the effects of television on voting trends before they made their proposals.

The future tense is used to write about events or conditions that have not yet begun:

They **will consider** her proposal.

The future perfect tense is used to write about a future event or condition that will end before another future event or condition begins or before a specified time in the future:

By next month, they **will have considered** all the proposals.

(See also 8b, 20c, and 21.)

Transitive Verb   *See* **verb.**

Verb   A word that expresses action or a state of being. An action verb expresses action:

The ballerina **danced** beautifully.

A linking verb expresses a state of being or a condition. It connects the subject of the sentence to a word that identifies or describes it:

Vitamin C **may be** *effective* against the common cold.

A transitive verb is an action verb that takes an object:

The fleet **secures** the *coasts* against invasion.

An intransitive verb is any verb that does not take an object:

After deregulation of the industry, prices **soared.**

(See also 8b.)

Verb Phrase   A phrase made up of the infinitive, the present participle or the past participle plus one or more auxiliaries or modals:

The candidate **will make** a speech tomorrow.
Jesse Jackson **had proved** himself an effective negotiator.
The gymnasts **have been practicing** regularly.

(See also 8b and 14.)

Verbal   A grammatical form that is based on a verb but that functions as a noun, an adjective, or an adverb, instead of as a verb, in a sentence. There are three types of verbals: participles, gerunds, and infinitives. The present participle and the past participle of most verbs can function as adjectives:

One of the most memorable figures in *Alice in Wonderland* is the **grinning** Cheshire cat.
The lawyer demanded a **written** contract.

A gerund is a verb form spelled the same way as the present participle but used as a noun in a sentence:

Walking is good for your health.

The present infinitive and the present perfect infinitive form of a verb can function as a noun, as an adjective, or as an adverb:

In *A Chorus Line,* the overriding ambition of each of the characters is **to dance.** Cassie was glad **to have gotten** the part.

(See also 8i.)

Verbal Phrase   A phrase consisting of a verbal and all its complements and modifiers. There are three types of verbal phrases: participial phrases, gerund phrases, and infinitive phrases. A participial phrase functions as an adjective in a sentence:

The image of a garden **filled with poisonous flowers** dominates "Rappaccini's Daughter."

A gerund phrase functions as a noun in a sentence:

Exercising in the noonday sun can be dangerous.

An infinitive phrase functions as a noun, an adjective, or an adverb:

To make the world safe for democracy was one of Wilson's goals.

(See also 9b.)

Voice   The indication of whether the subject performs or receives the action of the verb. If the subject performs the action, the verb and the clause are in the active voice:

Herman Melville **wrote** "Bartleby the Scrivener."

If the subject receives the action or is acted upon, the verb and the clause are in the passive voice:

"Bartleby the Scrivener" **was written** by Herman Melville.

(See also 8b and 20d.)

Index

531

Plan of the Book

After you have finished your final draft but before you proceed to draw up the final copy, reread your paper slowly and carefully. The following questions will assist you in revising and polishing your paper.

Purpose: Is the purpose clear and the *tone* consistent and appropriate for that purpose (**2a**)? Have you avoided errors in reasoning (*logical fallacies*) (**6b**)?

Title page: If required, have you included a title page that lists all pertinent information (**52**)?

Title: Is your title brief? Does it suggest the topic, tone, and purpose of the essay, or does it effectively challenge interpretation (**3e**)?

Outline: Does your instructor require an outline? If so, have you included one? (**2a, 52**)

Thesis: Is the thesis clear (**2a, 3e**)? Does it give your reader adequate direction regarding what is to follow (**3b**)?

Opening: Does your opening state the topic effectively (**3e**)?

Body: Does every part of the essay's body relate to the thesis and increase the reader's understanding of the problem being explored (**3e**)? Does the body follow, to some degree, the principle of generalization, narrower generalization, and *specific detail* (**3b**)? Is the body *coherent* (**3c**)?

Paragraphs: Is the *order* of paragraphs logical, each relating to the thesis (**2a**)? Are *transitions* between paragraphs clear and effective (**4d, e**)? Is *unity* apparent in each paragraph as it develops its one idea (**4a**)? Are *supporting details* specific, adequate, and logically arranged (**4b, c**)?

Sentences: Are sentences sufficiently *varied in form* to avoid monotony in style? Are your sentences constructed so that ideas are expressed forcefully and directly? Do you use action verbs and write in the *active voice*? Do your sentences emphasize important elements (**5a–c**)?

Words: Does your choice of words express your thoughts precisely (**43**)? Is the *diction* appropriate for purpose, tone, and audience (**42a–c; 43a–c, f**)? Have diction faults such as *wordiness, repetition, and vagueness* been avoided (**42d; 43d, e**)? Do you avoid malapropisms (**44**) and sexist language (**3b**)?

Conclusion: Does the closing effectively end the paper and emphasize your points without undue repetition of the thesis or main points (**3e**)?

Citations: Are all sources acknowledged according to accepted *guidelines* (**50**)? Is your *bibliography* complete and correct (**47, 48, 52, 53**)?

Manuscript form: Have you followed standard guidelines or your instructor's requirements in formatting your paper (**36**)?

Proofing: Have you re-read and edited your final version carefully, checking punctuation and mechanics (**III, IV**)? Have you checked for errors in usage (**II VI, glossary**)? Have you read your sentences backwards, from the bottom of the page up, to check spelling (**3f, V**)?